The Fragile Balance of Terror

A VOLUME IN THE SERIES

Cornell Studies in Security Affairs

Edited by Robert J. Art, Alexander B. Downes, Kelly M. Greenhill, Robert Jervis, Caitlin Talmadge, and Stephen M. Walt

Founding series editors: Robert J. Art and Robert Jervis

A list of titles in this series is available at cornellpress.cornell.edu.

The Fragile Balance of Terror

Deterrence in the New Nuclear Age

Edited by
VIPIN NARANG AND
SCOTT D. SAGAN

Cornell University Press

Ithaca and London

Copyright © 2022 by the American Academy of Arts and Sciences

Thanks to generous funding from the American Academy of Arts and Sciences, the ebook editions of this book are available as open access volumes through the Cornell Open initiative.

The text of this book is licensed under a Creative Commons Attribution-NonCommercial-NoDerivatives 4.0 International License: https://creativecommons.org/licenses/by-nc-nd/4.0/. To use this book, or parts of this book, in any way not covered by the license, please contact Cornell University Press, Sage House, 512 East State Street, Ithaca, New York 14850. Visit our website at cornellpress.cornell.edu.

Librarians: A CIP catalog record for this book is available from the Library of Congress.

ISBN 978-1-5017-6701-2 (hardcover)
ISBN 978-1-5017-6716-6 (paperback)
ISBN 978-1-5017-6703-6 (pdf)
ISBN 978-1-5017-6702-9 (epub)

Contents

Introduction: The Fragile Balance of Terror   1
VIPIN NARANG AND SCOTT D. SAGAN

PART I. NEW CHALLENGES IN THE NEW NUCLEAR AGE   11

1. Multipolar Deterrence in the Emerging Nuclear Era   13
CAITLIN TALMADGE

2. Psychology, Leaders, and New Deterrence Dilemmas   39
ROSE MCDERMOTT

3. Thermonuclear Twitter?   63
VIPIN NARANG AND HEATHER WILLIAMS

4. Understanding New Nuclear Threats: The Open Source Intelligence Revolution?   90
AMY ZEGART

PART II. ENDURING CHALLENGES WITH A NEW TWIST   121

5. How Much Is Enough? Revisiting Nuclear Reliability, Deterrence, and Preventive War   123
JEFFREY LEWIS AND ANKIT PANDA

6. Survivability in the New Era of Counterforce   154
CHRISTOPHER CLARY

CONTENTS

7. The Fulcrum of Fragility: Command and Control
   in Regional Nuclear Powers 182
   GILES DAVID ARCENEAUX AND PETER D. FEAVER

8. The Limits of Nuclear Learning in the New Nuclear Age 209
   MARK S. BELL AND NICHOLAS L. MILLER

   Conclusion: The Dangerous Nuclear Future 230
   VIPIN NARANG AND SCOTT D. SAGAN

   Acknowledgments 251
   Contributors 253
   Index 255

Introduction

The Fragile Balance of Terror

Vipin Narang and Scott D. Sagan

In 1958, Albert Wohlstetter published what was arguably the most influential paper on nuclear strategy during the Cold War. In "The Delicate Balance of Terror," Wohlstetter argued against the commonly held notion that the existence of thermonuclear weapons in the arsenals of both the United States and the Soviet Union had produced a "presumed automatic balance" of power, making nuclear war "extremely unlikely."[1] Instead, Wohlstetter maintained, the United States would have to spend significant intellectual capital and financial resources to ensure a "secure second-strike capability" permitting retaliation after a Soviet surprise attack. He warned, however, that his chosen strategy would increase "the accident problem": "In order to reduce the risk of a rational act of aggression, we are forced to undertake measures (increased alertness, dispersal, mobility) which, to a smaller extent, but still significant, increases the risk of an irrational or unintended act of war."[2] Wohlstetter's warning that the nuclear balance was precarious and that deterrence was complicated and imperfect had a profound effect on US nuclear doctrine and arms control policy during the Cold War.

Over sixty years after Wohlstetter's article was published, the world is on the cusp of a new nuclear age. China, Russia, and the United States are in the midst of a renewed arms race and nuclear modernization programs. Further, three new nuclear weapons powers have emerged since the end of the Cold War: India, Pakistan, and North Korea. Each has been involved in frequent, sometimes high intensity, crises in which escalation is not only possible but

---

1. Albert Wohlstetter, "The Delicate Balance of Terror," *Foreign Affairs* 37, no. 2 (1959): 211–34. https://doi.org/10.2307/20029345.
2. Wohlstetter, "Delicate Balance, 231."

increasingly likely. North Korea's 2017 nuclear and missile sprint to seek the capability to hold the United States homeland at risk sparked a major global crisis. India and Pakistan have engaged in more frequent militarized crises, with nuclear India making history when it used military airpower against the undisputed territory of another nuclear power for the first time in 2019. It is unlikely to be the last. A year after this intense crisis with nuclear Pakistan, the Indian military suffered at least twenty fatalities in a bloody clash with China. The restraining effects of classical deterrence theory appear to be eroding. Escalation has thus far been avoided not due to the skill with which these states believe they maneuver but largely through luck. And at some point, that luck may run out.

Furthermore, the nuclear aspirants that have so far failed to reach the finish line in the post–Cold War era—Iraq, Iran, Syria, and Libya—have perhaps disrupted the international system even more than the new nuclear powers, as terminating or stalling their nuclear weapons programs led to protracted wars and crises. Still, other potential nuclear weapons states lurk in the wings—US adversaries and allies alike—such as Saudi Arabia, Turkey, and perhaps South Korea, Japan, and Germany that may not indefinitely find America's extended deterrence commitments credible. These new and potentially future nuclear weapons powers—and the risk of what we term "nuclear contagion," or the further spread of nuclear weapons triggered by so-called index cases like North Korea or Iran—are a preview of the dangerous nuclear future.

We are unprepared for it. This is a more uncertain and complex nuclear world than we confronted during the Cold War. These new and potential nuclear powers reside in highly hostile environments. Many of these states have fewer resources and are characterized by more domestic instability than the first generation of nuclear powers. Some of these states are headed by personalist dictators who have few checks and balances on their decision-making authority. New technologies, including social media and cybersecurity, are complicating communication, command, and control. And the emergence of multiple nuclear states makes balances of power more complex and deterrence relationships more uncertain. Our theories and understanding derived from the Cold War bipolar nuclear competition leave us ill-equipped to handle the daunting challenges of this new nuclear age.

This new nuclear age demands new thinking and analysis about the challenges generated by the continued existence and spread of nuclear weapons. How does the prospect of more nuclear weapons powers—some led by personalist dictators driven by narcissism and megalomania and motivated by revenge—interacting with each other more frequently alter our confidence in our classic deterrence models? Can deterrence hold between these new nuclear states? What challenges will they face in building secure second-strike forces in the face of emerging counterforce and damage limitation incentives and technologies, in managing their arsenals, and in navigating crises? What are the risks of inadvertent escalation or accidental war in the new nuclear age? What mitigation steps are possible to reduce these risks?

These are the motivating questions for this book. The answers are worrying, and the conclusions grim, but together the chapters in this book leave no doubt that we should have reduced confidence in deterrence, preventing the first use of nuclear weapons in this new age. This introduction explains why deterrence with new nuclear states, and not the United States-Russia renewed rivalry—depending obviously on the outcome of the 2022 Russian Invasion of Ukraine and the resulting war—poses the greatest risk of deliberate and inadvertent or accidental nuclear war.[3] It then outlines the gaps in our theories and knowledge of new nuclear states and the structural, technical, and political sources of nuclear instability in the emerging nuclear world. It motivates the volume by highlighting why theories derived from the superpower nuclear balance are inapplicable to the emerging nuclear landscape—basic assumptions such as bipolarity, significant financial and technical resources, regime predictability, stable civil-military relations and competent nuclear organizations, and technological symmetries between rivals may not apply to new and emerging nuclear weapons powers.

The Eroding Foundations of Nuclear Stability

The nonuse of nuclear weapons since Hiroshima and Nagasaki in 1945 has generated significant overconfidence and complacency in the restraining and stabilizing effects of nuclear weapons and deterrence. We do not deny that nuclear weapons can induce, and have induced, caution among their possessors. Nuclear deterrence has been, and remains, a powerful constraint on decisions to go to war or escalate in a war. But that powerful deterrent is by no means a perfect deterrent. This volume demonstrates that there are many reasons to fear that deterrence will be far more precarious in the future than it has been in the past.

Four main lines of argument exist as to why nuclear weapons have not been used in war or inadvertently since 1945. All four arguments are challenged by emerging evidence in the contemporary nuclear age. The first is the inherently stabilizing features of nuclear weapons, the most destructive weapons on the planet—or the benefits of the "theory of the nuclear revolution."[4] Nuclear weapons are so destructive, the theory holds, that once a condition of mutually accepted survivable nuclear forces is obtained by

---

3. On great power (Russia, China, and United States) nuclear relations, see Robert Legvold and Christopher F. Chyba, eds., "Meeting the Challenges of a New Nuclear Age: A Special Issue," *Daedalus* 149, no. 2 (Spring 2020).

4. Robert Jervis, *The Meaning of the Nuclear Revolution: Statecraft and the Prospect of Armageddon* (Ithaca, NY: Cornell University Press, 1989); Kenneth N. Waltz, *The Spread of Nuclear*

two nuclear weapons powers, any strategic nuclear weapons use would be suicidal and would result in mutually assured destruction, thereby inhibiting nuclear use. This may have had purchase on the theoretical stability of the superpower nuclear competition, where the sheer size of the US and Soviet force structures—and their ability to devote enormous resources and organizational power to (barely) managing them securely—made the prospect of a disarming first strike practically impossible. But even during the Cold War, the theory of the nuclear revolution had a worrying number of "near misses," and failed to explain why nuclear weapons states refrained from using nuclear weapons against nonnuclear adversaries.[5]

With emerging technologies and the spread of nuclear weapons to small states with smaller arsenals, it is not at all obvious that the conditions of the theory of the nuclear revolution are met anywhere besides the United States-Russia balance—for technological, structural, and domestic political reasons.[6] First, many nuclear states may not be confident in the survivability of their nuclear forces, and the United States, in particular, may not accept vulnerability to them. The combination of smaller arsenals and improving counterforce technologies threaten one of the theoretical pillars of the theory of the nuclear revolution. In such asymmetric nuclear balances, the requirements necessary for the theory of the nuclear revolution to hold may be inapplicable, and these are the balances that characterize the contemporary and future nuclear world. For example, China and North Korea may not believe that they have survivable second-strike forces against the United States, while the latter repeatedly refuses to accept mutual vulnerability with them, reinforcing their fears.[7] Pakistan may fear that India does not accept the survivability of its forces as Indian decision-makers express interest in counterforce strategies.[8] This leads states to adopt dangerous arms racing behavior or, worse, during crises, may inject every dispute with "use them or lose them" fears. Furthermore, the theory of the nuclear revolution argues that the possession of nuclear weapons reduces uncertainty in the interaction between states but smuggles in the notion that it was the bipolar structure of the Cold War that did most of the work in reducing systemic uncertainty.

Weapons: More May Be Better, Adelphi Paper, no. 171 (London, UK: International Institute for Strategic Studies, 1981).

5. Scott D. Sagan, *The Limits of Safety: Organizations, Accidents, and Nuclear Weapons*, (Princeton, NJ: Princeton University Press, 1993).

6. See Brendan R. Green, *The Revolution that Failed: Nuclear Competition, Arms Control, and the Cold War* (Cambridge, UK: Cambridge University Press, 2020); Kier A. Lieber and Daryl G. Press, *The Myth of the Nuclear Revolution: Power Politics in the Atomic Age* (Ithaca, NY: Cornell University Press, 2020).

7. 2018 Nuclear Posture Review, https://dod.defense.gov/News/SpecialReports/2018 NuclearPostureReview.aspx.

8. Christopher O. Clary and Vipin Narang, "India's Counterforce Temptations: Strategic Dilemmas, Doctrine, and Capabilities," *International Security* 43, no. 3 (Winter 2018/2019): 7–52.

The new nuclear era, however, is marked by multipolar nuclear competition where uncertainty and miscalculation are endemic to nuclear interactions, increasing risks, as Caitlin Talmadge's chapter shows. Finally, the theory of the nuclear revolution makes assumptions about the domestic political stability of nuclear powers and their ability to securely manage nuclear weapons. With the prospect of nuclear weapons powers led by unstable regimes, such as Pakistan, or personalist dictators such as Kim Jong Un or the next Saddam Hussein—leaders driven sometimes by pathologies and paranoia rather than rational, national cost-benefit calculation and who may lack the resources to safely and securely manage their nuclear weapons—these assumptions are tenuous, at best. Whether the theoretical requirements posited by the theory of the nuclear revolution applied even during the Cold War is debatable, but in the contemporary and future nuclear world, relying on a deterrence model whose fundamental assumptions depart so significantly from reality may be a blueprint for catastrophe. Indefinitely relying on the restraining effects of nuclear weapons to spare the world nuclear use, without accounting for the changing character of the nuclear world, is increasingly untenable.

A second, related argument for why nuclear weapons have not been used since 1945 is that there has not been a crisis or war since World War II with high enough stakes for a nuclear weapons state to seriously contemplate the use of nuclear weapons.[9] In other words, no nuclear power has faced a significant enough threat to warrant the use of nuclear weapons. This selection effect flows from one implication of the theory of the nuclear revolution: the stability-instability paradox.[10] This paradox, scholars note, means that two nuclear weapons powers in a condition of mutual vulnerability may experience a higher frequency of lower intensity conflict, but that the constraining effects of mutual nuclearization inhibit escalation to a point where the use of nuclear weapons might be rationally considered. The argument posits that crises like the Cuban Missile Crisis so focused the superpowers' minds on avoiding escalation that they rarely put themselves in a position where the use of nuclear weapons could or would be contemplated. The contemporary nuclear landscape, however, is dotted with nuclear powers that show little fear of escalation. India, frustrated by the constraining effects of Pakistani nuclearization, has increasingly tried to push the line on how far it can escalate militarily in crises, reaching a worrying historical first in 2019 when it bombed undisputed mainland Pakistani territory, the first time that a nuclear weapons power has done so against another nuclear weapons power. The concerning feature of the new nuclear era—as Mark Bell and Nicholas

---

9. See Benjamin A. Valentino, "Moral Character or Character of War? American Public Opinion on Targeting Civilians in Times of War," *Daedalus*, vol. 145, no. 4 (Fall 2016): 127–138.

10. See Jervis, *The Theory of the Nuclear Revolution*, 19–22.

Miller argue in their chapter—is that states may no longer seek to avoid crises but to win them and may advertently or inadvertently stumble into high-intensity conflict where the use of nuclear weapons no longer becomes unthinkable.

A third line of argument explaining the nonuse of nuclear weapons since 1945 is what Nina Tannenwald called the "nuclear taboo," that the moral opprobrium of nuclear weapons grew over time and inhibited the United States in particular from contemplating nuclear use against both nuclear and nonnuclear adversaries.[11] That no state used nuclear weapons since 1945 is a fact. But whether it was due to moral or prudential reasons—the tradition of nonuse—continues to be debated.[12] Nevertheless, both the taboo argument and the tradition of nonuse arguments are under threat in the contemporary nuclear landscape. For one, the taboo was always a contested norm, and it is not necessarily a strong one across the world, as Tannenwald herself has noted when expressing concerns of a "vanishing" taboo.[13] States such as Pakistan and North Korea, which rely on the threat of nuclear first use for their day-to-day security, have every incentive to undermine both the taboo and the stability of the tradition of nonuse to enhance the credibility of their deterrent threats.[14] Second, survey experiments by Scott Sagan, Benjamin Valentino, and Janina Dill suggest that publics across the world—from the United States to Israel to India to France—are unconstrained by either a taboo or a tradition of nonuse in their support of nuclear use.[15] The moral underpinnings of any nuclear taboo may be eroding, if they ever existed. And the argument for the tradition of non-use faces challenges from regimes and leaders who may be motivated by personal considerations and whose shorter time horizons undercut the prudential calculations that may have restrained the United States and the Soviet Union.

Fourth, the risk of nuclear weapons use has been inhibited by the small number of nuclear weapons states. During the Cold War, there were effec-

---

11. Nina Tannenwald, *The Nuclear Taboo: The United States and the Non-Use of Nuclear Weapons since 1945* (Cambridge, UK: Cambridge University Press, 2007).

12. See T.V. Paul, *The Tradition of Non-Use of Nuclear Weapons* (Stanford, CA: Stanford University Press, 2009); and Scott D. Sagan, "Realist Perspectives on Ethical Norms and Weapons of Mass Destruction," in *Ethics and Weapons of Mass Destruction: Religious and Secular Perspectives*, ed. Sohail H. Hashmi and Steven P. Lee (Cambridge: Cambridge University Press, 2004), 73–95.

13. Nina Tannenwald, "The Vanishing Nuclear Taboo? How Disarmament Fell Apart," *Foreign Affairs* 97, no. 6 (November/December 2018): 16–24.

14. See Vipin Narang, *Nuclear Strategy in the Modern Era: Regional Powers and International Conflict* (Princeton, NJ: Princeton University Press, 2014).

15. See Scott D. Sagan and Benjamin A. Valentino, "Revisiting Hiroshima in Iran: What Americans Really Think about Using Nuclear Weapons and Killing Noncombatants," *International Security* 42, no. 1 (Summer 2017): 41–79, doi.org/10.1162/ISEC_a_00284; and Janina Dill, Scott D. Sagan, and Benjamin A. Valentino, "Kettles of Hawks: Public Opinion on the Nuclear Taboo and Non-Combatant Immunity in the United States, United Kingdom, France, and Israel," *Security Studies*: 31, no. 1 (2022): 1–31.

tively three nuclear states—the United States plus its NATO allies Britain and France, the Soviet Union, and China. And the primary competition was between the United States and the Soviet Union, while China was content with a minimal retaliatory force that gave it the freedom to lay unallied between the superpowers. Israel and South Africa possessed undeclared and untested nuclear weapons capabilities, but their experiences were largely peripheral to the nuclear landscape. The small number of nuclear weapons powers made the nuclear world, and each state's nuclear arsenals, easier to manage and reduced systemic risk of accidents or intentional nuclear use.

As of 2022, there are "effectively" nine nuclear weapons states, with the addition of India, Pakistan, and North Korea. The latter two are led by a de facto praetorian regime and a personalist dictator, respectively, each with their own pathologies that may lead them to depart from classic means-end rational behavior in crises. And the future may herald significantly more independent nuclear weapons powers as nuclear contagion increases the risk of the spread of nuclear weapons, from Iran, Turkey, and Saudi Arabia to South Korea, Japan, and Germany if they ever choose to escape from a US nuclear umbrella that they fear is unreliable. The existence of more nuclear weapons states, some with resource constraints and immature organizations, inherently increases the risk of use in the system.

More worrying are the types of future states that might populate the future nuclear world, especially personalist dictatorships. Democracies and autocracies alike have developed and deployed nuclear weapons. Democracies and autocracies alike have started nuclear weapons programs and then abandoned them. But only autocracies, and a particular kind of autocracy, a personalist dictatorship, have tried to develop nuclear weapons after having signed the Nuclear Non-Proliferation Treaty.[16] These are the most worrying types of proliferators because of what we term the personalist paradox. Personalistic regime leaders are more likely to want the bomb and are more likely to start illicit programs because they have fewer domestic constraints and may have less fear of being caught cheating on nonproliferation commitments. Yet they are less likely to succeed in building nuclear weapons because of weak bureaucratic structures and pathologies that make it difficult for such leaders to sustain major scientific, industrial projects.[17] But North Korea's success, and Bashar al-Assad's near success in hiding an above-ground nuclear

---

16. See Scott D. Sagan, "The Causes of Nuclear Weapons Proliferation," *Annual Review of Political Science* 14, (March 2011): 225–244; and Christopher Way and Jessica L.P. Weeks, "Making it Personal: Regime Type and Nuclear Proliferation," *American Journal of Political Science* no. 3 (July 2014): 705–719.

17. See Jacques E.C. Hymans, *Achieving Nuclear Ambitions: Scientists, Politicians, and Proliferation* (Cambridge, UK: Cambridge University Press, 2012); and Målfrid Braut-Hegghammer, *Unclear Physics: Why Iraq and Libya Failed to Build Nuclear Weapons* (Ithaca, NY: Cornell University Press, 2016).

reactor in 2007, have provided a blueprint for personalist dictators everywhere who seek the bomb.[18] If they succeed, personalistic regimes may be more likely to use nuclear weapons due to accident, faulty decision making, or emotion, as Rose McDermott argues in this volume.[19]

The past is a poor template for the future, and the future nuclear world has the potential to be distinctly different—and more fragile—from anything we have previously confronted. More nuclear states, interacting more frequently and intensely, possessing smaller and less sophisticated arsenals, led by regimes whose preferences may depart from classic rationality, who seek to win crises rather than avoid them, operating in the modern high-velocity information environment where misinformation may be rampant, characterizes this new, more dangerous, nuclear world. The theoretical foundations that gave us any confidence that nuclear weapons would continue to be effective deterrents with minimal risk of accidents or intentional use are all eroding. This volume is the first attempt to characterize the key features of this new nuclear age and analyze and assess its risks. To better manage this potentially unstable new nuclear age, we must first understand it.

The Plan of the Book

This book is organized into two parts. The first part identifies the unique challenges of this new nuclear landscape—the characteristics that make it distinct from the previous nuclear eras. Caitlin Talmadge offers a framework for thinking about nuclear deterrence in a multipolar world and about multipolar nuclear interactions—like that between India, Pakistan, and China—which our existing theories derived from the bipolar Cold War model fail to consider. The uncertainty in regional and global multipolar nuclear interactions is a sharp deviation from the relative ease of managing a bipolar Cold War nuclear competition. Rose McDermott assesses a troubling attribute of many of the new nuclear states: their leaders tend to be personalist dictators, and such autocrats can behave in ways that deviate dangerously from our standard rationalist models of deterrence. They may be more risk-seeking, motivated by pathologies such as megalomania, narcissism, and revenge, making them harder to deter and predict. Vipin Narang and Heather Williams analyze crises in the new media—especially social media—environment and explore how new tools such as Twitter and private chat apps can amplify nationalism and misinformation/disinformation, thereby

---

18. See Vipin Narang, "Strategies of Nuclear Proliferation: How States Pursue the Bomb," *International Security* 41, no. 3 (Winter 2016/2017): 110–150.

19. See also Scott D. Sagan, "Armed and Dangerous: When Dictators Get the Bomb," *Foreign Affairs* 97, no. 6 (November/December 2018): 35–43.

accelerating or decelerating crises in novel ways. Amy Zegart explores the rise of open-source intelligence (OSINT) and how that may affect our ability to predict the emergence of nuclear states. While this makes it more challenging for states to hide nuclear weapons programs, proliferators may also learn to adapt to the growth of these new tools and become better hiders. The rise of OSINT tools may also make crisis de-escalation more difficult, as governments may no longer be able to sustain convenient face-saving fictions that have previously enabled crisis de-escalation.

The second part explores how enduring challenges that have confronted nuclear states—achieving reliability, survivability, and command and control over their nuclear forces—take on a new salience in this new nuclear age. Jeffrey Lewis and Ankit Panda examine how new nuclear states think about how much is enough when they develop their initial nuclear arsenals, and what this means for arsenal vulnerability and crisis dynamics, particularly when there may be a discrepancy between when a state thinks it has enough, but its adversary does not agree and vice versa. Christopher Clary asks the related question about whether nuclear forces in new nuclear powers are survivable in the so-called new era of counterforce. He concludes that although they are likely to be, the fear over survivability concerns—fears intentionally stoked by stronger powers such as the United States and potentially others such as India toward Pakistan—will intensify in the new nuclear age, leading to worrying crisis dynamics as states may have itchy trigger fingers. Giles David Arceneaux and Peter Feaver explore the problem of command and control in new nuclear states, revisiting the theory and evidence from Feaver's seminal work on this topic, as three new nuclear states have emerged since then. They show that new nuclear states are unlikely to have static command and control arrangements that are either persistently assertive or persistently delegative. Rather, many will likely transform their arsenals from assertive arrangements to delegative arrangements at the worst possible time—during a crisis or war—in order to avoid the force being neutralized, raising nuclear risks that the command and control literature has previously overlooked. Mark Bell and Nicholas Miller examine whether new nuclear states can learn the institution of deterrence, and whether they are sufficiently chastened after crises. Their conclusions are concerning, showing that nuclear states rarely learn the right lessons from crises and, rather than seeking to avoid future crises, tend to believe they escaped significant escalation due to their own skill, rather than luck, leading them to potentially push the line in future crises. And at some point, the bill for mistakenly believing that escalation is good and easy to control may come due.

We conclude with a chapter outlining a series of steps—crisis management, operational arms control, nonproliferation, and counterproliferation—that can be taken to mitigate these dangers. The emerging nuclear age presents a series of daunting challenges, ones that our existing theories and understandings derived largely from the Cold War are ill-equipped to manage. This book tries to make sense of these worrying challenges and offer potential suggestions to help minimize the risk that a nuclear weapon may be used in anger or by accident for the first time since 1945 as we enter a dark new nuclear landscape.

I. NEW CHALLENGES IN THE NEW NUCLEAR AGE

CHAPTER 1

Multipolar Deterrence in the Emerging Nuclear Era

Caitlin Talmadge

The end of the Cold War ushered in what some observers have called the second nuclear age. India and Pakistan's dramatic nuclear tests, North Korea's steady progress toward the bomb, fears about further proliferation by Iraq and Iran, and the specter of so-called loose nukes falling into terrorists' hands all presented nuclear dangers different from those that had accompanied the relatively rigid alliance blocs of the US-Soviet rivalry.[1] Despite these new dangers, the total number of nuclear weapons worldwide declined in the 1990s and 2000s compared to the Cold War due to US-Russian arms control.[2] Even amid all the unsettling changes in the regional nuclear landscape, the political relationships among the actual or potential nuclear-armed great powers remained relatively benign. US unipolarity muted any broader great power competition, and even where relationships

---

I gratefully acknowledge the support of the American Academy of Arts and Sciences in preparing this chapter. For able research assistance, I thank David Bernstein and Samuel Seitz. For helpful discussions and feedback, I thank Brendan Green, Charles Glaser, Nuno Monteiro, John Mearsheimer, Steve Miller, Tim McDonnell, Vipin Narang, Barry Posen, Scott Sagan, Elizabeth Saunders, Amy Zegart, and participants in workshops held by Yale University, the Carnegie Corporation of New York, Harvard's Belfer Center, and the American Academy of Arts and Sciences.

1. On the general causes of proliferation, the literature is voluminous, but see Scott Sagan, "Why Do States Build Nuclear Weapons? Three Models in Search of a Bomb," *International Security* 21, no. 3 (Winter 1996–1997): 54–86; and Alexandre Debs and Nuno Monteiro, *Nuclear Politics: The Strategic Logic of Proliferation* (New York: Cambridge University Press, 2017), including literature discussion, 13–27. On loose nukes, see Matthew Bunn, *The Next Wave: Urgently Needed New Steps to Control Warheads and Fissile Material* (Washington, DC: Carnegie Endowment for International Peace and Project on Managing the Atom, Harvard University, April 2000).

2. Hans Kristensen and Matt Korda, "Status of World Nuclear Forces," Federation of American Scientists, May 2019, https://fas.org/issues/nuclear-weapons/status-world-nuclear-forces/.

between the major states were occasionally tense, nuclear weapons simply were not a focal point the way they had been during the bipolar struggle of the Cold War.[3]

Since at least 2010, a new nuclear era has been emerging, distinct from both the Cold War and the interregnum that followed. It is characterized not simply by a larger number of nuclear actors but also by important changes in the relationships among them. The most crucial change is the emergence of renewed geopolitical competition among three nuclear-armed great powers—the United States, Russia, and China—that structurally looks different from both the two-sided superpower rivalry in the Cold War and the diffuse nuclear threats of the immediate post–Cold War period.[4] This distinctly triangular nuclear relationship at the great power level is likely to have important consequences on its own but will also intersect with long-gestating regional nuclear developments in potentially new ways.

Overall, the dual presence of multisided nuclear competitions at both the global and regional levels—and the potential for intersections between the two—raises the possibility that emerging deterrence dynamics may look quite distinct from those of the past. What will this sort of world mean for the peacetime, crisis, and wartime behavior of nuclear-armed states? As the continuing and lively contestation of Cold War nuclear history demonstrates, the answers to this question are not always intuitive or obvious even in retrospect, much less when trying to consider the future.[5] With that caveat in mind, this chapter attempts to leverage international relations theory, strategic nuclear thought, and the historical record to propose at least some initial answers.

In general, it is unlikely that the effects of nuclear weapons in this new era will be categorically good or bad; for example, systematically enhancing stability by making arms races, crises, and wars all less likely, or systematically undermining stability by making all these dangers much more likely. Yet the cross-cutting effects will probably be more bad than good on net. This is because a world of multiple nuclear actors will likely strengthen the deterrent power of nuclear weapons, but this power is already strong; thus, the enhancement of peace and stability will be real but somewhat marginal. By contrast, the new era will actively open additional paths for nu-

---

3. On unipolarity, see William Wohlforth, "The Stability of a Unipolar World," *International Security* 24, no. 1 (Summer 1999), 5–41; and Nuno Monteiro, *Theory of Unipolar Politics* (New York: Cambridge University Press, 2014). On polarity in general and the relationship between the distribution of power and the propensity for conflict, see John Mearsheimer, *The Tragedy of Great Power Politics* (New York: W.W. Norton, 2001), chap. 2.

4. For an early assessment of this emerging structure, see Brad Roberts, "Tripolar Stability: The Future of Nuclear Relations among the United States, Russia, and China," Institute for Defense Analyses paper, September 2002.

5. Francis J. Gavin, *Nuclear Weapons and American Grand Strategy* (Washington, DC: Brookings Institution Press, 2020).

clear instabilities not present in past nuclear configurations and will exacerbate dangers that were always a risk in the Cold War. The implication, paraphrased in terms of the famous Waltz-Sagan debate over the effects proliferation, is that more may be somewhat better, until it is much worse.[6]

This chapter argues that the greater uncertainty inherent to a world with multiple, independent, rivalrous nuclear states, both at the global level of the great powers as well as in regional sub-systems, is likely to marginally bolster some of the stabilizing effects of nuclear weapons. International relations theory and classic works in nuclear strategy would all suggest that the heightened prospect of unpredictable escalation in such a world should strengthen deterrence and significantly lower the likelihood of any rational state deliberately starting not only nuclear war but any type of war or crisis with a nuclear-armed opponent.

Unfortunately, even as this world will give nuclear-armed states ever stronger reasons not to deliberately start a war, it will also provide more ways they can stumble into one. The presence of multiple nuclear competitors—arrayed in both a great-power triangle as well as several regional dyads or triangles, with the potential for interaction between the great power and regional relationships—raises greater risks of miscalculation about what other states see as their core interests and what constitutes a challenge to the status quo. No one will welcome a crisis, but crises may still occur.

Furthermore, this prospect is likely to motivate at least some states to pursue vigorous peacetime nuclear competition in anticipation that the nuclear balance may indeed matter one day for bargaining or warfighting. The resulting arms races are then likely to create other risks of accidental or unauthorized nuclear use, especially given potential military organizational dynamics. These arms races also have the potential to make crises or wars more escalatory if they do break out, compared to a world in which nuclear weapons did not exist, or even compared to the Cold War. All of these possibilities make it hard even for those who credit nuclear weapons with keeping the Cold War cold to rest easy when contemplating the future of nuclear deterrence.

The chapter proceeds in four parts. The first section defines in more detail the key features of the emerging era. The next two sections then theorize about what these characteristics will likely mean for, first, the peacetime and, second, the crisis/wartime behavior of nuclear-armed states. Several historical vignettes and forward-looking scenarios help to illustrate the empirical plausibility of the potential dynamics. The last section of the chapter briefly summarizes the findings and discusses what they mean more broadly for policy.

---

6. Scott Sagan and Kenneth Waltz, *The Spread of Nuclear Weapons: An Enduring Debate*, 3rd ed. (New York: W.W. Norton, 2013).

CHAPTER 1

Defining the Emerging Nuclear Era

Observers have struggled since the end of the Cold War to describe, much less predict, the key features of the nuclear landscape that would eventually replace the once-dominant US-Soviet struggle. The US government's effort to do so began with the term "tailored deterrence." An invention of the Clinton administration, this idea developed further in the Bush and Obama years, and occupied a prominent place in the Trump administration's 2018 Nuclear Posture Review.[7] The basic concept is that unlike in the Cold War, when US deterrence strategy focused overwhelmingly on the Soviet Union, it must now contend with a world of multiple potential adversaries with nuclear weapons, in which one size does not fit all. A State Department study proceeds from the same premise.[8]

It is hard to disagree with this general idea, and many scholars have concurred that the current nuclear environment presents new challenges, although they characterize those challenges in various ways.[9] Some have even described the new landscape as a "multipolar nuclear world" or a situation of "nuclear multipolarity."[10] These terms can be confusing despite their long lineage in strategic nuclear thought.[11] The main reason is that a state's power

---

7. U.S. Department of Defense, "Nuclear Posture Review Report 2018," February 5, 2018, 25–40, https://media.defense.gov/2018/Feb/02/2001872886/-1/-1/1/2018-NUCLEAR-POSTURE-REVIEW-FINAL-REPORT.PDF. On the evolution of the term, see Brad Roberts, *The Case for U.S. Nuclear Weapons in the 21st Century* (Stanford: Stanford Security Studies, 2016), 18–19.

8. U.S. State Department, International Security Advisory Board, "Report on The Nature of Multilateral Strategic Stability," April 27, 2016, https://2009-2017.state.gov/documents/organization/257667.pdf.

9. Steven Miller, "The Rise and Decline of Global Nuclear Order?" in *Meeting the Challenges of the New Nuclear Age: Nuclear Weapons in a Changing Global Order*, ed. Steven Miller, Robert Legvold, and Lawrence Freedman (Cambridge, MA: American Academy of Arts and Sciences, 2019): 1–27; Gregory Koblentz, "Strategic Stability in the Second Nuclear Age," *Council on Foreign Relations*, Council Special Report no. 71 (November 2014); Andrew Krepinevich, *The Decline of Deterrence* (Washington, DC: Hudson Institute, March 2019), 24–33; Stephen Peter Rosen, "After Proliferation: What to Do If More States Go Nuclear," *Foreign Affairs* 85, no. 5 (September–October 2006): 9–14; and Willie Curtis, "The Assured Vulnerability Paradigm: Can it Provide a Useful Basis for Deterrence in a World of Strategic Multi-Polarity?" *Defense Analysis* 16, no. 3 (2000): 239–256.

10. Stephen J. Cimbala, "Deterrence in a Multipolar Nuclear World: Prompt Attacks, Regional Challenges, and U.S.-Russian Deterrence," *Air & Space Power Journal* (July–August 2015): 51–62; Christopher Twomey, "Asia's Complex Strategic Environment: Nuclear Multipolarity and Other Dangers," *Asia Policy*, no. 11 (January 2011), 57; and James Acton, "Chapter Five: Nuclear Multipolarity," *Adelphi Series* 50, no. 417 (2010), 84.

11. John Weltman, "Managing Nuclear Multipolarity," *International Security* 6, no. 3 (Winter 1981/82), 182–194; Richard Rosecrance, "Bipolarity, Multipolarity, and the Future," *Conflict Resolution* 10, no. 3 (1966): 319–320; Richard Brody, "Some Systemic Effects of the Spread of Nuclear Weapons Technology: A Study through Simulation of a Multi-Nuclear

and its nuclear status are related but distinct. All nuclear weapons states are not great powers (e.g., North Korea and Pakistan); all powerful states do not have nuclear weapons (e.g., Germany and Japan); and a state's overall power can be declining even if its nuclear arsenal is improving (e.g., Russia). Therefore, it is difficult to speak of multipolarity in a nuclear context without getting sidetracked into a discussion about whether the world as a whole is becoming more multipolar or not, or who counts as a pole.

Furthermore, the defining feature of the current era cannot simply be the presence of multiple nuclear-armed states, as the term "nuclear multipolarity" might imply. There were already six nuclear powers by the 1970s (the United States, the Soviet Union, Britain, France, China, and Israel), but everyone still references the era overall as one of strict bipolarity. This is because even as states besides the superpowers acquired nuclear weapons, their arsenals remained dramatically smaller and less capable than those of the superpowers, and these countries also lacked the other economic and military dimensions of superpower status.[12]

Most important, during the Cold War each of these other nuclear weapons states aligned with or at least tilted heavily toward one of the superpowers.[13] For example, France and Britain were closely tied to the United States through the North Atlantic Treaty Organization, though the force de frappe tried hard to have it otherwise. For a variety of reasons, Israel's relationship with the United States also grew closer around the time it developed nuclear weapons. Likewise, China developed its early nuclear capabilities with active help from the Soviet Union, its staunch communist ally at the time.[14] Although the two grew estranged by the mid-1960s, the period of Chinese isolation was relatively brief, and by the early 1970s, China and the United States were pursuing rapprochement. China's internal political upheaval during the intervening years, and the resulting disarray of its military forces, meant that China never

---

Future," *Journal of Conflict Resolution* 7, no. 4 (December 1963): 663–753; and Ciro Elliott Zoppo, "Nuclear Technology, Multipolarity, and International Stability," *World Politics* 18, no. 4 (July 1966): 579–606.

12. On these other proliferants, see Avery Goldstein, *Deterrence and Security in the 21st Century: China, Britain, France, and the Enduring Legacy of the Nuclear Revolution* (Stanford, CA: Stanford University Press, 2000); and Vipin Narang, *Nuclear Strategy in the Modern Era: Regional Powers and International Conflict* (Princeton: Princeton University Press, 2014).

13. Major studies of proliferation at the time assumed that new proliferants would fold into the existing bipolar order, aligning with either the Soviet or US camps. Albert Wohlstetter et al., *Moving toward Life in a Nuclear Armed Crowd?* Report prepared for U.S. Arms Control and Disarmament Agency (Los Angeles, CA: Science Applications, April 22, 1976).

14. Goldstein, *Deterrence and Security in the 21st Century*; Taylor Fravel, *Active Defense: China's Military Strategy since 1949* (Princeton: Princeton University Press, 2019), chap. 8; Taylor Fravel and Evan Medeiros, "China's Search for Assured Retaliation: The Evolution of Chinese Nuclear Strategy and Force Structure," *International Security* 35, no. 2 (Fall 2010): 48–87; and Jeffrey Lewis, *The Minimum Means of Reprisal: China's Search for Security in the Nuclear Age* (Cambridge, MA: American Academy of Arts and Sciences, 2007).

really constituted an independent nuclear power capable of sustained competition with the two superpowers.[15]

Today, by contrast, the world is witnessing multiple distinct but interrelated nuclear competitions emerging—not just the presence of multiple nuclear-armed states. By nuclear competitions, I mean politically contentious relationships between independent, nuclear-armed states that display a persistent effort to achieve military, political, and strategic advantages over a rival, with nuclear weapons being one of the major tools in that effort. These nuclear competitions differ in many important respects, as do the competitors.

One competition is occurring at the level of the nuclear-armed great powers, states that control vast territory and possess overall military capabilities that clearly set them apart from the rest of the pack. The United States, Russia, and China fall into this exclusive club, and all are engaged in major long-term nuclear modernization programs that clearly are motivated by the actual or potential nuclear capabilities of the other two. At the political level, the US relationships with Russia and China are much more hostile than the relationship of those two countries with each other, but Russia and China eye each other warily as well.[16]

Most important, a stable alliance between any two of the three countries seems highly unlikely. In particular, it is unlikely that any two of these three states would cooperate in a nuclear strategy or a nuclear war against the other. The incentives for defection from this sort of cooperation would be high because it would always be in the interest of any of the three great powers to sit out a nuclear war fought between the other two. Thus, cooperation between two against a third would be hard to sustain. The likely result is that there are and will likely remain three independent nuclear-armed great powers. This fact makes the structure of any nuclear competition or confrontation among them different from that of the two-player Cold War.[17]

This is not to say that three are currently competing on equal footing. The nuclear postures of the United States, Russia, and China differ in important ways. The United States currently possesses the most advanced, survivable, and secure nuclear arsenal and is most capable of conducting ambitious nuclear missions such as counterforce, damage limitation, and extended deter-

---

15. Roderick MacFarquhar and Michael Schoenhals, *Mao's Last Revolution* (Cambridge: Harvard University Press, 2006).

16. Kathrin Hille et al., "US Urged to Exploit Cracks in Russia-China relationships," *Financial Times*, July 26, 2020, available online; Paul Haenle et al., "Are China-Russian Relations Getting Too Close for Comfort?" China in the World Podcast, Carnegie-Tsinghua Center for Global Policy, October 30, 2019, available online, https://www.chinafile.com/library/china-world-podcast/are-china-and-russia-getting-too-close-comfort.

17. On the general features of bipolarity versus multipolarity, see Kenneth Waltz, *Theory of International Politics* (New York: McGraw-Hill, 1979), especially chap. 8; and Barry R. Posen, "Emerging Multipolarity: Why Should We Care?" *Current History* (November 2009): 347–352.

rence.[18] Yet Russia still benefits from the Soviet nuclear inheritance, and the sheer size of its arsenal endows it with a strong claim to survivability unless it is caught completely by surprise in a massive, bolt-from-the-blue, peacetime first strike.[19] Furthermore, despite a shrinking economic base, Moscow has invested heavily in growing and improving its arsenal of so-called nonstrategic nuclear weapons in order to make threats of first use more credible.[20]

China, meanwhile, has the smallest and least sophisticated arsenal of the three by far and continues to publicly adhere to a doctrine of no first use.[21] China's arsenal is also the most vulnerable to preemption, and the United States has yet to acknowledge a state of mutual vulnerability with China.[22] But China is making rapid strides toward a larger arsenal and has the economic base to sustain much more substantial nuclear forces if it chooses to do so.[23] Moreover, China's growing conventional capabilities and regional assertiveness make its nuclear capabilities much more relevant to geopolitical competition with the United States than would otherwise be the case.[24]

---

18. Amy Woolf, "U.S. Strategic Nuclear Forces: Background Developments, and Issues," Congressional Research Service, January 3, 2020; Keir Lieber and Daryl Press, "The New Era of Counterforce: Technological Change and the Future of Nuclear Deterrence," *International Security* 41, no. 4 (Spring 2017): 9–49; and Hans Kristensen and Matt Korda, "United States nuclear forces, 2020," *Bulletin of the Atomic Scientists* 76, no. 1 (2020): 46–60.

19. This is an important and often overlooked assumption in an authoritative open-source analysis of Russian vulnerability to a US counterforce strike. As Lieber and Press note, "A preemptive strike on an alerted Russian arsenal would still likely fail." Keir Lieber and Daryl Press, "The End of MAD? The Nuclear Dimension of U.S. Primacy," *International Security* 30, no. 4 (Spring 2006): 8.

20. Hans Kristensen and Matt Korda, "Russian Nuclear Forces, 2019," *Bulletin of the Atomic Scientists* 74, no. 2 (2019): 73–84.

21. Hans Kristensen and Matt Korda, "Chinese Nuclear Forces, 2019," *Bulletin of the Atomic Scientists* 75, no. 4 (2019): 171–178.

22. Vince Manzo, *Nuclear Arms Control without a Treaty? Risks and Options after New START* (report from Center for Naval Analyses, 2019), pt. IV, https://www.cna.org/CNA_files/PDF/IRM-2019-U-019494.pdf.

23. Hans Kristensen and Matt Korda, "China's Nuclear Missile Silo Expansion: From Minimum Deterrence to Medium Deterrence," *Bulletin of the Atomic Scientists*, September 1, 2021, https://thebulletin.org/2021/09/chinas-nuclear-missile-silo-expansion-from-minimum-deterrence-to-medium-deterrence/; Austin Long, "Myths or Moving Targets? Continuity and Change in China's Nuclear Forces," War on the Rocks, December 4, 2020, http://warontherocks.com/2020/12/myths-or-moving-targets-continuity-and-change-in-chinas-nuclear-forces/; Caitlin Talmadge, "The U.S.-China Nuclear Relationship: Growing Escalation Risks and Implications for the Future," Testimony before the U.S.-China Economic and Security Review Commission, Hearing on China's Nuclear Forces, June 7, 2021, https://www.uscc.gov/sites/default/files/2021-06/Caitlin_Talmadge_Testimony.pdf; and Caitlin Talmadge, "The U.S.-China Nuclear Relationship: Why Competition Is Likely to Intensify," Brookings Series on Global China, September 2019, 1–15, https://www.brookings.edu/research/china-and-nuclear-weapons/.

24. Talmadge, "The U.S.-China Nuclear Relationship"; and Austin Long, "U.S. Nuclear Strategy toward China: Damage Limitation and Extended Deterrence," in *America's Nuclear*

CHAPTER 1

The overall picture is thus that of an emerging great power nuclear competition among three actors who stand out from the rest of the pack, even as they differ from one another.

Distinct from this great power nuclear triangle, a second set of regional nuclear competitors is also apparent.[25] The most important characteristic of these states is that their nuclear behavior is no longer channeled, shaped, and suppressed by an overarching superpower competition the way it was during the Cold War. Unleashed from the strictures of bipolarity, the regional nuclear powers are now pursuing their own nuclear capabilities and competitions, the nature and purposes of which vary widely.[26]

For example, India and Pakistan both have nuclear capabilities aimed primarily at influencing the other, although their nuclear arsenals also offer some protection against great power predation.[27] India, in particular, worries about China.[28] North Korea, meanwhile, seeks to leverage its increasingly diversified nuclear arsenal to deter the United States and possibly coerce South Korea while also seeking autonomy from China.[29] For its part, Israel has a small but sophisticated arsenal aimed mainly at deterring conventional threats in its region, not tangling with other nuclear powers—although future proliferation by Iran, Saudi Arabia, or Turkey could change that.[30] Britain and France also maintain small but sophisticated nuclear arsenals, both of which have global reach, although neither country is currently engaged in a major nuclear rivalry and the main security concerns of both are regional. Britain has de-emphasized the role of nuclear weapons in its security strategy since

---

Crossroads: A Forward-Looking Anthology, ed. Caroline Dorminey and Eric Gomez (Washington, DC: Cato Institute, 2019), 47–55.

25. Miller, "The Rise and Decline of Global Nuclear Order?"

26. On regional nuclear powers, see Goldstein, *Deterrence and Security in the 21st Century*; and Narang, *Nuclear Strategy in the Modern Era*.

27. Narang, *Nuclear Strategy in the Modern Era*, chaps. 3 and 4.

28. See Lisa Michelini, Vipin Narang, and Caitlin Talmadge, "When Actions Speak Loud Than Words: Adversary Perceptions of Nuclear No First Use Pledges," draft paper presented at University of Oslo, November 2021.

29. Vipin Narang, "Nuclear Strategies of Emerging Powers: North Korea and Iran," *Washington Quarterly* 38, no. 1 (2015): 73–91; and Vipin Narang and Ankit Panda, "North Korea Is a Nuclear Power. Get Used to It," *New York Times*, June 12, 2018.

30. Narang, *Nuclear Strategy in the Modern Era*, chap. 7. On fears of a Middle East proliferation cascade, see Dalia Dassa Kaye and Frederic M. Wehrey, "A Nuclear Iran: The Reactions of Neighbors," *Survival* 49, no. 2 (June 1, 2007): 111–128; Roberts, *The Case for U.S. Nuclear Weapons in the 21st Century*, 222–223; Henry Sokolski, "In the Middle East, Soon Everyone Will Want the Bomb," *Foreign Policy*, May 21, 2018, https://foreignpolicy.com/2018/05/21/in-the-middle-east-soon-everyone-will-want-the-bomb/; Eric S. Edelman, Andrew F. Krepinevich, and Evan Braden Montgomery, "The Dangers of a Nuclear Iran: The Limits of Containment," *Foreign Affairs*, no. 1 (January/February 2011): 66–81; and Yoel Guzansky, "The Saudi Nuclear Genie Is Out," *Washington Quarterly* 38, no. 1 (January 2, 2015): 93–106. For a contrary view, see Barry Posen, *A Nuclear-Armed Iran: A Difficult But Not Impossible Policy Problem* (New York: Century Foundation, 2006).

the end of the Cold War, hewing closely to the United States, while France relies on nuclear weapons mostly as a hedge against major changes in its security environment.[31]

I refer to all of these actors as regional nuclear powers because, with the possible eventual exception of India, none of these states has the potential to contest any of the nuclear-armed great powers in a serious long-term nuclear competition. In several cases, the regional powers likely do not even have secure second-strike forces versus the great powers. Certainly, the regional nuclear powers do not have the ability or even the potential ability to hold at risk the great powers' nuclear forces, though they might have or seek this capability versus their neighbors. They are not in the business of extended deterrence, but they also do not need to be since their grand strategies do not involve a global fight for allies. Each of these countries also lacks at least one of the other traditional inputs to great power status, whether it be strategic depth (Pakistan, Israel, North Korea, France, Britain), a highly advanced economy (Pakistan, North Korea, India), or a large population (Israel, North Korea).[32] Yet they remain important because they are rivalrous nuclear-armed states, not tightly yoked to the major powers, which see nuclear weapons as integral to the management of their security problems.

The regional arsenals thus form the second tier in the emerging structure of nuclear politics. The key question is what does this two-tiered, multi-actor nuclear world mean for both the peacetime and the crisis or wartime behavior of nuclear-armed states; in other words, for general deterrence, arms races, arms control, and the risks of escalation? It is hard to know for sure because such a world has not existed before, but in the next two sections I sketch some possibilities.

Peacetime Behavior in a World of Multiple Nuclear Competitors

The presence of multiple nuclear competitors at the great power and regional levels is likely to have cross-cutting effects in peacetime.[33] On the one hand, nuclear-armed states, particularly when arrayed in multisided rivalries against opponents with survivable nuclear forces, should work hard not to deliberately provoke their like into a crisis or war. This should strengthen

---

31. Narang, *Nuclear Strategy in the Modern Era*, chap. 6.
32. Although often considered less important today than in the past eras, these inputs remain relevant to a state's ability to sustain long-term competition, and especially resource-intensive nuclear competition. The size of a country's population is a major factor in its potential ability to limit damage in a nuclear exchange. States with small populations concentrated in tight geographical areas are inherently more vulnerable to relatively small nuclear attacks.
33. Michael Intriligator and Dagobert Brito, "Nuclear Proliferation and the Probability of Nuclear War," *Public Choice* 37 (1981): 247–260.

general deterrence by dampening the chance of any rational state initiating conflict. On the other hand, in a world of multiple nuclear competitors, there are more ways to stumble into a crisis or war due to misperceptions and miscalculations. Furthermore, this prospect of getting into a war, even one no one wants, means that states may see good reasons to arms race. Overall, these latter destabilizing effects are likely to be more pronounced than the benefits to general deterrence which, though real, are probably relatively more marginal, because there are already strong rational incentives to avoid conflict among nuclear-armed states.

GENERAL DETERRENCE

Everyone fears the specter of nuclear war that has hung over humanity since 1945, but influential scholars argue that it is this very prospect that has prevented great power conflict since that time. It is no coincidence, in this view, that great power competition led to two catastrophic global conflicts in the thirty years before nuclear weapons were invented, yet no such war has taken place in the seventy-five years since.[34] Nuclear weapons have, in the words of Robert Jervis, "revolutionized" international politics. Once two states each have secure second-strike forces, meaning nuclear arsenals that can absorb a first strike and still impose unacceptable retaliatory damage on the opponent, they enter a state of mutual vulnerability that radically changes the relationship between military force and foreign policy. Under this condition of mutually assured destruction (MAD), military victory becomes meaningless. The loser of a war can impose as much damage on the winner as the winner can on the loser. Thus, the goal of both sides is no longer to win wars but to avoid them.[35]

Strong versions of the argument suggest that states will avoid not only war but also lower-level tussling that could lead to war. As Jervis argues, "Nuclear threats may not have to be highly credible to be highly effective. Even a slight chance that a provocation could lead to nuclear war will be sufficient to deter all but the most highly motivated adversaries. Furthermore, because a high level of violence could result even if neither side sought that outcome, states need not threaten all-out war in order to have that dan-

---

34. It is important to remember that the Cold War was not peaceful for everyone. The period was brutal for those ensnared in the great powers' proxy wars. Paul Thomas Chamberlain, *The Cold War's Killing Fields: Rethinking the Long Peace* (New York: Harper, 2018).

35. Robert Jervis, *The Meaning of the Nuclear Revolution: Statecraft and the Prospect of Armageddon* (Ithaca: Cornell University Press, 1989); and Thomas Schelling, Thomas Schelling, *Arms and Influence* (New Haven: Yale University Press, 2008). On the emotional underpinnings of this deterrence logic, see Rose McDermott et al., "'Blunt Not the Heart, Enrage It': The Psychology of Revenge and Deterrence," *Texas National Security Review* 1, no. 1 (December 2017): 68–88.

ger loom large in the adversary's (and their own) mind."[36] In short, because nuclear escalation is always a possibility, and would be so devastating, two or more states entrenched in this condition of mutual vulnerability will be loath to challenge the status quo. And there is little reason for them to do so if they are simply seeking security, because nuclear weapons give both sides a virtual guarantee against being invaded. Thus, the relationship may be tense, but crises will be rare and wars virtually nonexistent, as nuclear stalemate drains the system of competition.[37]

From this perspective, the uncertainty associated with a world of multiple independent nuclear actors should strengthen the deterrent effects of the nuclear revolution, profoundly inhibiting rational states from initiating conflict.[38] Any state that embarked on a nuclear war (or even a crisis that posed the possibility of escalation to war) would have to contend not only with reaction from the target but also with the possibility of intervention by other nuclear-armed states. Waltz made this argument even in the bipolar context of the Cold War: "as soon as additional states joined the nuclear club . . . the question of who deterred whom could no longer be easily answered," he explained. "The Soviet Union had to worry lest a move made in Europe might cause France and Britain to retaliate, thus setting off American forces as well. Such worries at once complicated calculations and strengthened deterrence. Somebody might have retaliated, and that was all a would-be attacker needed to know."[39]

In a world with multiple autonomous nuclear actors, an opportunistic third party could even use the occasion of a nuclear exchange between two other states to improve its own position.[40] Such an exchange would leave both contenders greatly weakened, at best; one might emerge as the winner in the sense of having more of its military, economy, and nuclear weapons left intact, but relative to the other nuclear-armed states in the system that had not been involved in the war, this winner could be relatively more vulnerable to coercion and certainly would be much weaker overall than before the war.

To put it in simple terms, imagine that on the first day of a war, Side A and Side B each have twenty-five nuclear weapons, but after the war Side A is left with ten nuclear weapons and Side B with two nuclear weapons. Side A's postwar position, while bad, is much better in a world in which State B is the only other nuclear-armed state versus a world in which there is a State C that also had twenty-five weapons on the first day of the war and was not involved in the war. In this world of adversarial nuclear-armed states,

---

36. Jervis, *The Meaning of the Nuclear Revolution*, 38.
37. Jervis, *The Meaning of the Nuclear Revolution*.
38. Intriligator and Brito, "Nuclear Proliferation and the Probability of Nuclear War."
39. Sagan and Waltz, *The Spread of Nuclear Weapons*, 14.
40. Brad Roberts, "Nuclear Multipolarity and Stability," *Institute for Defense Analyses*, IDA Document D-2539 (November 2000), S-4; and Acton, "Chapter Five," 88–89.

State C's arsenal is now more than double the size of the other two states' combined residual arsenals. Such a lopsided ratio potentially endows State C with the ability to coerce both A and B, depending on the nature of each state's forces, and it is unlikely that A would consider the war to have improved its position in this scenario even though it ended the war with more of its arsenal left intact than B.[41] C might even have incentives to deliberately provoke A and B into this sort of fight, a danger that Henry Rowen once called the "catalytic nuclear war" problem.[42]

The point of this vignette is not that such a scenario is realistic. It is that rational states are likely to anticipate this type of scenario in a world of multiple nuclear competitors and restrain themselves accordingly. In addition to all of the reasons for nuclear caution that exist even in a two-sided nuclear competition, the presence of a third party introduces new possibilities for postwar predation. After all, in a three-sided nuclear competition, there is a way to win a nuclear war: by sitting it out while the other two fight. Recognition of this possibility should inhibit states even more strongly from deliberately starting such wars, or from anything that might entangle them in such a war.

From this perspective, then, it does not really matter that China's nuclear arsenal is currently much smaller than that of the United States or Russia. The question is not how many nuclear weapons China has versus the other two competitors in peacetime; it is how many China has after the United States and Russia fight a nuclear war, and whether this is enough to help China advance its foreign policy objectives. Again, this is not a prediction that the United States and Russia are going to fight a general nuclear war, or that China would then use its position afterward to push a much-weakened postwar United States out of the Pacific. It is simply noting that any reasonable US or Russian leader would have to think about this prospect before setting in motion events that could lead to such a war, and in so doing would probably step back from the precipice.

We now know that even in the bipolar environment of the Cold War, senior US military leaders thought about exactly this problem as they discussed revisions to the Single Integrated Operational Plan (SIOP) in the early 1970s. Declassified documents reference the need to develop a US option for striking China in the event of a war with the Soviet Union, to "negate any immediate Chinese communist nuclear threat to the United States and preclude the PRC from emerging as the dominant nuclear power fol-

---

41. I draw in this vignette on James N. Miller, "Zero and Minimal Nuclear Weapons," in *Fateful Visions: Avoiding Nuclear Catastrophe* (Cambridge, MA: Harper & Row, 1988), 19.

42. Henry Rowen, "Catalytic Nuclear War," in *Hawks, Doves, & Owls: An Agenda for Avoiding Nuclear War*, ed. Graham Allison, Albert Carnesale, and Joseph Nye (New York: Norton, 1995), 150–153.

lowing an exchange between the US and USSR."[43] In other words, despite China's rudimentary arsenal, which never remotely amounted to a third superpower during the Cold War, US officials worried that China could effectively end up the winner of a US-Soviet nuclear war unless the United States revised the SIOP to ensure otherwise.

This fear seems likely to be much more pronounced in a world where China's nuclear arsenal is growing and improving, and it seems inherent to the structure of three-sided nuclear competitions. A future India, too, will have to worry about predation from China if it exhausts itself in a nuclear war with Pakistan, and the winner of a nuclear war between a future nuclear-armed Saudi Arabia and a nuclear Iran would be Israel. These are all hypotheticals, and again, the point is not that these wars will happen. Rather, the point is that states will anticipate the postwar predation problem and not begin such wars in the first place.

That being said, the Cold War certainly demonstrates that nuclear-armed states can stumble into crises that they do not want, because they may have different definitions of the status quo or misunderstand how the opponent will perceive their actions.[44] In the early crises over Berlin, for example, neither side considered itself revisionist, but each was considered revisionist by the other, and they ended up on the brink of war twice. The Cuban Missile Crisis continued this theme. The Soviets saw the emplacement of missiles on the island as their answer to the US presence in Berlin and the ring of US bomber bases surrounding the Soviet periphery. Americans, in turn, viewed the introduction of Soviet nuclear forces in the western hemisphere as a sign of aggression, even though it did little to change the nuclear balance.[45]

Ultimately, general deterrence, while strong during the Cold War (strong enough that we are all still here to tell the tale), was probably not as strong as nuclear revolution adherents would expect. The rational incentives to avoid crises were high, yet crises still happened. The presence of multiple autonomous nuclear-armed states is likely to augment the incentives for any rational state to avoid deliberately starting a crisis or war, but these incentives are already strong, and a multisided nuclear competition could also multiply the ambiguities and miscalculations that produce unintended crises. The net effect of these competing influences over time is hard to predict in

---

43. Sayre A. Swartzrauber to JCS Chairman et al., "Single Integrated Operational Plan," February 25, 1972, Top Secret, enclosing memorandum from Secretary of Defense Laird to JCS Chairman on the same topic, February 25, 1972, and JCS message 3440, same topic, February 24, 1972, Top Secret, 1, National Security Archive, George Washington University.

44. Brendan Green, *The Revolution That Failed: Nuclear Competition, Arms Control, and the Cold War* (Cambridge: Cambridge University Press, 2020).

45. Marc Trachtenberg, *History and Strategy* (Princeton: Princeton University Press, 1991), chaps. 1, 3, 5, 6.

CHAPTER 1

any particular scenario but warrants more pessimism than optimism over time.

ARMS RACES

If, as just argued, states with nuclear weapons are likely to believe that there is still some chance of entering a nuclear crisis or war, even a crisis or war they do not see themselves as initiating and do not want, then they are unlikely to abandon peacetime nuclear competition. Even in the Cold War, neither side accepted nuclear stalemate.[46] Each perpetually worried that the other was irrational and aggressive and that technological change might someday render MAD obsolete. Thus they repeatedly sought to try to achieve a meaningful advantage in the nuclear balance, even though the nuclear revolution school of thought would suggest that no such advantages can exist once two states cross a relatively low threshold of nuclear capability. Through a combination of civil defenses, missile defenses, and, most important, counterforce capabilities against the other side's nuclear weapons, both sought to limit the costs they would suffer in the event of an all-out nuclear war.

The Soviet Union and especially the United States pursued this approach, known as damage limitation, for a variety of reasons.[47] But an important one may have been a belief that having such a capability—or having the adversary believe that one believed one had such a capability, whether one did or not—would improve their bargaining positions in a crisis. If one side had the ability to limit the damage it suffered in an all-out nuclear war, or could just convince the adversary that it believed it had this capability, it might have been possible to bargain more credibly over high-stakes issues by convincing the opponent that one was more willing to tolerate the risk of escalation. This pursuit of damage limitation and the reactions to it—that is, building ever-larger offensive forces to deny the adversary any hope of meaningfully limiting costs in an all-out war—became a major driver of the Cold War arms race.[48]

A three-sided nuclear competition could intensify this dynamic in three ways. First, given the postwar predation problem, having more nuclear-

---

46. Green, *The Revolution That Failed*; Austin Long and Brendan Green, "Stalking the Secure Second Strike: Intelligence, Counterforce, and Nuclear Strategy," *Journal of Strategic Studies* 38, no. 1 (2015): 38–73; Steven Zaolga, *The Kremlin's Nuclear Sword: The Rise and Fall of Russia's Strategic Nuclear Forces, 1945–2000* (Washington, DC: Smithsonian Institution Press, 2002).

47. On defining damage limitation, see Charles Glaser and Steve Fetter, "Should the United States Reject MAD? Damage Limitation and U.S. Nuclear Strategy toward China," *International Security* 41, no. 1 (Summer 2016): 49–50.

48. On this logic, and for a critique of it, see Charles Glaser, *Analyzing Strategic Nuclear Policy* (Princeton: Princeton University Press, 1990). For a more recent exposition, see Matthew Kroenig, *The Logic of American Nuclear Strategy: Why Strategic Superiority Matters* (Oxford: Oxford University Press, 2018).

armed adversaries probably expands what is required for a damage limitation capability that could meaningfully affect a state's credibility in bargaining. To return to the vignette, it is now not enough for State A to limit damage only with respect to State B; it also has to have enough left over to continue to influence State C. Only if State A can convince State B that it can tolerate more risk with respect to State B *and* State C will A improve its bargaining position versus B. That is a high bar and provides a rationale for building higher levels of arms than would be the case in a world without a nuclear-armed State C.

Yet nothing from the experience of the Cold War leads to the expectation that great powers will throw up their hands and shrink from this challenge.[49] In fact, despite the fragility of China's nascent nuclear forces in that era, both superpowers still expressed concern about a situation in which China might sit out a US-Soviet nuclear war and emerge the winner—and their anticipation of this problem probably led them both to build or retain somewhat larger forces than otherwise would have been the case. In initial arms control negotiations with the Americans, for example, "the Soviet leadership implied that at the end of the talks, the USSR would require a certain 'reserve' to account for the Chinese forces as well."[50] In other words, even the tentative prospect of another major nuclear-armed state apparently drove Soviet calculations of their needed force size upward, albeit probably not in dramatic fashion.

Similarly, according to an unusually well-sourced *Washington Post* article, and consistent with the SIOP revisions already discussed, the US military in the late 1970s developed "a special targeting plan for China that required U.S. weapons to be held in reserve for possible strikes against Beijing's handful of strategic warheads. . . . The aim of the plan was to ensure that China could not become the world's most powerful nation following a general nuclear war between Russia and the United States."[51] Again, this is not to say that China's minimal forces were the main driver of US arsenal size, but the fact that US officials thought in terms of a reserve force versus China, even at a time when rapprochement was well underway, is telling. It suggests that a full-blown nuclear competition among three great powers could drive arsenals upward in the future.

Regional powers, by definition, cannot compete in this sort of arms race with the great powers. But they certainly could engage in such arms races with one another, and would face largely the same set of incentives to do so

---

49. Some of this logic draws on Acton, "Chapter Five," 84; and Andrew Krepinevich, *The Decline of Deterrence* (Washington, DC: Hudson Institute, March 2019), 26–28.

50. Aleksandr' G. Savel'yev and Nikolay N. Detinov, *The Big Five: Arms Control Decision-Making in the Soviet Union* (Westport, CT: Praeger, 1995), 13.

51. R. Jeffrey Smith, "Clinton Directive Changes Strategy on Nuclear Arms," December 7, 1997, quoted in Timothy McDonnell, "The Terrible Swift Sword: U.S. Nuclear Posture and Foreign Policy," unpublished manuscript, 2020, 378, available from the author.

CHAPTER 1

if those competitions involved three or more players. If a regional power believed that there could someday be a crisis or war in which the nuclear balance mattered, it might seek an advantage in that balance over other states through the development of counterforce capabilities and strategic defenses. India already appears to be pursuing both.[52] The general point is that situations of three or more players drive arsenals up, not down.

Second, the presence of multiple nuclear competitions may generate overlapping arms races that feed into and off of one another. It is important to remember that the Cold War arms race, as intense as it was, was driven largely by the actions and reactions of the two superpowers, notwithstanding the US and Soviet considerations about China. By contrast, contemporary developments involving the United States, China, India, and Pakistan illustrate how the presence of multiple nuclear competitors could fuel multiple intersecting arms races across the two tiers of nuclear-armed states, especially if any of them pursue offensive counterforce capabilities as technology increasingly allows.[53]

For example, the United States points to China's nuclear modernization program as one of the justifications for its own nuclear modernization, including ever-growing counterforce capabilities for purposes of damage limitation.[54] China's modernization is at least partly a reaction to the United States' long-standing position of nuclear advantage vis-à-vis China, epitomized by the fact that the United States has not acknowledged a state of mutual vulnerability with China.[55] If the United States and China were the only two major rivalrous nuclear states in the system, this alone might be enough to generate an intense arms race, as it was in the Cold War. Yet China's simmering rivalry with India, another nuclear-armed state, adds another dimension because China's efforts to make its nuclear forces more survivable against the United States also make them potentially more threatening to India.[56] Unsurprisingly, therefore, India is showing signs of seeking to acquire a more credible deterrent against China. These nascent Indian capabilities directed at China, however, are also improving India's ability to engage in counterforce strikes

---

52. Christopher Clary and Vipin Narang, "India's Counterforce Temptations: Strategic Dilemmas, Doctrine, and Capabilities," *International Security* 43, no. 3 (Winter 2018/19): 7–52; and Charles Ferguson and Brue MacDonald, *Nuclear Dynamics in a Multipolar Strategic Ballistic Missile Defense World* (Washington, DC: Federation of American Scientists, 2017).

53. On the intersections, see Acton, "Chapter Five," 84. On counterforce, see Lieber and Press, "The New Era of Counterforce."

54. U.S. Department of Defense, "Nuclear Posture Review Report 2018."

55. Manzo, *Nuclear Arms Control without a Treaty?*

56. Robert Einhorn and W.P.S. Sidhu, "The Strategic Chain Linking Pakistan, India, China, and the United States," *Brookings Institution* (2017), 1. See also Tong Zhao, "China's Strategic Environment and Doctrine," annex to Einhorn and Sidhu, "The Strategic Chain Linking Pakistan, India, China, and the United States," 22; and P.K. Singh, "The India-Pakistan Nuclear Dyad and Regional Nuclear Dynamics," *Asia Policy*, no. 19 (2015): 37–44.

against Pakistan.⁵⁷ As a result, Pakistan now has incentives to enlarge its forces as well, which will only then stimulate further improvements in India's capabilities. Those Indian capabilities, in turn, will feed back into Chinese motivations for developing a more robust arsenal, which will then feed right back into US justifications for modernization.

Each country's armament decisions stem from multiple factors, both domestic and international, and this is a simplified sketch. Nevertheless, it is hard to ignore the sense that what happens in one dyad is cascading into the others and then ricocheting back, especially as nuclear forces increasingly are able to threaten an opponent's arsenal, not just its cities. Structurally, this dynamic seems even more likely today than in the Cold War, and it seems capable of generating a higher overall level of armament than the individual dyads otherwise would.

Third, alliance dynamics in a world of multiple nuclear competitors could also intensify pressures to arms race. Even in the Cold War, a situation in which structural realists would have expected alliances to be relatively peripheral, extended deterrence commitments were a major driver of larger and more capable superpower arsenals.⁵⁸ Higher force levels, and eventually the development of counterforce capabilities and the deployment theater nuclear capabilities, were seen as key to strengthening the US nuclear umbrella.⁵⁹

The basic reason was that extended deterrence commitments always have a credibility problem: both the adversary and the ally have to be convinced that the patron will expose its homeland to nuclear risk in defense of the ally.⁶⁰ This is a hard sell. A patron with a damage limitation capability can try to make this claim a bit more credible because the perceived ability to reduce the danger facing his own cities in a nuclear war may make it less costly for him to defend his ally in a way that might provoke such a war. The Soviet Union and especially the United States developed absurdly large arsenals in part because of this reasoning.

These dynamics could reappear in amplified form if the presence of more nuclear competitors leads to the emergence of new extended deterrence

---

57. Clary and Narang, "India's Counterforce Temptations."
58. Waltz, *Theory of International Politics*, chap. 8; and Posen, "Emerging Multipolarity." For an early take on extended deterrence commitments and the Cold War arms race, see Earl Ravenal, "Counterforce and Alliances: The Ultimate Connection," *International Security* 6, no. 4 (Spring 1982): 26–43.
59. Marc Trachtenberg, *A Constructed Peace: The Making of the European Settlement, 1945–1963* (Princeton: Princeton University Press, 1999); Ivo Daalder, *The Nature and Practice of Flexible Response: NATO Nuclear Strategy and Theater Nuclear Forces since 1967* (New York: Columbia University Press, 1991); and Brian Auten, *Carter's Conversion: The Hardening of American Defense Policy* (Columbia: University of Missouri Press, 2008).
60. Mira Rapp-Hooper, "Absolute Alliances: Extended Deterrence in International Politics," PhD diss., Columbia University, 2015.

commitments.[61] The result could be intense pressure for larger arsenals oriented toward counterforce, at least as substantial as what was seen in the Cold War, and probably more so given the considerations already described above. The emergence of such arsenals could then provide another mechanism for activating or intensifying the broader arms race dynamics.[62]

East Asia offers a glimpse of the potential role of alliances in this sort of world. The emergence of North Korea as a nuclear power has already catalyzed greater demands from South Korea and Japan for US protection. The United States points to these demands as one justification for its continued pursuit of damage limitation, including ever-improving counterforce capabilities. The United States has also deployed regional missile defenses that it states are designed for use against North Korean missiles. Many in China believe that both the missile defenses and counterforce capabilities stem from the US pursuit of a first-strike capability against China.[63] The logic is that effective defenses might enable the United States to mop up China's "ragged retaliation" in the aftermath of a US attack, making such an attack much less costly to the United States and its allies than it otherwise would be. China also probably fears that even the prospect of this sort of damage limitation capability could enhance the United States' bargaining leverage more generally, giving the latter a higher tolerance for bearing the risks of nuclear escalation even in disputes or crises that begin over non-nuclear issues.

Whether one takes expressed Chinese concerns at face value or not, US alliance commitments to South Korea and Japan due to North Korea's nuclear capabilities make it almost inevitable that the United States will acquire capabilities that China sees as threatening. These sorts of dilemmas, or "trilemmas" as Mira-Rapp Hooper and Linton Brooks call them, will become more common in the emerging nuclear environment, not less.[64] East Asia, in particular, demonstrates how great power nuclear competitions are likely to intersect with the emergence of regional nuclear powers in destabilizing ways. In short, a world of multiple nuclear competitors may be peaceful, but it may also be tense and characterized by unrelenting pressure to arms race by states that can afford to do so.

Unfortunately, these larger arsenals also will pose ever-greater management challenges to the states that possess them. Findings from organization theory applied to military behavior, as well as the US and Soviet experiences with nuclear weapons, should instill humility about what Scott Sagan calls

---

61. Roberts, *The Case for U.S. Nuclear Weapons in the 21st Century*, 232.
62. Acton, "Chapter Five," 88–89.
63. Fiona Cunningham and Taylor Fravel, "Assuring Assured Retaliation: China's Nuclear Strategy and U.S.-China Strategic Stability," *International Security* 40, no. 2 (Fall 2015): 7–50.
64. Linton Brooks and Mira Rapp-Hooper, "Extended Deterrence, Assurance, and Reassurance in the Pacific during the Second Nuclear Age," in *Strategic Asia 2013–2014* (Seattle, WA: National Bureau of Asian Research, 2014), X.

"the limits of safety."[65] More nuclear weapons possessed by more states introduces an inherently greater risk of accidental or unauthorized nuclear use, even if it also provides strong inhibitions against deliberate use. Although it is straightforward to deduce from rational deterrence theory the incentives that states will have to manage their nuclear arsenals competently, it is organizations—especially military organizations—that will often make the consequential decisions about arsenal composition, safety procedures, and security measures. It is possible that their political interests, worldviews, professional incentives, and standard operating procedures will lead to suboptimal behavior and even catastrophe. "The superpowers' experience with nuclear weapons in the Cold War was like walking across thin ice," Sagan writes. "The fact that two states performed this feat one time should not lead us to think that other states can safely do it nor that Russia and America can continue walking along that dangerous path forever."[66]

Crisis and Wartime Behavior in a World of Multiple Nuclear Competitors

Though a world of multiple nuclear competitors strengthens the incentives for states to avoid crises or wars, if such crises or wars do break out, the prospects for both horizontal and vertical escalation seem higher. The greater number of players increases the likelihood of misperceptions, such that a nuclear crisis that initially involves only two states could inadvertently come to involve other states, or that two separate, concurrent nuclear crises could inadvertently exacerbate each other. These dynamics could be destabilizing and make de-escalation harder than it would have been in the Cold War.

In a system with only two nuclear-armed great powers, nuclear crises can undoubtedly be dangerous, but there is a certain simplicity to nuclear signaling.[67] State A need only transmit to and receive information from State B. A can usually make a reasonable assumption that B's behavior is directed at A and vice versa. In a world of multiple nuclear competitors, however, nuclear signals that A sends to B may also be read by State C, which may be unaware of the ongoing A-B crisis and, believing itself to be the target of aggression, respond accordingly. C's response could then be read as the initiation of a new crisis by A or B or both. A could then respond to C, but B may interpret that action as directed at B, leading to escalation in both the A-B and the A-C crises.

Though a bit convoluted, this sort of dynamic is not particularly difficult to imagine in the future given various possible adversarial nuclear triangles

---

65. Scott Sagan, *The Limits of Safety: Organizations, Accidents, and Nuclear Weapons* (Princeton: Princeton University Press, 1993).
66. Sagan and Waltz, *The Spread of Nuclear Weapons*, 81.
67. Ciro Elliott Zoppo, "Nuclear Technology, Multipolarity, and International Stability," *World Politics* 18, no. 4 (July 1966), 601.

within and across the great power and regional power tiers of competition: the United States-Russia-China; the United States-North Korea-China; China-India-Pakistan; or, in a future nuclear Middle East, Israel-Iran-Turkey, Israel-Iran-Saudi Arabia, or Israel-Saudi Arabia-Turkey. In all of these trios, what started as a crisis between two of the states could quickly draw in the third state (or even a fourth or fifth), which would then contribute further to the action-reaction dynamic. For example, if China started to mobilize its nuclear forces in a crisis with the United States, India would certainly take notice, but if India were not aware of the crisis with the United States, its interpretation of and reaction to China's mobilization could be ominous. Or, India could be aware of the US-China crisis and choose to alert its forces simply to reduce vulnerability at a time that its nuclear-armed neighbor might also be going on alert. Either way, the question of China's reaction to the Indian alert would then be important, particularly if China inferred the possibility of coordination between the United States and India against China. This sort of potential chain reaction demonstrates how the structure of the emerging nuclear environment could exacerbate crises rather than contain them.

There is also the possibility that two nuclear crises could arise in separate dyads concurrently and then exacerbate each other. In the worst-case scenario, a state with limited or inaccurate situational awareness might even mistakenly attribute the source of an attack (especially a cyberattack) on its nuclear forces or command and control to the wrong opponent and retaliate accordingly.[68] For example, will a future nuclear Saudi Arabia have the ability to distinguish an Iranian cyberattack on its nuclear command and control from an Israeli one? The persistent confusion over the 2019 Abqaiq attack does not inspire confidence. In general, there is no guarantee that the regional nuclear powers will develop the national technical means needed to attribute incoming attacks on their nuclear arsenals at the same rate that they acquire the weapons themselves.

In a more mild but still troubling scenario, the simultaneity of crises could make both harder to de-escalate. For example, a US-China crisis could be much harder to resolve if it arose at the same time as an India-Pakistan crisis because China and India are also nuclear rivals. China might be reluctant to take steps to de-escalate the crisis with the United States if these also opened a window of vulnerability to India at a time when India was already at a high level of nuclear readiness.

Even in the Cold War, crisis communication and de-escalation proved difficult, with signals often misunderstood or simply not received. Nothing about the emerging nuclear landscape will ease these challenges. An un-

---

68. Wohlstetter identified this basic problem early in the Cold War. Albert Wohlstetter, "Nuclear Sharing: NATO and the N+1 Country," *Foreign Affairs* 39, no. 3 (April 1961), 371.

usual moment in the Cold War offers a glimpse into the challenges of managing multiplayer nuclear crises. The fall of 1969 witnessed two separate showdowns between two different nuclear-armed dyads: a border clash between the Soviet Union and China, and a tense negotiation over Vietnam between the Soviet Union and the United States. Both developed a nuclear dimension.[69]

In the Sino-Soviet dispute, the Soviets resorted to nuclear threats against China's arsenal in an attempt to get China to back down.[70] Although initially skeptical of the Soviet saber-rattling, the Chinese grew alarmed after learning through diplomatic backchannels that the Soviets were floating the notion of a nuclear attack on China to the Americans. Although the United States threw cold water on the idea, Chinese leaders did not know that. Chinese leaders "concluded—wrongly—that the United States not only supported the Soviet Union but was deliberately waiting for the two communist rivals to go to war in order to join the conflict late on the winning side, as it presumably had done in the First and Second World Wars."[71] Furthermore, Chinese leaders feared that Moscow's subsequent efforts to negotiate were actually a smokescreen for conducting a surprise nuclear attack. On three different occasions, Chinese leaders convinced themselves that such an attack was imminent.[72] Growing more paranoid by the day about the prospect of war, Chinese leaders evacuated the cities and initiated a massive civil defense effort. Most important, China's rudimentary nuclear forces went on alert—a dangerous step in itself, given the reliance on volatile, liquid-fueled missiles—and China test-fired a nuclear weapon at Lop Nor.[73]

Meanwhile, at the same time that this crisis was unfolding between the Soviet Union and China, the Nixon administration was struggling mightily to end the Vietnam War. Nixon decided to try to convince Hanoi that he was a madman who might just turn to nuclear weapons if the North Vietnamese did not come to terms. In order to try to make this threat credible, Nixon secretly alerted US nuclear forces (the alert had to be secret, and therefore

---

69. For background on each, see Michael Gerson, *The Sino-Soviet Border Conflict: Deterrence, Escalation, and the Threat of Nuclear War in 1969* (Center for Naval Analyses, November 2010); M. Taylor Fravel, *Strong Borders, Secure Nation: Cooperation and Conflict in China's Territorial Disputes* (Princeton: Princeton University Press, 2008), 211–217; and William Burr and Jeffrey Kimball, *Nixon's Nuclear Specter: The Secret Alert of 1969, Madman Diplomacy, and the Vietnam War* (Lawrence: University of Kansas Press, 2015).

70. Gerson, *The Sino-Soviet Border Conflict*.

71. Lorenz Luthi, "Restoring Chaos to History: Sino-Soviet-American Relations, 1969," *The China Quarterly*, 2012, 393.

72. Gerson, *The Sino-Soviet Border Conflict*, 46, 50; and John Wilson Lewis and Litai Xue, *Imagined Enemies: China Prepares for Uncertain War* (Stanford: Stanford University Press, 2006), 58–64.

73. See sources and discussion in Caitlin Talmadge, "Would China Go Nuclear? Assessing the Risk of Chinese Nuclear Escalation in a Conventional War with the United States," *International Security* 41, no. 4 (Spring 2017): 88–89.

CHAPTER 1

limited in some significant ways, because it would have been deeply politically unpopular had the public learned of it). He knew the North Vietnamese would have little ability to detect the heightened state of readiness, but their patron, the Soviet Union, likely would and might then pressure them to accede to Washington's demands.[74]

What the Americans transmitted may not have been what the Soviets received, however. The Americans at first were not sure the Soviets even detected the limited alert. Documents from the time reveal ongoing efforts by Washington to observe a Soviet political or military response.[75] We now know based on interviews conducted after the end of the Cold War that Soviet leaders were aware of the US alert, but they also were uncertain of the intentions behind it.[76]

More specifically, the Soviets did not register the US alert as connected to negotiations over Vietnam. From the US perspective, it was clear that Vietnam was the top issue of concern, as National Security Advisor Henry Kissinger had repeatedly stressed to his Soviet counterpart Anatoly Dobrynin in the weeks leading up to the alert; thus, the Americans expected that the Soviets would infer that the alert was an attempt to apply pressure on Hanoi.[77] But this did not occur. When Dobrynin met with Kissinger and Nixon after the alert was well underway, the former said nothing new on Vietnam, disappointing and perplexing the Americans. The Soviet documentary record remains inaccessible, as do US intelligence assessments of Soviet reactions to the alert, so it is hard to know for sure why the Soviets did not appear to move at all on Vietnam in response to the alert. They may just have been tough negotiators. But another explanation is that the Soviets simply did not recognize the secret alert as a signal about Vietnam, because the Americans did not identify it explicitly as such; indeed, precisely

---

74. Scott Sagan and Jeremi Suri, "The Madman Nuclear Alert: Secrecy, Signaling, and Safety in October 1969," *International Security* 27, no. 4 (Spring 2003): 150–183; William Burr and Jeffrey Kimball, "Nixon's Secret Nuclear Alert: Vietnam War Diplomacy and the Joint Chiefs of Staff Readiness Test, October 1969," *Cold War History* 3, no. 2 (January 2003): 113–156; William Burr and Jeffrey Kimball, "Nixon's Nuclear Ploy," *Bulletin of the Atomic Scientists*, vol. 59 (no. 1): 28–73; and Burr and Kimball, *Nixon's Nuclear Specter*, especially introduction and chap. 8.

75. Memorandum to Secretary of Defense from JCS Chairman Earle Wheeler, "US Military Readiness Tests—Worldwide," October 22, 1969, Top Secret/Noforn/Sensitive, NARA, Record Group 218. Records of the Chairman Joint Chiefs of Staff, Earle Wheeler Papers, box 109, "381 World-Wide Increased Readiness Posture (October 69)," National Security Archive Electronic Briefing, book no. 81, document 10.

76. Bruce Blair, *The Logic of Accidental Nuclear War* (Washington, DC: Brookings Institute, 1993), 180n16.

77. Memorandum from Henry A. Kissinger for the President, "Conversation with Soviet Ambassador Dobrynin," October 1, 1969, enclosing memorandum of conversation between Dobrynin and Kissinger, September 27, 1969, Top Secret Sensitive, NSCF, box 489, Dobrynin/Kissinger 1969 (Part II), National Security Archive Electronic Briefing, book no. 81, document 4.

because the alert was kept secret, the Americans could not discuss its purpose explicitly.

Moreover, it is plausible that the Soviets viewed the alert as being a signal about the simultaneous crisis with China. In the same October meeting in which Dobrynin said "nothing new" on Vietnam, Kissinger noted that the Soviets went out of their way to "again give vent to their underlying suspicion that we are trying to flirt with China in order to bring pressure on them. They warn us 'in advance' that any such idea can lead to grave miscalculations and would interfere with the improvement of US-Soviet relations."[78] One reasonable interpretation of this Soviet vent is that it might have reflected a Soviet fear that the US nuclear alert was an effort to get the Soviets to back off on their nuclear threats against China; after all, the Soviets had recently floated the idea of a nuclear attack on China to the Americans. Kissinger, however, does not appear to have considered this possibility. He instead dismissed the stated Soviet concerns as part of the Soviets' larger worries about US-China rapprochement: "You have already answered this point," he advised the president, "and I believe there is no advantage in giving the Soviets excessive reassurance. In any case we should not be diverted from our China policy."[79]

This myopic reaction shows that Nixon and his senior aides viewed almost everything unfolding in October 1969 through the lens of their pressure campaign against the Soviets on Vietnam, despite the simultaneous Sino-Soviet crisis occurring.[80] Upon learning of China's nuclear alert, for instance, the historians William Burr and Jeffrey Kimball report that "Kissinger said he 'didn't know whether it was a reaction to us or what the Soviets did in reaction to the US.' Laird said 'he didn't know either.'"[81] Neither of these explanations was right; the Chinese alerted their forces in response to fears of a Soviet attack, and those fears would have arisen with or without the US alert, because they stemmed from the Sino-Soviet border conflict. But the US surprise at the Chinese alert is remarkable. In addition to not considering that the Soviets might view the US alert as a signal about

---

78. Memorandum From the President's Assistant for National Security Affairs (Kissinger) to President Nixon, Washington, October 21, 1969, National Archives, Nixon Presidential Materials, NSC Files, Box 489, President's Trip Files, Dobrynin/Kissinger, 1969, Part 1. Secret; Nodis, available in the *Foreign Relations of the United States 1969–1976*, vol. 12: *Soviet Union, January 1969–October 1970*, ed. Erin Mahan and Edward Keefer (Washington, DC: Government Printing Office, 2006).
79. Memorandum From the President's Assistant for National Security Affairs (Kissinger) to President Nixon, Washington, October 21, 1969.
80. Memorandum from Henry Kissinger to President Nixon, "The US Role in Soviet Maneuvering Against Peking," September 29, 1969, attached to Memorandum to Kissinger from Alexander Haig, October 11, 1969, National Archives, Nixon Presidential Materials Project, National Security Council Files, box 337, HAK/Richardson Meeting May 1969-December 1969, National Security Archive Electronic Briefing, book no. 49, document 24.
81. Burr and Kimball, *Nixon's Nuclear Specter*, 303.

China, the United States also interpreted Chinese actions only as responses to US actions, not as responses to the separate crisis with the Soviets. In short, the Americans initiated a nuclear alert directed at another nuclear-armed state—at the same time that that state was known to be in a nuclear crisis with a third nuclear-armed state—and yet this other crisis barely seemed to factor into US decision making.

The story has a happy ending in this case because the Soviets either ignored the US alert, or misinterpreted it in a manner that led them to stand down in their threats against China. But as a whole the episode demonstrates how complicated nuclear signaling can become once there are multiple players or multiple concurrent crises. Sometimes miscalculation may lead to restraint, which may have been what happened in this case and what Waltz would predict. But there is no guarantee that similar misperceptions in the future would lead to de-escalation rather than escalation, especially when set against the backdrop of a more complex nuclear world. In the 1969 case, for example, had China been able to detect the US alert, it was primed to interpret US preparations as threatening. Given advances in open-source intelligence and even the emergence of social media, it seems less likely in the future that a nuclear-armed state would remain as isolated and unaware of another nuclear state's alert as China was of the United States' alert in 1969.

Furthermore, it seems at least as likely in the future as it was in 1969 that two overlapping pairs of nuclear-armed states could become involved in simultaneous crises, which is not to say that it is likely in absolute terms, only that it is far from impossible. After all, there was only a brief period of a few years in the Cold War in which China did not tilt heavily toward the United States or the Soviet Union, yet in this short interval two major, concurrent nuclear crises arose that ensnared all three countries. In the future, China could end up in crises with India and the United States at the same time; the United States could find itself in crises with North Korea and China at the same time; or a future nuclear Iran could experience crises with Israel and a future nuclear Saudi Arabia at the same time. Dual crises could feed into each other and make de-escalation more difficult than it would be in a simpler two-player game.

Conclusions and Implications

This chapter has examined the future of nuclear deterrence in a world of multiple, autonomous, nuclear-armed states, and in particular a world in which there are three rather than two nuclear-armed great powers in addition to a growing number of nuclear-armed regional powers. It is hard to reach a place of optimism when contemplating this landscape. The good news about such a world is that it somewhat strengthens the incentives for rational states to simply avoid crises or wars. The prospect of escalation and the fear of postwar predation by nuclear-armed states that sit out a nuclear conflict should induce even greater caution and restraint among nuclear-armed states than was seen in the Cold War.

The bad news is that this stabilizing effect seems likely to be marginal—it amounts to strengthening a general deterrent effect that is already strong—while instabilities will intensify or arise in new forms. Inadvertent crises and wars are still possible in a world of nuclear-armed great powers, as they were in the Cold War, and such wars are likely to bring greater risks of miscalculation and escalation as the number of players grows. Furthermore, states' anticipation of this prospect is likely to lead them to arms race in the expectation that the nuclear balance might matter someday. Especially when combined with potential alliance dynamics and the presence of multiple nuclear rivalries, peacetime nuclear competition in this world is likely to be intense. This competition brings its own risks of accidental or unauthorized use.

In policy terms, this sort of world also renders the prospects for arms control dim.[82] During the Cold War, the United States and the Soviet Union labored to secure a series of modest but important arms control agreements starting in the early 1970s. Yet even this feat required the repeated alignment of strategic and political incentives in both Moscow and Washington and was not a foregone conclusion. Interwoven into the bargaining process were additional arms buildups by both sides in particular areas that they thought might generate concessions from the other.[83] Today's environment introduces more veto players to arms control, making the process of getting to yes more difficult. No state is likely to agree to significant arsenal reductions with respect to any of its potential adversaries unless an agreement ensures those reductions are undertaken by all potential adversaries. Otherwise, the state could be left vulnerable.

This dynamic is emerging in the US-Russia-China triangle. In 2010 the United States and Russia signed the New START treaty, which caps strategic nuclear weapons on both sides well below their Cold War levels, but US concerns about growth in China's arsenal are at least part of the stated reason that the United States under the Trump administration came close to allowing the treaty to lapse.[84] China, for its part, has repeatedly indicated that it has no interest in becoming a party to New START, given that its arsenal is much smaller than that of the United States or Russia.[85] It is unclear

---

82. For similar logic, see Einhorn and Sidhu, "The Strategic Chain Linking Pakistan, India, China, and the United States" 14; and Michael Krepon, "Is Cold War Experience Applicable to Southern Asia?" in *Nuclear Risk Reduction in South Asia* (New York: Palgrave Macmillan, 2004), 11.

83. Green, *The Revolution That Failed*.

84. Manzo, *Nuclear Arms Control without a Treaty?*

85. Tom O'Connor, "China 'Will Never' Join Arms Control Deal with U.S. and Russia," *Newsweek*, May 20, 2019.

if what was once a bilateral strategic arms control framework will survive what is increasingly becoming a trilateral nuclear competition. It is also worth noting that this competitive dynamic is emerging even though one of the competitors (China) is nowhere near parity with the other two (Russia and the United States) despite recent growth.[86]

Furthermore, alliance considerations in a three-sided nuclear competition are especially relevant to arms control. US extended deterrence commitments were and continue to be a roadblock to nuclear arms control. In the Cold War, for example, NATO members' reactions to SALT I, and fears of what SALT II and the Mutual and Balanced Force Reductions talks would bring, were a major reason for the eventual US deployment of long-range theater nuclear forces to Europe, which then ramped up the arms race in the early 1980s.[87] The US commitments to South Korea and Japan (not to mention NATO) are a significant reason the United States has not adopted a nuclear No First Use Policy and is unlikely to reduce its arsenal to the levels China claims would galvanize progress.[88]

If a three-sided nuclear competition results in greater extended deterrence commitments by the great powers, particularly in situations where the great powers seek to prevent non-nuclear allies from acquiring the bomb, then those allies could become additional veto players in any attempt at arms control. Even in the bipolar world of the Cold War—again, the sort of world in which a major power is supposed to be relatively dismissive of alliance concerns—the United States paid these concerns great heed in sizing and shaping its nuclear force. The dynamics of a three-sided competition are likely to make the great powers even more sensitive to their allies' fears that arms control spells the abandonment of extended deterrence commitments.

In sum, nuclear weapons are likely to exert cross-cutting effects in the emerging environment. Although some of these effects could be stabilizing in terms of marginally strengthening rational deterrence, instabilities seem likely to dominate over time. A world of multiple, potentially intersecting nuclear rivalries introduces a sobering set of potential dangers that will pose vexing challenges for policymakers.

---

86. Hans M. Kristensen and Matt Korda, "Chinese Nuclear Forces, 2020," *Bulletin of the Atomic Scientists* 76, no. 6 (November 2020), 443–457, doi:10.1080/00963402.2020.1846432.

87. Daalder, *The Nature and Practice of Flexible Response*; and Brendan Green and Caitlin Talmadge, "Alliances, Arms Control, and Nuclear Escalation: Evidence from the Cold War, Implications for Today," draft paper.

88. Brad Roberts, "Debating No-First-Use, Again," *Survival* 61, no. 3: 39–56.

CHAPTER 2

Psychology, Leaders, and New Deterrence Dilemmas

Rose McDermott

Does the emergence of new nuclear states change the fundamental basis of the deterrence dynamics that have existed in the past between the more established nuclear states? One of the most important ways in which new nuclear states present challenges results from the disproportionate prevalence of more personalistic leaders heading such states.[1] Individuals such as Saddam Hussein of Iraq, Kim Jong Un in North Korea, Muammar al-Qaddafi of Libya, and Mohammad bin Salman in Saudi Arabia exemplify the kinds of personalistic leaders who have sought or are currently seeking nuclear weapons. Although classic deterrence theory assumes a unified rational actor in charge of a given state, empirically this has not been the case. Clearly all behavior is a function of both personality and environment, and some leaders are more constrained by their bureaucracies or domestic constituencies than others. But psychological factors matter as well, especially when leaders are less constrained by such forces. For our purposes, leaders might be plotted on distribution of personalities that combine elements of impulsiveness, vengefulness, degree of psychic numbing, and the extent to which they privilege security over other values. The creation of such a scale could then be used to assess the likelihood of conflict and the kinds of consequences that might ensue. Such an index would be difficult to quantify but might be used to rank nuclear leaders, or incipient ones, in terms of their tendency to take a bad situation and make it worse.

Most of the existing debate around the effect of personalistic leaders on nuclear deterrence has focused on proliferation issues, with some providing more optimistic views and others remaining more pessimistic. Jacques Hymans, Malfrid Braut-Hegghammer, and Christopher Way and Jessica

---

1. Scott D. Sagan. "Armed and Dangerous," *Foreign Affairs* 97, no. 6 (2018): 35–43.

Weeks show that personalistic leaders are less likely to succeed in their goals, even if they are more likely to cheat, precisely because it proves difficult to succeed in achieving complex technological projects such as the successful creation of a nuclear weapon.[2] The following analysis falls on the more pessimistic side of the ledger, but the discussion does not revolve around risks associated with the likelihood of proliferation. Rather, it examines the inherent structural and psychological challenges posed by personalistic leaders, especially those of new nuclear states, including the challenges associated with deterring such regimes, and argues that these kinds of leaders will be harder and less likely to be deterred from conflict.

The central question posed by this chapter asks whether such leaders pose new and different kinds of threats and challenges for nuclear stability? The answer is yes for three reasons. First, personalistic leaders have fewer organizational constraints. There are fewer checks and balances imposed on such leaders, at least in part because they tend to rely on family members and other loyal followers. Under such circumstances, corruption runs rampant and expertise remains limited. Second, this lack of constraint gives free rein and unfettered access to a panoply of psychological mechanisms that play out more prominently and potently because institutions are not able to buffer or constrain their behavior as effectively. These features are not restricted to narcissism and paranoia but also encompass pathological versions of natural human tendencies such as pride and shame.[3] Although all leaders may tend toward an increasing preference for personalistic control over time, such tendencies are certainly variable, and different regime types provide different degrees of structural constraint on these impulses. Third, such leaders turn out to be poor learners, at least partly because they tend to surround themselves with sycophants, privileging loyalty over competence, and thus reducing both the safety and reliability of nuclear arsenals. The risk of internal threats to the regime raises the stakes under such conditions, forcing personalistic leaders to privilege internal security over external threat or stability. As a result, such personalistic leaders are easier to antagonize, more prone to conflict, aggression, and reckless behavior, and less stable. As a result, they make deterrence less stable and thus create a more dangerous world.

This chapter explores the challenges posed by the acquisition of nuclear weapons by personalistic leadership through an investigation of these three

---

2. Jacques Hymans, *Achieving Nuclear Ambitions: Scientists, Politicians, and Proliferation* (New York: Cambridge University Press, 2012); Malfrid Braut-Hegghammer, *Unclear Physics: Why Iraq and Libya Failed to Build Nuclear Weapons* (Ithaca: Cornell University Press, 2016); Way, Christopher, and Jessica LP Weeks. "Making It Personal: Regime Type and Nuclear Proliferation," *American Journal of Political Science* 58, no. 3 (2014): 705–719.

3. Rose McDermott, *Presidential Leadership, Illness, and Decisionmaking* (New York: Cambridge University Press, 2007); Uri Bar-Joseph and Rose McDermott, *Intelligence Success and Failure: The Human Factor* (New York: Oxford University Press, 2017).

features: some of the typical organizational features and challenges faced by these kinds of leaders; the reciprocal roles of pride and shame in driving choice and behavior; and the limits on learning.[4] In all attempts to examine leaders, humility suggests that simply because Western leaders and publics interpret events in one way does not necessarily mean that other leaders and cultures see things in a similar manner. Understanding another's goals and motives is tricky under the best of circumstances.[5] Nonetheless, it can prove useful to explore some of the organizational factors and universal characteristics of human behavior and learning that might affect personalistic leaders in variable ways that pose risks to all of us in a world of increasing nuclear proliferation and conflict.

Regime Type and State Structure

Although I focus on leaders and their pathologies, this does not mean that state structures and institutions do not matter. Leaders operate within such contexts, but these relationships are often reciprocal: state structures and processes enable or constrain certain types of leaders, who themselves strive to create and reshape politics and state structures in ways they prefer. Leaders can be more or less successful at achieving these ends. As Braut-Hegghammer demonstrates, personalistic leaders are more likely to flourish within the institutional structure of weak states. She argues that it is this mix of lack of state capacity married to the unwillingness on the part of state leaders to strengthen a state's formal institutions that allow such leaders to gain and maintain power. Personalistic leaders not only neglect the creation and maintenance of state structures that might otherwise constrain them but actively work to undermine these institutions. In this way, they strive to govern through informal structures of patronage and control.[6] Personalistic leaders prefer state structures they can control and manipulate and try to create and strengthen these kinds of cultures.

Within this context of a weak or easily manipulated state, leader proclivity can exert an outsized influence. At the outset, it is important to distinguish

---

4. For related work examining authoritarian leadership styles on various outcomes, see Jessica Weeks, "Autocratic Audience Costs: Regime Type and Signaling Resolve," *International Organization*, 62. no. 1 (2008): 35–64. For casework examining the role of learning in personalistic and non-personalistic regimes, see Bar-Joseph and McDermott, *Intelligence Success and Failure*.

5. For work on the problems posed by mirror imaging, see Robert Jervis, *The Logic of Images in International Relations* (New York: Columbia University Press, 1989); Lee Ross. "The Intuitive Psychologist and His Shortcomings: Distortions in the Attribution Process," in *Advances in Experimental Social Psychology* 10 (1977): 173–220.

6. Braut-Hegghammer, *Unclear Physics*.

between autocrats, dictators, and personalistic leaders.[7] The distinction is subtle but important, although sometimes types overlap. Dictators often have domestic constituencies to whom they must be responsive, even if only to pay off, to stay in power. Furthermore, as Caitlin Talmadge argues, even one-party states often behave like democracies, providing some constraint on the behavior of leaders.[8] These constituencies may be much smaller than those in democracies but can nonetheless still organize against leaders they oppose.

Personalistic regimes have many fewer restraints on leader preferences, and this has profound implications. As Weeks writes, "In personalist regimes in which there is no effective domestic audience, no predictable mechanism exists for restraining or removing overly belligerent leaders, and leaders tend to be selected for personal characteristics that make them more likely to use military force."[9] This insight remains particularly relevant here because many of the new nuclear states, both existing and potential, remain highly personalistic and suffer from the flaws and weaknesses Weeks identifies. Importantly, both self and societal mechanisms leading to selection for power privilege types who are more likely to use military force to gain and maintain control, both internally and externally. Weeks goes on to make a useful distinction among personalist leaders between "bosses" and "strongmen" based on whether the audience or leader is civilian or military, respectively. For our purposes, this distinction does not prove dispositive because it speaks to issues of training and culture, and is applicable to underlying psychological mechanisms, which are posited to apply universally across professions or positions.

State capacity can interact with regime type in various ways as well. Although democracies tend to have strong and well-established institutions, personalistic regimes tend to flourish in environments of weak states with underdeveloped institutions offering little countervailing power. This is particularly true when personalistic leaders retain control over instruments of state coercion such as the military and police, even if they only do so by providing special privileges or payments to such groups. Autocratic dictatorships such as those that prevail in places like Russia and China can exist within the context of strong state structures (i.e., Mao or Stalin) or weak ones, such as in Pakistan. However, personalistic leaders of the type considered here, who raise concerns as a result of their actual or proposed acquisition of nuclear weapons, exist almost entirely within the context of weak state institutions and structures.

---

7. The following argument rests heavily on Weeks's work: Jessica Weeks, "Strongmen and Straw Men: Authoritarian Regimes and the Initiation of International Conflict," *American Political Science Review* 106, no. 2 (2012): 326–347; Jessica Weeks, *Dictators at War and Peace* (Ithaca: Cornell University Press, 2014); Weeks, "Autocratic Audience Costs."

8. Caitlin Talmadge, *The Dictator's Army: Battlefield Effectiveness in Authoritarian Regimes* (Ithaca: Cornell University Press, 2015).

9. Weeks, "Autocratic Audience Costs."

In addition, states themselves exist within an international structure. Starting at the dawn of the nuclear age, scholarship on nuclear deterrence traditionally discussed stability within the context of the bipolarity between the United States and the Soviet Union (and Russia since its collapse) during and after the Cold War.[10] New nuclear states now emerge in the context of a multipolar world.[11]

Moreover, the mere existence of more nuclear states poses new challenges for the kind of interactions that take place between such leaders. Past nuclear states mutually acknowledged a degree of peer status; new nuclear states seek such status in the context of clear asymmetries in economic and social power and influence. How might nonpersonalist regimes interact with personalist ones who possess nuclear capability? This can be particularly fraught when a democracy might consider the personalist regime to be "less than" in terms of legitimacy, status, or morality. This assessment can be made even more challenging if one side or the other believes the other to be irrational? How does the nature of mutual nuclear vulnerability in the context of other forms of power imbalance affect the relationships between leaders, and the goals they seek through the acquisition of nuclear technology? For example, personalistic leaders may be driven by the desire to achieve great power status without having to provide all the typical accoutrements associated with this status on the international stage, including a certain standard of living for their population; they may be trying to use nuclear weapons as a cheaper shortcut to international status as opposed to treating them as genuine weapons of war. Notably, there are conditions under which this motivation might prove stabilizing if it encourages leaders to see nuclear weapons more as a shortcut to international status than as instruments of coercion.

The prevalence of personalistic leaders in nuclear states holds additional implications. First, such leaders will be much more concerned about the possibility of an overthrow from within their domestic constituency since they incorporate few, if any, of those interests in their larger decision making. In personalist regimes, leaders may wonder whether their orders will be followed or whether a sufficiently independent military might launch a coup. In this way, personalistic leaders exacerbate the principal-agent problem because decision making may appear unitary when in fact it is by the constant threat and risk of overthrow.[12] This means that one of the challenges

---

10. Thomas Schelling, *The Strategy of Conflict* (Cambridge, MA: Harvard University Press, 1980); Robert Jervis, *The Illogic of American Nuclear Strategy* (Ithaca: Cornell University Press, 1984).

11. Charles Kegley and Gregory Raymond, "Must We Fear a Post-Cold War Multipolar System?," *Journal of Conflict Resolution* 36, no. 3 (1992): 573–585.

12. For an overview of the challenges posed by the asymmetry in information and incentives embedded in principal-agent problems, see Gary Miller, "The Political Evolution of Principal-Agent Models," *Annual Review of Political Science* 8 (2005): 203–225.

posed in such regimes revolves around the ways they must manage their arsenals against internal threats. What new or additional risks do strategies built with an eye to maximizing internal control pose for preventing the initiation of conflict if such leaders are challenged either internally or externally? As Weeks documents, civilian dictatorships appear less belligerent than military juntas. But personalism married to militarism poses particular dangers, especially when enhanced by widespread surveillance and coercive control over the public, allowing little room for any opposing ideas or perspectives to emerge.

The phenomenon of personalistic leaders is no longer one merely restricted to the developing world but now affects emerging and new nuclear states as well. Are serious risks of nuclear proliferation or use higher with some types of leaders than others? Does it matter that now there are more personalistic leaders at the helm of countries that are seeking, or have already acquired, nuclear weapons? As Way and Weeks demonstrate, personalistic leaders are more likely to violate the nonproliferation treaty, although they are not clear on the causal mechanism by which this occurs; it may be that such leaders care less about audience costs, or because they are convinced to do so by the sycophants that surround them.[13] Does this mean that personalistic leaders are less likely to be deterred? The answer again is yes, precisely because there is less constraint on their psychological pathologies and less ability to learn from their own and others' behavior and mistakes.

CHALLENGES FOR PERSONALISTIC LEADERSHIP

The first question that should be addressed about the control of nuclear weapons by personalistic leaders is whether this is a new problem. Even in the early days of the Cold War, Josef Stalin had a stranglehold over his country, operating as a dictator who made all meaningful decisions almost entirely on his own, often assassinating those who disagreed with him or showed any real or imagined disloyalty.[14] However, the enormity of the institutional and state bureaucracy that existed in the Soviet Union also induced a certain degree of stability. Thus, there is some historical precedent for a dictator having complete control over a nuclear-armed state. Just because a nuclear conflict did not erupt at the time does not mean that risks do not exist in the future as a result of similar kinds of personalistic leadership, particularly if a higher percentage of them emerge. And each age faces its own unique environmental stresses and pressures.

---

13. Christopher Way and Jessica Weeks, "Making It Personal: Regime Type and Nuclear Proliferation," in *Nonproliferation Policy and Nuclear Posture*, ed. Neil Narang, Erik Gartzke and Matthew Kroenig (New York: Routledge, 2015), 165–188.
14. Sagan, "Armed and Dangerous."

A few characteristics distinguish personalistic leaders from democratic ones. First, they are not elected with a broad constituency to which they need to be responsive. Rather, they often come to power in a hereditary fashion, as is the case with Kim Jong Un in North Korea and Mohammed bin Salman in Saudi Arabia, or they rise as a result of successful political or military fighting against rival factions internally or externally, as with Saddam or Qaddafi.

Second, the organizational structure of personalistic regimes differs from traditional democracies. In rational choice terms, democracies need larger winning coalitions than personalistic regimes require to stay in power.[15] Democracies also tend to include many institutions that function to balance the power of the executive through courts, parliaments, and other bureaucracies. By contrast, personalistic leaders thrive in environments without such constraints. Personalistic regimes typically involve leaders who are surrounded by yes men or other sycophants who remain fiercely loyal to the leader because their survival often depends on his patronage. Such close supporters often include family members or other tribal kin whose loyalty remains unquestioned. Such family members may be corrupt, and the information leaders receive may be biased or narrow as a result of fear, ignorance, or sheer greed on the part of advisers. But given the constant risk of overthrow, loyalty will always trump expertise in the eyes of personalist leaders. This means not only do such personalistic leaders have much more leeway than democratic leaders in their decisions and actions, but they also have fewer sources of independent information, support, or constraint in potential areas of ignorance or incompetence. This increases the likelihood that such leaders will not even be aware of their blind spots, technical or otherwise since no one around them will risk informing them of their ignorance. When followers and supporters fear being killed if they go against the leaders' will, few corrections will be possible when the leader makes a mistake or demonstrates poor judgment. Such an organizational structure increases the odds of bad decision making precipitously, particularly when supporters are chosen not for their skill or competence but rather for their loyalty or family relationship to the leader. This means that the skilled hand of professionals will not provide as much constraint or capability as it should.

This also means that trust becomes a much more critical issue for leaders in such regimes. It becomes risky for them to delegate decisions or actions to others whose loyalty is not assured. This inner circle may be limited to family members or to a limited group of loyal followers who may not have expertise on important topics, including technical issues involving the development, maintenance, or safety of nuclear weapons. This becomes an even more potent problem when contemplating the use of such weapons,

---

15. Bruce Bueno De Mesquita, Alastair Smith, James D. Morrow, and Randolph M. Siverson, *The Logic of Political Survival* (Cambridge: MIT Press, 2005).

where certain leaders may possess near total discretion as well as ignorance over the deployment of weapons of mass destruction as well as their military, political, and environmental consequences. In addition, total control of such weapons by a single individual introduces greater potential for accidents if leaders can act on a whim, or as the result of a strong impulse driven by fear of threat, anger over disrespect or maltreatment, or a desire to showcase a display of strength.

The challenges that confront personalistic leaders fall into at least three potential camps. First, they have informational problems of the sort implied above. If no one risks telling them anything they do not want to hear or do not already know, they may miss critically important information about all kinds of things, from the technological reliability of their weapons to the nature of any threats they might confront. For example, the design of the Iraqi bomb could have allowed it to go off accidentally if it were to fall off the back of a truck.[16] And worse, over time, they will become increasingly less aware that there are things they do not know because all their opinions are continually validated by everyone around them and they get used to and expect such deference. The constant and unwavering external validation increases already overblown tendencies toward arrogance and boosts their beliefs into the realm of overconfidence. Even if they want to obtain additional information, they may not know where or how to get such information without risking embarrassment. Even if they are able to obtain such information, they likely will not know how to judge its reliability. Because personalistic systems mean that leaders must always be on the lookout for threats to their regime, trade-offs between competence and loyalty will typically swing toward privileging security over all else. The documents that came out of Iraq provide rich documentation of this proclivity.[17] In a telling illustration, Benjamin Buch and Scott Sagan reveal that Saddam thought his chemical and biological weapons were much more powerful than they were, believing they actually did operate to deter the United States from regime change in Iraq after the invasion in 1991. In compelling tapes, Saddam argued that he "would have been called stupid" had he used these weapons outside of such existential threats.[18] This statement demonstrates that Saddam was more concerned with what other people thought of him than with the destruction he might have provoked.

---

16. Scott Sagan and Kenneth Waltz, *The Spread of Nuclear Weapons: A Debate Renewed; with New Sections on India and Pakistan, Terrorism, and Missile Defense* (New York: W.W. Norton, 2003), 78.

17. Kevin Woods, David Palkki, and Mark Stout, eds., *The Saddam Tapes: The Inner Workings of a Tyrant's Regime, 1978–2001* (New York: Cambridge University Press, 2011).

18. Benjamin Buch and Scott D. Sagan. "Our Red Lines and Theirs: New Information Reveals Why Saddam Hussein Never Used Chemical Weapons in the Gulf War," *Foreign Policy* (2013): 5, http://foreignpolicy.com/2013/12/13/our-red-lines-and-theirs/.

Second, personalistic leaders have an additional, more subtle but potentially more influential challenge. Any intrinsic personality flaw they may have, be it narcissism, paranoia, or some other factor, will become exacerbated and magnified in its effect on decision making because few, if any, checks and balances exist to curtail its influence on outcomes.[19] For example, Steven Rosen writes extensively on how evolution shapes responses to crisis in ways that have special importance for tyrants.[20] By examining how emotional arousal, stress, and time pressure exert predictable influences on decision making, Rosen highlights how personalistic regimes may suffer the disproportionate effects of their leaders' pathologies. Moreover, such personality defects are most likely to appear in personalistic leaders because it is those very antisocial characteristics that often allow them to gain power initially, especially if they have come to power by achieving victory through internecine infighting.

Classic examples like Hitler and Stalin are easy to generate, but more nuanced versions of personality disorders may play out in ways that exert a systematic and decisive influence on decision making without advisers being able to do anything about it. Worse, such leaders will not recognize these effects as deviant in any way since they simply represent what they have always known and experienced. Narcissism, for example, inclines a person to strongly believe that whatever is best for themselves is best for everyone else, without regard to the actual opinion of others. Such leaders are characterized by a persistent display of grandiosity, a constant need for validation and admiration, and a clear lack of empathy. Here, too, leaders will not be aware of the effect of their behavior on others' responses by definition, so they may not realize how changing their own behavior might lead to a better result since one of the defining hallmarks of a personality disorder is the inability to change patterns of behavior in response to external circumstances. Instead, narcissistic leaders are likely to blame everyone else for the problems they caused.[21] Furthermore, personalistic leaders need to be paranoid to stay in power; the very structure of their systems demands that much, if not all, of their behavior and decisions must be shaped by the constant requirement of guarding against a coup, an overthrow, or an assassination attempt.

---

19. A great deal has been written on the influence of illness, including psychological illness, on leader behavior, including Jerrold Post and Robert Robins, *When Illness Strikes the Leader: The Dilemma of the Captive King* (New Haven: Yale University Press, 1995); Robert Robins, and Jerrold Post, *Political Paranoia: The Psychopolitics of Hatred* (New Haven: Yale University Press, 1997); McDermott, *Presidential Leadership*.

20. Stephen Rosen, *War and Human Nature* (Princeton: Princeton University Press, 2009).

21. A great deal of work has been done on narcissism and leadership. For overarching theoretical work, see Jerrold Post, "Current Concepts of the Narcissistic Personality: Implications for Political Psychology," *Political Psychology* 14, no. 1 (1993): 99–121.

This leads to a third challenge such leaders confront. The factors that personalistic leaders must consider in deciding what to do are vastly more limited than those democratic leaders have to contemplate. Democratic leaders represent, by definition, much broader coalitions that can throw them out of power if they do not approve of their behavior. Personalistic leaders confront a different set of calculations in two important ways. First, they do not have to do what is best for their broader constituencies. Some may have to pay off small groups of elites, but many, such as Kim Jung Un, appear to only have to please themselves. This means that the kinds of persuasive strategies advocating for the value of a particular policy to a broader public that might appeal to a democratic leader would be utterly impervious to a personalistic one. So trying to convince such a leader of the objective value of a particular policy for their wider constituency will prove meaningless and unpersuasive to them. It also means that the give and take of democratic systems designed to produce better arguments fail to make policies adopted by personalistic leaders stronger, leading to weaker policy overall. Second, such leaders recognize that they do not simply confront a retirement of neglect and possible ridicule if they lose control, but rather risk literal decapitation if overthrown, since many such rulers are often assassinated or imprisoned by domestic opponents or foreign intervention once they lose power.

Pride and Shame

Because personalistic leaders have more freedom to exert their personal preferences through state actions than democratic leaders, it is worth examining the effect of emotional factors on decision making.[22] Two particular emotional forces appear clearly and deeply relevant to decision making in the realm of conflict and have received less attention but merit more serious examination: the role of pride and shame in shaping choice and guiding behavior. These psychological mechanisms prove particularly potent and powerful in personalistic regimes precisely because such individuals are less constrained by those organizational and state structures that might otherwise buffer or inhibit their personal proclivities. This is true for psychological features such as paranoia and narcissism, as well as pride and shame. The reason these individual factors help illuminate our understand-

---

22. The following discussion is based in large part on work on pride and shame, including Daniel Sznycer, Laith Al-Shawaf, Yoella Bereby-Meyer, Oliver Curry, Delphine De Smet, Elsa Ermer, Sangin Kim, et al., "Cross-Cultural Regularities in the Cognitive Architecture of Pride," *Proceedings of the National Academy of Sciences* 114, no. 8 (2017): 1874–1879; Daniel Sznycer, John Tooby, Leda Cosmides, Roni Porat, Shaul Shalvi, and Eran Halperin, "Shame Closely Tracks the Threat of Devaluation by Others, Even across Cultures," *Proceedings of the National Academy of Sciences* 113, no. 10 (2016): 2625–2630.

ing of nuclear crisis brinksmanship is precisely because they help provide the micro-foundational basis for revenge motivations and other over-reactions that risk escalation and war in times of conflict. In short, pride and shame provide proximate explanations for why individual leaders make the choices they do and engage in the behavior they pursue.

Pride and shame are fundamentally and primarily social emotions designed to calibrate and elicit a particular response from others. This is what makes them especially relevant when considering issues of bargaining, negotiation, initiation or escalation of conflict, or nuclear brinksmanship. For example, a personalistic leader who has been humiliated or made to feel ashamed by an adversary will be more likely to seek revenge, raising the risk for unanticipated or unnecessary escalation. Therefore, these emotions hold particular import for understanding the influence of leader's style on nuclear stability and deterrence, in addition to other outcomes.

Throughout human history, where reversals of fortune occurred frequently and precipitously, and most often in the absence of institutions like police, hospitals, and insurance designed to help strangers in need, people needed to rely on each other for mutual help and support in times of trouble or conflict. Individual willingness to help others depended in large part on various characteristics that were considered valuable (i.e., attractiveness, strength, generosity) or dangerous (i.e., greed, laziness, infidelity). Status on these variables holds concrete value in many ways more precious than material possessions, because other people's willingness to help or hurt you in time of danger or trouble affects one's chances for survival. In addition, there is a critical element of strategic interaction in these assessments: other's inclination to help depends in part on your reputation on these dimensions as well, since potential reciprocation plays a large part in calculations regarding the risk of helping others at a potential cost to the self. As a result, other people's evaluation of one's behavior becomes a key to individual survival, not only in our ancestral past but in many environments, including war zones, where the only help available comes from those close at hand and money loses meaning in the absence of material goods for purchase.

SHAME

First, it is important to distinguish shame from guilt. Shame is typically interpreted to represent a public emotion; a reaction people have when others evaluate them negatively. By contrast, guilt results from an internal discrepancy between one's values and behavior; in this way, a person can feel guilt even if no one else is aware of their bad behavior. Conversely, shame can be experienced even if a person believes they did nothing wrong. In this way, shame is much closer to humiliation because that too results from public admonishment. Blema Steinberg writes about the role that shame and humiliation played over the course of three presidencies with regard to US intervention in Vietnam.[23] Her discussion of narcissism is particularly apt with reference to personalistic leaders. Specifically, she notes from a psychodynamic perspective that narcissists strive to replace the parental love that was lacking by striving for a series of public successes and accomplishments.[24] This strategy inevitably fails; however, it highlights the critical role that public accolades and approval hold for narcissistic leaders who are overly sensitive to slights, while also illustrating the lengths to which such individuals will go, ignoring or causing pain and suffering, in order to obtain the external validation they find both so necessary and so lacking.

The challenge is to understand how these emotions function to anticipate the effect of behavior on social bonds in an accurate manner. The psychological calculation cannot become too extreme in either direction without risking harm: if we only consider others' evaluations, we risk total exploitation; if we only care about our own preferences, we risk exclusion and ostracism. Therefore, over the vast majority of human history, individuals needed to assure that any benefits they might receive from a given action would be more valuable than any social cost that might occur as a result of it, precisely because the long-term social costs of both exploitation and social alienation posed a serious threat to survival. As a result, people need to consider not just personal but also social consequences when contemplating a given action, especially those that might have severe social repercussions.

Two of the most powerful emotional motivational mechanisms identified by evolutionary theorists that appear to calibrate this calculation of other people's response to our behavior are pride and shame, which are in many ways flip sides of the same coin. This argument asserts that shame and pride represent universal human responses to social exchange. However, such universal responses vary and are calibrated based on assessments of local values. In other words, the psychological mechanism that recognizes and regulates the response of pride and shame are universal, but the specific environmental circumstances that trigger their expression differ by both individual as well as situational circumstances. This allows for cultural factors to affect their manifestation but also explains how variance can arise in their expression and how misunderstandings can arise in their interpretation. Equally important, pride can elicit a specific kind of backlash under certain circumstances that risk retaliation.

23. Blema Steinberg, *Shame and Humiliation: Presidential Decisionmaking on Vietnam* (Montreal: McGill-Queen's Press, 1996).
24. Note the theoretical similarity of this argument as applied to Dwight Eisenhower, John F. Kennedy, and Richard Nixon with the argument the Georges put forward to explain Woodrow Wilson's behavior during the course of his presidency in Alexander George and Juliette George, *Woodrow Wilson and Colonel House: A Personality Study* (New York: Random House, 1956).

Work in evolutionary psychology and biological anthropology has provided extensive documentation of the mental architecture of both shame and pride. Both of these emotions demonstrate remarkable cross-cultural similarity not only in their manifestation but also in the kinds of traits and behaviors that trigger them. The underlying cognitive architecture of both remains similar precisely because both evolved to help calibrate others' likely responses to our actions and to assess whether these evaluations would operate to our individual benefit or detriment. When leaders have a perverted sense of what constitutes benefit, cost, or risk, and no one around them has the courage to correct them, profoundly destabilizing effects can easily result.

Evolutionary psychologists argue that shame operates as a kind of self-defense system, forcing people to incorporate the values of others into the decisions they make about future actions. If people fail to do this, they would risk the willingness of others to help them during times of crisis, threat, or illness. This so-called information threat theory of shame allows individuals to avoid socially costly actions by predicting how others will react and thus avoiding behaviors that might hurt their social standing. This emotion encourages individuals to balance direct personal benefit from an action, like cheating, against the social sanction and reaction such behavior might cause, such as social ostracism. Note that this is calibrated to one's sense of personal value, worth, and status, and when such assessment is outsized, it can lead to important miscalculations about others' willingness to defer or make accommodations to retain the relationship.

Experimental work across many diverse cultures has demonstrated the remarkably consistent operation of this motivational mechanism. For example, work on shame examined not only culturally diverse democracies such as the United States, Israel, and India but also included fifteen small-scale societies around the world that differed in geography, language, and culture. Daniel Sznycer and colleagues showed that experiences of shame closely matched assessments of how others in the local community might devalue them based on particular behaviors.[25] Although evaluations of certain behaviors emerged remarkably consistent across cultures, the insight that evaluations are pegged to local values offers critical insight into how universal human characteristics can still produce variant responses across time and place. The tendency for shame to function in reaction to the anticipation of public censure can remain a human constant, but the kinds of behavior that might receive sanction, or the precise nature of that sanction, might still differ across cultures, locales, or even social classes.

---

25. Daniel Sznycer et al., "Cross-Cultural Invariances in the Architecture of Shame," *Proceedings of the National Academy of Sciences* 115, no. 39 (2018): 9702–9707.

From this perspective, shame functions as a defense against being negatively evaluated or ostracized by others. Note the similarity this theoretical approach shares with the dominant view in sociology, which also holds that shame operates as a signal to prevent fractures in social relationships. Thus, shame functions to deter an individual from making choices or taking actions that can reasonably be anticipated to result in negative evaluations by others. All other considerations fall by the wayside when compared with the critical value of maintaining strong social relationships where one is valued, included, and protected.

Experimental work demonstrates that this social evaluation represents the central element sparking shame; doing something wrong does not produce shame independent of the social response of others.[26] Specifically, when someone contemplates doing something that others will not like, but is morally irreproachable, shame results. This would not be the case if shame resulted from solely internal evaluations of the rectitude of the self, as might be the case with guilt. Similarly, if someone considers doing something that is wrong but believes no one will know or find out, shame does not result. When people play a public goods game, for example, shame is predicted by the degree of social exclusion, not by the person's degree of contribution. In other words, people can do the right thing, such as contribute more than their fair share, and still feel shame if others evaluate them negatively, just as they avoid feeling any shame at all for doing something objectively wrong, such as under-contributing in a public goods game, as long as they believe no one else will find out about their behavior or evaluate it negatively. In this way, publicity more than immorality precipitates shame in most people most of the time.

PRIDE

The cognitive architecture of pride mirrors that of shame. As Sznycer et al. write: "Pride occurs in every known culture, appears early in development, is reliably triggered by achievements and formidability, and causes a characteristic display that is recognized everywhere."[27] Like shame, pride helps direct and shape decisions and behavior to increase the value that others place on the self. Like shame, pride is a public social emotion. As these authors note: "Ancestrally, enhanced evaluations would have led to increased assistance and deference from others."[28] In experimental tests involving sixteen countries across four continents, as well as ten small-scale societies across the world, pride mirrored positive evaluations from others. Though this may

---

26. Theresa Robertson, Daniel Sznycer, Andrew Delton, John Tooby, and Leda Cosmides, "The True Trigger of Shame: Social Devaluation Is Sufficient, Wrongdoing Is Unnecessary," *Evolution and Human Behavior* 39, no. 5 (2018): 566–573.
27. Sznycer et al., "The True Trigger of Shame," 1874.
28. Sznycer et al., "The True Trigger of Shame."

seem obvious in some ways, it also documents the motivational role offered by the desire for pride. People will strive to take actions that increase their respect, admiration, and status in the eyes of others. They also tend to want to advertise these behaviors so as to derive the positive evaluations of others so that they can take advantage of the social, especially reproductive, benefits that accrue in the wake of such recognition. This is known as the advertisement recalibration theory of pride.

Note here the critical but opposite role that publicity plays in shame and pride. People want to hide behavior that they know others will not approve of and publicize those they anticipate others will like. This helps explain the way in which social media, with its widespread and immediate effect, can shift the balance of power between followers and leaders in calculations of public response to given behaviors.

However, such behaviors do not have to be positive as judged by some kind of universal moral metric in order to elicit pride. For example, leaders who demonstrate aggression toward enemies may receive a great deal of positive approval even if their actions kill a lot of opponents. This is because not just good actions and intentions but also aggressive capability can operate to protect the group from enemies and earn accolades on the part of other members of a group, including followers. In ancestral environments, or even modern ones where cooperation is less common, raising the cost of conflict for rivals works to preserve scarce resources for members of the group. For example, shame may work to enhance rather than diminish the prospect of a leader acquiring or using nuclear weapons if he knows his supporters and followers support this, as they often do.[29] The experimental work clearly shows that individuals can just as easily feel enormous pride as a result of their aggressive behavior as they can for acts of kindness and generosity toward others.

The most potentially destructive aspect of pride occurs when it functions merely to dominate others without offering commensurate group benefits. Pride often encourages individuals to help each other, but it can just as easily motivate people to take advantage of others. When individuals become overconfident, convinced of their superior value, or captivated by their unrivaled capacity to wreak destruction on the enemy, they can become overly confident in their ability to exploit others with impunity. In the animal kingdom, this may look like an alpha male engaging in aggressive mate guarding; in human cultures, such individuals often display the classic characteristics of narcissists who value their own welfare above that of all others.

---

29. For evidence that the US public supports the use of nuclear weapons, see Scott Sagan and Benjamin Valentino, "Revisiting Hiroshima in Iran: What Americans Really Think about Using Nuclear Weapons and Killing Noncombatants," *International Security* 42, no. 1 (2017): 41–79.

This is where the backlash of pride can result. Individuals who dislike or resent the social subordination that results from others' pride can feel envious of other people's success. This can produce a sense of grievous indignation and a subsequent desire to kick the dominant person down a few pegs on the social ladder. This impulse likely both results from, as well as enhances, the self-domestication witnessed in humans across time.[30] Human history is replete with examples of leaders who, having exploited their constituencies, were deposed or assassinated by their followers; such consequences have resulted in increased egalitarianism and preferences for a fairer allocation of resources across millennial time.[31] Thus, when leaders demonstrate too much pride resulting from personal factors rather than activities taken on behalf of the collective, they run higher risks of decapitation by those who feel aggrieved by the social subordination imposed on them by the leader's pride. Thus, from the perspective of evolutionary psychology shame and pride function as a kind of social pricing signal. As a result, individuals automatically, instinctually, and intuitively incorporate others' preferences and values into their own calculations in deciding how to act. However, some individuals are more able to accurately assess how various behaviors will be interpreted by others or read others' responses to them. Both power and narcissism reduce the ability of individuals to accurately read the emotions and intentions of others.[32] For obvious reasons, personalistic leaders will not need to be as good at judging others' reactions since high power people require others to defer to them rather than the reverse. This inability to read social signals can help explain, in part, why so many high power personalistic leaders nonetheless eventually lose control, often in ignominious ways.

STATUS AND NUCLEAR WEAPONS

The role of pride and shame are often underestimated because of the premium placed on material goods by most observers and analysts, especially

---

30. Richard Wrangham, "Two Types of Aggression in Human Evolution," *Proceedings of the National Academy of Sciences* 115, no. 2 (2018): 245–253; Richard Wrangham, *The Goodness Paradox: The Strange Relationship between Virtue and Violence in Human Evolution* (New York: Pantheon, 2019).

31. Christopher Boehm, *Hierarchy in the Forest: The Evolution of Egalitarian Behavior* (Cambridge, MA: Harvard University Press, 2009).

32. There is quite a body of work on how power distorts perception, the best of which comes out of Dacher Keltner's lab. A representative sample includes Gerben Van Kleef, Christopher Oveis, Ilmo Van Der Löwe, Aleksandr LuoKogan, Jennifer Goetz, and Dacher Keltner, "Power, Distress, and Compassion: Turning a Blind Eye to the Suffering of Others," *Psychological Science* 19, no. 12 (2008): 1315–1322; Dacher Keltner and Robert Robinson, "Extremism, Power, and the Imagined Basis of Social Conflict," *Current Directions in Psychological Science* 5, no. 4 (1996): 101–105; Dacher Keltner and Robert Robinson. "Defending the Status Quo: Power and Bias in Social Conflict," *Personality and Social Psychology Bulletin* 23, no. 10 (1997): 1066–1077.

economists. The critical insight offered by a full appreciation of the role of social approval on human survival over time lies in the recognition that social status has an inherent value that far exceeds any given material resource. Status may appear ephemeral and hard to measure, but individuals constantly calibrate their relative standing in the social hierarchy through the psychological mechanisms of pride and shame, among other characteristics. Since social acceptance and approval proved more essential for survival than material goods, especially in the ancestral conditions that shaped human psychology, status counts for much more than territory, livestock, or other resources such as money. This is because social status represents not only the extent to which others are willing to come to your aid under conditions of threat or trouble but also their willingness to mate with you, influencing the prime driver of natural selection. Though it may be impossible to accurately measure status in the way that money, numbers of weapons, or acres of land can be consistently and comparatively counted, it represents the most valuable commodity anybody can marshal for their own and their offspring's prospects for survival and well-being. And shame and pride represent two of the most potent and automatic mechanisms by which individuals calibrate relative social status.

In practical terms, this means that less constrained leaders should prove more willing to fight for status than for material resources, including weapons. It also means they may be more willing to take risks to preserve their status. This is important because not all wars start by accident. Not all personalistic leaders are mad or crazy, nor do they need to be so to incite a conflict. Rather, war can result from a process of imperfect decision making whereby personalistic leaders are willing to manipulate risk to demonstrate strength, power, resolve or attain, secure or enhance their international status. A leader does not have to be crazy to manipulate risk in a way that replaces control with chance. Therein lies the distinction between Daniel Ellsberg's idea of the madman theory and Thomas Schelling's notion of a threat that leaves something to chance.[33] A meaningful distinction exists between being crazy and being unpredictable. Personalistic leaders will be more willing to replace control with chance in order to maintain their internal control or secure their international status, for without both they risk death at the hands of their domestic rivals or followers in a way that is not typically true of democratic leaders.

This implies that it may require different strategies and techniques of deterrence to dissuade leaders who feel that their status is threatened, as opposed to those who experience material deprivations such as economic

---

33. Daniel Ellsberg, "The Political Uses of Madness," lecture given at the Lowell Institute of the Boston Public Library, March 26, 1959, https://ia800102.us.archive.org/20/items/ThePoliticalUsesOfMadness/ELS005-001.pdf; Schelling, *The Strategy of Conflict*.

sanctions, which are less likely to affect personalistic leaders who care less about their constituencies.[34] Indeed, the use of economic sanctions represents the mirror imaging that fails to accurately recognize that the kinds of material pressures that work for democracies do not necessarily work the same way for personalistic regime types that must operate under different organizational and psychological imperatives.

This raises an additional consideration regarding the extent to which nuclear weapons serve as signals of status, as opposed to weapons that might realistically be used in conflict. If the acquisition of nuclear weapons is designed not only to protect and defend a country from a feared attack or incursion but also symbolically serve to enhance the international standing of leaders of such countries, this means that some leaders likely pursue such weapons not for obvious military or strategic reasons, but rather for the social status they confer. Such a perspective offers some unexpected insights. First, one of the challenging aspects that new nuclear states present to existing ones revolves around issues of power asymmetry. Existing nuclear states may resist having to consider new nuclear states who are weaker along other dimensions such as economic power as equal, yet this may be a large part of the goal of their acquisition for personalistic regimes. Part of this resistance on the part of so-called great powers no doubt derives from the strong aversion everyone has to feeling vulnerable or to losing status, especially if they feel they have no control over the source of the threat. Leaders of established nuclear states may have a hard time accepting the acquisition of nuclear weapons by states they consider inferior, and thus remain reluctant to treat them with the logic of deterrence that has governed great power nuclear balance since the Soviets developed retaliatory capacity. By contrast, the new nuclear states may expect exactly such commensurate status treatment, at least personally, because of their acquisition of nuclear weapons. In this regard, note Turkish President Recep Tayyip Erdogan's statement that Turkey deserved nuclear weapons, a statement that reflected more a desire to achieve a particular kind of great power status, as opposed to an argument built on military capacity or requirements. Here, as with other leaders such as Nikita Khrushchev, the distinction between national and personal status conflates. This discrepancy in perception may exacerbate an objective military threat and raise it to the level of an existential one precisely because what is being threatened is less physical and material and more social and status oriented. In this way, social status easily emerges as more powerful than material concerns, psychologically, even if this preference remains largely unconscious and often ignored in more material negotiations. The crux may come down to the fact that existing nuclear powers do not want to be rendered equal, much less subordinate, to an economically

---

34. Rosen, *War and Human Nature*.

or socially inferior country, while new nuclear powers expect to be treated as equals for just that reason.

Second, in hopes of motivating states that have already acquired nuclear weapons to disarm, offering status enhancement may be a necessary part of any successful settlement, perhaps more valuable to personalistic leaders than lifting sanctions since they tend to be more concerned with themselves than with their citizens. Such status acknowledgments may be hard for existing states to offer, and the nature of the offerings demanded or accepted might differ across cultures and countries. Ironically, such enticements may objectively be less financially expensive than alternatives such as sanctions, arms races, or denuclearization, but may be less likely to occur because the psychological cost may be too high for many democratic leaders to bear, either personally or in the eyes of their mass publics. This asymmetry illustrates the intrinsically superior value of status over material factors.

Finally, status issues may influence escalation and retaliation strategies should conflict erupt. This highlights the important distinction between retribution and revenge. Retribution targets individuals or states that one feels has wronged them or have done something objectively objectionable in a tit-for-tat manner and seeks justice in retaliation.[35] Revenge is less targeted and more indiscriminate, seeking suffering on the part of victims, and not simply a return to the previous state as might be possible with restrained retribution.[36] Personalistic leaders, who privilege emotional motives over moral ones, and are less likely to be subjected to institutional constraints, are thus more likely to engage in revenge when their status is threatened, particularly if they are also narcissists. It is not pride that provokes aggression but rather narcissism. It is not narcissism per se that instigates aggression, but rather social rejection and other threats to the ego that reliably precipitate aggression.[37]

Learning

Personalistic leaders are not only less constrained and more likely to manifest their psychological proclivities in unfettered and belligerent ways. They are also less likely to be able to learn from history, others, or their own mistakes. This is because they may be ignorant or disinterested in history,

---

35. Peter Liberman and Linda Skitka, "Vicarious Retribution in US Public Support for War Against Iraq," *Security Studies* 28, no. 2 (2019): 189–215; Peter Liberman, "Retributive Support for International Punishment and Torture," *Journal of Conflict Resolution* 57, no. 2 (2013): 285–306.

36. Rose McDermott, Anthony Lopez, and Peter Hatemi, "'Blunt Not the Heart, Enrage It': The Psychology of Revenge and Deterrence," *Texas National Security Review* 1, no. 1 (2017): 68–88.

37. Jean Twenge and W. Keith Campbell. "'Isn't It Fun to Get the Respect That We're Going to Deserve?' Narcissism, Social Rejection, and Aggression," *Personality and Social Psychology Bulletin* 29, no. 2 (2003): 261–272.

feel that other cases, events, or decisions by other leaders have little or no relevance to them, fail to understand or acknowledge their own mistakes, or some combination. It is also because the sycophants and family members who surround them are less likely to understand these larger forces, believe they are relevant, or be interested or willing to challenge the leader even if they are aware of various limitations or problems confronting him. This lack of learning poses threats not only to the stability of the international environment but also to models that assume leaders can learn the correct (i.e., stabilizing) lessons either from history or vicariously from others.

Learning is a complex phenomenon. Western leaders cannot assume, for example, that leaders from other cultures will interpret events in the same way or extract the same lessons moving forward as they might. Analysts cannot assume that the lessons we think people learn, or the ones we think they should learn, are what they do take away from their own experiences or those derived from observing others.

Learning in the realm of nuclear deterrence proves especially tricky because it has to be, by definition, historically informed and vicarious, at least so far. Such information leaves huge gaps in anticipating the fallout, both literal and figurative, that might result from any future nuclear attack. Here, research on learning can provide some insight.

First, learning takes place within particular organizational structures and cultures that differ predictably by regime type. This means that learning is rarely an individual process, but rather one that integrates information in reciprocal ways between producers and consumers of intelligence, in addition to learning derived from actual experience.

Many factors, both conscious and not, can influence the learning process. Of course, the most powerful teacher for most people is failure. This poses the most profound of questions with regard to the use of nuclear weapons. Do states need a crisis, or some kind of near miss such as the Cuban Missile Crisis, to be socialized into the virtues and values of embracing a deterrence posture? For example, Michael Cohen argues that while the acquisition of nuclear weapons can indeed spur nations to become more belligerent and aggressive, their behavior becomes chastened over time as they learn the limits of nuclear coercion and the risks of brinksmanship.[38] If this learning process is to take place, then states need to be able to extract the correct lesson from a past failure or vicarious observation. But that is neither easy nor automatic. Failure improves performance because stress focuses attention and increases motivation. Arousal resulting from failure helps improve performance, at least initially, but too much stress for too long a period of time can induce depression and helplessness and can thus work against optimal decision making.

---

38. Michael Cohen, *When Proliferation Causes Peace: The Psychology of Nuclear Crises* (Washington, DC: Georgetown University Press, 2017).

As noted above, personalistic leaders tend to surround themselves with sycophants, privileging loyalty over competence. This means that the vast majority of advisers that personalistic leaders rely on for guidance lack critical skills or are outright incompetent. Such leaders may not even be informed of incipient or actual failure because advisers possess an (accurate) fear of reprisal. For example, Saddam apparently thought he won the first Gulf War.[39] This means that personalistic leaders are more likely to lack critical information than leaders in democratic regimes who are constantly exposed to a barrage of different voices, opinions, and information.

A more critical aspect of learning from failure revolves around social rejection. When failure occurs, individuals are more likely to attribute hostile intent to others they believe inflicted that harm or failure. This perceived sense of injury makes them more likely to respond aggressively. Ambiguity makes this tendency worse. One of the few forces that can ameliorate this proclivity is accountability, the very factor present in democracies but lacking in personalistic regimes.[40] Individuals who are forced to be accountable for their actions show less overconfidence and greater analytic complexity in their thinking. This means not only that democratic leaders, on average, may display different characteristics in their dealings than personalistic leaders, but neither side may understand that the other is operating under a different series of personal, as well as organizational, constraints. The tendency for mirror imaging may induce additional misunderstandings around this exact issue of accountability and the effects it can exert on decision making.

Amy Edmondson shows that certain factors inhibit prospects for learning within organizations.[41] The most potent of these include interpersonal fear, emotional beliefs about failure, groupthink, destructive power dynamics, and information hoarding. It should be immediately obvious that this list constitutes a litany of the factors most likely to characterize personalistic regimes defined by destructive power dynamics. In such regime types, interpersonal fear of failure permeates the atmosphere precisely because subordinates think their lives may be at risk if they do not do what the leader wants, do not tell him what he wants to hear, or oppose him in any way. Such fear induces information hoarding because no one wants to be responsible for communicating bad information, so fearful individuals simply keep negative information to themselves.

---

39. Harold Brands and David Palkki, "'Conspiring Bastards': Saddam Hussein's Strategic View of the United States," *Diplomatic History* 36, no. 3 (2012): 625–659.

40. Philip Tetlock, "Accountability and Complexity of Thought," *Journal of Personality and Social Psychology* 45, no. 1 (1983): 74–83.

41. Edmondson and colleagues have conducted extensive work on learning in organizations. The following discussion draws primarily and extensively from work summarized in Amy C. Edmondson's *Teaming: How Organizations Learn, Innovate, and Compete in the Knowledge Economy* (New York: Jossey-Bass, 2012).

CHAPTER 2

There are several important aspects of this analysis of organizational learning when applied to personalistic versus democratic regimes. First involves the power of social norms and emotional factors in encouraging or stifling creativity and complex analytic thought. Adequate learning, especially from failure, will be vastly more restricted under conditions of fear and social exclusion. Learning is both a personal and an interpersonal process; when power dynamics between leaders and followers interfere with the free and open exchange of ideas, including admissions of failure, creativity is hampered, and productive learning is truncated. All learning incorporates elements of risk and prospects for failure. Leaders whose behavior and risks of retaliation restrict open discussions of errors or mistakes make the possibility of learning and improvement much less likely.

Conclusion

The challenges posed by new nuclear states run by personalistic leaders may not pose entirely new kinds of risks, but the prevalence of such leaders does indeed increase the probability of more negative interactions between and among nuclear states, particularly as they proliferate in number and potential interactions and conflicts become more statistically likely.

We are not entirely without history when it comes to personalistic leaders in possession of nuclear weapons. Some might argue that some of those threats have been overblown and did not materialize, such as those surrounding Mao after Chinese acquisition in 1964, or current debates around the threat posed by Pakistan or North Korea, which have not (yet) resulted in nuclear conflagration. However, the absence of evidence, as the saying goes, does not constitute evidence of absence. Specifically, Mao engaged in exceptionally risky behavior when he sparked the Ussuri River clash with the Soviet Union in 1969.[42] In that instance, Mao provoked the Soviets, moving troops and evacuating Beijing, and almost instigated a war between the two nuclear powers. Other examples abound, including Kim Jung Un's provocations in 2017, which risked nuclear exchange as well.[43] These examples of nuclear crisis do not provide assurance that personalistic leaders are particularly easy to deter. Just because bad things did not occur in the past does not mean they will not happen in the future.

Personalistic leaders are not the only ones who pose a threat to nuclear stability, and even democratic leaders can possess concerning personality

---

42. M. Taylor Fravel, *Strong Borders, Secure Nation* (Princeton: Princeton University Press, 2008), chap. 4.

43. Ankit Panda, *Kim Jong Un and the Bomb: Survival and Deterrence in North Korea* (New York: Oxford University Press, 2020); Victor Cha and David Kang, *Nuclear North Korea* (New York: Columbia University Press, 2018).

flaws that can exert a destructive effect in a crisis. Similarly, emotionally labile or unstable democratic leaders such as Donald Trump raise concerns about the stability of deterrence. But here again it is important to keep in mind that these effects exist on a spectrum. Kim Jung Un appears to have few constraints on his predilections and has murdered many rivals. Mao, Stalin, and Hitler were not constrained by courts or parliaments, but they did operate within vast bureaucracies, which dampened some of their flexibility. Leaders of aspiring nuclear powers may find themselves with internal constraints imposed by other sources of power within their regimes. In other words, behavior emerges from a combination of personal tendencies within particular organizational contexts, just as crises erupt from immediate circumstances embedded in particular historical environments. Whether and how these interactions led to cooperative or destructive outcomes thus depends on a number of factors that may be difficult to control or predict. But certain personality characteristics tend to induce predictable responses, and these can be managed if properly controlled. For example, narcissists who are insulted or humiliated tend to react with rage and aggression but are easily manipulated with flattery. Having psychological consultants equivalent to the economic ones who populate the National Council could prove especially helpful in potentiating peace by helping to establish standard guidelines for interactions with particular personality types.

Important considerations arise from the recognition that personalistic leaders may have fewer institutional and organizational constraints than leaders in more established democratic nuclear states. This means that the factors that influence their decision making, and the pressures that operate on them, will not necessarily closely mirror those experienced by established nuclear states, making communication and understanding between established and new nuclear states more challenging. In particular, personalistic leaders will have much more leeway to pursue policies that they believe will enhance their stature among their small local band of cronies and family members. These forces may not appear relevant from the perspective of great power politics but may nonetheless represent the driving force in shaping personalistic leaders' choices and behavior. In addition, because they operate with fewer organizational constraints than democratic leaders, they have the ability to manifest their psychological proclivities in unfettered manners that risk a higher probability of conflict. They are also less able to learn from history or from others for those same organizational and psychological reasons.

Status appears to be an especially critical factor when dealing with all parties in a nuclear conflict. When new nuclear powers expect to be given equal status because of the acquisition of nuclear weapons, and such recognition is not forthcoming by established nuclear powers, achieving the kind of stable deterrence that characterized the great powers in the latter half of the twentieth century will prove much more challenging. New nuclear leaders who head more personalistic regimes will prove harder to deter and easier to antagonize. They will be more prone to conflict, aggression, and reckless behavior, rendering nuclear deterrence and stability more precarious and making the world a more dangerous place going forward.

In that regard, observers should remain humble about the prospects for democratic institutions to save us from the destructive force of personalistic leaders. As problematic as personalistic leaders in autocratic or totalitarian regimes may be, individuals with such proclivities who exist in democratic structures still hold the potential for deeply disturbing outcomes. No one need be reminded that Hitler was democratically elected before seizing full power for himself, just as Vladimir Putin's ostensibly democratic support may reside in name only. Trump may be an aspiring dictator but operated at least nominally within democratic institutions until he lost the 2020 election. Investigations following these events show how close the country came to successful insurrection and the complete destruction of democratic norms; but for a few key individuals, including critical military leaders, the institutions we rely on to keep democratic leaders in check might have failed and could still fail in the future.[44] This illustrates the capricious nature of organizational and institutional constraints; norms may not hold in the absence of commitment to democratic values and stronger rules, laws, and institutions designed to constrain personalistic leaders, regardless of the regime types in which they operate.

---

44. Bob Woodward and Robert Costa, *Peril* (New York: Simon and Schuster, 2021).

CHAPTER 3

Thermonuclear Twitter?

Vipin Narang and Heather Williams

Social media platforms such as Twitter, Facebook, and WhatsApp—and their local variants worldwide—have injected new dynamics into the way leaders, governments, and media interact with citizens and vice versa. Leaders and organizations can bypass official bureaucratic channels and communicate, in real time, directly not only with their constituents, but also with anyone in the world with a smartphone or, in the case of open platforms such as Twitter, anyone with access to the internet and a social media account. Crisis tweeting by leaders as a form of communication is a novel feature of the information landscape. During the January 2020 crisis between the United States and Iran, for example, following the assassination of General Qasem Soleimani, President Donald Trump sent 182 tweets, including one on January 4, threatening to target fifty-two Iranian cultural sites.[1] In addition to serving as a unique communications platform for leaders, ordinary citizens can interact with, disseminate, like, ridicule, or otherwise reach leaders and organizations that they previously could never dream of directly interacting with—and not just celebrities, but their elected (or unelected) leaders.

How have these platforms affected international politics, particularly crises involving one or more nuclear powers? Do they trigger crises and serve

---

1. Donald Trump, Twitter, January 4, 2020. The full thread reads, "Iran is talking very boldly about targeting certain USA assets as revenge for our ridding the world of their terrorist leader who had just killed an American, & badly wounded many others, not to mention all of the people he had killed over his lifetime, including recently . . . hundreds of Iranian protesters. He was already attacking our Embassy, and preparing for additional hits in other locations. Iran has been nothing but problems for many years. Let this serve as a WARNING that if Iran strikes any Americans, or American assets, we have . . . targeted 52 Iranian sites (representing the 52 American hostages taken by Iran many years ago), some at a very high level & important to Iran & the Iranian culture, and those targets, and Iran itself, WILL BE HIT VERY FAST AND VERY HARD. The USA wants no more threats!"

as rocket fuel for their escalation? Or are they just noise that thickens the fog of war without fundamentally altering crisis dynamics? And how do different platforms affect crisis dynamics as the sheer volume of information—some of which is of dubious quality and produced by an unsubstantiated rumor mill—pollinates and pollutes the media and popular discourse?[2] These are questions on which we have little scholarship or thinking in international security. This chapter attempts to fill this gap by disaggregating social media platforms along three relevant dimensions in crises—whether they are open or closed platforms (platform properties), whether the event is discrete or ongoing (crisis properties), and whether the intended audience is international or domestic (audience properties). We provide evidence from South Asia, notably the 2019 Pulwama/Balakot crisis, the 2018 Hawaii missile alert, and the 2017 fake evacuation order on the Korean Peninsula, to illustrate how and whether social media platforms affect crisis dynamics.

We hypothesize and provide preliminary evidence that social media does not have a uniform effect on crisis dynamics but can have varying impacts depending on the specific type of platform and the nature of the crisis. In particular, open social media platforms such as Twitter have the potential to thicken the fog of war in discrete crises. But open platforms are also more likely to assemble and disseminate accurate information more broadly in ongoing crises. Closed platforms such as WhatsApp and Facebook may reinforce incorrect information even over protracted crises, as users gravitate toward social clusters that reinforce preexisting beliefs and opinions rather than seeking accurate information. Open platforms may also be more useful for external signaling to adversaries and a broader international community; their wide reach allows for deterrence or coercive signals to be more quickly and directly transmitted to target audiences. Closed platforms, by contrast, can be exploited to generate nationalism or domestic audience costs by specifically and privately targeting and potentially monopolizing the information constituents receive. All these platforms are also vulnerable to manipulation either by governments to generate domestic support or by malicious actors that can employ them to spread potentially dangerous disinformation.

Do social media platforms affect the outbreak or course of nuclear crises? For example, would the existence of Twitter or WhatsApp during the 1999 Kargil war or 2008 Mumbai attack between India and Pakistan have led to a different outcome, namely escalation or even nuclear use? The media environment during Kargil, or during the 2008 terrorist attack in Mumbai, was riddled with substantial misinformation. Ultimately, Kargil did not escalate

---

2. See David M. J. Lazer et al., "The Science of Fake News: Addressing Fake News Requires a Multidisciplinary Effort," *Science* 359, no. 6380 (March 2018), 1094–1096.

because India's prime minister Atal Bihari Vajpayee did not want to escalate and ordered a highly constrained Indian response to the Pakistani infiltration.[3] It is hard to envision that if live streaming television of these events in both Hindi and English at the time did not generate pressure for escalation, Twitter would have. In another counterfactual, if social media did not exist during the 2018 Hawaii missile alert, traditional media and communication platforms, such as television, radio, and text messaging, might have achieved the same outcome and de-escalated a potential crisis. Although social media platforms may not independently cause crises or escalation, they can contribute to the broader information and misinformation environment, notably by cross-pollinating (or cross-polluting) more mainstream media platforms such as television or print news. They can also be manipulated by governments and malicious actors to affect crisis dynamics, serving as accelerants or amplifiers, with both risks and benefits. They provide a mechanism to de-escalate crises quickly and serve as a propellant to spin them up, with the risk of nuclear powers tweeting their way to war.

Social media platforms as a whole inject a level of complexity and information velocity into nuclear-tinged crises that nuclear weapons powers have not previously had to manage. Our overall conclusion is a simple but underappreciated point thus far: different social media platforms can work at cross-purposes against each other in crises, making a uniform effect difficult to measure or even theorize.[4] In aggregate, the new social media ecosystem may simply generate noise and ambiguity, which can sometimes make navigating a crisis difficult but may also provide states face-saving ways to de-escalate. Each platform may have differential effects depending on the type and duration of the crisis, as well as which audience is being targeted. This chapter undertakes a brush-clearing exercise to systematically think about how different social media platforms may impact different types of nuclear crises. We disaggregate social media platforms—since social media is not a monolithic concept or tool—and crisis types to theorize about the different ways in which social media may affect crises between nuclear actors.[5] These dynamics may apply to all types of militarized crises between states, but we restrict our focus to crises with a nuclear component, given the risks involved with rapid or unintended escalation in such crises.

---

3. See, for example, Vipin Narang, *Nuclear Strategy in the Modern Era* (Princeton: Princeton University Press, 2014), chap. 10.

4. See, for example, Harold A. Trinkunas, Herbert S. Lin, and Benjamin Loehrke, *Three Tweets to Midnight: Effects of the Global Information Ecosystem on the Risk of Nuclear Conflict* (Stanford, CA: Hoover Institution Press, 2020), which offers a variety of excellent perspectives, many of which treat social media platforms as monolithic.

5. On disaggregating crisis types, see Mark S. Bell and Julia MacDonald, "How to Think about Nuclear Crises," *Texas National Security Review* 2, no. 2 (February 2019), 1–26.

CHAPTER 3

Social Media and Escalation Risks: Existing Pathways

Escalation is ultimately a political activity. Although it is typically thought of as a linear process, "the sequential expansion of the scope or intensity of conflict," the increasing speed of conflict and emergence of new technologies has complicated the notion of an "escalation ladder" and replaced it with something more akin to an "escalation web."[6] Escalation is typically categorized as being either deliberate, such as a preemptive nuclear attack, or in the face of defeat; or inadvertent, to include accidents, unintended use of force from apex political authorities, "mechanical failure, unauthorized (nuclear) use, or insanity."[7] The election of US president Trump, accompanied by his novel approach to tweeting, brought attention to the intersection of social media and politics, particularly nuclear weapons postures—whose button is really bigger?—and nuclear threats such as "fire and fury." But Trump is hardly the only world leader to use social media in an inflammatory way, and in 2019 Twitter issued guidelines for "World Leaders: Principles and approaches" warning them against tweets that could promote terrorism, threaten violence, encourage self-harm, or risk an enforcement response by Twitter.[8] For violations of these guidelines and due to the risk of further incitement of violence in the United States, Twitter suspended President Trump's account—terminating his ability to tweet—shortly after the events of January 6, 2021, with two weeks left in office, an unprecedented move.

At its core, social media is a means of virtually connecting people in real time with limited, if any restrictions, on content. The most common social media platforms include Facebook, YouTube, WhatsApp, Instagram, and Twitter.[9] Platforms are differentiated by a variety of factors: accessibility of information (open or closed), censorship and government oversight, content (visuals, videos, or text), sponsorship, and human versus bot-generated content, among others. Social media is increasingly present in international politics and conflicts, such as the 2014 Ukraine crisis with activists,

---

6. See, for example, Robert E. Osgood and Robert W. Tucker, *Force, Order, and Justice* (Baltimore: Johns Hopkins University Press, 1967); Heather Williams and Alexi Drew, "Escalation by Tweet: Managing the New Nuclear Diplomacy," King's College London Occasional Paper, July 2020.

7. Barry R. Posen, "Inadvertent Nuclear War?: Escalation and NATO's Northern Flank," *International Security* 7, no. 2 (Fall 1982): 29.

8. "World Leaders: Principles and Approaches," October 15, 2019, Twitter, https://blog.twitter.com/official/en_us/topics/company/2019/worldleaders2019.html.

9. Statista, "Most Popular Social Networks Worldwide as of April 2020, Ranked by Number of Users," https://www.statista.com/statistics/272014/global-social-networks-ranked-by-number-of-users/. Interestingly, although Twitter is one of the most commonly studied platforms with regards to politics, it is only the twelfth most popular social media platform, behind QZone, TikTok, and Reddit.

experts, politicians, and even armed fighters taking to platforms such as Twitter, Facebook, and YouTube to document and circulate their experiences in real time with multimedia tools.

Scholarship into the impact of social media on politics and nuclear weapons, specifically, is relatively nascent. A handful of studies across disciplines highlight at least four related ways social media may have an escalatory effect in crises, and their combination may be both figurative and literal confusion: disinformation, ambiguity, impact on decision making, and public pressure. First, social media is a primary vehicle for disseminating outright disinformation. Lanoszka defines disinformation as "a systematic government effort aimed at using disinformation to mislead a particular audience—whether a government or key members of society—in order to influence the policy process."[10] On social media, the disinformation need not originate from the government; in some cases the government may propagate it, but in others, the government may be embattled to correct or fight disinformation campaigns that originate from malicious nonstate actors or influencers. Disinformation can range from rumors to deep fakes. A 2018 study by MIT researchers based on 126,000 stories tweeted by 3 million people between 2006 and 2017 found that "Falsehood diffused significantly farther, faster, deeper, and more broadly than truth in all categories of information, and the effects were more pronounced for false political news than for false news about terrorism, natural disasters, science, urban legends, or financial information."[11] Interestingly, the study also found that it took the truth six times as long as the falsehood to reach 1,500 people, perhaps confirming the old adage that the truth is boring, while disinformation is often spectacular and shocking.[12] It remains unclear if this wider and faster dissemination of disinformation has a significant impact on politics. Lanoszka demonstrates that "disinformation is ineffective in terms of changing the policies of a target as regards to its foreign policy alignments and armaments—that is, the balance of power."[13] Rather than create new tensions and pressure escalation, rumor typically reinforces preexisting views.[14] Of particular concern is the spread of disinformation during a crisis, when rumors have been shown to flourish and propagate virally.[15]

---

10. Alexander Lanoszka, "Disinformation in International Politics," *European Journal of International Security* 4, no. 2 (2019): 3.

11. Soroush Vosoughi, Deb Roy, and Sinan Aral, "The Spread of True and False News Online," *Science* 359, no. 6380 (2018): 1146–1151.

12. Vosoughi, Roy, and Aral, "True and False News Online."

13. Lanoszka, "Disinformation," 1.

14. K. Hazel Kwon, C. Chris Bang, Michael Egnoto, and H. Raghav Rao, "Social Media Rumors as Improvised Public Opinion: Semantic Network Analyses of Twitter Discourses during Korean Saber Rattling 2013," *Asian Journal of Communication* (February 2016): 5.

15. Kwan et al., "Social Media," 4.

A second concern is that social media platforms may contribute to unintended escalation due to enhanced ambiguity, or the thickening of the fog of war where leaders or governments are less certain as to the facts on the ground and are forced to assume the worst, erring on the side of escalation. Posen explored inadvertent escalation scenarios during the Cold War that involved targeting nuclear systems due to the inability to discriminate facts and systems in real time.[16] Social media might provide information in real time; however, this is not necessarily accurate information, nor can it help differentiate offensive from defensive acts.[17] By flooding the information space, sowing uncertainty, and generating mixed messages in the midst of an already chaotic crisis environment, social media certainly can have escalatory consequences as states assume the worst about the situation or their adversary in the face of ambiguity.[18]

Current scholarship is mixed on whether ambiguous messaging has a stabilizing or destabilizing effect during crises. On the one hand, it may force states to assume the worst-case scenario and overreact; on the other hand, it may allow for face-saving pathways to de-escalation. The conventional wisdom tends to support the former, arguing that in the absence of reliable or consistent information, actors may misperceive an adversary's capabilities or willingness to respond.[19] Misperception occurs when there is an unintentional discrepancy between a state's actions and the adversary's understanding of those actions.[20] By potentially injecting more noise into the system, social media may increase the propensity that such a discrepancy will not only exist but be larger than in the past. Although deliberate ambiguity is central to nuclear deterrence theory, such as Thomas Schelling's "threat that leaves something to chance," social media amplifies the risk that states perceive a threat when none was made, or vice versa.

Inherent within this concern about unintentional escalation is the impact of social media on decision making, a third theme in the emerging literature on social media. A 2020 edited volume identifies the impact on decision-making calculus as the "most worrisome possibility" due to the spread of disinformation.[21] Malicious actors—whether a state actor, state-supported nonstate actor,

---

16. Barry R. Posen, *Inadvertent Escalation: Conventional War and Nuclear Risks* (Ithaca: Cornell University Press, 1991).
17. Posen, "Inadvertent Nuclear War?," 35.
18. Keir A. Lieber, *War and the Engineers: The Primacy of Politics over Technology* (Ithaca: Cornell University Press, 2005), 5.
19. Sarah Kreps and Jacquelyn Schneider, "Escalation Firebreaks in the Cyber, Conventional, and Nuclear Domains: Moving Beyond Effects-Based Logic," *Journal of Cybersecurity* 5, no. 1 (2019).
20. Daniel S. Geller, "Nuclear Weapons, Deterrence, and Crisis Escalation," *Journal of Conflict Resolution* 34, no. 2 (June 1990), 293.
21. Trinkunas, Lin, and Loehrke, *Three Tweets to Midnight*, 4.

or independent actor—can manipulate social media to distort messaging throughout an ongoing crisis. At the onset of a crisis, in particular, social media may increase pressure on decision makers to "do something," whereas silence on social media could prompt worst-case thinking and preemptive attacks.[22] But if the conflict escalates to a limited war, Lawrence Freedman identifies increasing complexity confronting decision makers as they are forced to account for a rich mix of factors: military logic, commitments, international law, domestic politics, casualty levels, economics, and dangers of a wider conflict.[23] But what if images—or fakes—shared via Twitter or Instagram suggest a higher casualty level than official figures? How might this impact a leader's perception of the crisis, absent definitive intelligence? These questions are exacerbated when the stakes (and emotions) are higher, and social media may complicate opportunities for dialogue and interaction among political leaders.[24]

It is possible that social media does not necessarily change crisis outcomes or significantly change leaders' preferences about escalation. A historical counterfactual may be illustrative, such as if John F. Kennedy and Nikita Khrushchev had the ability to tweet during the Cuban Missile Crisis. According to Freedman, "in Cuba the drive to escalation was inhibited by keen awareness on both sides that the political stakes were simply not worth taking matters to a decisive showdown."[25] Unless social media affects underlying political stakes, it is not obvious that it will change crisis behavior. Indeed, the Cuban Missile Crisis counterfactual has to also account for the possibility that Kennedy could have just as easily tweeted de-escalatory messages to more rapidly end the crisis: "I want the missiles out, but I do not want a war Nikita," with Khrushchev replying back, "Me neither Jack, let's talk." Therefore, the pathways to rapid escalation imbued within social media in crises allow for equally rapid de-escalation if both sides have a common preference for it.

A fourth and final theme is the concern that social media might amplify nationalism and public pressure for escalation. Social media could influence escalation dynamics by negatively shaping public opinion, largely through rumors and increasing calls for deliberate escalation to preempt an anticipated attack or stop a costly conflict. Social rumor can be defined as "improvised and expressive forms of public opinion that especially arise under

---

22. Herbert Lin, "Escalation Dynamics and Conflict Termination in Cyberspace," *Strategic Studies Quarterly* 6, no. 3 (Fall 2012): 58.

23. Lawrence Freedman, "Escalators and Quagmires: Expectations and the Use of Force," *International Affairs* 67, no. 1 (January 1991), 28.

24. Paul Slovic and Herbert S. Lin, "The Caveman and the Bomb in the Digital Age," in *Three Tweets to Midnight*, 40.

25. Freedman, "Escalators," 27.

uncertain socio-political situations" and has been proven to exacerbate conflict.[26] In addition, research demonstrated that visual images and videos are five times as likely to be shared.[27] In a crisis that the public can see, Instagram may prove more useful than Twitter—and together they can be, quite literally, deadly. And rapid (private or public) dissemination of accurate or fake images/videos as opposed to just text descriptions of the same in a crisis—especially of death or suffering—can mobilize emotions and revenge motives in ways that generate escalatory pressures.[28] Research into nonnuclear crises demonstrates that whether publics believe a rumor on social media "is determined by pre-existing cognitive schemes and attitudes rather than simply by credulity or gullibility."[29] For the most part, publics use social media during a crisis to reduce uncertainty by verifying information and disproving false rumors, foster a shared "keynote" narrative of events, and most—but not all—emergency information on Twitter was found to be accurate, and audiences can largely identify and dismiss untrue rumors.[30]

A confounder in any analysis of social media dynamics is cross-pollination with mainstream media since many journalists and television outlets now derive information from, as well as break news on, platforms such as Twitter. This cross-pollination dynamic can serve as rocket fuel for misinformation and rumormongering, spreading misinformation to much wider audiences and making it even more difficult to correct. Mainstream media and its relationship to social media outlets means all are competing for breaking news, and seemingly credible, but sensational tweets often cross-pollinate the mainstream media, amplifying their reach and impact. In many ways the current impact of social media is comparable to the "CNN effect" and the advent of the 24/7 news cycle in the late 1980s and early 1990s. Arguably, the CNN effect increased public pressure on governments to shift their foreign policies, particularly military interventions based on what people were seeing—visually in ways they had not previously—at home. This might entail sending humanitarian aid to Somalia or drawing down operations in Afghanistan with visuals of body counts. Where social media differs from the CNN effect, of course, is that in the current climate, governments are just as subject to the "Twitter effect" as the public—they are

---

26. Kwon et al., "Social Media"; G. A. Fine, "Rumor Matters: An Introductory Essay," in *Rumor Mills: The Social Impact of Rumor and Legend*, ed. G. A. Fine and V. C. Heath (New Brunswick, NJ: Transaction, 2005).
27. See, for example, Williams and Drew, "Escalation by Tweet."
28. Rose McDermott, Anthony C. Lopez, and Peter K. Hatemi, "'Blunt Not the Heart, Enrage It': The Psychology of Revenge and Deterrence," *Texas National Security Review* 1, no. 1 (November 2017): 66–88.
29. Kwon et al., "Social Media," 5.
30. Tanja Schreiner, "Information, Opinion, or Rumor? The Role of Twitter During the Post-Electoral Crisis in Cote D'Ivoire," *Social Media and Society* (January–March 2018), 1–16; Kwon et al., "Social Media," 4.

reading the same messages and might be victim to the same disinformation campaigns.

This review of contemporary scholarship also reveals gaps and points of tension in understanding the impact of social media on crises. The majority of scholarship treats social media as monolithic or focuses on a single platform, with no differentiation between platforms such as Twitter or Tik Tok.[31] Similarly, the social media literature fails to disaggregate the impact of social media on short, sharp crises versus longer ones.[32] We hypothesize that not only does the type of social media platform matter for escalation dynamics, but the type of crisis matters as well. A significant reason for the confusion within the literature on the impact of social media on crises is that it treats all social media platforms and all crises as uniform. We aim to correct these mistaken assumptions by disaggregating both social media and crises, hypothesizing that different types of social media platforms can have varied effects in different types of crises.

Toward a More Fine-Grained Treatment of Thermonuclear Twitter

This chapter offers an original framework to systematically analyze the impact of social media on escalation based on the properties of three dimensions: the type of platform, the type of crisis, and the target audience. Our goal is to offer a useful framework for thinking about the impact of social media on crises in a more granular fashion, which can be applied across platforms, regions, and audiences.

First, the type of platform matters. Namely, is the platform open or closed? We treat this as a binary variable, but it is admittedly potentially continuous, as Twitter has completely open reach—even despite echo chambers—whereas Facebook has potentially several nodes of reach from the user, and text message apps such as WhatsApp can have large private groups or single users. Open platforms, such as Twitter, are often an opportunity to engage with strangers, whereas closed platforms, such as WhatsApp, are how we communicate with those we know and trust. As demonstrated in the study by Hunt Allcott, Matthew Gentzkow, and Chuan Yu, disinformation is more likely to

---

31. An exception to this is Hunt Allcott, Matthew Gentzkow, and Chuan Yu, "Trends in the Diffusion of Misinformation on Social Media," *Research and Politics* (2019): 108. They analyzed 569 cases of fake news websites and 9,540 fake stories on Facebook and Twitter between January 2015 and July 2018 and found that misinformation had a limited impact over Facebook compared to Twitter—one explanation for this was changes to the Facebook platform after the 2016 US presidential election.

32. For work on the effects of cyberweapons and emerging technologies on escalation, see Kreps and Schneider, "Escalation Firebreaks"; and Caitlin Talmadge, "Emerging Technology and Intra-War Escalation Risks: Evidence from the Cold War, Implications for Today," *Journal of Strategic Studies* 42, no. 6 (August 2019): 864–887.

be spread via Twitter than Facebook.[33] But it is theoretically possible that open platforms like Twitter more easily "revert to the mean" over time as disinformation can be publicly corrected in ways that closed platforms such as Facebook and WhatsApp may not enable. In general, we hypothesize that Twitter users seek, and eventually receive, more accurate information in crises as misinformation is corrected—even if dissemination is imperfect—whereas closed platforms are more likely to have misinformation persist and be deployed to reinforce preexisting beliefs, such as hypernationalism.

Second, the nature of the crisis also matters.[34] This is supported by literature on escalation, whereby the political context and stakes affect the outcome of the conflict. Studies on the impact of social media from different disciplines also reinforce this point. A study on Twitter usage during a political crisis in Côte d'Ivoire in 2010–2011, for example, found that social media usage and its impact shifted with the nature of the conflict. At the outset of the conflict, it was primarily used for political signaling for domestic audiences, but as the conflict escalated it shifted to being a vehicle for providing information about humanitarian aid to the public along with sharing information about the nature of the conflict with international audiences.[35] We hypothesize that crisis duration is the relevant property involving the differential impact of social media. We differentiate between short crises ranging from hours to several days, and long crises going beyond that. In short crises focused on a discrete event, such as a singular terrorist attack or explosion (such as the August 2020 ammonium nitrate explosion in Beirut), we hypothesize that misinformation will spread rapidly as "hot takes" make the rounds on both open and closed platforms. But in long crises, involving iterated and longer interaction between adversaries, open platforms are more likely to revert to the mean and widely disseminate more accurate (not necessarily entirely accurate, but a relatively more accurate version) of events than closed platforms, where conspiracy theories and misinformation are likely to persist. We differentiate crises as either discrete or ongoing, but obviously there is a spectrum of duration and intensity, though we hypothesize that duration is the more relevant variable as information reverts to the mean.

The third dimension we focus on is domestic versus international audiences. Whether or not a social media message has an impact begs the question: impact on whom? Scholarship to date focuses on two audiences: international actors, particularly political leaders and decision makers, and the domestic public. Russian president Vladimir Putin is likely to be impacted by a Trump tweet differently than a Trump voter in Florida. That said, there will likely be spillover between domestic and international au-

---

33. Allcott, Gentzkov, and Yu, "Trends."
34. See Bell and MacDonald, "Escalation."
35. Schreiner, "Information," 1.

Table 3.1 Short Crisis

	Domestic	International
Open (Twitter)	Hot takes/misinformation	Alerting international actors (risk of spillover)
Closed (WhatsApp)	Fearmongering	Diasporic nationalism?

Table 3.2 Long Crisis

	Domestic	International
Open (Twitter)	Information improves	Deterrence/coercion signaling (risk of spillover)
Closed (WhatsApp)	Preexisting beliefs/conspiracy theories	Diasporic patriotism?

diences on open platforms, as the messages targeted at one group will also be read by the other one. In general, social media in crises involve communication, signals, and spillover between leaders to leaders, leaders to the public, the public to leaders, and the public to each other.[36] And, in some cases, messages intended for domestic consumption can have unintentional consequences if misinterpreted by the leaders of the adversary.

Based on these variables, we identify two main sets of hypotheses about how social media impacts nuclear crises. We orient these dimensions in tables 3.1 and 3.2 to generate hypothesized effects based on these three properties of nuclear crises in an era of social media.

- H1: Social media does not have a uniform effect on crisis dynamics but can have varying impacts depending on the specific type of platform and the nature of the crisis.
    - H1a: Open social media platforms are more likely to thicken the fog of war than closed platforms during short crises.
    - H1b: Closed social media platforms will reinforce existing views over long crises to include conspiracy theories.
- H2: Social media does not have a uniform effect on international and domestic audiences.
    - H2a: Open platforms are more useful for signaling to the international community than closed platforms.
    - H2b: Closed platforms are more likely to be used to exacerbate domestic public opinion and nationalism during a crisis.

---

36. Christian Reuter, Stefan Stieglitz, and Muhammad Imran, "Social Media in Conflicts and Crises," *Behavior and Information Technology* 39, no. 3 (2020): 241–251.

Depending on the properties of the platform, the crisis, and the audience, we hypothesize differential effects and dynamics in crises. The aim of this theoretical framework is to offer more fine-grained predictions and mechanisms for how different social media tools affect nuclear crisis dynamics, rather than simply assuming that there is an overall effect and that all platforms have a uniform effect. The dissatisfaction is that there may not be an overall effect, but we believe it is more accurate to treat the impact of social media on crisis dynamics at a more granular, platform level than search for aggregate effects, which may be difficult to identify and isolate.

To explore these hypotheses and illustrate these mechanisms, we examine three empirical cases: the 2019 India-Pakistan crisis, the 2018 Hawaii missile alert, and the 2017 United States Forces Korea (USFK) evacuation order from the Korean Peninsula. The case studies were selected because they all have a nuclear component involving two nuclear actors, at least in the background, and otherwise offer useful variation. The Pulwama/Balakot crisis was a discrete crisis on the day of the attack on Indian security services on February 14, 2019, followed by a several-day crisis when India retaliated on February 26, 2019. The 2018 Hawaii missile alert originated with a push notification through cellular carriers but not via a public platform, thus it almost uniquely had the properties of a universal private network. All cell phone users received an official emergency alert, which was inadvertently sent during a test warning of an incoming North Korean ballistic missile, closing with "This is not a drill." This generated understandable panic. Although there was no reason to otherwise believe North Korea would launch a first strike against Hawaii, the message was disseminated through an official state channel six weeks after North Korea tested its longest-range missile, the Hwasong-15 ICBM, and before Kim Jong Un initiated the so-called charm offensive. And just four months earlier in 2017, at the height of tensions between the United States and North Korea, a fake message ordering the evacuation of nonessential US military personnel from South Korea—the leading indicator of a potential US-led attack against North Korea—circulated on closed platforms such as WhatsApp and Facebook, generating fears of an impending war at a time when it was plausible that the United States may initiate a surprise attack on Kim Jong Un's North Korea.[37] Within the cases, we look for indicators of social media impact, to include (1) responses from international actors over social media; (2) spread of misinformation, disinformation, and "deep fakes"; (3) shifts in public opinion and attitudes; and (4) military responses and escalatory (or de-escalatory) actions.

---

37. Kim Gamel, "US Forces Korea Warns of Fake Evacuation Message," *Stars and Stripes*, September 21, 2017, https://www.military.com/daily-news/2017/09/21/us-forces-korea-warns-fake-evacuation-messages.html.

FROM PULWAMA TO BALAKOT 2019

On February 14, 2019, a local twenty-two-year-old Kashmir man, Adil Ahmad Dar, drove a minivan laden with RDX into a bus carrying paramilitary forces from the Central Reserve Police Force (CRPF) near the Kashmir village of Pulwama, killing over forty personnel in the worst terrorist attack in Indian Kashmir in decades. Within hours, the attack was claimed by the Pakistani militant group, the Jaish-e-Mohammed (JeM), which radicalized Dar and purportedly assisted him with logistics and planning. Indian social media went into hyperdrive. After initial ambiguity about the nature of the attack, India's major media figures on Twitter arrived at a relatively accurate accounting of what happened: the JeM took responsibility for an attack in Kashmir that killed about forty (the final count ended up being forty-two) CRPF personnel.[38] Initial accounts underreported the number killed, rather than exaggerating them, so the figure circulating on Twitter by the end of the day had been revised up from "over a dozen" to the nearly accurate forty CRPF soldiers. This seems to have been consistent in both English and Hindi language accounts and is consistent with what we expect with open platforms in a relatively discrete crisis, where confusion eventually leads to convergence through crowdsourcing and viral propagation of more updated information.

The dynamics on WhatsApp appear to have been different and illustrate the perils of closed social media platforms during discrete crises.[39] In closed WhatsApp groups a variety of misinformation and disinformation campaigns were circulating virulently and virally. For example, a fake picture of India's main opposition candidate, Congress's Rahul Gandhi, who was about to run a national election against the wildly popular BJP incumbent prime minister, Narendra Modi, was photoshopped as meeting Dar, the suicide terrorist.[40] It is unclear how widely this was propagated or believed, as this is difficult to measure. But it was making the rounds on highly popular and widely subscribed BJP linked WhatsApp groups. Older videos, which will only get more realistic with so-called deep fake technology, were circulating that appeared to show Congress celebrating the attack and shouting "Pakistan zindabad" (long live Pakistan) as part of a concerted political effort to

---

38. NDTV, Twitter, February 14, 2019, https://twitter.com/ndtv/status/1096147017145798656?s=20.
39. Kunal Purohit, "After Pulwama Terror Attack, WhatsApp Groups Are Fueling Hypernationalism, Hatred, and Warmongering," *Firstpost*, February 16, 2019, https://www.firstpost.com/india/after-pulwama-attack-whatsapp-groups-are-fuelling-hypernationalism-hatred-and-war-mongering-6099461.html.
40. Jignesh Patel, "Rahul Gandhi's Image Photoshopped; Shown Posing with Pulwama Suicide Bomber," *alt news*, February 15, 2019, https://www.altnews.in/rahul-gandhis-image-photoshopped-shown-posing-with-pulwama-suicide-bomber/.

paint the Congress Party as Pakistan sympathizers.[41] What was not fake was a message that seems to have circulated millions of times in India on various WhatsApp groups calling for India to destroy Pakistan, fueling hypernationalism and warmongering. Citing each previous war that Pakistan "started" and India "finished," the message closed with "2019: They Started, and we will BLOODY HELL FINISH IT."[42] Others demanded 400 Pakistanis killed for 40 Indians, still others demanded that Modi do a "Gujarat" on Pakistan (i.e., massacre Muslims). These were shared virally in multiple groups in both English and Hindi, and all aimed at seemingly one thing: whipping up nationalism and revenge emotions against Pakistan and, dangerously, against Muslims within India. Some were preceded with the hashtag #IndiaNeedsNuclearStrike. Equally worrying were the messages going viral that purported to show the Muslims of India celebrating the attack—creating the real possibility of internal violence and reprisals against Indian Muslims, which did happen sporadically but was thankfully not widespread.

Although Twitter had its fair share of rabble-rousing, the public and open nature of the platform tended to moderate it compared to WhatsApp. The latter, in addition to being a closed network, is also perceived to be a more private space, which has led people to share and say what they would otherwise not say publicly, revealing a widespread virulent nationalism and othering of Pakistan and Indian Muslims. Facebook was also a platform for particularly nationalist comments, and an NDTV editor was suspended for posting racist comments on her Facebook page.[43] Twitter at least allows for a possible pathway for users to be exposed to alternative information and perspectives since the nature of retweets and the platform tends to revert to the mean over time. To be sure, this effect will be moderated by the echo chamber effect—it is those accounts in extreme networks that have the lowest probability of receiving moderating information. But on WhatsApp, such a pathway may not even exist; a user's potential exposure is limited by the groups that they are in. As such, it is easy to select into groups that reinforce preexisting beliefs, where conspiracy theories and virulent narratives take hold and are difficult to dislodge.

Twelve days later, India struck back at a JeM Madrassa outside a Pakistani town, Balakot. For the first time in history, a nuclear weapons power used airpower directly on the undisputed sovereign territory of another nuclear

41. BOOM FACT Check Team, "No, Police Did Not Lathicharge Congress Workers for Saying 'Pakistan Zindabad,'" *Boom*, February 13, 2019, https://www.boomlive.in/no-police-did-not-lathicharge-congress-workers-for-saying-pakistan-zindabad/.

42. Purohit, "After Pulwama."

43. JKR Staff, "NDTV Suspends Editor for Facebook Post on Pulwama Terror Attack," *Janta Ka Reporter*, February 15, 2019, http://www.jantakareporter.com/entertainment/ndtv-suspends-editor-for-facebook-post-on-pulwama/232537/.

weapons power. Interestingly, the first inkling of the attack came from the Twitter account of the official Pakistan Army spokesman, Major General Asif Ghafoor, thereby alerting the world via social media that India had retaliated.[44] For India it was the first time that it had used airpower against mainland Pakistan since the 1971 war. It is probably unsustainable to argue that social media put pressure on Modi to hit back in this fashion since, with or without Twitter or WhatsApp, Modi seems to have been itching to retaliate. This is consistent with our general hypothesis that social media pressure is endogenous to what states may otherwise prefer to do. What social media likely did was prepare the domestic political battlefield to overwhelmingly support a relatively aggressive retaliation. The BJP IT cell went into hyperdrive after the attack, propagating both bot-driven tweets and WhatsApp messages hailing Modi's retaliation—with his fifty-six-inch chest—as historic after Congress's failure to do anything, especially after the 2008 Mumbai attack that killed 173 civilians. Immediately, the news and bot-driven tweets (distinguishable by their verbatim language) were deployed on Twitter to claim that Modi had killed 500 or 600 terrorists at Balakot—very close to the 400 deaths demanded by nationalist WhatsApp groups after Pulwama. The same purportedly went out over the WhatsApp groups.

The problem for both the Indian and Pakistani governments was that, at least on Twitter, the global analytical community was watching, analyzing, and weighing in. The Pakistani claim that India's Air Force turned around after being intercepted was quickly debunked when the official army spokesman later tweeted pictures of Indian missiles hitting trees deep into Pakistani territory, roughly 60 kilometers from the Line of Control (LoC).[45] This was both for domestic political purposes in Pakistan—the Indian Air Force (IAF) did not hit anything except some trees and maybe a goat—but was also the first report to the international community that India had retaliated. On February 26, Major General Ghafoor announced in an official Pakistan Army press conference that was live-streamed, live-tweeted, and later put on YouTube that Pakistan was convening the National Command Authority (NCA), ominously adding—cutting from Urdu to English for maximum international signaling effect—"I hope you understand what is National Command Authority, what does it constitute."[46] The NCA is the body in charge of Pakistan's nuclear weapons. This was clearly a signal to

---

44. Major General Ghafoor, Twitter, February 25, 2019, https://twitter.com/OfficialDGISPR/status/1100179216375693318?s=20.

45. Major General Ghafoor, Twitter, February 25, 2019, https://twitter.com/OfficialDGISPR/status/1100179216375693318?s=20 and Twitter, February 26, 2019, https://twitter.com/OfficialDGISPR/status/1100231826348617728?s=20.

46. See Ankit Panda, Twitter, February 26, 2019, https://twitter.com/nktpnd/status/1100496202154631170?s=20.

India, but more important, the United States, whose intervention in South Asian crises Pakistan has routinely attempted to catalyze in order to prevent Indian escalation.[47]

However, the Indian claim that it brought down the Balakot structure was also quickly debunked because it was still standing, and every commercial satellite could still see it, a new feature Zegart explores in her chapter. Within a couple of days, India's Air Force claimed it used a penetrator version of the Spice standoff missiles that were not designed to bring down the structure. Commercial satellite imagery detected several ground scars on the side of the hill where the structure stood, leading to speculation that most, if not all, of the Spices missed the target. It is possible one or more penetrated the building, but it became obvious that the BJP's initial claim of several hundred terrorists killed (which was later sourced to how many cell phones the National Technical Research Organization [NTRO] detected several days before the strike, not on the day of the strike) was likely inaccurate and exaggerated.[48] On Twitter, open-source analysts eventually concluded that the IAF either completely missed, or largely missed, the target at Balakot. But this was mostly in English. Major Hindi language accounts did not bother correcting the original estimate.[49] On WhatsApp and closed platforms, however, this outside analysis did not find its way into the narrative, and the "man on the street" across India continues to largely believe that Modi killed hundreds of terrorists at Balakot.[50]

On February 27, the Pakistan Air Force (PAF) retaliated for India's Balakot strike by crossing the LoC and, it claims, "intentionally missing" an Indian Brigade Headquarters, just to demonstrate that it could hit it if so desired. In the ensuing dogfight, India shot down one of its own Mi-17 helicopters in a tragic friendly fire incident and lost a MiG-21 Bison that had crossed the LoC in hot pursuit of the PAF. The pilot, Wing Commander Abhinandan Varthaman, was captured alive by Pakistan, whose official media spokesman tweeted that there were multiple Indian pilots in custody but then clarified that there was only one.[51] He was wounded but then expeditiously returned to India on March 1 as a de-escalatory measure. Var-

47. See Narang, *Nuclear Strategy in the Modern Era*.
48. "Rajnath Singh Says NTRO Surveillance of JeM Camp in Balakot before IAF Air Strikes Confirmed 300 Active Mobile Phones," *Press Trust of India*, March 5, 2019.
49. See, for example, ABP News, Twitter, February 27, 2019, https://twitter.com/ABPNews/status/1100765012572815360?s=20.
50. See, for example, Pooja Chaudhuri, "Fake WhatsApp Chat Shared on Social Media to Claim 292 Terrorists Killed in Balakot Airstrike," *alt news*, March 5, 2019, https://www.altnews.in/fake-whatsapp-chat-shared-on-social-media-to-claim-292-terrorists-killed-in-balakot-airstrike/.
51. Major General Asif Ghafoor, Twitter, February 27, 2019, https://twitter.com/OfficialDGISPR/status/1100641491679150080?s=20, and Twitter, February 27, 2019, https://twitter.com/OfficialDGISPR/status/1100739613486915584?s=20.

thaman then claimed that he shot down a PAF F-16 before he went down. Thus began one of the great social media mysteries of the Balakot crisis: was there actually a second pilot, or #doosraBanda, as Pakistan's official military spokesman initially claimed, and if so was it a Pakistani Air Force pilot who ejected from an F-16 that was shot down? Reputable Indian journalists continued to tweet about the #doosraBanda months later, and the IAF offered official briefings showing circumstantial evidence the F-16 was shot down.[52] Pakistan continues to deny that an F-16 pilot was killed and is bolstered by a US Department of Defense (DoD) leak that all US-origin (meaning all) PAF F-16s were later accounted for and operational.[53] WhatsApp groups circulated fake videos of a PAF parachute, and the belief that India shot down an F-16 persists on closed social media platforms. Many Indian journalists and military on open platforms such as Twitter continue to believe so. This debate spilled over into mainstream media outlets, illustrating the cross-pollination effect of social media to mainstream media, which would reproduce tweets and potentially doctored images on-screen during live broadcasts. Much of the WhatsApp activity was designed to whip up patriotism and pride in India's Armed Forces after spinning up the hypernationalism before the Balakot strike. Anecdotal evidence suggests that almost all Indians adamantly believe that Varthaman killed a PAF F-16, because it aligns with preexisting beliefs in the superiority of India and its Air Force, and that the DoD audit was motivated by Lockheed's refusal to admit that an F-16 could be killed by a vintage MiG-21 Bison.

A curious episode then emerged after the crisis seemingly de-escalated. Reports surfaced that India may have threatened to escalate the crisis with surface-to-surface missile strikes if Abhinandan had not been expeditiously returned by Pakistan. Pakistan allegedly threatened privately to retaliate "three times over" if India breached that red line.[54] During the campaign trail, Prime Minister Modi seemingly confirmed this threat when he stated that he was prepared to order a missile strike that would have been a "qatal ki raat," or night of murder. But none of this occurred through social media, suggesting that significant deterrence threats between governments can still be conveyed privately, the old-fashioned way, and not make its way to social media. When this threat was made public, it was for domestic political purposes for

---

52. See, for example, Vishnu Som, Twitter, October 8, 2019, https://twitter.com/VishnuNDTV/status/1181495301456023553?s=20.

53. Lara Seligman, "Did India Shoot Down a Pakistani Jet? US Count Says No," *Foreign Policy*, April 4, 2019, https://foreignpolicy.com/2019/04/04/did-india-shoot-down-a-pakistani-jet-u-s-count-says-no/.

54. Sanjeev Miglani and Drazen Jorgic, "India, Pakistan Threatened to Unleash Missiles at Each other: Sources," Reuters, March 16, 2019, https://www.reuters.com/article/us-india-kashmir-crisis-insight/india-pakistan-threatened-to-unleash-missiles-at-each-other-sources-idUSKCN1QY03T.

Modi's reelection campaign to illustrate his resolve and aggressiveness against fighting terrorism.

What can we learn from the social media dynamics during the Pulwama/Balakot crisis in February 2019? For one, different platforms had different dynamics. Open platforms such as Twitter served largely, over time, to generate relatively accurate information for those who wished to find it. There is no doubt a lot of trolling and nationalism on Twitter, but basic facts tended to revert to their true values over time and correct initial misinformation. Here the audiences were domestic and international, for both deterrence signaling, and making the international community aware of events—Pakistan's official army spokesperson was the first to alert the world to India's strike at Balakot and mention, in English, Pakistan's convening of the NCA, perhaps as a signal to catalyze international efforts to intervene in the crisis. Closed groups, such as WhatsApp, were a completely different story and aimed primarily at domestic audiences. Coordinated groups and messages attempted to whip up hypernationalism following the Pulwama attack, and then circulated government propaganda after the Balakot strike and retaliation, with little if any effort by anyone to verify information. This may have largely served to reinforce preexisting beliefs. In a country where a majority of respondents, according to Sagan and Valentino, would have no problem using nuclear weapons first even if there is no military advantage, those preexisting beliefs provide a domestic political base to support quite aggressive policies.[55] This mechanism is potentially escalatory.

But there was a de-escalatory mechanism provided by social media platforms as well. Both sides could convey narratives to their publics that allowed for them to walk away from the crisis claiming they won. India convinced its public that it killed over 300 terrorists at Balakot and shot down a Pakistani F-16. There was enough ambiguity around it that people who wanted to believe that narrative—a substantial portion of India's electorate presumably—could. And these tools allowed the BJP to monopolize that narrative, particularly on WhatsApp. Pakistan was able to credibly claim the converse; the international open-source community concluded that India largely missed at Balakot and failed to kill an F-16, ratifying the Pakistan Army's narrative. For Pakistan, Twitter worked in its favor, so it promoted tweets by "foreign experts" that validated Pakistan's claims. Both sides were able to walk down from the crisis without further escalation despite it being the most kinetically aggressive engagement between two nuclear powers, perhaps in history. As Mark Bell and Nicholas Miller's chapter in this volume suggests, it is unclear whether both governments opportunistically

---

55. Benjamin Valentino and Scott Sagan, "Atomic Attraction," *Indian Express*, June 3, 2016, https://indianexpress.com/article/opinion/columns/barack-obama-hiroshima-speech-india-nuclear-weapon-terrorism-atomic-attraction-2831348/.

used these fictions as cover to de-escalate or whether, more concerningly, they actually believed these fictitious narratives, which may incentivize future escalation. Nevertheless, this episode shows that social media platforms do not have a uniform effect on crisis dynamics and that platform properties, crisis properties, and audience properties interact in interesting ways to generate different dynamics.

HAWAII MISSILE ALERT 2018

On January 13, 2018, at 8:07 a.m. Hawaii time, every cell phone user in Hawaii received an alert through the official state government Emergency Alert System: "Emergency Alert: BALLISTIC MISSILE THREAT INBOUND TO HAWAII. SEEK IMMEDIATE SHELTER. THIS IS NOT A DRILL." This was a push notification through the state's cell networks, which essentially served as a universal text message to every cell phone on the Hawaiian Islands. At the same time, an emergency message scrolled on all local Hawaiian television stations: "If you are indoors, stay indoors. If you are outdoors, seek immediate shelter in a building. Remain indoors well away from windows. If you are driving, pull safely to the side of the road and seek shelter in a building or lay on the floor." The alert was pushed with no context and no ability to otherwise determine whether the alert was genuine. It seemed authentic, and it was also plausible that North Korea had launched a missile at the United States, given recent events and barbs exchanged between Trump and Kim Jong Un. Many people took to social media to try to confirm the alert, but confusion ensued for what may have been excruciating minutes for the residents of Hawaii. This panic was exacerbated by the medium of text messaging, a platform akin to a social media tool: one with almost universal reach but on a closed platform with no ability to crowdsource accuracy such as on Twitter. It was not until thirty-eight minutes later, at 8:45 a.m. that a follow-up notification was sent to cell phones and TV emergency message scrolls that it was a false alarm.[56]

During those thirty-eight minutes, some social media platforms proved to be a more reliable source of information than official channels, and traditional news media largely relied on messages from Facebook and Twitter. Between 8:07 a.m. and 8:12 a.m., employees at the Hawaii Emergency Management Agency (Hi-EMA) notified state and local officials that it was a false alert and used the Hawaii Warning System to notify counties, "Attention all stations—This is the state warning point—There is no ballistic missile threat

---

56. Amy Wang, "Hawaii Missile Alert: How One Employee 'Pushed the Wrong Button' and Caused a Wave of Panic," *Washington Post*, January 14, 2018, https://www.washingtonpost.com/news/post-nation/wp/2018/01/14/hawaii-missile-alert-how-one-employee-pushed-the-wrong-button-and-caused-a-wave-of-panic/.

to Hawaii—this is a drill—I repeat, this is a drill."[57] At 8:13 a.m., an employee at Hi-EMA posted that it was a "false alert" on their personal Facebook page, and five minutes later the agency's PR team began sending notifications via social media. One of the first tweets confirming it was a false alert came from Rep. Tulsi Gabbard at 8:19 a.m.: "HAWAII—THIS IS A FALSE ALARM. THERE IS NO INCOMING MISSILE TO HAWAII. I HAVE CONFIRMED WITH OFFICIALS THERE IS NO INCOMING MISSILE." This was confirmed one minute later by Hi-EMA and five minutes later by the governor. US Indo-Pacific Command apparently sent an email—with limited distribution by definition—stating it was a false alarm at 8:35 a.m., and at 9:08 a.m. it finally tweeted, "US Pacific Command has detected no ballistic missile threat to #Hawaii. Earlier message was sent in error and was a false alarm."[58] Traditional media sources and TV stations called on people to retweet their messages that it was a false alert in a classic example of cross-pollination between social media and news outlets.[59]

Individuals and traditional news agencies were quick to respond, while the government response was relatively slow and careless. One reason for the delay between the two push notifications was that the Hi-EMA checklist for drills did not include a protocol response to false alerts. In order to issue a Civil Emergency Message (CEM) retracting the earlier alert, they needed confirmation of the code and requested additional guidance from the Federal Emergency Management Agency (FEMA). Hi-EMA first contacted FEMA for approval at 8:26 a.m., but could not get through until 8:30 a.m., at which time FEMA advised to issue a CEM. The CEM was drafted at 8:32 a.m. and pushed at 8:45 a.m.[60] In an additional blunder, at 11.15 a.m. Hi-EMA tweeted that there would be a press conference at 1:00 p.m. about the "missile launch." This was subsequently removed.[61]

Both state and federal reports on the false alert blame "human error." The original message was sent because an operator inadvertently selected "test message" instead of the "drill" option on a drop-down menu. Further, the

---

57. Brigadier General (ret) Bruce E. Oliveira, "False Ballistic Missile Alert Investigation for January 13, 2018 Findings and Recommendations," January 29, 2018, https://dod.hawaii.gov/wp-content/uploads/2018/01/report2018-01-29-181149.pdf.

58. Ankit Panda, Twitter, January 13, 2018, https://twitter.com/nktpnd/status/952247826557390854?s=20; US Indo-Pacific Command, Twitter, January 13, 2018, https://twitter.com/INDOPACOM/status/952256032859832320?s=20.

59. 9 News Denver, Twitter, January 13, 2018, https://twitter.com/9NEWS/status/952245328396222464.

60. Interestingly, the timings of the state and FEMA reports differ slightly on when the call was received. See U.S. Department of Homeland Security Inspector General, "FEMA's Oversight of the Integrated Public Alert & Warning System (IPAWS)," Report OIG-19-08, November 19, 2018, https://www.oig.dhs.gov/sites/default/files/assets/2018-11/OIG-19-08-Nov18.pdf; Oliveira, "False Ballistic Missile Report Investigation."

61. Hawaii EMA, Twitter, January 13, 2018, https://web.archive.org/web/20180113214335/https://twitter.com/hawaii_ema/status/952287925777063936.

operator claims not to have heard, "EXERCISE EXERCISE EXERCISE," and instead heard, "This is not a drill." He had a record of poor performance, and according to a colleague, "He is unable to comprehend the situation at hand and has confused real life events and drills on at least two separate occasions."[62] After accidentally sending the missile alert message, the employee allegedly "just sat there" and did not "assist in the process" of canceling the alert.[63] The employee later told NBC, "I was 100 percent sure that it was the right decision, that it was real."[64]

Although there was no other indication that Kim Jong Un's North Korea was about to launch a first strike against Hawaii or the United States, this accidental alert came just six weeks after North Korea tested its third and longest range ICBM, the Hwasong-15. And it came only ten days after President Trump tweeted: "North Korean Leader Kim Jong Un just stated that the 'Nuclear Button is on his desk at all times.' Will someone from his depleted and food starved regime please inform him that I too have a Nuclear Button, but it is a much bigger & more powerful one than his, and my Button works!"[65] For almost an entire year, the general public had been subjected to reports of almost biweekly missile tests (seventeen in total), a (likely) thermonuclear test in September, media reports painting Kim Jong Un as "crazy," and presidential threats of "fire and fury." The diplomatic charm offensive that Kim Jong Un would soon initiate had not yet begun. Furthermore, Hawaii was a ripe first target for North Korea due to its centrality for Pacific Command and its proximity to North Korea. It would have been plausible for an average citizen in Hawaii to believe that Kim Jong Un had decided to launch a first strike at the state.

In an added twist, it was roughly 2 p.m. on the East Coast of the United States when reports of the alert circulated on social media. President Trump was reportedly at Trump International Golf Course in Florida when those tweets began, though where he was precisely at this time is publicly unknown. At the time, Trump did not address the false alert. Gabbard tweeted, "Donald Trump is taking too long. Now is not the time for posturing. He must take this threat seriously and begin direct talks with North Korea, without preconditions, to de-escalate and denuclearize the Korean peninsula. There is no time to waste. . . . The people of Hawai'i should never have had to go through this."[66] North Korea's official outlet, Rodung Sinmun, took

---

62. Oliveira, "False Ballistic Missile Report," 10.
63. Oliveira, "False Ballistic Missile Report," 10.
64. As discussed in "FEMA's Oversight of the Integrated Public Alert & Warning System (IPAWS)."
65. Donald J. Trump, Twitter, January 2, 2018, https://twitter.com/realDonaldTrump/status/948355557022420992?s=20.
66. Tulsi Gabbard, Twitter, January 13, 2018, https://twitter.com/TulsiGabbard/status/952289562843328513.

particular delight in the "tragicomedy" and that "The entire island was thrown into an utter chaos at the news that a ballistic missile was coming in."

But a hypothetical scenario helps demonstrate how dangerous this false alert could have been: what if President Trump had logged onto his personal Twitter account on the back nine and saw a screenshot posted by reputable users in Hawaii of the inbound missile alert and thought, "time to launch a counterforce strike against North Korea." On the golf course, his chief of staff is nowhere to be found, but he summons his military aide with the nuclear satchel and orders to be patched through to the National Military Command Center (NMCC). He cracks open the "biscuit" that he keeps in his oversized golfing pants, validates and authenticates himself to the duty officer at the NMCC, and orders a first strike against North Korea, citing the inbound missile alert he has seen confirmed by the Hawaiian government officials. It is a legal and valid order, and no one could legally stop him.[67]

What does this incident reveal about social media during crisis? First, open social media platforms can provide an important source of information and quickly revert to the mean in disseminating accurate information. In this case, Twitter proved to be a better means of alerting the public than government officials or traditional news platforms. While the initial push message, essentially a closed platform, was alarming, subsequent open and closed platform messaging was highly effective in de-escalating tensions rather than stirring up fears of an incoming North Korean missile.

US FORCES KOREA NONESSENTIAL PERSONNEL EVACUATION ORDER 2017

Several months earlier, at the height of US-North Korean tensions, on the morning of September 21, 2017, a message was sent from the USFK Facebook account, on WhatsApp and via text message, calling for a noncombatant evacuation operation order (NEO). The order appeared to be official and from legitimate USFK and DoD accounts. It stated: "Real World Noncombatant evacuation operation order issued. All DoD family members and non-emergency essential DoD on the Korean Peninsula, an evacuation order has been issued" and was received from "USFK Official Alert."[68] The order requires family members and all noncombat essential personnel to evacuate in anticipation of a conflict and is considered to be the leading indicator

---

67. Bruce Blair and Jon Wolfsthal, "Trump Can Launch Nuclear Weapons Whenever He Wants, with or without Mattis," *Washington Post*, December 23, 2018, https://www.washingtonpost.com/outlook/2018/12/23/trump-can-launch-nuclear-weapons-whenever-he-wants-with-or-without-mattis/.

68. "Fake Evacuation Orders sent to US Military Personnel in South Korea," Fox News, September 22, 2017, https://www.foxnews.com/world/fake-evacuation-orders-sent-to-us-military-personnel-in-south-korea.

of a possibly imminent conflict—and a potential attack by the United States and South Korea against North Korea. It is one of the first steps the Pentagon takes in anticipation of conflict. The order was distributed from seemingly legitimate (compromised) accounts. There was no reason to believe it was not true.

Upon reports of the NEO order spreading virally within the USFK community, the latter quickly issued a denial on Facebook, which read:

> On Thursday, 21 SEP, we received multiple reports of a fake text-to-cell and social media message regarding a "real world noncombatant evacuation operation (NEO) order issued" which instructed DoD family members and non-emergency essential DoD civilians on the Korean peninsula that an evacuation order had been issued. USFK did NOT issue this message. All US Department of Defense (DoD) family members are reminded to confirm any evacuation-related communications with their service member and unit non-combatant evacuation (NEO) representatives. Anyone receiving this false message should not click any links or open any attachments included in the correspondence.[69]

The closed nature of the platforms made it difficult to immediately counter the disinformation as it went viral with no widespread correction. Luckily, USFK acted swiftly and, interestingly, used the same platform—Facebook—on which the initial fake orders were posted, to correct the misinformation rather than sending an internal email or posting the correction on Twitter. An internal email may not reach as far as the original misinformation, failing to fully correct it, while tweeting a clarification may have reached too broad an audience, creating more panic than it solved by alerting those that did not see the initial Facebook message that there was a fake evacuation order even issued in the first place. Therefore, the sensible strategy was to use the same platform that propagated the disinformation in order to correct it. The DoD opened an investigation as to the source of the false message, and suspicion turned to a North Korean psychological operation, though as far as the authors are aware, there has been no official confirmation of this. If it was North Korean psyops, using legitimate and trusted, but compromised, social media accounts of USFK personnel added credibility and generated real concern that the evacuation order—and an imminent conflict—was genuine.

Given the intensity of tensions at the time, it would have been perfectly believable that the Trump administration had decided that military force was the only way to remove Kim Jong Un and his nuclear weapons. The order came at the height of the 2017 crisis between North Korea and the United States when it appeared that a war between the two was more than just a

---

69. USFK, Facebook post, September 21, 2017, https://www.facebook.com/myusfk/posts/10159342075800223.

remote possibility. Three weeks earlier, North Korea tested a purported thermonuclear weapon with a yield over 150kt.

Moreover, the United States conducted numerous exercises in the region immediately prior to and after the incident. In June and again in October 2017, it conducted genuine NEO drills, although officially the exercises are not in relation to any current events. A spokeswoman for the 2nd Combat Aviation Bridge told *Stars and Stripes* during the April exercise, "Obviously the one (scenario) that is forefront in our mind is a resumption of hostilities with North Korea or rising political tension leading to the feeling that American citizens might not be safe."[70] Earlier that year, in April 2017, Trump tweeted, "North Korea is looking for trouble. If China decides to help, that would be great. If not, we will solve the problem without them! U.S.A."[71] At the same time he told Fox News, "We're sending an Armada" to include an aircraft carrier to deter North Korean aggression and further escalation. The announcement came only two days after a Trump-Xi summit in Mar-a-Lago, during which Trump expressed his frustration and waning patience with Kim Jong Un. The news about the carrier prompted a flurry of news stories, sparking fears of a US preemptive attack; however, the aircraft carrier, the USS *Carl Vinson*, was 3,500 miles away, traveling in the opposite direction.[72] It was not until a week later, after completing a joint exercise in the Southern Pacific region, that the *Carl Vinson* began sailing north. During this time, Trump's tweets and the clear confusion within the administration heightened fears of a possible escalation.

This episode shows how social media platforms can be misused to spread malicious and potentially war-hysterical information quickly, but also how that misinformation can be corrected relatively quickly as well. In this case, the crisis was embedded within a larger North Korea-US crisis, but the nature of the disinformation did not require action on the order of minutes—as in the Hawaii missile alert—since evacuations take days. Therefore, a considered denial on the same social media platform from the official USFK account sufficiently corrected the disinformation campaign. Twitter was used only once by USFK during the confusion, linking to the Facebook post clarifying that the message was fake. Similarly, the Navy and other Services retweeted the USFK message or news stories from *Stars and Stripes* and *Military Times* about the fake order.[73] Again, this points to a cross-pollination

---

70. Gamel, "US Forces Korea Warns of Fake Evacuation Message."
71. Donald Trump, Twitter, April 11, 2017, https://twitter.com/realDonaldTrump/status/851767718248361986.
72. Mark Landler and Eric Schmitt, "Aircraft Carrier Wasn't Sailing to Deter North Korea, as U.S. Suggested," *New York Times*, April 18, 2017, https://www.nytimes.com/2017/04/18/world/asia/aircraft-carrier-north-korea-carl-vinson.html.
73. Gamel, "US Forces Korea Warns of Fake Evacuation Message"; Charlsy Panzino, "U.S. Forces Korea: Evacuation Message Is Fake," *Military Times*, September 21, 2017, https://www.militarytimes.com/news/2017/09/21/us-forces-korea-evacuation-message-is-fake/.

relationship between social media and more traditional media sources, such as *Stars and Stripes*. Whereas in the Hawaii false alert case, social media was out in front of traditional media and played an important role in public communications, military news outlets were the main source of information for the USFK case, aside from the Facebook post by USFK. This case is striking in the lack of social media activity it generated, and the *Stars and Stripes* story dominated Twitter activity about the case, accounting for the top three most frequently tweeted/retweeted posts about it in the immediate aftermath, aside from the USFK original tweet and link to the Facebook story.[74]

Conclusion

This chapter has attempted to illustrate that social media and its impact on crises between nuclear actors is complex and not a monolithic phenomenon. We make the simple but powerful point that properties of the platform, the crisis, and the intended audience can interact in interesting ways to lead to different types of dynamics in crises between nuclear powers, some escalatory and some de-escalatory. They do not have a uniform effect. The analysis of the three cases demonstrates the open and closed social media platforms were used differently and to different effects. This provides strong support for our first hypothesis, that social media does not have a uniform effect on crisis dynamics but can have varying impact depending on the specific type of platform and the nature of the crisis.

Did open social media platforms do more to thicken the fog of war than closed platforms during discrete crises? Not exactly. Open platforms, such as Twitter, during both acute and ongoing crises, invite more information sharing so as to ascertain a holistic picture closer to the truth. This, too, is reinforced by studies into the use of Twitter, with one study finding that "far from safely agreeing with the dominant opinions in their respective social communities or merely being expressive, users debated with and challenged one another, even inviting disagreement."[75] And did closed social media platforms reinforce existing views over ongoing crises to include conspiracy theories? Yes, at least in the Pulwama/Balakot case.

It was more challenging to prove or disprove our second hypothesis that social media does not have a uniform effect on international and domestic audiences. We have hypothesized directions and effects of these dynamics,

---

74. One of the other most retweeted stories was by a prominent Japanese academic confirming that the order was fake. Okyuyama Masashi, Twitter, September 21, 2017, https://twitter.com/masatheman/status/911001313231564802.

75. Chang Wan Woo, Matthew P. Brigham, and Michael Gulotta, "Twitter Talk and Twitter Sharing in Times of Crisis: Exploring Rhetorical Motive and Agenda-Setting in the Ray Rice Scandal," *Communication Studies* 71, no. 1 (2020): 40–58.

CHAPTER 3

but do not have enough data—some of which is incredibly difficult to observe and collect—to conclusively answer these questions, which are critical to future nuclear-tinged crises. In addition to these questions, the research also raises important questions about wider nuclear strategy in two specific ways. First, it highlights risks and important questions about chain of command and leadership during crises. In the Hawaii case, for example, the first person to publicly announce that the alert was fake was one of the employees at Hi-EMA who posted to his personal Facebook account. And the USFK example suggests that social media can be manipulated potentially by malicious actors. This begs the question: if orders can be issued via social media, will they be subject to similar vulnerabilities? The Twitter hack on July 15, 2020, in which several hundred high-profile "verified" accounts, including the then-presidential candidate Joe Biden's, were taken over in a bitcoin scam—perpetrated with insider help by a Florida teenager—raises terrifying prospects. What if that hack were executed at the height of a military crisis and the perpetrator did not want bitcoin but to start a war? Imagine if President Trump's account had been taken over and a hacker simply tweeted "Game over Iran" or "Your time is up Kim." North Korea appeared to monitor President Trump's Twitter account in real time and having little early warning capability, may be forced to have an itchy trigger finger if it fears an imminent US attack. The power of some of these platforms, and their inherent insecurity, can generate some hair-raising scenarios.

If social media can contribute to nuclear escalation, should governments close down social media during a crisis? There are no easy answers to this question as a shutdown may create more rumors or risks—and remove potential pathways to de-escalation—than keeping the platform fully operational. In late 2019, for example, Iran shut down the country's access to the internet, including both Iranian and international sites, for a week amid ongoing protests over rising fuel prices. Iran, Russia, and potentially other countries are refitting their national internets to make it easier to shutdown access at the government's behest, similar to China's "Great Firewall."[76] According to internet freedom groups, outages are becoming increasingly common and jumped from 75 to 196 between 2016 and 2017.[77] Social media and its cross-pollinating effects will remain an important force that governments will have to contend with in future nuclear-tinged crises.

Social media is rich in variance. Different platforms—by design—make it harder to control the narrative, whether to deploy nationalist fictions or withhold inconvenient facts. Some platforms are dangerous vectors for dis-

---

76. Lily Hay Newman, "How the Iranian Government Shut Off the Internet," *Wired*, November 17, 2019, https://www.wired.com/story/iran-internet-shutoff/.

77. Michael Safi, "Iran's Digital Shutdown: Other Regimes Will Be Watching Closely," *Guardian*, November 21, 2019, https://www.theguardian.com/world/2019/nov/21/irans-digital-shutdown-other-regimes-will-be-watching-closely.

information, as suggested by two of the incidents offered here, which were false alerts. This may change the ways leaders communicate the crisis and spill over to public or use public domain for communicating, making private diplomacy ever more challenging and complicated. For example, Vladimir Putin's order to increase Russia's nuclear alert level during the 2022 Ukraine war went viral on Twitter, generating anxiety about a nuclear crisis between the United States and Russia. Yet it was also nuclear experts on Twitter that reduced global anxiety by explaining that Putin's order was largely rhetorical, with no practical impact on Russia's force posture. In this case Twitter served as a platform that both increased and subsequently reduced public anxiety about the nuclear crisis. Our fundamental conclusion is that different social media platforms have varied volume, accuracy, and speed of information leading to distinct effects and potential pathways to escalation and de-escalation in international crises. The only uniform effect that social media as a whole injects into nuclear crises is complexity. And over time, complexity in more frequent and potentially intense nuclear crises can generate a bill no one wants due.

CHAPTER 4

Understanding New Nuclear Threats

The Open-Source Intelligence Revolution?

Amy Zegart

In February 2001, Gwynne Roberts published a bombshell investigation in Britain's *Sunday Times* suggesting that Iraqi leader Saddam Hussein had "hoodwinked the West" and secretly tested a nuclear bomb on September 19, 1989.[1] The story appeared amid heightened tensions and mounting concerns over Iraq's weapons of mass destruction (WMD) programs. After years of dodging United Nations weapons inspectors, the Iraqi regime had kicked inspectors out of the country in 1998. As a result, for three years before the *Sunday Times* story broke, information about Iraq's nuclear program had ground to a halt.

Roberts, a journalist and filmmaker, recounted how a "mysterious visitor" appeared at his hotel in northern Iraq one night claiming to be a nuclear scientist from Hussein's nuclear program. The visitor, called "Leone," was shivering and afraid. "If I reveal secrets to you, my life is at risk," he said. But "Leone" worked through the night, sketching nuclear bomb designs, describing organizational details of Saddam's WMD program, showing a photograph of warhead allegedly bought from Russia, and providing the exact time and location of Saddam's alleged nuclear test. For the final stage of his investigation, Roberts went high tech. He bought commercial satellite images of the test site "Leone" described before and after the claimed test date and had them analyzed by Professor Bhupendra Jasani of King's Col-

---

The author gratefully acknowledges the support of the American Academy of Arts and Sciences for this project and the valuable feedback on earlier drafts provided by Robert Cardillo, Tom Fingar, Rose Gottemoeller, Siegfried Hecker, Jeffrey Lewis, Steve Miller, Vipin Narang, Frank Pabian, Allison Puccioni, Joshua Rovner, Scott Sagan, and all the participants in the Academy's November 2019 and July 2020 workshops.

1. Gwynne Roberts, "Was This Saddam's Bomb?" *Sunday Times*, February 25, 2001.

lege London. Jasani's imagery analysis seemed like it came straight from the television show *CSI*. He found evidence confirming the test site, including the existence of a wide tunnel stretching under the lake—exactly as "Leone" had described—and a railway line with roads leading to a shaft entrance, which was a huge rectangular structure; and evidence of an "unusually sensitive military zone," an army base with forty buildings. "If you wanted to hide something, I guess this is exactly what you would do," said Jasani in the *Sunday Times*.[2]

But Jasani was mistaken. Frank Pabian, the former nuclear chief inspector for the UN's International Atomic Energy Agency in Iraq and a leading satellite imagery expert, reviewed the same images and found absolutely no evidence the area had been used to conduct an underground nuclear test. Jasani had misinterpreted the satellite photos. The tunnel was actually an agricultural area served by a natural spring. The rail lines were a dual lane paved highway. The huge rectangular structure was an irrigated field. The unusually sensitive military zone with forty buildings had just two conventional ammunitions storage facilities with several typical storage bunkers nearby. And if the tunnel's dimensions were what Jasani believed them to be from the satellite imagery, excavation would have required the removal of enormous volumes of earth that would be impossible to conceal. Yet nothing in any imagery showed the removal, storage, or replacement of massive quantities of earth when the alleged underground testing facility was constructed and used.[3] Pabian and Terry Wallace, then a geophysics professor and forensic seismologist and now Director Emeritus at Los Alamos National Laboratory, later also debunked the *Sunday Times* story using seismological evidence and sent their information to the International Atomic Energy Agency. Still, Roberts's investigation appeared on BBC in March 2001, and in 2022 it was still available online, uncorrected, long after additional evidence showed conclusively that Saddam tried but never succeeded in developing a nuclear bomb.[4]

---

2. Gwynne Roberts, "Saddam's Bomb," BBC News, March 2, 2001, http://news.bbc.co.uk/2/hi/programmes/correspondent/1191203.stm.

3. Frank V. Pabian, unclassified email to author, October 17, 2019; Frank V. Pabian, "Commercial Satellite Imagery: Another Tool in the Nonproliferation Verification and Monitoring Tool-Kit," in *Nuclear Safeguards, Security, and Nonproliferation*, ed. James Doyle (Burlington, MA: Elsevier, 2008), 247, http://www.elsevier.com/books/nuclear-safeguards-security-and-nonproliferation/doyle/978-0-7506-8673-0#description; Larry O'Hanlon, "Seismic Sleuths," *Nature* 411 (June 14, 2001), 734–736, https://www.nature.com/articles/35081281.pdf.

4. Roberts, "Saddam's Bomb." For Iraq's failed nuclear program, see Målfrid Braut-Hegghammer, *Unclear Physics: Why Iraq and Libya Failed to Build Nuclear Weapons* (Ithaca: Cornell University Press, 2016); Charles Duelfer, *Comprehensive Report of the Special Advisor to the DCI on Iraq's WMD*, September 30, 2004, https://www.govinfo.gov/app/details/GPO-DUELFERREPORT; Joseph Cirincione et al., "WMD in Iraq: Evidence and Implications," Carnegie Endowment for International Peace, January 2004, https://carnegieendowment.org/files/Iraq3FullText.pdf.

CHAPTER 4

Roberts' story and its undoing were an early example of a rapidly growing phenomenon: the rise of nuclear threat intelligence providers operating outside of governments. Thanks to internet-powered global communications, the explosion of unclassified information online (including social media), the commercialization and advancement of satellite imagery, and developments in automated analytics like machine learning, all sorts of nongovernmental organizations and individuals are playing an ever-larger role. In the erroneous Saddam bomb story described above, claims were first reported by a British journalist, reinforced by a British professor, and discredited by a former UN weapons inspector with the help of a future US national nuclear lab director. All of them drew only from publicly available unclassified sources.

This chapter examines the emerging world of nongovernmental intelligence players in the nuclear arena. It examines why estimating nuclear threats is challenging, even for governments with sophisticated technical collection platforms, and how well US intelligence agencies have done in the past. Further, it describes major changes that have ushered in the rise of nongovernmental intelligence collectors and analysts. Finally, it examines the attributes, benefits, and risks of this emerging ecosystem and implications for the future.

Taking stock of the current moment is crucial. On the one hand, nongovernmental nuclear sleuths offer valuable information that can be shared with publics, policymakers, and international organizations—highlighting nuclear dangers and potentially generating better policies to address them. On the other hand, this ecosystem may increase nuclear dangers when its information is wrong as well as when it is right. The key factor is transparency. Public errors can raise tensions, distract intelligence officials, and lead policymakers astray. Accurate information can be dangerous, too, ending useful fictions that enable face-saving ways out and forcing premature decisions during sensitive negotiations and crises.

Hard Targets: Estimating Nuclear Dangers

Estimating nuclear threats is one of the most important intelligence missions. From Germany's race to develop an atomic bomb in World War II to North Korea's recent nuclear provocations, US intelligence officials have spent more than half a century trying to understand the capabilities, intentions, and activities of allies, adversaries, terrorist groups, and individuals seeking to develop the world's most dangerous weapons.

Nuclear-related intelligence falls into four broad categories: (1) understanding vertical nuclear proliferation, or the development of new weapons, programs, or capabilities within a known nuclear state such as Russia or China; (2) understanding horizontal proliferation or the spread of nuclear materials, technologies, equipment, or know-how from one nuclear nation to another country or non-state actor; (3) understanding nuclear risks related to accidents (such as the 1986 Chernobyl disaster) and crisis escalation; and (4) preventing strategic surprise by anticipating major nuclear developments with large geopolitical and national security ramifications, such as the 1962 Cuban missile crisis or the 1998 Indian and Pakistani nuclear tests.

How well have US intelligence agencies done? It is hard to say. As Sherman Kent, the founding father of the CIA's analytic branch, once noted, estimating is by nature a "hazardous occupation," an "excursion out beyond established fact into the unknown."[5]

Nuclear activities are especially challenging because states go to great lengths to conceal them. The Manhattan Project was so highly classified, Vice President Harry Truman had no idea it existed until Franklin Roosevelt died in office and Truman became president.[6] During the Cold War, the Soviet Union built three plutonium production reactors entirely underground, inside a mountain.[7] Nikita Khrushchev's secret operation to deploy nuclear missiles to Cuba in 1962 employed a deception operation so elaborate, planning documents were hand carried to a tight inner circle, ship crews were told to pack for a cold climate, and even ship captains carrying the missiles were not told their final destination until they were in the middle of the Atlantic Ocean.[8] Saddam Hussein hid some of his facilities in a large date palm grove and buried telltale power line connections underground to obscure them from overhead observation.[9]

Assessing the record is also difficult because intelligence failures are public and well-known, but successes are often silent or obscured by events. The U.S. Intelligence Community's Iraq WMD assessments in the early 2000s will forever be remembered as one of the greatest intelligence failures in history. At the same time, US intelligence agencies scored a major WMD success that has gone largely overlooked: Libya's relinquishing of its nuclear, chemical, and longer-range ballistic missile programs. "Intelligence was the key that opened the door to Libya's clandestine programs," noted CIA

---

5. Sherman Kent, "A Crucial Estimate Relived," *Studies in Intelligence* 9, no. 2 (Spring 1964), 1–18, https://www.cia.gov/static/f547ed3bcd5793ff5456dc381c2df789/A-Crucial-Estimate-Relived.pdf.

6. "Harry Truman," Atomic Heritage Foundation, https://www.atomicheritage.org/profile/harry-truman.

7. Frank V. Pabian, "Commercial Satellite Imagery as an Evolving Open-Source Verification Technology," *Joint Research Centre*, European Commission, 2015, 34. See also Oleg A. Bukharin, "The Cold War Atomic Intelligence Game, 1945–1970, from the Russian Perspective," *Studies in Intelligence* 48, no. 2 (2004), https://www.cia.gov/static/826e930085a20f893b891b25417c0a1f/Cold-War-Atomic-Intel.pdf.

8. James H. Hansen, "Learning from the Past: Soviet Deception in the Cuban Missile Crisis," *Studies in Intelligence* 46, no. 1 (2002), https://www.cia.gov/static/205b8c27be0286b9a0d19fbf90d2382a/Soviet-Deception-Cuban-Missile.pdf.

9. Hansen, "Learning from the Past," *Studies in Intelligence* 46, no. 1 (2002): 34–35.

director George Tenet in February 2004.[10] He was right. In the fall of 2003, the CIA discovered that Pakistani scientist A. Q. Khan was planning to illegally ship uranium centrifuge parts to Libya on a German merchant ship named the *BBC China* as part of a worldwide nuclear smuggling operation. US officials had the ship interdicted, and together with British intelligence, confronted Muammar Qaddafi with the evidence. US intelligence officials went on to play a major role in assessing whether Qaddafi's expressed desires to give up his WMD programs and rejoin the family of nations were sincere. By December 2003, they successfully engineered Qaddafi's abandonment of his nuclear ambitions and rollback of his missile program. Then in 2011, eight years after Qaddafi came clean, the United States and its NATO allies became embroiled in Libya's civil war. Qaddafi was killed, order within the country unraveled, and the Libyan nuclear intelligence success story faded in the face of subsequent policy failures.[11]

Intelligence successes and failures, moreover, are often hard to distinguish. The historical record is never complete, classification can distort what records are known, and vital information often comes to light only in the fullness of time. Was the Cuban missile crisis an intelligence success or failure? For years, most analysts considered it an unmitigated success. US U-2 surveillance planes discovered telltale signs of Soviet nuclear missile sites before they became operational, giving President John F. Kennedy time and leverage to demand their removal. Yet as time passes, we learn more about what was not known back in 1962, including the existence of operational tactical nuclear missiles on Cuba, the presence of more than 40,000 Soviet troops there, the predelegation of nuclear launch authority to Soviet submarine captains and the near-launch of a Soviet nuclear torpedo amid the crisis.[12] All of this newly discovered information suggests that had the US naval blockade failed and the United States invaded Cuba as planned, the risks of general nuclear war between the United States and Soviet Union would have been far higher than US intelligence officials and policymakers believed at the time.

10. George J. Tenet, "DCI Remarks on Iraq's WMD Programs," February 5, 2004, https://irp.fas.org/cia/product/dci020504.html.
11. William Tobey, "Cooperation in the Libya WMD Disarmament Case," *Studies in Intelligence* 61, no. 4 (December 2017), https://www.cia.gov/static/c134fac60c8d3634a28629e6082d19eb/Cooperation-in-Libya-WMD.pdf.
12. Jessica Sleight, "The Cuban Missile Crisis: Five Things You Didn't Know," *Ploughshares Fund*, October 15, 2012, https://www.ploughshares.org/issues-analysis/article/cuban-missile-crisis-five-things-you-didn%E2%80%99t-know; Anatoli I. Gribkov and William Y. Smith, *Operation ANADYR: U.S. and Soviet Generals Recount the Cuban Missile Crisis* (Chicago: Edition Q, 1993), 28; James G. Hershberg, "The Global Cuban Missile Crisis—Surfing the Third Wave of Missile Crisis Scholarship," *Cold War International History Project Bulletin: The Global Cuban Missile Crisis at 50*, issue 17–18 (Fall 2012), https://www.wilsoncenter.org/sites/default/files/CWIHP_Cuban_Missile_Crisis_Bulletin_17–18.pdf. Thomas S. Blanton, "The Cuban Missile Crisis: 40 Years Later," *Washington Post*, October 16, 2002, https://www.washingtonpost.com/wp-srv/liveonline/02/special/world/sp_world_blanton101602.htm.

Sometimes, even intelligence improvements can look like failures. In November 2007, a National Intelligence Estimate (NIE) reversed some previous judgments about Iran's nuclear activities. Earlier, the Intelligence Community believed Iran was "determined to develop nuclear weapons."[13] But newly collected intelligence suggested that Iran had halted its nuclear weapons design and weaponization activities back in 2003. The revised estimate drew fire from just about all sides. Some believed the Intelligence Community was "sabotaging" the administration as it sought a harder line, including international sanctions, against Iran.[14] President George W. Bush called the language "eye-popping."[15] Others questioned why the intelligence was not known earlier. Some wondered if the new judgments were compensation for the mistaken assessment of Iraq's WMD programs in 2002. Almost nobody considered the possibility that analytic views had changed in light of new and better information.[16] As former National Intelligence Council chairman Greg Treverton notes, "the primary findings of the 2007 NIE were neither retracted nor superseded, and were in fact reiterated by senior intelligence officials, including the director of national intelligence (DNI), many times through early 2012."[17]

All of this is to say that humility is in order. Estimating nuclear threats is exceptionally challenging and assessing the track record of intelligence agencies is far more complicated than it may seem.[18]

AN INTELLIGENCE AGENCY SCORECARD: WHAT ACADEMIC ANALYSES FIND

For years, studies of nuclear threat intelligence have looked at individual cases in isolation, examining what intelligence agencies got right or wrong about Country X or Event Y. The 1962 Cuban Missile Crisis is the granddaddy of them all, remaining the most studied event of the nuclear age. Academics have written so much about that eyeball-to-eyeball moment, there is

---

13. Gregory F. Treverton, "The 2007 National Intelligence Estimate on Iran's Nuclear Intentions and Capabilities," *Center for the Study of Intelligence*, Central Intelligence Agency, May 2013, appendix A, https://www.cia.gov/static/a6c09ab8eb00a08b8ba5ad1a5055f527/2007-Iran-Nuclear-Intentions.pdf, 19.
14. Greg Simmons, "Bush Administration Credibility Suffers after Iran NIE Report," Fox News, December 7, 2007, https://www.foxnews.com/story/bush-administration-credibility-suffers-after-iran-nie-report.
15. George W. Bush, *Decision Points* (New York: Crown Publishers, 2010), 418.
16. Mark Lowenthal, *From Secrets to Policy* (Los Angeles: CQ Press, 2010), 123.
17. Treverton, "The 2007 National Intelligence Estimate on Iran's Nuclear Intentions and Capabilities."
18. For a discussion of limitations of academic studies of nuclear proliferation, see Alexander H. Montgomery and Scott D. Sagan, "The Perils of Predicting Proliferation," *Journal of Conflict Resolution* 53, no. 2 (April 2009): 302–328.

even an article about why we should stop writing articles about it.[19] Over time, however, research has advanced scholarship significantly by moving beyond single cases to better assess the overall record of US nuclear threat analysis and to more carefully examine the underlying causes of error. In 2006, Jeffrey Richelson was the first to offer a broader historical overview of US intelligence assessments, examining thirteen nuclear cases ranging from Nazi Germany to North Korea.[20] Building on that work, Montgomery and Mount provide the best existing assessment of how well US intelligence agencies assessed nuclear threats over six decades, examining seventeen cases where countries are known to have pursued the development of a nuclear weapon—some of them successfully. Using declassified US intelligence estimates, other government documents, and secondary sources, they find that US intelligence agencies correctly identified the nature and timing of three cases (China in the 1950s–1960s, Pakistan in the 1970s–1980s, and Brazil's pursuit and abandonment of its nuclear ambitions in the 1970s–1980s).[21] US intelligence agencies underestimated nuclear programs in five cases (the Soviet Union, Israel, Taiwan, South Korea, and Iraq before the First Gulf War of 1990–91) and overestimated in nine (Germany, France, India, South Africa, Argentina, Libya, North Korea, Iran, and Iraq before Operation Iraqi Freedom in 2003). "The U.S. intelligence agencies' experience with foreign nuclear weapons programs have been poor," Montgomery and Mount conclude. "The overall patterns of estimation indicate that not only have estimations been generally off, but that they are biased toward overestimation."[22] Testing twelve hypotheses about the causes of estimation errors, they find the most consistent evidence for two: US policy toward a country can lead to collection and analysis blind spots, and intelligence officials tend to err by misestimating the intent, motives, or resolve of the target state.

Although an important step forward, the study defines accuracy in unrealistic and problematic ways. For example, Montgomery and Mount call a 1959 assessment of France's nuclear test an "overestimation" because it concluded a test would "be possible" by November 1959 when the test occurred just three months later.[23] Similarly, they claim an August US intelligence document "underestimated" China's atomic test which occurred on Octo-

---

19. Eliot A. Cohen, "Why We Should Stop Studying the Cuban Missile Crisis," *National Interest*, no. 2 (Winter 1985–86): 3–13.
20. Jeffrey Richelson, *Spying on the Bomb: American Nuclear Intelligence from Nazi Germany to Iran and North Korea* (New York: W.W. Norton, 2006).
21. Alexander H. Montgomery and Adam Mount, "Misestimation: Explaining U.S. Failures to Predict Nuclear Weapons Programs," *Intelligence and National Security* 29, no. 3 (2014), 357–386, Appendix, http://people.reed.edu/~ahm/Projects/ProlifIntel/ProlifIntelAppendix.pdf.
22. Montgomery and Mount, "Misestimation," 383.
23. Montgomery and Mount, "Misestimation," 371.

ber 16, 1964 even though the estimate said it believed the test would probably come after the end of 1964, or just ten weeks later than it actually occurred. The estimate also explicitly noted that "the possibility of . . . a detonation before the end of this year cannot be ruled out."[24] Such exacting standards of pinpoint accuracy are often unhelpful and occasionally misleading. Even when intelligence assessments are accurate, other factors can intervene that change the timing and nature of outcomes—factors that are unknown to even the leaders of the target country. Consequently, intelligence estimates can look wrong in hindsight even though they were correct at the time. In World War II, for example, General Dwight Eisenhower decided that the allies would land at Normandy on June 5, 1944. They did not because bad weather delayed the invasion for twenty-four hours. Had German intelligence analysts estimated that D-Day would be June 5, they would have been wrong, but not really.

Cullen Nutt looks across cases and finds that intelligence agencies are prone to overcorrection: underestimating one nuclear threat can lead to overestimating the next. The key mechanism at work is judgment. Nutt finds that intelligence officials and agencies adopt different standards for rendering judgments based on prior experiences. Underestimation failures of the past can lead intelligence analysts to become "urgent judges" who reach definitive conclusions about evidence more quickly and with less evidence. Conversely, prior overestimation failures can lead analysts to become "skeptical judges" who require higher standards of proof and more effort to discern nuclear dangers. Nutt finds that overestimating Iraq's nuclear weapons program in 2003 led US intelligence officials in 2007 to become skeptical judges of Syria's nuclear program. Israeli intelligence, by contrast, veered from underestimating Libya's nuclear program to adopting an "urgent judgment" approach to Syria, which led to the discovery of that Syria was secretly building a nuclear reactor.[25]

In short, academic research is moving toward a better and more systematic understanding of how well US intelligence agencies have estimated nuclear dangers over time, and why. The problem is that current work is better situated to understanding the past than the future. Although intelligence agencies are still critical players in the nuclear threat assessment landscape, they are no longer the only critical players. Technological advances are democratizing the collection and analysis of intelligence, with potential far-reaching implications for US intelligence and the future assessment of nuclear dangers.

---

24. Central Intelligence Agency, "The Chances of an Imminent Communist Chinese Nuclear Explosion," Special National Intelligence Estimate (SNIE)13-4-64, August 26, 1964, https://fas.org/irp/cia/product/frus_30_043.htm.
25. Cullen G. Nutt, "Proof of the Bomb: The Influence of Previous Failure on Intelligence Judgments of Nuclear Programs," *Security Studies* 28, no. 2 (2019): 321–359.

CHAPTER 4

The Democratization of Intelligence

Three trends have democratized the collection and analysis of nuclear threat intelligence to places and people outside of governments: Rising commercial satellite quantities and capabilities; the explosion of connectivity and other open-source information on the internet; and advances in automated analytics like machine learning. Together these and other tools have been called "public technical means."[26]

LOW-COST EYES IN THE SKY

Governments of major powers used to corner the nuclear-related intelligence collection and analysis market. In the early Cold War, the United States deployed U-2 photoreconnaissance airplanes over the Soviet Union to ascertain how many nuclear missiles and bombers the Soviets had and where they were deployed.[27] In 1960, America's CORONA satellite program ushered in the era of "remote sensing" from space. CORONA was essentially a large camera sent into orbit that photographed areas over the earth's surface and returned film in a parachuting capsule that had to be captured in midair over the Pacific Ocean to be developed. Though the first thirteen missions failed, CORONA's first success provided more coverage of the Soviet Union in a single mission than all previous U-2 flights combined.[28] Albert Wheelon, the CIA's first deputy director of science and technology, remarked that "it was as if an enormous floodlight had been turned on in a darkened warehouse."[29] Satellite imagery quickly became the cornerstone of nuclear arms control verification, compensating for the lack of reliable on-the-ground intelligence inside the Soviet Union.[30] The Soviets soon followed, developing a CORONA counterpart named Zenit-2, which returned its first usable photographs (after several failed attempts) in 1962. Like CORONA, the Soviet program provided leaders essential intelligence about US capabilities.[31]

---

26. Christopher Stubbs and Sidney Drell, "Public Domain Treaty Compliance Verification in the Digital Age," *IEEE Technology and Society Magazine* 32, no. 4 (Winter 2013): 57–64, https://ieeexplore.ieee.org/document/6679319.

27. Central Intelligence Agency, *CORONA: America's First Imaging Satellite Program*, CIA Museum, November 21, 2012, https://www.cia.gov/legacy/museum/exhibit/corona-americas-first-imaging-satellite-program/.

28. CIA, *CORONA*.

29. Philip Taubman, *Secret Empire: Eisenhower, the CIA, and the Hidden Story of America's Space Espionage* (New York: Simon & Schuster, 2003), 35.

30. Oleg Bukharin, "From the Russian Perspective: The Cold War Atomic Intelligence Game, 1945–70," *Center for the Study of Intelligence*, Central Intelligence Agency, July 27, 2008, https://www.cia.gov/static/826e930085a20f893b891b25417c0a1f/Cold-War-Atomic-Intel.pdf.

31. Peter A. Gorin, "ZENIT: Corona's Soviet Counterpart," in *CORONA Between the Sun and the Earth*, ed. Robert A. MacDonald (Bethesda, MD: American Society for Photogrammetry

Although imagery resolution improved and the first commercial satellite made imagery publicly available in 1972, the United States and Soviet Union continued to dominate the space market, each operating a small number of large spy satellites that were the size of a bus, cost billions apiece to design and launch, used highly advanced technology, and produced classified information.[32]

It was not until the early 2000s that technological advances and commercialization opportunities converged, giving rise to a dramatic increase in the capabilities, quality, and number of small satellites operated by private firms. The first CORONA satellite had a resolution of twelve meters, which meant that the image could not distinguish between two adjacent objects on the ground unless they were at least twelve meters (or thirty-nine feet) apart.[33] In the 1990s, the first commercial satellites offered sub-ten meter electro-optical imagery.[34] In 2000 one commercial satellite offered sub-two meter resolution.[35] By 2019, there were twenty-five commercial satellites offering sub-2 meter resolutions. Most of them (nineteen of the twenty-five) offered resolutions under one meter. Starting in 2014, commercial satellites offered imagery with thirty-one centimeter resolution (or about one foot).[36] As Pabian notes, thirty-one centimeter resolution constitutes a 900 percent improvement over what was available just fifteen years earlier. That level of resolution can enable an analyst to detect objects like manhole covers, utility lines, and building vents; identify details of equipment needed for the nuclear fuel cycle such as different types of cylinders in open storage, and details of electrical power, cooling, heating, and ventilation equipment. It could even enable differentiation between types of cars driving on the road.[37]

---

and Remote Sensing, 1997), 84–107; Peter A. Gorin, "Zenit: The Soviet Response to CORONA," in *Eye in the Sky: The Story of the CORONA Spy Satellites*, ed. Dwayne A. Day, John M. Logsdon, and Brian Latell (Washington, DC: Smithsonian Institution Press, 1998), 157–172.

32. Allison Puccioni, "Commercial Lift-Off," *IHS Jane's Intelligence Review*, December 2015, 53. China more recently has joined that elite group. See Amy B. Zegart and Michael Morell, "Spies, Lies, and Algorithms," *Foreign Affairs* 98, no. 3, (May/June 2019): 85–96.

33. Frank V. Pabian, "Commercial Satellite Imagery as an Evolving Open-Source Verification Technology," *Joint Research Centre*, European Commission, 2015, 6.

34. Pabian, "Commercial Satellite Imagery," 10.

35. Pabian, "Commercial Satellite Imagery," 11.

36. Satellites launch dates and resolution data from "Satellite Sensors," Satellite Imaging Corporation, https://www.satimagingcorp.com/satellite-sensors/; Pabian, "Commercial Satellite Imagery," 11.

37. Philip Bump, "Here's Why the Resolution of Satellite Images Never Seems to Improve," *Washington Post*, April 21, 2017, https://www.washingtonpost.com/news/politics/wp/2017/04/21/heres-why-the-resolution-of-satellite-images-never-seems-to-improve/; Pabian, "Commercial Satellite Imagery," 11. It is important to note that commercial satellite imagery resolution is both a matter of technology and law. Satellites operated by the U.S. Intelligence Community produce even sharper resolutions, but the precise specifications are classified. Commercial satellite operators must be cleared to sell photographs at certain resolutions.

Other improvements in satellite capabilities include video, which can facilitate observation of dynamic activities like vehicle movement, construction, and nuclear facility cooling plumes; and Synthetic Aperture Radar (SAR), which enables imaging even in cloudy weather, through dense vegetation, and at night.[38] SAR can also detect otherwise imperceptible micro changes of the earth's surface over time, enabling better detection of hidden nuclear activities such as underground tunnel construction.[39] Although most nongovernmental nuclear threat organizations rely on basic, inexpensive electro-optical imagery which can only capture imagery in clear weather, some are starting to use SAR and other more advanced capabilities.[40,41]

Satellites are not just getting better. They are getting more plentiful. According to then-director of National Intelligence Daniel Coats, the number of satellite launches more than doubled between 2016 and 2018 (see figure 4.1). In 2018 alone, 322 small satellites about the size of a shoebox were hurled into space.[42] The Paris-based firm Euroconsult estimates that more than 8,000 small satellites will be launched between 2019 and 2028.[43] Although most of these small satellites are used for weather and communications, the number of imagery satellites is growing, too.[44]

For nuclear-related intelligence, increasing satellite quantity has a quality all its own. The more commercial satellites there are, the shorter the time lag between images of a single location on earth. And that allows more finely tuned before/after comparisons of suspect facilities or geographic areas, potentially capturing on-the-ground activity that would not otherwise be observable.[45] Some companies are already moving into the "high revisit rate" market, offering constellations of satellites that offer lower quality resolutions but higher frequency imaging. San Francisco startup Planet, founded by former NASA employees in 2010, has more than 150 satellites in orbit and offers imaging of any target up to two times a day, at three meters and seventy-two-centimeter

---

38. Pabian, "Commercial Satellite Imagery," 16; Allison Puccioni, "Penetrating Vision," *IHS Jane's Intelligence Review*, May 2016; Wisconsin Project on Nuclear Arms Control, "More Eyes on More Data: Prospects for Restricting Iran's Missile Program Using Open Sources," February 13, 2019.
39. Puccioni, "Penetrating Vision," 57.
40. Electro-optimal imagery is inherently limited because 50 percent of the earth's surface is cloud-covered at any given time. Puccioni, "Penetrating Vision," 54.
41. United States Geospatial Intelligence Foundation, *2019 State and Future of GEOINT Report*, 2019, https://usgif.org/system/uploads/6904/original/2020-SaFoG.pdf, 8.
42. Maxime Puteaux and Alexandre Najar, "Are Smallsats Entering the Maturity Stage?" *Space News*, August 6, 2019, https://spacenews.com/analysis-are-smallsats-entering-the-maturity-stage/.
43. Puteaux and Najar, "Smallsats."
44. See Puccioni and Ashdown, "Raising Standards," 8.
45. Pabian, "Commercial Satellite Imagery," 14.

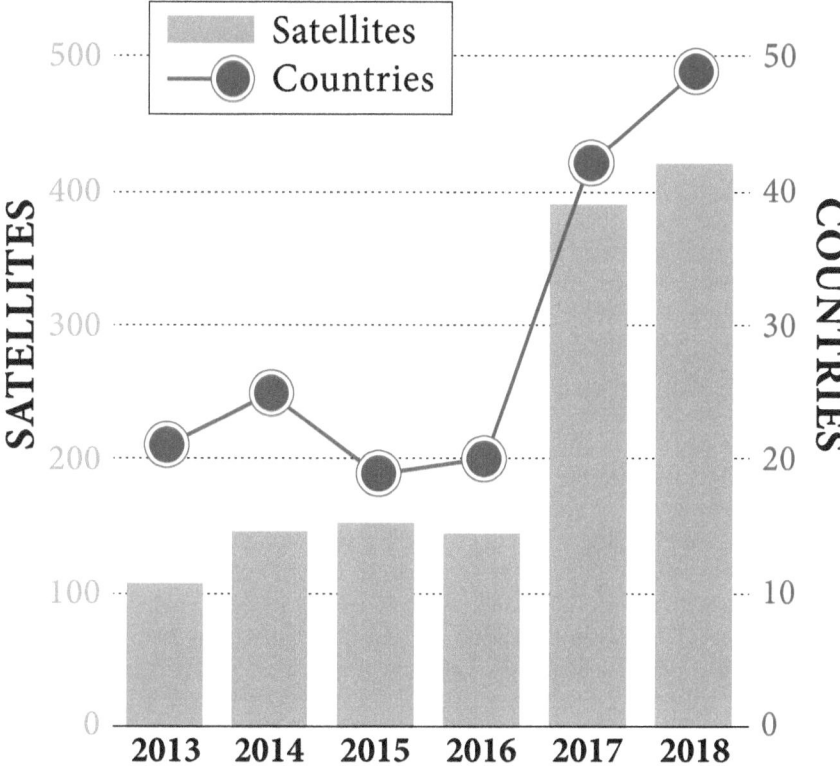

Figure 4.1. Countries that own the satellites and the number of satellites launched, 2013–2018.
Source: Daniel R. Coats, "Statement for the Record: Worldwide Assessment of the US Intelligence Community," US Senate Select Committee on Intelligence, January 29, 2019, 17.

resolution.[46] Seattle-based startup BlackSky has four imagery satellites in orbit and plans to eventually build a sixty-satellite constellation capable of revisiting the same city every ten to fifteen minutes with sub-1 meter resolution.[47]

Perhaps the most revolutionary change in satellite imagery is that just about anyone can use it. The costs of acquiring satellite images have plummeted, from nearly $4,000 per frame to as little as $10.[48] Some high-resolution imagery is free; anyone with an internet connection can access Google Earth, which has satellite and airplane overhead imagery with resolutions ranging from fifteen meters to

---

46. Found at planet.com, a company that provides commercial satellite imagery. See "Monitoring," Plant Labs, https://www.planet.com/products/monitoring/.
47. Caleb Henry, "BlackSky Launching Two Satellites on June Starlink Mission," *Space News*, June 5, 2020 https://spacenews.com/blacksky-launching-two-satellites-on-june-starlink-mission/; "Products and Services," BlackSky, https://www.blacksky.com/.
48. Pabian, "Commercial Satellite Imagery."

CHAPTER 4

30 centimeters. Google Earth also offers applications to conduct analysis, including 3D building modeling of facilities in its Earth maps and historical satellite image comparisons dating back thirty-five years. In short, commercial satellites now offer low-cost eyes in the sky for anyone who wants them.

CONNECTIVITY: MORE INFORMATION, MORE AVAILABLE, TO MORE PEOPLE

The second major trend democratizing nuclear threat intelligence is the internet, which has powered an explosion in open-source information and the connectivity to make it widely available and sharable. In 2000, approximately 15 percent of the world's population was connected to the internet.[49] By 2022, more than half the world was online, and more people were estimated to have mobile phones than access to running water.[50] As Amy Zegart and Michael Morell note in *Foreign Affairs*, connectivity turns everyday citizens into intelligence collectors whether they know it or not. "Cell phones can videotape events and even record seismic activities, such as underground nuclear tests, in real time. Surveillance cameras capture much of what takes place in cities around the world. Social media, search engines, and online retail platforms expose a great deal of information about users," they write.[51] In addition, metadata—such as the time, location, and equipment used to take a photograph posted online—downloadable 3D modeling applications, and community data sharing sites like Open Street Map, which allows users to post their GPS coordinates from their phones, all offer new clues and tools for nuclear sleuths.

The online information ecosystem makes possible exciting new opportunities for societal verification or open crowdsourcing to assess nuclear threat information. But it is also making misinformation and disinformation easier to manufacture and spread. In the new online ecosystem, information anywhere can go viral, regardless of its quality or credibility.

AUTOMATED ANALYTICS: MACHINE LEARNING, COMPUTER MODELING, AND MORE

Large increases in compute power and training data have spawned the creation of publicly available machine learning techniques that can analyze massive quantities of data at machine speed. Once algorithms are trained on a dataset to look for certain patterns, they can process thousands of images faster than humans by orders of magnitude. For nuclear threat intelligence, machine learning techniques offer particular promise to analyze

---

49. Niall McCarthy, "Giant Chart: Global Internet Usage by the Numbers," *Forbes*, August 27, 2014, https://www.forbes.com/sites/niallmccarthy/2014/08/27/giant-chart-global-internet-usage-by-the-numbers/#1cb1938a7f7b.
50. Zegart and Morell, "Spies, Lies, and Algorithms."
51. Zegart and Morell, "Spies, Lies, and Algorithms," 90.

satellite imagery of known missile sites or facilities to detect changes over time.[52] In 2017, for example, US intelligence officials from the National Geospatial-Intelligence Agency asked researchers at the University of Missouri to develop machine learning tools to see how fast and accurately they could identify surface-to-air missile sites over a vast area in Southwest China. The research team developed a deep learning neural network (essentially, a collection of algorithms working together) and used only commercially available satellite imagery with one-meter resolution. The computer and the human team correctly identified 90 percent of the missile sites. But the computer completed the job eighty times faster than humans, taking just forty-two minutes to scan an area of approximately 90,000 square kilometers (about three-quarters the size of North Korea).[53] Machine learning also holds promise for faster sifting of large quantities of written information—everything from trade documents that might suggest illicit financing schemes to the metadata of photos online—such as the date and time stamp on the picture, the type of camera used, the software that processed the image, and where the camera was placed when the picture was taken.[54]

In addition, computer modeling enables analysts to better understand the specifications and functions of structures already built. Online crowdsourcing is offering promising new avenues, too. Already, thousands of citizen scientists have successfully sifted through massive quantities of data to help a Cal Tech and UC Santa Cruz team identify several new exoplanets and an international team of physicists identify new gravitational lenses.[55] In 2016, Melissa Hanham at the Center for Nonproliferation Studies began a crowdsourcing initiative for nuclear proliferation-related imagery called Geo4Nonpro, which drew several hundred imagery experts together. Among its achievements was discovering the geolocation of North Korea's clandestine Kangson uranium enrichment facility.[56]

---

52. Wisconsin Project on Nuclear Arms Control, "More Eyes on More Data."

53. Sandra Erwin, "With Commercial Satellite Imagery, Computer Learns to Quickly Find Missile Sites in China," *Space News*, October 19, 2017. North Korea is 120,000 square kilometers. Fixed sites can be found by machines. Mobile launchers are much harder and still require human skills.

54. Jeffrey Lewis, "Applying New Tools to Nonproliferation: A Nuclear Detective Story," *Nuclear Threat Initiative*, May 2, 2016, chap. 4.

55. Enaie Azambuja, "Exoplanet Explorers Discover Five-Planet System," Electronic Specifier, January 12, 2018, https://www.electronicspecifier.com/industries/aerospace-defence/exoplanet-explorers-discover-five-planet-system; Phillip J. Marshal et al., "SPACE WARPS—I. Crowdsourcing the Discovery of Gravitational Lenses," *Monthly Notices of the Royal Astronomical Society* 255, no. 2 (January 11, 2016): 1171–1190, https://doi.org/10.1093/mnras/stv2009; Adam Hadhazy, "Crowdsourcing the Universe: How Citizen Scientists Are Driving Discovery (Kavli Roundtable)," Space.com, January 15, 2016, https://www.space.com/31626-crowdsourced-astronomy-finding-faint-galaxies-in-deep-space.html.

56. Melissa Hanham et al., "Geo4Nonpro 2.0," CNS Occasional Paper #38, October 2018, Middlebury Institute of International Studies at Monterey, 19–20.

CHAPTER 4

The New Nuclear Sleuths: Who Is Who and What Is Different

Advances in satellites, connectivity, and automated analytics have given rise to a cottage industry of nongovernmental nuclear intelligence collectors and analysts. These actors can be classified into six major categories: academic researchers and former government officials, commercial analysis providers for profit, nongovernmental organizations (NGOs), journalists, advocacy groups, and hobbyists (see table 4.1).[57]

No publicly available study yet compares the utility of nongovernmental nuclear threat intelligence to classified analysis. However, evidence suggests that nongovernmental open source nuclear intelligence has distinctive attributes, benefits, and risks compared to classified intelligence.[58]

ATTRIBUTES

Nongovernmental nuclear intelligence collectors and analysts comprise an ecosystem that differs from the classified world along important organizational and technical dimensions (see table 4.2).

In the nongovernmental ecosystem, participants' motives run the gamut: informing the global public, securing nonprofit grants, selling analysis for profit, advancing a political objective, and having fun, to name a few. Membership is wide open to anyone with an internet connection. Although many participants are experts from the United States and allied countries who take their responsibilities seriously, they are not alone. Analysts include amateurs and experts from various fields with varying incentives. Some are former government officials, intelligence analysts and nuclear inspectors. Others have limited prior background or training, and there are no formal open-source training programs or quality control processes in place.[59] Quality control mechanisms like peer review exist, but they are informal and voluntary.[60]

Members of this ecosystem can move quickly, publishing what they want, whenever they want, without bureaucratic approvals or required vetting. "The process for evaluation within the US government or international military-intelligence communities is vastly more standardized than it is in

---

57. I do not include international organizations such as UN's International Atomic Energy Agency or the Comprehensive Test Ban Treaty Organization.

58. Allison Puccioni and Melissa Hanham, "OSINT Transparency Raises Ethical Questions," *Jane's Intelligence Review*, February 12, 2018, 5.

59. Puccioni and Ashdown, "Raising Standards"; Ben Loehrke et al., "The Gray Spectrum: Ethical Decision Making with Geospatial and Open Source Analysis," workshop sponsored by the Stanley Center for Peace and Security and the Open Nuclear Network, Readout & Recommendations, July 2019.

60. Puccioni and Ashdown, "Raising Standards."

Table 4.1 Major Nongovernmental Nuclear Intelligence Collectors and Analysts

Organization	Type	Website
Center for International Security and Cooperation (CISAC), Stanford University	Academic	https://cisac.fsi.stanford.edu/research/organization/6069/6716
James Martin Center for Nonproliferation Studies, Middlebury Institute of International Studies at Monterey	Academic	https://www.middlebury.edu/institute/academics/centers-initiatives/nonproliferation-studies
Project Alpha, King's College London	Academic	https://www.kcl.ac.uk/alpha/research
Armillary Services	Commercial Analysis	armillaryservices.com
All Source Analysis (Maxar)	Commercial Analysis	https://allsourceanalysis.com/channels/security/
The Diplomat (Ankit Panda)	Commercial Analysis, Journalism	https://thediplomat.com/
Jane's	Commercial Analysis, Journalism	https://www.janes.com/
Bellingcat	Journalism	https://www.bellingcat.com/
Gwynne Roberts	Journalism (and filmmaker)	https://www.imdb.com/name/nm1142546/
38 North (focuses on North Korea)	NGO	https://www.38north.org
Atlantic Council Digital Forensic Lab	NGO	https://www.atlanticcouncil.org/programs/digital-forensic-research-lab/
Center for Strategic and International Studies (CSIS): Beyond Parallel (focuses on North Korea); Asia Maritime Transparency Initiative	NGO	https://beyondparallel.csis.org; https://amti.csis.org/
Institute for Science and International Security (ISIS)	NGO	http://isis-online.org

(continued)

Table 4.1 Major Nongovernmental Nuclear Intelligence Collectors and Analysts (continued)

Organization	Type	Website
The Verification Research, Training, and Information Centre	NGO	https://css.ethz.ch/en/services/css-partners/partner.html/13368
Wisconsin Project on Nuclear Arms Control	NGO	https://www.wisconsinproject.org/about-us/
Access DPRK (Jacob Bogle is a coin dealer who is mapping North Korea using satellite imagery and claims to have discovered new military installations)	Hobbyist	http://www.jacobbogle.com/accessdprk.html http://mynorthkorea.blogspot.com
National Council for the Resistance of Iran (Iranian Opposition Parliament in Exile)	Advocacy group	https://www.maryam-rajavi.com/en/national-council-resistance-iran

Table 4.2 Attributes of Nongovernmental versus Government Ecosystems in Nuclear Threat Analysis

	Nongovernmental	US Government
Organizational objectives	Diverse: e.g., securing funding, informing public, pursuing hobby interests	Focused: informing US government to provide decision advantage
Membership	Open: anyone can join from anywhere	Closed: strict hiring rules and security clearances
Analyst backgrounds	Broader	Narrower
Analyst formal training	None	Extensive
Product quality control	Peer review is voluntary and informal	Peer review is mandatory and formal
Quantity of technical collection assets	Large	Small*
Capability of technical collection assets	Limited but improving	Highly sophisticated
Ecosystem speed	Faster	Slower

*Collection platforms owned and operated by the US government are few in number, but government agencies are increasingly purchasing commercial data as well.

the open source world," said Allison Puccioni, a former government imagery analyst who now works in the nongovernmental ecosystem.[61] "For the most part, very few articles are refuted in the open source community ever."[62] On the technical side, nongovernmental actors have access to commercial sensors that are far more numerous but lower quality than government platforms.[63]

The classified ecosystem looks different. Motives in the open-source nuclear intelligence world vary, but government employees share one mission objective: giving US policymakers decision advantage. Participation requires security clearances and adherence to strict government hiring and information policies. Analysts come with a narrower set of backgrounds but a higher average skill level. Because government analysts operate in bureaucracies, they receive formal, extensive training in tradecraft and must adhere to standardized quality control processes like peer review—though as the Iraq WMD intelligence failure shows, peer review does not guarantee

61. Author interview, July 2, 2020.
62. Author interview, July 2, 2020.
63. Author interviews and emails with several open-source nuclear analysts, June–July 2020; Zegart and Morell, "Spies, Lies, and Algorithms," 91.

quality.[64] Government analysts have access to the most sophisticated spy satellites and other collection platforms as well as commercial imagery.[65] This classified environment is designed to induce caution and confidence in analysis, but it moves at a slower pace.[66]

In sum, one ecosystem is more open, diffuse, diverse, and fast-moving. The other is more closed, tailored, trained, and slow-moving.

BENEFITS OF NONGOVERNMENTAL NUCLEAR SLEUTHS

The nongovernmental intelligence ecosystem offers several significant benefits. Diverse backgrounds can improve analysis by bringing different perspectives on problems and evidence. Some of the best organizations in this space—like Jeffery Lewis's team at the Center for Nonproliferation Studies, former Los Alamos National Laboratory director Siegfried Hecker and his team at Stanford's Center for International Security and Cooperation, and David Albright at the Institute for Science and International Security—bring together imagery analysts, country specialists, and experts in the nuclear fuel cycle.

These groups also provide more knowledgeable hands on deck, help intelligence officials and policymakers identify false positives and fake claims, verify treaty compliance, monitor ongoing nuclear-related activities, and surface clandestine developments that might not otherwise be discovered. As Vipin Narang notes, "Knowing the launch location for a test or one that failed used to be the monopoly of intelligence agencies."[67] That is no longer true.

Nongovernmental intelligence collectors and analysts have played a major role in correcting mistakes and debunking misinformation. In 2013, a *Wired Magazine* post by someone claiming to be an ex-CIA analyst sparked a furor

---

64. Puccioni and Ashdown, "Raising Standards," 7. For an analysis of Iraq WMD analytic failures, see the Commission on the Intelligence Capabilities of the United States regarding Weapons of Mass Destruction (Silberman-Robb Commission), Report to the President, March 31, 2005.

65. In 2019, US intelligence agencies spent $300 million on commercial imagery and experts expect spending to increase in the next several years. Sandra Erwin, "Analysts: NRO's Commercial Imagery Purchases Could Reach $400 Million by 2023," *Space News*, June 29, 2020, https://spacenews.com/analysts-nros-commercial-imagery-purchases-could-reach-400-million-by-2023/; Sarah Erwin, "Satellite Imagery Startups to Challenge Maxar for Big Government Contracts," *Space News*, June 6, 2019, https://spacenews.com/satellite-imagery-startups-to-challenge-maxar-for-big-government-contracts/.

66. US laws currently restrict the resolutions of American commercial satellites, the locations they can capture with remote sensing, and the foreign nationals allowed to purchase their products. Puccioni and Ashdown, "Raising Standards," 8; Allison Puccioni, "Steady Gaze," *Janes Intelligence Review*, December 2017, 56-57. For a dataset building on this chapter, see Katharine Leede, "Spies in the Public Eye: A Comparative Community Analysis of Nuclear Sleuths and Government Intelligence Agencies" (undergraduate thesis, Stanford University, June 2022).

67. Zachary Dorfman, "True Detectives," *Middlebury Magazine*, May 3, 2018, https://middleburymagazine.com/features/true-detectives/.

that China may have a "mystery complex." To stop the nonstory from going viral, the geospatial blogger Stefan Greens posted evidence online that the complex was nothing more than an industrial park. Similar efforts revealed that a suspected gas centrifuge facility in Syria was a cotton textile plant, a cylindrical foundation in Iran that could have indicated the beginnings of a nuclear reactor was the foundation of a hotel being built near a shopping mall, and an Israeli television report showing a satellite image of an Iranian missile launch pad big enough to send a nuclear weapon to the United States was just a massive elevator that resembled a rocket in a blurry image.[68]

Commercial imagery is an important asset, but it is not the only one. Many of these analyses use a variety of data types and tools. On February 24, 2015, for example, an Iranian opposition group called the National Council for the Resistance of Iran (NCRI) tried to derail international negotiations finalizing a nuclear freeze in Iran. NCRI claimed that a company called Matiran was secretly housing a nuclear facility in the basement of its Tehran office. NCRI's evidence of this clandestine nuclear site included satellite imagery of the facility as well as photographs of its hallways and a large lead-lined door to prevent radiation leakage. Within a week, Lewis's team showed conclusively that all of the evidence was fabricated. Lewis's team found that Matiran was a real company all right; it even had employees on LinkedIn. But Matiran had nothing to do with nuclear enrichment. It specialized in making secure documents like national identification cards. Analyzing commercial satellite imagery, Lewis's team found no unusual construction activity at the site during the alleged construction timeframe or obvious signatures of nuclear enrichment activities found at other known Iranian sites, such as ventilation systems or an electrical substation to power nuclear centrifuges. Using 3D modeling, they showed how the photos and description of the claimed facility looked too small to fit the machines and infrastructure required. They noted that none of Iran's known enrichment facilities used lead doors because they did not need them; radiation leakage had never been a concern. Lewis's team also found that the lead door photograph had been copied from a promotional photograph used on a commercial Iranian website. Metadata from the photograph suggested the actual door was from a different company's warehouse elsewhere in Iran that had nothing to do with any illicit nuclear activities. Finally, the team used crowdsourcing and social media to find someone whose self-posted GPS coordinates from his cell phone showed he had been to the Matiran facility. They contacted the visitor via email and verified through social media that he really worked in the secure documents business and was who

---

68. Pabian, "Commercial Satellite Imagery," 31–32; Lewis, "Applying New Tools to Nonproliferation" chap. 3, https://www.nti.org/analysis/reports/applying-new-tools-nonproliferation-nuclear-detective-story/.

he claimed to be. They found information about his marital status, his volunteer activities and hobbies, and even obtained his photograph. The source confirmed that Matiran really did make secure documents, and that many foreign contractors routinely visited its location, making it highly unlikely that Matiran would put a secret nuclear enrichment facility in the basement.[69]

Nongovernmental nuclear sleuths have also uncovered important new information about clandestine nuclear activities that have aided intelligence agencies and influenced policy.[70] In 2002, NCRI, the same Iranian opposition group that was behind the false report of a secret Iranian enrichment facility, publicly disclosed two actual ones—at Natanz and Arak. The researchers David Albright and Corey Hinderstein at the Institute for Science and International Security then followed this lead, unearthing archival satellite imagery from Digital Globe of the Natanz site, and using other sources to conclude that the Natanz facility was a highly sophisticated, secret facility that was producing enriched uranium that could be used for either nuclear power reactors or nuclear weapons. Albright and Hinderstein's analysis provided important new technical details about the function, size, and capacity of the underground facility—including that it was a gas centrifuge facility, that it was designed to hold tens of thousands of centrifuges, and that it was built in ways designed to conceal its discovery.[71]

In 2012, Siegfried Hecker and Frank Pabian determined the locations and supporting tunnels of North Korea's first two nuclear tests using commercial imagery and publicly available seismological information—assessments

---

69. Jeffrey Lewis, "That Secret Iranian 'Nuclear Faculty' You Just Found? Not o Much," *Foreign Policy*, March 3, 2015, https://foreignpolicy.com/2015/03/03/that-secret-iranian-nuclear-facility-you-just-found-not-so-much/; Lewis, "Applying New Tools to Nonproliferation." Lewis's team has published several significant studies. One was instrumental in proving that North Korea's 2016 submarine-launched ballistic missile test had failed, and that Kim Jong-Un's claims of success were based on a doctored video, James Pearson, "North Korea Faked Missile Test Footage: U.S. Experts," Reuters, July 11, 2016, https://www.reuters.com/article/us-northkorea-missile-analysis-idUSKCN0UQ0CC20160112; Anna Fifield, "With Technology, These Researchers Are Figuring Out North Korea's Nuclear Secrets," *Washington Post*, November 21, 2017, https://www.washingtonpost.com/world/asia_pacific/with-technology-these-researchers-are-figuring-out-north-koreas-nuclear-secrets/2017/11/20/274d9786-c9e2-11e7-b244-2d22ac912500_story.html. See also Ellen Nakashima and Joby Warrick. "U.S. Spy Agencies: North Korea Is Working on New Missiles," *Washington Post*, July 30, 2018, https://www.washingtonpost.com/world/national-security/us-spy-agencies-north-korea-is-working-on-new-missiles/2018/07/30/b3542696-940d-11e8-a679-b09212fb69c2_story.html.

70. Pabian, "Commercial Satellite Imagery," 38.

71. David Albright and Corey Hinderstein, "The Iranian Gas Centrifuge Uranium Enrichment Plant at Natanz: Drawing from Commercial Satellite Images," working paper, *Institute for Science and International Security*, March 14, 2003; Jeffrey Lewis, "NCRI still Didn't Discover Natanz," *Arms Control Wonk*, December 12, 2007, https://www.armscontrolwonk.com/archive/201737/ncri-still-didnt-discover-natanz/; Frank V. Pabian, "Commercial Satellite Imagery: Another Tool in the Nonproliferation Verification Toolkit," in *Nuclear Safeguards, Security, and Nonproliferation*, ed. James E. Doyle (Oxford: Elsevier, 2008), 234–238.

that proved highly accurate when North Korea revealed the test locations six years later.[72] Hecker and colleagues also utilized commercial satellite imagery and Google Sketchup, a 3D modeling program, to track the construction of a new nuclear reactor at North Korea's Yongbyon complex in 2012 and model the uranium centrifuge facility they were shown. No foreigners are known to have been allowed into the Yongbyon facilities after Hecker and Stanford colleagues visited in November 2010. But by tracking the facility using overhead photography combined with what they learned during their visit, they concluded that the reactor was still a long way from operations and that North Korea must also have an undisclosed pilot centrifuge plant.[73]

Finally, these nongovernmental actors offer more than just the benefits of information. They offer information that can be shared. Because they operate in the unclassified world, their findings can be publicized, alerting the general public and generating policy attention to an issue. Indeed, many of them already have extensive relationship networks with senior US officials, international inspectors, and journalists. Just as important, their information can also be more easily shared across the US government, as well as with allies, international organizations, and even adversaries—without jeopardizing classified intelligence sources and methods.[74] Particularly because nuclear threats are so dangerous, intelligence about them is often highly classified. And the more classified something becomes, the less analysis it gets, because so few people have access; going black runs the risk of going dark. Indeed, evidence suggests that US intelligence officials are well aware of these challenges, and the benefits of sharing nongovernmental unclassified intelligence. While current information sharing is informal and discretionary, in 2018, the Center for Strategic and International Studies and the National Geospatial-Intelligence Agency took a step toward more formalized arrangements, announcing a partnership to "produce unclassified reporting on issues of importance in North Korea."[75]

---

72. Frank V. Pabian and Siegfried S. Hecker, "Contemplating a Third Nuclear Test in North Korea," *Bulletin*, August 6, 2012, https://thebulletin.org/2012/08/contemplating-a-third-nuclear-test-in-north-korea/. Frank V. Pabian, Joseph S. Bermudez Jr., and Jack Liu, "The Punggye-ri Nuclear Test Site Destroyed: A Good Start but New Questions Raised about Irreversibility," *38 North*, May 31, 2018, https://www.38north.org/2018/05/punggye053118/.

73. Niko Minopoulos, Siegfried S. Hecker, and Robert Carlin, "North Korea from 30,000 Feet," *Bulletin of the Atomic Scientists*, January 6, 2012, https://thebulletin.org/2012/01/north-korea-from-30000-feet/.

74. United States Geospatial Intelligence Foundation, *2019 State and Future of GEOINT Report*, 9. Good unclassified technical intelligence allows policymakers to bring evidence to international debates more quickly because they don't need to request declassification. Cortney Weinbaum, John V. Parachini, Richard S. Girven, Michael H. Decker, and Richard C. Baffa, "Perspectives and Opportunities in Intelligence for U.S. Leaders," RAND Corporation, 2018, https://www.rand.org/pubs/perspectives/PE287.html.

75. Center for Strategic & International Studies, "CSIS Korea Chair Announces Research Partnership with National Geospatial-Intelligence Agency (NGA)," CSIS, May 22, 2018,

CHAPTER 4

KEY RISKS: WHEN INFORMATION IS WRONG,
WHEN INFORMATION IS RIGHT

This nongovernmental ecosystem also offers substantial risks. Some arise when information is wrong. Others arise when information is right.

First and most obviously, this ecosystem could inject and amplify errors in the policymaking world. Although the examples above highlight the best nongovernmental nuclear intelligence, the landscape is vast and filled with questionable data, shoddy analyses, pet theories, and political agendas. Skill levels vary considerably. Many amateur imagery analysts are well intentioned but poorly trained. As Pabian writes, there's a common misperception that "anyone can look at pictures."[76] In truth, imagery analysis requires considerable skill and training to know how shapes, shadows, sizes, scales, textures, perspectives, and contexts can obscure or delineate different objects seen from space, viewed from directly overhead, which is generally an unfamiliar vantage point.[77] Furthermore, different imagery technologies require different, specialized training and experience. Interpreting electro-optical imagery is not the same as interpreting images taken by Synthetic Aperture Radar satellites.[78]

Nuclear imagery analysis also requires expertise about the technical requirements of the nuclear fuel cycle so that the analyst knows what to look for. For example, gas centrifuge facilities like the one at Yongbyon in North Korea require large open halls for machinery like autoclaves and centrifuges. Underground gas centrifuge facilities like both Natanz and Fordow in Iran require additional heating, ventilation, and air conditioning systems to support subsurface operations of both equipment and personnel.[79] Without significant training, misinterpretation is easy. David Sandalow, who served in senior positions at the Department of Energy, Department of State, and the White House noted, "Without strong experience and training, it can be relatively easy to see proof of sinister intent in a benign image, or to miss details that would be conclusive to a knowledgeable photo interpreter."[80]

---

https://www.csis.org/news/csis-korea-chair-announces-research-partnership-national-geospatial-intelligence-agency-nga.
76. Pabian, "Commercial Satellite Imagery," 25.
77. Pabian, "Commercial Satellite Imagery," 27.
78. Puccioni, "Penetrating Vision," 56.
79. David Albright, Frank V. Pabian, and Andrea Stricker, "The Fordow Enrichment Plant, aka Al Ghadir: Iran's Nuclear Archive Reveals Site Originally Purposed to Produce Weapon-Grade Uranium for 1–2 Nuclear Weapons per Year," Institute for Science and International Security, March 13, 2009, http://isis-online.org/isis-reports/detail/the-fordow-enrichment-plant-aka-al-ghadir/.
80. David B. Sandalow, "Remote Sensing and Foreign Policy," paper presented at the Symposium on Viewing the Earth: The Role of Satellite Earth Observations and Global Monitoring in International Affairs, June 6, 2000, at George Washington University, Washington, DC,

The cost of mistakes can be high. "Satellite images have the potential, if interpreted incorrectly, to increase tensions among nations and create confusion during periods of crisis, rather than to promote stability," argues Sandalow. "This is not just a theoretical problem: in one incident, an image that a magazine claimed was the site of India's 1998 nuclear test turned out to be a livestock pen."[81] In short, while commercial satellites are making pixels a commodity, analysis is not. The real value of satellite imagery comes not from the photograph, but from the analysis of what it means.[82]

In June 2018, several nuclear proliferation experts warned in an Iran roundtable that "open source analysis by NGOs may introduce inaccurate information that can be disseminated rapidly in a political environment in which suspicion, disinformation, and unfounded accusations flourish."[83] The injection of inaccurate information that became disseminated rapidly had already happened. In 2011, Phillip Karber, a former Pentagon strategist, led a group of Georgetown students in his class to study China's vast underground tunnel system known as the "underground great wall." Although the tunnel's existence was well known—it had even been reported on China's state-run television—debate swirled about its purpose. Karber's students used commercial imagery, blogs, military journals, and even a fictional Chinese television drama about the military. They concluded that the tunnels were probably being used to hide nuclear weapons—3,000 of them, an estimate far higher than any official US government or international assessment. The Georgetown study produced headlines and heartburn. The *Washington Post* reported that the study had "sparked a congressional hearing and been circulated among top officials in the Pentagon, including the Air Force vice chief of staff."[84] As one Department of Defense official commented, "It's not quite a bombshell, but those thoughts and estimates are being checked against what people think they know based on classified information."[85]

Experts immediately highlighted several serious analytic errors. Hui Zhang, a physicist and senior research associate at Harvard's Managing the Atom Project, wrote that Karber's students based their 3,000 weapon number on a US intelligence projection from the 1960s, assumed it was accurate, and then kept adding weapons assuming a constant rate of growth—even

---

quoted in Pabian "Commercial Satellite Imagery," 29, and Laurie J. Schmidt, "New Tools for Diplomacy," NASA, 2019, https://earthdata.nasa.gov/learn/sensing-our-planet/new-tools-for-diplomacy.

81. Sandalow "Remote Sensing."
82. Pabian, "Commercial Satellite Imagery," 25.
83. Wisconsin Project on Nuclear Arms Control, "More Eyes on More Data."
84. William Wan, "Georgetown Students Shed Light on China's Tunnel System for Nuclear Weapons," *Washington Post*, November 29, 2011, https://www.washingtonpost.com/world/national-security/georgetown-students-shed-light-on-chinas-tunnel-system-for-nuclear-weapons/2011/11/16/gIQA6AmKAO_story.html.
85. Wan, "Georgetown."

though several subsequent, declassified US intelligence estimates, as well as international NGO estimates, consistently forecast that China likely had around 200 warheads, not 3,000. Lewis notes that based on the amount of plutonium China was known to use in its weapons testing, the country did not have sufficient fissile material to produce anywhere near that many weapons. And it turns out Karber's plutonium estimates relied on Chinese blog posts discussing a single anonymous 1995 Usenet post that was then plagiarized by a Singapore college student. The use of this suspect source was "so wildly incompetent as to invite laughter," wrote Lewis.[86] So why did China build the tunnels? According to Hui Zhang, a more likely explanation is that the tunnels were designed to protect China's vulnerable land-based missiles from a crippling first strike. Because China had a stated doctrine of no first use of nuclear weapons, survivable forces were essential for deterrence. And since China lacked reliable sea-based and air-based nuclear forces, the logical solution to ensure China retained a survivable second-strike force was to move its missiles deeper underground, where they could be better protected.[87] "Their research has value, but it also shows the danger of the Internet," said Hans. M. Kristensen of the Federation of American Scientists.[88] Lewis was more critical, writing, "Karber's claims are utter nonsense, and [he] is unbelievably successful at generating unwarranted publicity."[89]

Second, the nongovernmental ecosystem increases the risks of deliberate deception. Thanks to the rise of social media and advances in artificial intelligence, spreading lies and confusing the truth have never been easier. Russia's interference in the 2016 US presidential election was the first warning sign of the coming deception revolution.[90] The Kremlin's weaponization of social media, which included impersonating Americans, spreading false narratives, inflaming political divides, and favoring one presidential candidate, reached more than 120 million Americans. News suggests that Russia's deception playbook is not just for Russia anymore; in October 2019, Facebook publicly acknowledged its discovery of foreign influence campaigns on its platform waged by Iran and China.[91] In addition, advances in artificial intelligence have given rise to deepfakes, digitally manipulated audio, photographs, and videos which are highly realistic and difficult to

86. Jeffrey Lewis, "Collected Thoughts on Phil Karber," *Arms Control Wonk*, December 7, 2011, https://www.armscontrolwonk.com/archive/204799/collected-thoughts-on-phil-karber/.
87. Hui Zhang, "The Defensive Nature of China's Underground Great Wall," *Bulletin*, January 16, 2012, https://thebulletin.org/2012/01/the-defensive-nature-of-chinas-underground-great-wall/.
88. Wan, "Georgetown."
89. Lewis, "Collected Thoughts on Phil Karber."
90. Zegart and Morell, "Spies, Lies, and Algorithms."
91. Mike Isaac, "Facebook Finds New Disinformation Campaigns and Braces for 2020 Torrent," *New York Times*, October 21, 2019, https://www.nytimes.com/2019/10/21/technology/facebook-disinformation-russia-iran.html.

authenticate. Deepfake application tools online are now widely available and so simple to use, high school students with no coding background can create convincing forgeries. In May 2019, anonymous users doctored a video, which went viral on Facebook, to make House Speaker Nancy Pelosi appear drunk. When the social media giant refused to take it down after it went viral, two artists and a small technology start-up created a deepfake of Mark Zuckerberg and posted it on Instagram. In August, the *Wall Street Journal* reported the first known use of deepfake audio to impersonate a voice in a cyber heist. Believing he was talking to his boss, an energy executive transferred $243,000. The voice turned out to be an AI-based imitation that was so real, it even had the boss's slight German accent and lilt.

It does not take much to realize the manipulative potential these technologies for nuclear-related issues. In a world of cheap satellite imagery, deepfakes, and the weaponization of social media, foreign governments, their proxies, and third-party organizations and individuals will all be able to inject convincing, false information and narratives into the public domain at speed and scale. If their goal is to confuse rather than convince, a little deception can go a long way. Imagine a deepfake video depicting a foreign leader secretly discussing a clandestine nuclear program with his inner circle. Although the leader issues vehement denials, doubt lingers because seeing is believing and nobody can be completely sure whether the video is real or fake.

In this emerging world of accidental errors and deliberate misinformation, US intelligence agencies will increasingly have to serve as verifiers of last resort. As one expert nuclear panel noted, "Only governments can satisfactorily validate the results of open source analysis using classified sources and methods and only governments can make verification judgments."[92] This, too, poses significant challenges for effective nuclear intelligence. The more time government intelligence agencies spend debunking, validating, or adjudicating the work of others, the less time they have to advance their intelligence collection and analysis priorities. One consequence is that net production of reliable, verified nuclear threat intelligence could go down, not up. In the Karber case alone, the poorly researched claims of a few Georgetown students sent several senior Pentagon officials and at least one congressional committee on a wild goose chase that took time, resources, and attention away from everything else.

Third, this ecosystem can generate significant policy risks even when the information it uncovers is accurate. Particularly in crises and sensitive diplomatic negotiations, policymakers rely on useful fictions to buy time and save face, giving one or both sides a way out. After the Soviet Union invaded Afghanistan, the CIA began arming Afghan mujahideen. The Soviets knew

---

92. Wisconsin Project on Nuclear Arms Control, "More Eyes on More Data," 3.

it, and the Americans knew the Soviets knew. But the useful fiction kept a proxy war from becoming a superpower war with the potential for nuclear escalation.[93] As Bruce Berkowitz and Allan Goodman write, "The fact . . . covertness is sometimes no more than a fig leaf does not necessarily alter the fact that it is a useful fig leaf."[94]

Even accurate information, if revealed, can make these situations more dangerous, by forcing action too soon and narrowing the range of political outcomes for each side. Imagine what would have happened during the Cuban missile crisis if nongovernmental nuclear sleuths had discovered the secret deal between President Kennedy and Soviet leader Khrushchev to remove US Jupiter missiles from Turkey in exchange for dismantling Soviet nuclear weapons from Cuba. With congressional midterm elections just days away, Kennedy was under intense pressure to stand tough against the Soviets. Real-time fact-checking could have derailed that agreement, escalating a nuclear standoff already teetering on the brink of war.

The fourth risk is related and happens when nongovernmental organizations make public information that is already well known to the Intelligence Community. The need to generate attention, demonstrate impact, and attract funding creates perverse incentives for open-source nuclear sleuths to announce seemingly sudden discoveries and ostensible efforts to prove the government wrong—even when discoveries are not new and the government was right all along. When this happens, intelligence officials have to burn up time explaining to executive branch officials and members of Congress "what we already know about Subject X."

This, too, is not a hypothetical problem. It became an actual one in January 2019 when the Center for Strategic and International Studies announced the "discovery" of an undeclared missile site in North Korea and estimated that there may be nineteen more.[95] Even though many undeclared missile sites were already known, the story made *New York Times* and *Washington Post* headlines and national television news.[96] "The Intelligence Commu-

---

93. It also made it harder for the Soviets to retaliate against Pakistan and Egypt for assisting the American covert effort.

94. Bruce D. Berkowitz and Allan E. Goodman, "The Logic of Covert Action," *National Interest*, March 1, 1998, https://nationalinterest.org/article/the-logic-of-covert-action-333. See also Austin Carson, *Secret Wars* (Princeton: Princeton University Press, 2018) and Lindsey A. O'Rourke, *Covert Regime Change* (Ithaca: Cornell University Press, 2018).

95. Joseph Bermudez, Victor Cha and Lisa Collins, "Undeclared North Korea: The Sinori Missile Operating Base and Strategic Force Facilities," CSIS, January 21, 2019, https://beyondparallel.csis.org/undeclared-north-korea-the-sino-ri-missile-operating-base-and-strategic-force-facilities/.

96. Interview by author with two nonproliferation experts, October 2019. Lena H. Sun, "Report Identifies Another Secret North Korea Missile Site, One of 20," *Washington Post*, January 21, 2019, https://www.washingtonpost.com/politics/report-identifies-another-secret-north-korea

nity, I am sure, had to do a lot of explaining with the DC government community," said one former official.[97] The costs of distraction can be high: the more time intelligence officials spend going over what they already know, the less time they spend on what they do not.

Fifth and finally, there is the countermeasure risk: clever nuclear sleuthing in the public domain can alert adversaries about weaknesses in their camouflage, concealment, and deception techniques that they did not know existed. Militaries are always thinking about how to overcome vulnerabilities and negate the other side's advantage. The invention of submarines led to sonar, bombers led to radar, tanks led to anti-tank missiles. Evidence suggests that the advent of Google Earth has prompted new Chinese efforts to conceal military facilities from more frequent satellite shooting intervals, and Western media reports using open-source imagery led North Korea to conceal a hot water cooling line from one of its nuclear reactors so analysts could no longer use it to tell whether the reactor was making weapons-grade plutonium.[98] In 2016, Dave Schmerler, a researcher at the Center for Nonproliferation Studies, measured the size of North Korea's first nuclear device (called a "disco ball") and locate the building where it was photographed by using objects in the room as telltale markers. The next North Korean photo of a warhead was taken in a completely white room with nothing to measure.[99] Whether Schmerler's research prompted the change is impossible to know. But the dynamics are well-known; any time new indicators or monitoring methods are revealed, countermeasures are likely to follow, making future monitoring even more difficult. The upshot is that short-term intelligence gains could unwittingly generate far greater long-term intelligence losses.[100]

-missile-site-one-of-20/2019/01/21/4066aeec-1db0-11e9-9145-3f74070bbdb9_story.html; David E. Sanger and William J. Broad, "In North Korea, Missile Bases Suggest a Great Deception," *New York Times*, November 12, 2018, https://www.nytimes.com/2018/11/12/us/politics/north-korea-missile-bases.html; Courtney Kube and Carol E. Lee, "Report Finds Another Undisclosed North Korea Missile Site, Says There Are 19 More," NBC News, January 21, 2019, https://www.nbcnews.com/news/north-korea/report-finds-another-undisclosed-north-korea-missile-site-says-there-n958801.

97. Interview by author, October 2019.

98. Pabian, "Commercial Satellite Imagery," 35; Puccioni and Ashdown, "Raising Standards," 9.

99. Anna Fifield, "With Technology, These Researchers Are Figuring Out North Korea's Nuclear Secrets," *Washington Post*, November 21, 2017, https://www.washingtonpost.com/world/asia_pacific/with-technology-these-researchers-are-figuring-out-north-koreas-nuclear-secrets/2017/11/20/274d9786-c9e2-11e7-b244-2d22ac912500_story.html.

100. For more on this point, see Wisconsin Project on Nuclear Arms Control, "More Eyes on More Data."

CHAPTER 4

Conclusion

Estimating nuclear dangers is not just for governments anymore. Thanks to the small satellite revolution, the rise of online information and connectivity, and advances in automated analytics, individuals and organizations outside of governments are playing new and important roles. Leading nongovernmental nuclear intelligence organizations have become essential partners to US intelligence agencies and international nonproliferation organizations, enabling faster and better intelligence assessments of illicit nuclear activities in North Korea, Iran, and elsewhere. Nongovernmental nuclear intelligence organizations also play pivotal roles in monitoring treaty compliance, identifying false positives and debunking false claims. Several of these nongovernmental nuclear intelligence groups have amassed a breadth of expertise that rivals, and in some cases, exceeds the capabilities of the U.S. Intelligence Community, harnessing the talents of former international weapons inspectors, nuclear physicists, senior government officials, imagery analysts, geolocation specialists, and emerging scholars at the forefront of using advanced technological tools. Because their work is unclassified, it provides new avenues for information sharing both within and between governments. Their work also makes it more difficult for policymakers to misuse intelligence by cherry-picking, mischaracterizing, mistakenly interpreting, or selectively publicizing information that advances a particular policy position.

But this ecosystem also brings risks, particularly as technological tools spread, and more individuals and organizations use them. In the unclassified world, there is no legal or bureaucratic firewall preventing information from getting into the wild. Consequently, erroneous analyses can go viral before they can be verified, and deception can flourish. As this world evolves, US intelligence agencies may suffer degraded effectiveness as they spend more time validating the work of others rather than doing their own. Even good open-source information can backfire, escalating crises, derailing sensitive negotiations, and leading adversaries to take countermeasures that make future nuclear intelligence collection more difficult for everyone.

These are early days. Much about the effects of open-source nuclear threat intelligence on US policymaking remains unknown. When, where, and how is open-source intelligence likely to be redundant? Additive? Clarifying? Confirming or disconfirming? Under what circumstances does information transparency help and when does it hurt? As nuclear seeking becomes more sophisticated and pervasive, how will nuclear hiding change? Will open-source nuclear threat intelligence increase costs to proliferators, adding more security burdens that slow their programs down? As these questions suggest, there is much more academic and policy work to be done.

Looking ahead, maximizing the benefits and mitigating the risks of the evolving open-source nuclear intelligence landscape will be essential. That process starts by recognizing that the future may not look like the present, and the present system has weaknesses.

Open-source nuclear threat intelligence is dominated by the United States and its Western democratic allies. Many of the leading organizations in this space are filled with experts who are driven by a sense of responsibility to the nonproliferation mission, who have exacting quality standards, and who work closely with US and allied government officials. All of this, however, is informal. There is no official tasking of priorities to these organizations; each decides what to collect and analyze, and how, based on what individuals personally think is important or interesting or necessary to keep their organizations going. There is no formalized or standardized quality control handbook for open-source nuclear threat intelligence. The standards are often set high; yet they are self-determined.

This informal US-led ecosystem serves the country's national interests well. But the future is likely to bring more players from more countries with less expertise, less responsibility, and less connectivity to US and allied intelligence officials and policymakers. China already operates commercial satellites, and the internationalization of the commercial satellite business is expected to grow significantly in the next several years.[101] It is important to ask now, "What would the future look like in a more crowded, less benign open-source world?"

Doing so suggests that finding ways to codify and institutionalize current best practices, norms, and networks among leading nongovernmental nuclear intelligence collectors and analysts is an important first step. The good news is that nascent efforts are underway to establish standards, develop shared norms, and improve skills.[102] In July 2019, the Stanley Foundation began a series of international stakeholder workshops to examine ethical challenges in the open-source community and develop recommendations for addressing them.[103] The bad news is that such initiatives cut in two directions, improving standards and tradecraft for well-meaning nongovernmental actors as well as potential adversaries.

---

101. Puccioni and Ashdown, "Raising Standards," 8.
102. Puccioni and Ashdown, "Raising Standards"; Loehrke et al., "The Gray Spectrum."
103. Puccioni and Ashdown, "Raising Standards"; Loehrke et al., "The Gray Spectrum."

II. ENDURING CHALLENGES WITH A NEW TWIST

CHAPTER 5

How Much Is Enough?

Revisiting Nuclear Reliability, Deterrence, and Preventive War

Jeffrey Lewis and Ankit Panda

Shortly after the first flight test of North Korea's *Hwasong-15* on November 28, 2017, an intercontinental ballistic missile (ICBM) that could strike targets throughout the United States, Kim Jong Un declared that his country had "finally realized the great historic cause of completing the state nuclear force."[1] For Kim, the test of a missile capable of ranging the entirety of the US homeland with a nuclear device marked an important milestone in North Korea's development as a new nuclear state. Others were less impressed. Weeks later, when Kim Jong Un boasted that he had a nuclear button ready for use, US president Donald Trump pushed back, saying, "I too have a Nuclear Button, but it is a much bigger & more powerful one than his, and my Button works!"[2] Why did Kim Jong Un choose November 2017 to be the qualitative "finish line" for his nuclear deterrent? Did subsequent insinuations from the US president undercut his confidence in his deterrent? What considerations led Kim—and other leaders of new nuclear states—to identify a given moment where their countries were nuclear capabilities were enough to deter their adversaries? And can we generalize from those considerations anything at all about the decisions other new nuclear states may make?

---

1. Mark Landler and Choe Sang-Hun, "North Korea Says It's Now a Nuclear State. Could That Mean It's Ready to Talk?," *New York Times*, November 29, 2017, sec. World, https://www.nytimes.com/2017/11/29/world/asia/north-korea-nuclear-missile-.html.
2. "North Korean Leader Kim Jong Un just stated that the 'Nuclear Button is on his desk at all times.' Will someone from his depleted and food starved regime please inform him that I too have a Nuclear Button, but it is a much bigger & more powerful one than his, and my Button works!" Donald Trump, Twitter, January 2, 2018, https://web.archive.org/web/20180104001627/https://twitter.com/realDonaldTrump/status/948355557022420992.

CHAPTER 5

In this chapter, we interrogate the fundamentals of "enoughness" for new nuclear states seeking the deterrent benefits of nuclear weapons. Though the requirements for deterrence were exhaustively debated in the context of the Cold War dyad between Washington and Moscow, they are less understood in the context of new nuclear states like India, Pakistan, and North Korea, and near-nuclear states. When do political and military leaders in these states think they have built a nuclear force capable of sufficiently deterring aggression against them? When do their adversaries accept that these states have built such a force and acknowledge—either explicitly or tacitly—that some deterrence now obtains between them? Finally, what phenomena manifest when there's a gap between these two moments? By comparatively examining case studies from South Asia and the Korean Peninsula, we seek to interrogate these questions. We find little evidence to support the conventional wisdom that new nuclear states adopt the same quantitative and qualitative measures that the United States did during the Cold War. At the same time, US analysts continue to use those measures to understand new nuclear states. That apparent inconsistency presents an interesting challenge for the stable functioning of deterrence.

Deterrence and Enoughness

Broadly, in asking how states think of how much is enough, qualitatively and quantitatively, when it comes to nuclear weapons and deterrence, we must first ascertain what their goals are. Identifying the specific goals that new nuclear states are seeking to accomplish with their nuclear weapons helps understand how they think about how much is enough. A state seeking to deter existential conventional attacks against its national leadership, like North Korea, will think about nuclear weapons and their sufficiency differently from one seeking to deter the use of nuclear weapons and other weapons of mass destruction against its territory. So, in defining enoughness, the place to begin is not capabilities but objectives. More narrowly, the notion of enoughness can be conceptualized as a threshold and is akin to, but not precisely, the notion of sufficiency. In general, sufficiency is closely tied to concepts about qualitative and quantitative measures of capability and risk tolerances. It often exists as an abstract concept, isolated from any notion of cost. Deterrence is ultimately a political condition, not a technical one. By enoughness, we hope to also capture the other factors that shape the decisions of leaders as to when they have enough to achieve the benefits they seek from nuclear armaments.

When this threshold is met or exceeded, the leader (or leaders) may enjoy many of the benefits of successful deterrence, viewing the marginal benefit of further qualitative refinement or quantitative buildup as decreasing sharply per unit of additional investment in a nuclear force buildup. This may change, particularly as certain costs fall over time. But at least initially, new nuclear states usually face more acute resource constraints than the United States and the Soviet Union ever did while also facing normative, political, and legal constraints to their pursuit of a nuclear weapons capability. For such states, this threshold should matter deeply. Defining this threshold is challenging, but we surmise that states will concern themselves with attaining certain types of weapons and attaining a certain level of reliability. In general, for basic deterrence to obtain against their adversaries, states will seek to demonstrate a minimally credible capability to hold at risk their adversary's population centers and major military nodes. In reasoning about the survivability of their forces under resource constraints, new nuclear states will tolerate and accept some level of risk; this level of risk acceptance is not fixed and can vary with systemic and domestic political developments.

The foundational notions of what nuclear deterrence requires may not apply to new nuclear states. For instance, the emphasis that Albert Wohlstetter gives to the "stringent" requirements of nuclear deterrence, for instance, may mislead in making sense of how new nuclear states have navigated the problem of enoughness when it comes to their nuclear weapons capabilities.[3] Others, such as John Steinbruner, argued that US analysts vastly overstate the importance of details such as "relative force levels, the payloads of delivery systems, the accuracy/yield characteristics of warheads, the aggregate warhead numbers, and similar widely utilized measures" matter little at the margin.[4] For new nuclear states under acute resource constraints and facing international opprobrium and sanction in their pursuit of nuclear weapons, the propensity to favor uncertainty in force development—realizing a capability but leaving the use of that capability or the threat that it represents to chance—may be most appealing. If reasoning about nuclear sufficiency varies across states, where many might converge is in the pursuit of realizing Thomas Schelling's "threat that leaves something to chance."[5] The testing, development, and evaluation of nuclear weapons and delivery systems with this in mind would accept that even low—but nonzero—levels of credibility can yield significant deterrent effects, securing a state's most critical national interests.

The threshold concept may render elegant what is ultimately a deeply uncertain process for newer nuclear states, particularly as they go about developing, testing, evaluating, and operating nuclear weapons and delivery

---

3. Albert Wohlstetter, "The Delicate Balance of Terror," *Foreign Affairs*, January 1959, https://www.foreignaffairs.com/articles/1959-01-01/delicate-balance-terror.
4. John D. Steinbruner, "National Security and the Concept of Strategic Stability," *Journal of Conflict Resolution* 22, no. 3 (September 1, 1978): 411–428, https://doi.org/10.1177/00220027 7802200303.
5. Thomas C. Schelling, *The Strategy of Conflict* (Cambridge, MA: Harvard University Press, 1981), 187.

systems. Over the course of their nuclear development, these states will experience constant friction. Certain technological pathways for delivery systems, for instance, may prove to be dead-ends, requiring expensive rethinks, or a return to the drawing board. Nuclear tests, similarly, can fizzle or fail, requiring either an adjustment in plans or continued testing. Scientific and technical expertise in these endeavors should amass over time and prove largely irreversible, but nontechnical sources of friction—including from nuclear and nonnuclear adversaries, and international institutions and norms—can also render imprecise how states self-conceive of the notion of a large enough nuclear force.

In answering how much is enough, we must also consider the nuclear postures certain states envisage and factors beyond an abstract and hyperrationalized conception of deterrence. For instance, as Vipin Narang explains, the diversity of nuclear postures adopted by regional nuclear powers may be an optimization response to "external security and internal domestic political and financial constraints."[6] But ultimately, a state that optimizes for an assured retaliation posture, for instance, will calculate its deterrence requirements differently from another optimizing for asymmetric escalation—down to the specific types of delivery systems and nuclear weapons that may be developed. Geography, too, can bear on state decision making. States seeking to operationalize a deterrent against a territorially contiguous adversary (such as India and Pakistan) will have a different set of requirements versus states seeking to exercise deterrence against both regional and intercontinental adversaries (such as North Korea).

Further, just as the United States and the Soviet Union faced early uncertainties about whether nuclear deterrence was working as theorized, so too do new nuclear states face difficulties in verifying deterrent effects. It is often clear when deterrence fails, but what is less clear is why a crisis does not escalate. Explicit statements by the adversary concerning their decision making or assessment of the situation can be informative, but even then we must wonder whether such statements are truthful.

Empirically, there is also reason to believe that enoughness can hold salience under conditions of nuclear latency or the existence of recessed nuclear deterrents.[7] New nuclear states can choose—or by technical necessity opt for—a delayed breakout while maintaining unassembled and untested nuclear weapons and related facilities in good order. In South Asia, for example, we see evidence of India and Pakistan considering these questions of enoughness both before and after their weaponized nuclear tests in May 1998.

---

6. Vipin Narang, *Nuclear Strategy in the Modern Era: Regional Powers and International Conflict* (Princeton: Princeton University Press, 2014), 8.

7. Ashley J. Tellis, "India's Emerging Nuclear Posture: Between Recessed Deterrent and Ready Arsenal," Product Page, RAND Corporation, 2001, https://www.rand.org/pubs/monograph_reports/MR1127.html.

North Korea presents a particularly interesting case given that its October 2006 inaugural nuclear test is widely regarded as a fizzle: a development that should have been a worst-case outcome for Pyongyang at the time.

Threats, Reliability, and Enoughness

Writing in 1958 on the requirements of deterrence—and the problem of credibility—Bernard Brodie observed that when it came to nuclear forces, the notion of force-sizing wasn't as simple as counting: "What counts in basic deterrence is not so much the size and efficiency of one's striking force before it is hit as the size and condition to which the enemy thinks he can reduce it by a surprise attack—as well as his confidence in the correctness of his predictions."[8] Brodie's observation was not merely theoretical but actively weighed on how US military planners conceived of the risks of first strikes, the survivability of their nuclear forces, and, consequently, force sizing and structure questions. At the core of Brodie's observation is the idea that the size of a nuclear arsenal is not measured against some absolute scale, but rather is assessed through the perceptions by both parties: the defender must reason about his own force requirements based on the attacker's offensive means. For new nuclear states, similar concerns should—and do—exist. Based on the empirical record, these concerns manifest in certain developmental decisions observable across nuclear weapons and delivery system development programs.

Unlike the early nuclear states—and the United States and the Soviet Union/Russia, in particular—the testing and verification of certain capabilities are highly limited in the case of new nuclear states (see Table 5.1). India, Pakistan, and North Korea, for instance, each have conducted six nuclear detonations (India over two discrete test events, Pakistan with one, and North Korea over six). The United States conducted 1,054 nuclear tests.[9] Even today, there remain voices within the United States who do not believe that the data collected from these tests is sufficient and argue that the United States should resume nuclear explosive testing.[10] Other states have stockpiled weapons with either no explosive tests or extremely limited tests. South Africa, for example, stockpiled six nuclear weapons over the course of the 1980s without testing them. South African leaders believed that a nuclear explosion would be an important political signal that should be withheld

---

8. Bernard Brodie, "The Anatomy of Deterrence," Product Page, RAND Corporation, 1958, https://www.rand.org/pubs/research_memoranda/RM2218.html.

9. United States Nuclear Tests, July 1945 through September 1992, DOE/NV 209 Rev 16, September 2015.

10. James Glanz, "Rick Perry, as Energy Secretary, May Be Pressed to Resume Nuclear Tests," *New York Times*, December 27, 2016.

CHAPTER 5

Table 5.1 Nuclear Tests and Explosions by Country

Nuclear Tests and Explosions by Country		
	Tests	Explosions
United States (a)	1,054	1,149
Soviet Union/Russia	715	969
United Kingdom (b)	45	45
France	210	
China	45	
India (c)	2	6
Pakistan	1	6
North Korea	6	6
Israel	(d)	
South Africa	0	0

Countries count nuclear tests and explosions differently, with many countries counting simultaneous explosions as a single test. For consistency, both numbers are presented where available. These figures also exclude so-called hydronuclear explosions.
(a) Excludes the two combat uses but includes twenty-eight joint US-UK nuclear explosions.
(b) Also includes twenty-eight joint US-UK nuclear explosions.
(c) India considers the five explosions conducted on May 11 and 13 to be a single test series.
(d) There are allegations that Israel conducted one or more tests in the South Atlantic in 1979.
Sources: United States Nuclear Tests, July 1945 through September 1992, DOE/NV 209 Rev 16 (September 2015); USSR Nuclear Weapon Tests and Peaceful Nuclear Explosions: 1949 through 1990 (Sarov: Russian Federal Nuclear Center-VNIIEF, 1996); China Today: Nuclear Industry (Beijing, China: China Social. Science Press, 1987).

until that signal was needed.[11] Similarly, Pakistan stockpiled an unknown number of nuclear weapons during the 1980s and 1990s, testing them at yield only after India's 1998 nuclear tests created what Pakistani officials saw as a political imperative to respond.

For new nuclear states, quantitative concerns on force sizing loom large. These include practical considerations pertaining to resource constraints—such as available fissile material stocks—but also nuclear strategy concerns. For practical and strategic reasons, however, all new nuclear states have maintained relatively small and simple nuclear arsenals. Apart from the United States and the Soviet Union/Russia, no nuclear states have felt the need to develop warheads into the four- or five-digit ranges for stockpiling. According to contemporary open-source estimates, the nuclear forces in India and Pakistan number in the mid-hundreds each, while North Korea possesses

---

11. Lydia Von Wielligh-Steyn and Nic Von Wielligh, *The Bomb: South Africa's Nuclear Weapons Programme* (Pretoria: Litera, 2015).

scores of nuclear warheads. These states may have come to appreciate that "Small numbers of nuclear weapons produce dramatic effects," and that in "times of crisis, they compel statesmen to act with restraint."[12]

The South Asian dyad over decades and, over the last decade, the case of North Korea exhibit that the "dramatic effects" of even a small, unproven nuclear capability can very much be real. Inasmuch as raw capabilities and the perception thereof matter for effective deterrence, so too does the ability for leaders and decision makers to manipulate risk in crises and actively shape the "curved slope" that leads to the brink, as Schelling argues.[13] Herman Kahn's escalation dominance theory does not appear to greatly influence how these states have gone about developing their early nuclear capabilities. These states may then be less concerned with the choices that the United States and the Soviet Union made in honing the reliability and credibility of their deterrents. It is not surprising that it is the experience of those states that went first to inform our ideas about which technical paths are feasible and which are not for nuclear breakout. Yet the US and Soviet experiences may also be misleading.

South Asia

Much of what we discuss above is richly observable in the case of the India-Pakistan dyad. The South Asian case is particularly useful because both countries not only opted for exclusively different nuclear postures at all times of their coexistence—including as latent nuclear states, recessed deterrent nuclear states, and, finally, after 1998, as overt nuclear powers. To more closely examine how political, technical, and military stakeholders in these countries reasoned about the deterrent effects of nuclear weapons over time, we examine nuclear dynamics across all three areas.

1974: THE EFFECTS OF INDIA'S "PEACEFUL NUCLEAR EXPLOSION"

In December 1971, India and Pakistan fought an intense conflict that resulted in nothing short of a transformation of South Asia's political map. Pakistan was cleaved in two, as the erstwhile exclave of East Pakistan was

---

12. James Wood Forsyth Jr., Colonel B. Chance Saltzman, and Gary Schaub Jr., "Remembrance of Things Past: The Enduring Value of Nuclear Weapons," *Strategic Studies Quarterly* 4, no. 1 (Spring 2010): 74–89.

13. "The brink is not, in this view, the sharp edge of a cliff where one can stand firmly, look down, and decide whether or not to plunge. The brink is a curved slope that one can stand on with some risk of slipping, the slope gets steeper and the risk of slipping greater as one moves toward the chasm. But the slope and the risk of slipping are rather irregular." Schelling, *The Strategy of Conflict*, 200.

rendered independent and became the state of Bangladesh. India, meanwhile, seized on the victory as a moment of arrival as a regional power in its own right. Concerns about national defense and self-sufficiency, in particular, loomed large for New Delhi in the lead-up to and the aftermath of the war.[14] Despite the victory in the war, India had strategic misgivings about the apparent strategic rapprochement between the United States and China in the early 1970s. Perceptions of US support for Pakistan were high in New Delhi at the time, and India took Washington's decision to deploy an aircraft carrier strike group to the Indian Ocean as a signal of the Nixon administration's apparent hostility.[15] It was against this background that New Delhi set in place the series of events that would culminate in its first-ever detonation of a nuclear device.

On May 18, 1974, at 8:05 a.m., Indian scientists oversaw what would become the first known detonation of a nuclear device by a country other than five permanent members of the United Nations Security Council.[16] Officially dubbed a peaceful nuclear explosion (PNE) with the innocuous-sounding code name *Smiling Buddha*, the test was approved by India's civilian political leadership—specifically, Prime Minister Indira Gandhi—after a series of internal deliberations about the wisdom of proceeding with such a test.[17] These discussions were largely political in nature. At least three years before the 1974 test, the basic design for the device had been prepared.[18] In September 1972, Gandhi had specifically sanctioned that a physical nuclear device be prepared and assembled for a possible test and do so "near the peak of her post-war popularity."[19] The test was overseen by civilian scientists with the Bhabha Atomic Research Center.

The device was of a simple fission design and used twelve explosive lenses to compress a roughly 6 kilograms plutonium pit, a slightly smaller amount than the 6.2 kilograms used in "Fat Man."[20] The physical dimensions of the spherical implosion device stood at 1.25 meters and 1,400 kilograms.

---

14. Anit Mukherjee, *The Absent Dialogue: Politicians, Bureaucrats, and the Military in India* (New York: Oxford University Press, 2019), 152–156.

15. Jacques E. C. Hymans, *The Psychology of Nuclear Proliferation: Identity, Emotions and Foreign Policy* (New York: Cambridge University Press, 2006), 184.

16. George Perkovich, *India's Nuclear Bomb: The Impact on Global Proliferation* (Berkeley: University of California Press, 1999), 149–150.

17. Harsh V. Pant and Yogesh Joshi, *Indian Nuclear Policy: Oxford India Short Introductions* (New Delhi, India: Oxford University Press, 2018), 72–78.

18. Perkovich, *India's Nuclear Bomb*, 156.

19. "India's Nuclear Weapons Program. India's First Bomb: 1967–1974," Nuclear Weapon Archive, March 30, 2001, http://nuclearweaponarchive.org/India/IndiaFirstBomb.html.

20. Let us introduce a distinction: A simple fission device is a heavy and inefficient nuclear weapon similar to "Fat Man." A compact fission device is a lighter, more efficient nuclear weapon such as the US Mark 7. A compact fission device is small enough to fit a typical early generation ballistic missile such as a Scud. For comparison, the payload of a Scud missile is about 1,000 kilograms.

After the successful test, the Indian government claimed a yield of 12kT at the chosen test site at Pokhran, in the desert of Rajasthan in India's northwest, but authoritative accounts suggest that the actual yield may have been smaller.[21]

For a country like India in 1974, the notion of deploying a small number of 1,400 kilograms, 1.25 meter nuclear devices as a primitive gravity bomb in the service of existential deterrence through assured retaliation—less than thirty years after Fat Man was used against Imperial Japan—would not have prima facie been absurd. But this never happened. Some problems were technical. After diverting plutonium from apparent civil reactors for use in the 1974 test, India's ability to procure additional plutonium would have been limited, making quantitative expansion costly. To justify this cost, New Delhi may have needed certain assurances on reliability and operational deployment that were also out of reach in 1974. For instance, scientists involved in preparing the *Smiling Buddha* PNE device "had trouble stabilizing the polonium-beryllium neutron initiator."[22]

To this day, Indian accounts of the purpose of the PNE largely hew to the narrative that the test was not demonstrative for deterrence ends, but something akin to a prestige-bestowing scientific undertaking: a means to show that New Delhi, too, could enter the nuclear club. As Harsh Joshi and Yogesh Pant write, the nonaligned world applauded as a "Third World country had finally broken into the club of nuclear elites."[23] India's "insistence on using nuclear technology for peaceful purposes even after the test allowed her to sustain her moral leadership on nuclear disarmament," they add.[24] Other analysts entertain the possibility of other motives; Gurmeet Kanwal, for instance, notes the test "was conducted ostensibly for civilian purposes," leaving open the possibility that India benefited in other ways.[25] The all civilian-led decision-making process that led to the PNE and the fact that most preparatory work was led by civilian scientists gives this narrative some credibility. If India sought to communicate deterrent signals, it didn't do so with the PNE.

But what exactly did May 18, 1974, represent as a milestone in the then-nascent India-Pakistan nuclear dyad? Narang marks that date as the moment that India came to possess "the technical capacity to develop and deliver a plutonium fission weapon from its sizeable reactor capacity."[26] George Perkovich largely concurs, noting that the moment marked a "capacity to develop

---

21. Tellis, "India's Emerging Nuclear Posture," 196–198.
22. Vipin Narang, *Nuclear Strategy in the Modern Era: Regional Powers and International Conflict* (Princeton: Princeton University Press, 2014), 95.
23. Pant and Joshi, *Indian Nuclear Policy*, 82.
24. Pant and Joshi, *Indian Nuclear Policy*, 82.
25. Gurmeet Kanwal, "India's Nuclear Force Structure 2025," Carnegie Endowment for International Peace, June 30, 2016, https://carnegieendowment.org/2016/06/30/india-s-nuclear-force-structure-2025-pub-63988.
26. Narang, *Nuclear Strategy in the Modern Era*, 95.

nuclear weapons if security interests required it."[27] In terms of deterrence and enoughness, there is thin evidence to suggest that India sought to explicitly present itself to its primary adversary, Pakistan, and the world as a nuclear power after the PNE. The explicit decision to describe the test as peaceful and the subsequent twenty-four-year gap before New Delhi's weaponized tests in May 1998 had real effects on deterrence. As we suggest in our framing of how states self-conceive of their deterrents versus how their adversaries might, there is little doubt in the case of the Indian 1974 demonstration that Pakistan—wounds fresh from its dismemberment at the hands of India's conventional forces in 1971—took matters seriously. May 18 then represented a moment where India's self-conception in nuclear capability diverged considerably from how Pakistan perceived matters.

Days after the May 18 demonstration, it appeared that US national security decision makers were reasoning about possible Indian operationalization of a variant of the PNE device as a gravity bomb. A May 30 US National Security Council memorandum suggested that the Indian Air Force's Canberra medium bombers could reasonably deliver such a device.[28] But just as the physics package's potential neutron initiator problems would have likely kept Indian policymakers from pushing ahead with operationalization, the Canberra option would come with wrinkles: for instance, could New Delhi assure retaliation to adequately high confidence with a small number of bombs and bombers to deliver them in a shooting war? The inelegance of the solutions available to India aside, Pakistan took the demonstration as a dire development. The moment played a role in accelerating Islamabad's then-ongoing work on nuclear weaponization, including by specifically catalyzing a career move for Abdul Qadeer Khan to leave behind his work on uranium enrichment centrifuges in Europe and move to midwife Pakistan's bomb full-time.[29]

The early Pakistani public reaction described the PNE as an attempt at nuclear "blackmail" by India.[30] A spokesperson for the Pakistani Foreign Office said the PNE "cannot but be viewed with the degree of concern marching its magnitude by the whole world and more specifically, by India's immediate neighbors."[31] Zulfikar Ali Bhutto, the Pakistani prime minister at the time, decried an Indian attempt to seek "hegemony over the subcontinent."[32] Gan-

---

27. Perkovich, *India's Nuclear Bomb*, 189.
28. Narang, *Nuclear Strategy in the Modern Era*, 96.
29. Joshua Pollack, "The Secret Treachery of A.Q. Khan," Playboy, February 2012, http://carnegieendowment.org/files/the_secret%20treachery%20of%20aq%20khan.pdf.
30. Bhumitra Chakma, "Road to Chagai: Pakistan's Nuclear Programme, Its Sources and Motivations," *Modern Asian Studies* 36, no. 4 (2002): 871–912.
31. *The Pakistan Times*, May 19, 1974, quoted in Chakma, "Road to Chagai," 888.
32. Iram Khalid and Zakia Bano, "Pakistan's Nuclear Development (1974–1998): External Pressures," *South Asian Studies* 30, no. 1 (June 2015): 221–235.

dhi, perhaps having anticipated such a response, wrote Bhutto, reiterating the apparent mundane motives for the PNE. Underscoring that Pakistan's concerns did not solely vary with Indian intentions alone, Bhutto replied that "it is a question not only of intentions but of capabilities." He remained explicit about the implications for Pakistan: "But the acquisition of a capability, which has direct and immediate military consequences, becomes a permanent factor to be reckoned with. I need hardly recall that no non-nuclear-weapon state, including India, considered mere declarations of intent as sufficient to ensure their security in the nuclear age."[33]

This exchange between the two leaders underscored the perceptual gap that had opened up in South Asia, where the Pakistani leadership's perception of India's nuclear capability was likely greater in scope than India's self-conception as a nuclear power. Bhutto's view was not an outlier. As Bhumitra Chakma observes, the "general public, political parties, and media in Pakistan" all shared this view, as did the Pakistani military.[34] Given the generally poor background conditions in 1974 for Pakistan after its defeat in 1971, the PNE not only had the effect of increasing Islamabad's resolve in seeking the bomb but did so by accentuating security concerns. But, in the end, what India had after the PNE was not enough for its nuclear deterrence requirements, but neither was Pakistan—already proven to have been conventionally inferior—satisfied without its own capability.

1980s–1998 IN SOUTH ASIA: RECESSED DETERRENTS AND ENOUGHNESS

By the end of the 1980s, both India and Pakistan had progressed sufficiently in their indigenous nuclear weapons development efforts to the point that both countries had recessed nuclear deterrents; their weapons could be manufactured, tested, and deployed over a relatively short duration. Pakistan stockpiled nuclear weapons based initially on a compact uranium implosion design provided by China, which was tested on DF-2 ballistic missile in 1966. The first Pakistani highly enriched uranium (HEU) devices may have been assembled as early as 1985.[35] According to Feroz Khan, Pakistan subsequently developed a smaller version of this device largely by improving the electronics and reducing the "jitter" among the detonators. Pakistan conducted a series of twenty-four "cold test" of compact devices between 1983 and 1995. Samar Mubarakmand argued that cold tests are sufficient to establish confidence in nuclear weapons designs. "If you have a cold test and

---

33. Bhutto's letter to Gandhi was printed in a 1974 edition of *Pakistan Horizon*. Chakma, "Road to Chagai," 888.
34. Chakma, "Road to Chagai," 888.
35. Feroz Khan, *Eating Grass: The Making of the Pakistani Bomb* (Stanford, CA: Stanford Security Studies, 2012), 188.

CHAPTER 5

you detect neutrons," Mubarakmand told Feroz Khan, "you can be more than 100% sure that if you put enriched uranium in the same bomb, it is bound to give you fission."[36] These devices were validated in nuclear explosions in 1998 after India's nuclear test created domestic political pressure within Pakistan to follow suit. The general consensus is that these devices all used HEU, although there is reportedly a debate within the intelligence community about the final test.[37] In any case, by 1986, Pakistan's ability to manufacture a working nuclear weapon was, in the US view, effectively complete; one US official memorably characterized Islamabad's technical proximity to the bomb as being "two screwdriver turns" away from complete.[38]

On the Indian side, the final work toward the country's initial nuclear weapons was ordered by Prime Minister Rajiv Gandhi in 1988–89 as a response to Indian fears concerning Pakistan's weaponization. The Indian Atomic Energy Commission and Defense Research & Development Organization were charged with weaponization and are thought to have produced the final components necessary for a missile-deliverable weapon around this time. India's indigenously developed first-generation ballistic missiles began flight testing by 1988. The liquid-propellant-based Prithvi-I was first tested in 1988, and the solid-propellant-based Agni-I was first tested in 1989.[39] During this period, India's ability to assemble and deliver a nuclear weapon was thought to be achievable in seventy-two hours, allowing New Delhi to practice deterrence by assuring retaliation.[40] While these developments were ongoing in both countries, nuclear signaling remained muddled. Multiple crises between India and Pakistan around these times—notably, the Indian capture of the Siachen Glacier in Operation Meghdoot (1984), the Brasstacks Crisis (1986–1987), and the start of the Kashmir insurgency (1988–1990)—took place under the shadow of recessed deterrents and weaponization.

36. Khan, *Eating Grass*, 185.
37. According to press reports, Los Alamos National Laboratory conducted the preliminary analysis and concluded that Pakistan had tested a device involving plutonium. But analysts at Lawrence Livermore National Laboratory disagreed with the Los Alamos conclusion, "alleging that Los Alamos contaminated and then lost the air sample from the Pakistan blast." One official explained that "there is some disagreement here, and experts at the labs need to sort it out." See Dana Priest, "U.S. Labs at Odds on Whether Pakistani Blast Used Plutonium," *Washington Post*, January 17, 1999, A2. According to Mark Hibbs, the dispute was eventually resolved in favor of contamination. "It is currently believed that the plutonium found in the environmental samples in Pakistan was instead of Indian origin," Hibbs wrote, "and that comparative isotopic analysis suggests the plutonium was vented to the atmosphere by the explosions at Pokhran carried out two weeks before." Mark Hibbs, "Vented Indian Plutonium Deemed Source of Reports Pakistan Tested PU Weapons," *Nuclear Fuel*, February 7, 2000.
38. Bob Woodward, "Pakistan Reported Near Atom Arms Production," *Washington Post*, November 4, 1986, https://www.washingtonpost.com/archive/politics/1986/11/04/pakistan-reported-near-atom-arms-production/acd69089-dff0-424c-ba59-bd3fcac02b76/.
39. Narang, *Nuclear Strategy in the Modern Era*, 96–97.
40. Narang, *Nuclear Strategy in the Modern Era*, 97.

The precise role of nuclear deterrence in this era between India and Pakistan remains contested but, in a subjective sense, senior decision makers in South Asia appeared to understand that nuclear capabilities played a role in shaping these crises.[41] After an Indian military mobilization during the 1990 Kashmir uprising, Pakistani officials feared the prospect of a preventive Indian attack against its primary uranium enrichment facility. General Mirza Aslam Beg, Pakistan's chief of army staff, would later describe a set of steps Pakistan took to imply the possible dispersal of nuclear weapons, "not to precipitate a crisis but to deter."[42] In Beg's telling, the signal was meant for Indian interpretation as much as it was for American interpretation.[43] Feroz Khan, reflecting on this episode, which was partially disputed by other prominent Pakistani officials, including the then foreign minister Sahabzada Yaqub-Khan, notes that these types of "veiled messages" were an attempt to deter and may have been abetted by the lack of an ability by either India or Pakistan to verify the other's nuclear capabilities with any high level of confidence of precision. "Neither country had the national technical means to detect the exact progress of the other's nuclear program," Khan writes.[44] In Pakistan's case, Khan, citing Mubarakmand, concludes that through 1990, there was considerable uncertainty within Pakistan's nuclear weapons complex about whether the devices that had been cold tested to the point were "deliverable with any degree of assurance or performance."[45] But even if Pakistan had doubts about its nuclear capability, Beg's retelling of crises during this time suggests that nuclear signaling appeared to play a role.

1998 ON: A NEW NORMAL

The nuclear competition between India and Pakistan in the twenty-two years since the 1998 tests has come to resemble the more conventional nuclear dyadic relationship seen between the United States and the Soviet Union. In techno-military terms, the two countries remain mired in a security dilemma, whereby Indian pursuit of improved survivability for its second strike and development of damage limitation capabilities has been met with the ongoing testing, development, and evaluation in Pakistan of a range of new systems, from low-yield battlefield nuclear weapons like the Hatf-IX Nasr and the multiple independently targetable reentry vehicle capable Ababeel medium-range ballistic missile. Advances in conventional precision strike platforms, intelligence, surveillance, and reconnaissance capabilities

---

41. Khan, *Eating Grass*, 229–231.
42. Khan, *Eating Grass*, 230.
43. Beg, in his discussion of this episode with Feroz Khan, also expresses concern about Indian coordination with Israel to carry out a preventive attack. See Khan, *Eating Grass*, 230.
44. Khan, *Eating Grass*, 233.
45. Khan, *Eating Grass*, 232–233.

in India, too, stand to keep Pakistani anxieties about the survivability of its own deterrent—and, by proxy, the qualitative and quantitative sufficiency of its deterrent—high.[46] Both countries have also taken steps to gradually develop a sea-based deterrent.[47] In qualitative terms, especially, the post-1998 era has seen a substantial technical change in the delivery systems available to each side.

In technical terms, both India and Pakistan have sought to improve survivability and nuclear force responsiveness; Pakistan, owing to its offensively oriented posture, has doctrinally moved from a minimum credible deterrent to "full spectrum deterrence," enabled by longer-range delivery vehicles and lower-yield options, like the medium-range Shaheen-III and the suspected 5–12 kT yield Nasr.[48] In the Indian case, it is less clear that many of post-1998 developments were driven by unease about the credibility of its assured retaliation posture versus other factors, including bureaucratic interests in the country's Defense Research and Development Organisation (DRDO) to continue developing newer delivery systems, many of which were tested as "technology demonstrators" without full political sanction for development and deployment.[49] Given that India has concerned itself not only with Pakistan but with practicing credible minimum deterrence against China, many developments were driven by perceived deterrence requirements vis-à-vis Beijing.[50]

46. Christopher Clary and Vipin Narang, "India's Counterforce Temptations: Strategic Dilemmas, Doctrine, and Capabilities," *International Security* 43, no. 3 (February 1, 2019): 7–52, https://doi.org/10.1162/isec_a_00340.

47. Diana Wueger, "India's Nuclear-Armed Submarines: Deterrence or Danger?," *Washington Quarterly* 39, no. 3 (July 2, 2016): 77–90, https://doi.org/10.1080/0163660X.2016.1232636; Christopher Clary and Ankit Panda, "Safer at Sea? Pakistan's Sea-Based Deterrent and Nuclear Weapons Security," *Washington Quarterly* 40, no. 3 (July 3, 2017): 149–168, https://doi.org/10.1080/0163660X.2017.1370344.

48. Hans M. Kristensen, Robert S. Norris, and Julia Diamond, "Pakistani Nuclear Forces, 2018," *Bulletin of the Atomic Scientists* 74, no. 5 (September 3, 2018), 348–258, https://doi.org/10.1080/00963402.2018.1507796. Some Indian analysts have expressed skepticism about the Nasr as a real capability, citing fissile material constraints in Pakistan and a potentially inefficient HEU gun-type design for the weapon's sub-300 millimeter diameter physics package. See Aditya Ramanathan and Kunal Kini, "Are Pakistan's Battlefield Nuclear Weapons a Mirage?," *Diplomat*, May 7, 2019, https://thediplomat.com/2019/05/are-pakistans-battlefield-nuclear-weapons-a-mirage/.

49. See, for example, former Indian defense minister A. K. Antony on Arihant, India's first SSBN, quoted in Sandeep Unnithan, "The Secret Undersea Weapon," *India Today*, January 17, 2008, https://www.indiatoday.in/magazine/defence/story/20080128-the-secret-undersea-weapon-735178-2008-01-17. Rajesh Basur argued that "there is no evidence that the question of credibility significantly shaped the thinking of either side." See Rajesh M. Basrur, *South Asia's Cold War: Nuclear Weapons and Conflict in Comparative Perspective* (London: Routledge, 2008).

50. For background on Indian views of Chinese nuclear forces, see discussion in Manjeet S. Pardesi, "China's Nuclear Forces and Their Significance to India," *Nonproliferation Review* 21, no. 3–4 (October 2, 2014): 337–354, https://doi.org/10.1080/10736700.2014.1072996.

India's self-assessment of the sufficiency of its nuclear forces, early in the post-1998 era, did not focus on available yield packages or delivery systems in the Pakistan case but more on the adequacy of nuclear command and control (NC2). K. Subrahmanyam, a prominent advocate of India's nuclear deterrent and an instrumental voice in the development of India's 1999 draft nuclear doctrine, writing in 2003 emphasized that the core of India's credibility lay in its NC2 capabilities.[51] "The credibility of the Indian retaliatory ability which would deter a sabre-rattling Islamabad depends on the explicit and transparent projection of such a survivable command and control system," he wrote.[52] Subrahmanyam was primarily concerned about India's ability to retaliate after a decapitation strike—the worst-case scenario in his view—which might have posed particular challenges in the Indian context given the robustness of civilian control over the nuclear enterprise. Concern over NC2 is not unique to India and is a natural area of focus for a new nuclear state, but developments in India early in the post-1998 era underscore this point.[53]

One of the five detonations that India conducted in 1998 during the two Pokhran-II test events was later revealed authoritatively to have been a fizzled thermonuclear design. K. Santhanam, the DRDO field director for Pokhran-II, revealed in 2009 that "not only was the yield of the second fusion (H-bomb) stage of the thermonuclear (TN) device tested in May 1998 was . . . far below the design prediction made by the Bhabha Atomic Research Centre (BARC), but that it actually failed."[54] P. K. Iyengar, a former chairman of India's Atomic Energy Commission, concurred with that assessment.[55] In the eleven years between Santhanam's authoritative disclosure and the May 1998 test, few Indian scientists, civilian leaders, or military officers grumbled about nuclear insufficiency. As far as anyone in a position to have influence in India was concerned, the country was a nuclear power, even though rumors of a thermonuclear fizzle had been apparent for years. In September 1998, the US seismologist Terry C. Wallace cast doubt that the Indian claim of having tested a forty-three kiloton thermonuclear weapon on May 11—the first of the two days of the Pokhran-II tests—was likely not the

---

51. K. Subrahmanyam, "Essence of Deterrence," Ministry of External Affairs Government of India (originally appeared in *Times of India*), January 7, 2003, https://mea.gov.in/articles-in-indian-media.htm?dtl/15232/Essence+of+Deterrence.

52. Subrahmanyam, "Essence of Deterrence."

53. Peter D. Feaver, "Command and Control in Emerging Nuclear Nations," *International Security* 17, no. 3 (1992): 160–187, https://doi.org/10.2307/2539133.

54. K. Santhanam and Ashok Parthasarathi, "Pokhran-II Thermonuclear Test, a Failure," *Hindu*, September 17, 2009, sec. Comment, https://www.thehindu.com/opinion/op-ed/Pokhran-II-thermonuclear-test-a-failure/article13736892.ece.

55. P. K. Iyengar, "Non-Fissile Doubts," *Outlook India Magazine*, October 26, 2009, https://www.outlookindia.com/magazine/story/non-fissile-doubts/262331.

case.⁵⁶ A month later, a report noted that further analysis at Lawrence Livermore National Laboratory "concluded that the second stage of a two-stage Indian hydrogen bomb device failed to ignite as planned."⁵⁷ Indian scientists subsequently pushed back on these analyses, claiming a lack of specific knowledge about the geological qualities of the Pokhran test site had skewed the seismic analysis.⁵⁸

Both Santhanam and Iyengar extended their assessments of the failed thermonuclear weapon test to make the case that India's deterrent, contrary to its post-1998 presentation as credible, may be lacking. "Thermonuclear weapons are crucial to a credible deterrent because they are much lighter than fission weapons and therefore more suitable for deployment on missiles," Iyengar wrote.⁵⁹ Santhanam was unequivocal: "No country having undertaken only two weapon related tests of which the core TN device failed, can claim to have a [Credible Minimum Deterrent]."⁶⁰ But these exhortations largely fell on deaf ears, and India's civilian leadership did not acknowledge any major deficiencies. In the aftermath of the 2005 US-India nuclear deal, in particular, Indian prime minister Manmohan Singh was keen to maintain goodwill, and any suggestion that New Delhi could resume nuclear testing despite an earlier announced unilateral moratorium would have had significant diplomatic consequences. Despite the technical shortcoming of India's apparent thermonuclear test in 1998, New Delhi appeared to retain confidence in the deterrent effects of its nuclear arsenal.

In the immediate aftermath of India's 1998 tests—and before Pakistan's Chagai-I and Chagai-II tests later that month—it appeared that Indian officials did not take seriously the possibility that Pakistan would demonstrate a nuclear capability as well. L. K. Advani, the Indian home minister at the time and an influential leader within the then governing Bharatiya Janata Party, delivered remarks in the week after the Pokhran-II tests implying that India's nuclear status had decisively transformed the geopolitical status quo in South Asia—apparently with little expectation that New Delhi would have to contend with a nuclear deterrence relationship with Islamabad in a matter of days. The tests have "brought about a qualitatively new stage in

---

56. Terry C. Wallace, "The May 1998 India and Pakistan Nuclear Tests," *Seismological Research Letters* 69, no. 5 (September 1, 1998): 386–393, https://doi.org/10.1785/gssrl.69.5.386.

57. November 1998 *Nucleonics Week* report, quoted in Praful Bidwai and Achin Vanaik, *New Nukes: India, Pakistan and Global Nuclear Disarmament* (Oxford: Signal Books, 2000), 101.

58. S. K. Sikka, Falguni Roy, and G. J. Nair. 1998. "Indian Explosions of 11 May 1998: An Analysis of Global Seismic Body Wave Magnitude Estimates," *Current Science* 75, no. 5, September 10, 1998, http://web.archive.org/web/20010524095558/www.barc.ernet.in/webpages/milestones/drs_03.html, 481.

59. Iyengar, "Non-Fissile Doubts."

60. Santhanam and Parthasarathi, "Pokhran-II Thermonuclear Test, a Failure."

Indo-Pakistan relations," Advani said.[61] He further counseled Pakistan to "realize the change in the geo-strategic situation in the region and the world [and] roll back its anti-India policy, especially with regard to Kashmir."[62] Advani's apparent lack of concern with imminent Pakistani breakout contrasts with Rajiv Gandhi's weaponization directives in the late-1980s, which were driven directly by well-placed Indian concern about then-ongoing Pakistani weaponization activities. Days later, Advani's attempts to leverage India's nuclear monopoly in South Asia to extract concessions on Kashmir and other issues would appear overstated as Pakistan conducted its tests. It is possible instead that Advani's posturing was intended for domestic consumption since the party had retained the option to "exercise the option to induct nuclear weapons" in its 1998 election manifesto.[63]

Post-1998 crises in South Asia have explicitly contended with nuclear pressures. Although scholarly accounts of the 1999 Kargil War and major crises in 2001–2002, 2008, and 2019 differ on the precise intensity of nuclear escalation risks, policymakers in both countries were well aware of the possibility for escalation.[64] Given divergent doctrines and postures—in particular, India's adoption of no first-use and massive retaliation since 2003—Pakistan has retained the nuclear initiative. Senior Indian decision makers have indicated openly that the prospect of Pakistani nuclear first-use has effectively "deterred India" in crises, including from mobilizing conventional military forces after the 2008 Mumbai terror attacks when Lashkar-e-Taiba terrorists killed approximately 166 people.[65] The prospect of credible Pakistani nuclear first-use has vexed India; however, contemporary debates in New Delhi have not focused overwhelmingly on the technical capacity for effective deterrence but on posture and doctrine.[66] Although some prominent Indian

---

61. Kenneth J. Cooper, "Key Indian Official Warns Pakistan," *Washington Post*, May 19, 1998, https://www.washingtonpost.com/archive/politics/1998/05/19/key-indian-official-warns-pakistan/c5774a66-c376-443a-b2a5-e443f0528b77/.

62. Cooper, "Key Indian Official Warns Pakistan."

63. Bharatiya Janata Party, *BJP Election Manifesto 1998*, 1998, http://library.bjp.org/jspui/handle/123456789/241.

64. For a study of Kargil deemphasizing nuclear status, see T. Negeen Pegahi, "Pakistan's Nuclear Weapons and the Kargil Conflict: Reassessing Their Role in the Two Sides' Decision-Making," *Asian Survey* 60, no. 2 (April 2020), 245–264, https://doi.org/10.1525/as.2020.60.2.245. For the authoritative study of the 2001–2002 crisis, see Polly Nayak and Michael Krepon, "US Crisis Management in South Asia's Twin Peaks Crisis," in *The India-Pakistan Military Standoff*, ed. Zachary S. Davis (New York: Palgrave Macmillan US, 2011), 143–186, https://doi.org/10.1057/9780230118768_7. For a diverse treatment of the 2019 Balakot crisis, see Vijay Shankar et al., "South Asia Post-Crisis Brief," Global Zero, June 2019, https://www.globalzero.org/wp-content/uploads/2019/06/South-Asia-Post-Crisis-Brief.pdf.

65. "'Pak's N-Bomb Prevented Indian Retaliation after 26/11,'" *Indian Express*, March 9, 2009, http://archive.indianexpress.com/news/paks-nbomb-prevented-indian-retaliation-after-2611/432730/.

66. For summaries of this debate, see Shashank Joshi, "India's Nuclear Anxieties: The Debate Over Doctrine," Arms Control Association, May 2015, https://www.armscontrol.org/act/2015

voices have advocated for continued nuclear testing at some point in the future, particularly to demonstrate a successful, fully staged, high-yield thermonuclear weapon capability, reliability does not appear to be a primary Indian concern.[67]

North Korea's Deterrent

There are three distinct periods in North Korea's nuclear development; each period is marked by the advance of North Korea's nuclear weapons capabilities, which causes a crisis that results in an attempted diplomatic settlement that quickly gives way to another crisis.

This structure is probably not a series of coincidences. Narushige Michishita argues that North Korea uses force when it wants something, and when it believes that a use of force—married with diplomatic efforts—will achieve it.[68] He calls these periods "military-diplomatic campaigns." Issues such as the broad international environment or domestic politics are likely secondary factors and, over time, North Korea's choice in tactics has changed. The important idea is that the decision to explode a nuclear weapon or launch a ballistic missile is better understood as a political demonstration rather than a test. The benefit sought by North Korea from these events is chiefly political, not technical—even if North Korean scientists do appreciate the technical gain from testing.

The first period began in the late 1970s, as North Korea responded to South Korea's nuclear weapons program by seeking its own nuclear reactor and ballistic missiles. This is the period in which North Korea built the reactor at Yongbyon and successfully developed a series of ballistic missiles based on the Soviet-produced Scud short-range ballistic missile. This period concluded with a series of diplomatic efforts by the Clinton administration to freeze North Korea's capabilities at a latent deterrent, with North Korea possessing all the necessary technologies for a very minimal deterrent but having not fashioned a force that would normally be considered sufficient for an operational deterrent.[69] These diplomatic efforts included the 1994

-05/features/india%E2%80%99s-nuclear-anxieties-debate-over-doctrine; Rajesh Rajagopalan, "India's Nuclear Doctrine Debate," Carnegie Endowment for International Peace, June 30, 2016, https://carnegieendowment.org/2016/06/30/india-s-nuclear-doctrine-debate-pub-63950.

67. Bharat Karnad, "Slumping Modi Needs Thermonuclear Tests," *Security Wise* (blog), June 3, 2018, https://bharatkarnad.com/2018/06/03/slumping-modi-needs-thermonuclear-tests/.

68. Narushige Michishita, *North Korea's Military-Diplomatic Campaigns, 1966–2008* (New York: Routledge, 2009).

69. For background on this period, see Joel S. Wit, Daniel B. Poneman, and Robert L. Gallucci, *Going Critical: The First North Korean Nuclear Crisis* (Washington, DC: Brookings Institution Press, 2004).

Agreed Framework as well as the effort to negotiate an agreement to address North Korea's development of ballistic missiles.

This diplomatic process unraveled over the course of about a decade. There is no single moment separating this first period from the one to follow. As the diplomatic agreements that marked the end of the first phase were collapsing, North Korea resumed the progress toward more advanced capabilities that would begin the next phase. As diplomacy faltered, North Korea resumed its advance toward nuclear weapons by developing a uranium enrichment program to offer a second path to nuclear weapons, importing expertise and technology for ballistic missile engines that use more advanced propellants than the Scud-based missiles, and ultimately designing and testing a nuclear warhead compact enough to fit on a ballistic missile.[70] North Korea conducted nuclear tests in 2006 and 2009. These capabilities allowed North Korea to move from a latent to what might be called a rudimentary and small but operational force of missile-deliverable nuclear warheads. This period concluded with another series of diplomatic efforts by the Bush and Obama administrations. Both sought to reimpose a freeze on North Korea's nuclear capabilities and its development of ballistic missiles. Although both agreements—2007 Six Party Talks and 2012 Leap Day Deal—were presented as steps toward the elimination of North Korea's nuclear programs, each agreement was in practice a partial freeze that left in place North Korea's progress from latency to a what might be called a rudimentary deterrent.

As in the case of the transition from the latency to a rudimentary deterrent, there is no single moment when diplomacy failed, and North Korea resumed its nuclear programs. The collapse of the Six Party and Leap Day agreements were each followed, in about a year's time, with North Korea's second and third nuclear tests, respectively. During this period, North Korea worked to significantly improve its nuclear weapons designs, developing a more reliable compact design as well as a thermonuclear weapon. These designs made more efficient use of North Korea's growing stockpile of plutonium and HEU. North Korea advanced to a third engine design for its ballistic missiles, importing a Soviet-era liquid propellant engine that finally allowed Pyongyang to develop a credible ICBM that could threaten the United States. Although these capabilities are modest by the standards of other nuclear powers, by 2017 North Korea had a small arsenal of nuclear and thermonuclear weapons that could credibly threaten US forces in South Korea and Japan, as well as targets in the United States. As in the preceding periods, North Korea again froze aspects of its program while opening negotiations with the Trump administration, including summits in Singapore,

---

70. See Jonathan D. Pollack, *No Exit: North Korea, Nuclear Weapons, and International Security* (London: International Institute for Strategic Studies, 2011).

Hanoi, and Panmunjom.[71] What North Korea offered was, again, a freeze in its capabilities; although continuing the pattern of past agreements, the freeze was even less comprehensive than its predecessors. North Korea committed to ending the testing of nuclear weapons and ICBMs and offered to close its plutonium and uranium production facilities at the Yongbyon complex, but it continued to produce fissile material for nuclear weapons and to develop its missile capabilities.

As in the case of all the preceding periods, the new era in North Korea's nuclear program is emerging as the old era's diplomatic denouement unravels. It is unclear what the new era will bring, although Kim Jong Un has promised it will be "shocking."[72]

The Path to Latency and the 1994 Agreed Framework

North Korea's interest in ballistic missiles and nuclear weapons most likely dates to 1965; although this interest appears to have entered a much more serious phase in the mid-1970s. At that time, South Korea had a program to seek a nuclear weapons capability, including an attempted purchase of a nuclear reactor and a program to develop ballistic missiles. Archives from former Warsaw Pact states reveal North Korean officials expressing interest in acquiring similar capabilities and focusing on South Korea's programs. One North Korean official even asserted, not convincingly, that North Korea had already developed missiles and nuclear weapons.[73]

Kim Il Sung's efforts to acquire these capabilities from North Korea's traditional patrons, the Soviet Union and China, were initially unsuccessful. Archival documents from former Warsaw Pact states show that North Korean officials repeatedly asked the Soviet Union to provide a research reactor—a request that was repeatedly denied.[74] One 1976 meeting seems to

---

71. Ankit Panda, *Kim Jong Un and the Bomb: Survival and Deterrence in North Korea* (New York: Oxford University Press, 2020), 253–283.

72. A state media summary of Kim Jong Un's remarks at a December 2019 Workers' Party of Korea meeting included the following account: "He said that we will never allow the impudent US to abuse the DPRK-US dialogue for meeting its sordid aim but will shift to a shocking actual action to make it pay for the pains sustained by our people so far and for the development so far restrained." See "Report of the Fifth Plenary Meeting of the 7th Central Committee of the WPK (Kim Jong Un's 2020 New Year Address)," NCNK, January 2, 2020, https://www.ncnk.org/resources/publications/kju_2020_new_years_plenum_report.pdf/file_view.

73. *Memorandum, Hungarian Foreign Ministry*, February 16, 1976, https://digitalarchive.wilsoncenter.org/document/111471.

74. *Report, Embassy Of Hungary In North Korea To The Hungarian Foreign Ministry*, December 8, 1976, https://digitalarchive.wilsoncenter.org/document/110125. The Soviet Union had supplied North Korea with a small IRT reactor and provided some training and assistance to North Korean scientists. But on the issue of a larger research reactor that could

have been especially heated.[75] The Soviet Union supplied North Korea with FROG artillery rockets and Styx cruise missiles; however, Moscow appears to have refused to supply Scud missiles that might form the basis of a nuclear force. An effort to codevelop a ballistic missile with China also fell through.[76]

The result was that North Korea acquired these technologies from outside the traditional patron channels. North Korea ultimately acquired a pair of Scud missiles from Egypt. Egypt had lost the Soviet Union as a supplier of military equipment after the Camp David Accords. The two countries appear to have worked out a barter arrangement, in which North Korea would reverse engineer the missiles and then aid Egypt in maintaining and producing them. The origin of the gas-graphite reactor at Yongbyon is murkier. It is evidently a gas-graphite reactor modeled on the British Calder Hall design. The UK sold Calder Hall-type reactors to Italy and Japan. The Yongbyon reactors bear a much closer resemblance to the gas-graphite reactor at Tokai-mura in Japan than it does to the Italian reactor at Latina or the parent designs in the UK. Analysts usually observe that the information about such reactors was easily found in the open literature.[77] Much of that literature was available in Japanese publications. North Korea has long used sympathetic Korean residents living in Japan as a source of technology.

These two capabilities—a gas-graphite reactor at Yongbyon and a series of *Scud*-based ballistic missiles—were the capabilities around which North Korea built its early nuclear weapons program and that ultimately drove the nuclear crisis during the Clinton administration, which negotiated the 1994 Agreed Framework to freeze North Korea's plutonium production infrastructure and sought, unsuccessfully, an agreement to resolve issues arising from North Korea's ballistic missile program. In the early 1990s, North Korea's domestic and international situation deteriorated rapidly. The collapse of the Soviet Union damaged the North Korean economy and left Pyongyang exposed to international pressure. North Korea had in place a latent deterrent—the basic elements of a nuclear weapons capability, but it had not yet rendered those elements into an operational force. North Korea

---

produce amounts of plutonium significant enough for a nuclear weapon, the Soviet Union repeatedly declined the request. Eventually, in 1985, the Soviet Union would agree to supply a reactor, but this was after North Korea had constructed the research reactor at Yongbyon. The Soviet reactor was not supplied.

75. *Report, Embassy of Hungary in North Korea to the Hungarian Foreign Ministry*, April 15, 1976, https://digitalarchive.wilsoncenter.org/document/111473.

76. John Wilson Lewis and Hua Di, "China's Ballistic Missile Programs: Technologies, Strategies, Goals," *International Security* 17, no. 2 (Fall 1992): 5–40.

77. Joshua Pollack, "Why Does North Korea Have A Gas-Graphite Reactor?" *ArmsControlWonk.com* (blog), October 16, 2009, https://www.armscontrolwonk.com/archive/502504/why-does-north-korea-have-a-gas-graphite-reactor/.

possessed around six kilograms of plutonium—enough, according to US estimates, for "one, possibly two" nuclear weapons.[78] There was a joke at the time, making the rounds of the Pentagon, that captured North Korea's vulnerability: "What would you do if North Korea tested a nuclear weapon? Tell them to test the other one."

Former intelligence analysts have noted that there was a hardening of views inside the US intelligence community about North Korea's determination to develop nuclear weapons around 1991.[79] There had been substantial evidence prior to 1991 that North Korea was seeking nuclear weapons, such as implosion experiments at Yongbyon. It is not clear what changed, but it is possible that North Korea's reaction to the collapse of the Soviet Union may have had a profound effect. North Korea's foreign minister reported that the loss of the protection provided by Moscow compelled North Korea to seek nuclear weapons.[80]

The foreign minister did not elaborate on the role that North Korean leaders saw for nuclear weapons, but two defectors later described widespread views throughout North Korea during the Kim Jong Il era.[81] One, Choi Juh-wal, explained that the purpose of North Korea's nuclear forces was to target US forces in South Korea and Japan, particularly to interdict supply lines. "On the military front, the North can deal a blow to the 40,000 US forces stationed in the South and target the US defense facilities and the Japanese defense facilities in Japan, thereby effectively destroying supply based in times of war." Choi also argued that North Korean leaders believed that the casualties in such an attack would cause the United States to stop an invasion. "If a war breaks out in the Korean Peninsula, the North's main

---

78. See Central Intelligence Agency, Unclassified document provided to Congress (2002). The U.S. Joint Atomic Energy Intelligence Committee had assessed that in a worst-case scenario, North Korea might have as many as 8.3–8.5 kilograms of plutonium. David Albright and Kevin O'Neill, eds., *Solving the North Korean Nuclear Puzzle* (Institute for Science and International Security, 2000), 93–96. This served as the basis for the assessment that North Korea had "one, possibly two" nuclear weapons. How much fissile material a first North Korea nuclear weapon would require is, of course, based on a technical judgment. The US "Fat Man" device had six kilograms of plutonium. Kim Il Do, a defector, claimed that North Korea's first nuclear weapon used only four kilograms of plutonium. According to the North Koreans, the amount was two kilograms.

79. Torrey Froscher, "North Korea's Nuclear Program: The Early Days, 1984–2002," *Studies in Intelligence* 63, no. 4 (Extracts, December 2019): 17–32.

80. In February 1991, Kim Yong-ham, at the time the DPRK foreign minister, told Tanzanian officials that "Now that the U.S.S.R. no longer provided security, the D.P.RK. was going ahead with a program to acquire its own nuclear weapons." "North Korean Nuclear Potential," State Department Cable, March 11, 1991, https://totalwonkerr.net/wp-content/uploads/2020/05/North_Korean_Nuclear_Potential.pdf.

81. "North Korean Missile Proliferation," Hearing before the Subcommittee on International Security, Proliferation, and Federal Services of the Committee on Governmental Affairs, United States Senate, S. Hrg. 105-241 (October 21, 1997), https://www.govinfo.gov/content/pkg/CHRG-105shrg44649/pdf/CHRG-105shrg44649.pdf.

target will be the US forces based in the South and Japan. That is the reason why the North has been working furiously on its missile programs. Kim Jong Il believes that if North Korea creates more than 20,000 American casualties in the region, the US will roll back and the North Korea will win the war." Young-Hwan Ko, a former North Korean diplomat who also testified at the same hearing, claimed that such views were widely shared inside the North Korean government.[82]

Still, North Korea agreed, in 1994, to the Agreed Framework under which it froze operations at Yongbyon and suspended construction at two larger reactors based on the same design in exchange for the promise of improved relations with the United States. Although this agreement held out the eventual possibility of eliminating the plutonium that North Korea was suspected of having separated covertly, it was a forward-looking document that was designed to freeze North Korea's production of plutonium. Almost immediately, the agreement—which also called for the United States and its partners in South Korea and Japan to provide fuel assistance and to construct a pair of relatively proliferation-resistant light-water reactors—ran into severe political opposition within the United States. The Clinton administration attempted to preserve the Agreed Framework by negotiating a series of supplemental agreements. Allegations that North Korea was constructing a covert reactor underground, which proved false, resulted in an inspection by US experts. North Korea's development, and export, of ballistic missiles led the Clinton administration to attempt to negotiate an agreement limiting North Korea's ballistic missiles. Like the Agreed Framework, the prospective agreement held out the possibility of addressing missiles produced in the past but was fundamentally a forward-looking effort to freeze production and export.

While the Agreed Framework faltered in the face of congressional opposition, North Korea opened a second route to producing nuclear weapons in this period, acquiring technology for the enrichment of uranium using gas centrifuges. North Korea imported sample centrifuges from Pakistan, critical components from several countries, and began constructing a series of facilities, including a covert enrichment site near Kangson.[83] At the same time, North Korea was attempting to shift its missile program from Scud-based missiles, which use relatively poor propellants, to a new generation of missiles that use a more energetic propellant combination. North Korea did this, in large part, by importing technology and expertise from post-Soviet Russia.[84]

---

82. "North Korean Missile Proliferation."
83. Ankit Panda, "Exclusive: Revealing Kangson, North Korea's First Covert Uranium Enrichment Site," July 13, 2018, https://thediplomat.com/2018/07/exclusive-revealing-kangson-north-koreas-first-covert-uranium-enrichment-site/.
84. Panda, *Kim Jong Un and the Bomb*, 157.

CHAPTER 5

THE PATH TO RUDIMENTARY DETERRENCE AND THE 2007 SIX PARTY AGREEMENT

As the Clinton administration's diplomatic efforts collapsed, North Korea embarked on a path toward a rudimentary deterrent. The Bush administration formally abandoned the agreement after intelligence came to light, indicating that North Korea had begun to import large numbers of aluminum tubes suitable for the centrifuge program that we now know existed.

North Korea was now free to complete its withdrawal from the 1970 Nuclear Nonproliferation Treaty, which it effectuated in early 2003, and harvest the kilograms of plutonium that had been canned under the Agreed Framework. North Korea appears to have converted some amount of the material into a small number of nuclear weapons.

North Korea also appears to have made a relatively surprising decision—the device that North Korea constructed was reportedly 1,000 kilograms—compact enough to arm a ballistic missile. North Korea later released an image that appears to show Kim Jong Il posing with such a device. US intelligence assessments have consistently argued that a compact device constructed without prior testing is likely to produce a disappointing yield. A disappointing yield was, in fact, the result when North Korea tested a nuclear weapon for the first time in October 2006. The device exploded, but its yield was low, probably less than two kilotons.

Why did North Korea choose a technically risky path? The failure of the test surprised many analysts. It seems that North Korea was particularly sensitive to the international cost of testing relative to the technical gain. In some ways, this decision is not unusual for states that acquired nuclear weapons after the 1964 Chinese nuclear explosion. Though the first five nuclear powers all tested large "Fat Man" style implosion devices, none of the subsequent states to build nuclear weapons have done so. Rabinowitz has documented the role of US bargaining in constraining testing in second-wave nuclear states—Israel, South Africa, and Pakistan.[85] Rabinowitz argues that the United States chose to turn a blind eye to the existence of these programs provided that they did not conduct tests. Although we continue to use the term "tests" to describe these nuclear explosions, new nuclear states regarded them instead as more of a demonstration.

North Korean leaders acted as though this is how they, too, saw nuclear explosions. Kim Jong Il may well have believed that he could continue to develop nuclear weapons as Israel, South Africa, and Pakistan all did as long as he refrained from conducting nuclear explosions. This probably reflected both conversations with Chinese officials, as well as how North Korean of-

---

85. Or Rabinowitz, *Bargaining on Nuclear Tests: Washington and Its Cold War Deals* (New York: Oxford University Press, 2014).

ficials interpreted US positions in negotiations. North Korean leaders, at least initially, seem to have concluded that they could develop and deploy certain nuclear-armed ballistic missiles, while minimizing external pressure by refraining from tests or demonstrations.

The decision to conduct a nuclear explosion in 2006, by contrast, appears to have been driven by the conclusion that the situation with the United States was trending in an unfavorable direction with the collapse of the Agreed Framework. For Michishita, the nuclear test in 2006 was a military part of a military-diplomatic campaign to return the United States to negotiations, one outcome of which was that the Bush administration would eventually remove North Korea from the list of state sponsors of terror. North Korean leaders also saw the test as a means to strengthen deterrence by demonstrating resolve.

This pattern is also evident in North Korea's testing of ballistic missiles. As part of the Clinton-era diplomacy, North Korea had accepted a moratorium on the launches of long-range missiles "of any kind" after its test of a space launch vehicle in August 1998. This moratorium lasted until July 2006. During this period, North Korea developed a new intermediate-range ballistic missile—the Musudan—based on the Soviet SS-N-6. The missile was first spotted by the US intelligence community in satellite images in 2003. North Korea even sold a 2,500 kilometer-range variant of the missile to Iran in 2005. US and South Korean officials increasingly began describing the missile as deployed beginning in 2007. North Korea still had not, at this point, tested this system. Despite the absence of any flight tests, North Korea developed two road-mobile ICBMs that used a pair of Musudan/SS-N-6 engines clustered in a first stage. As with North Korea's first nuclear weapon, when North Korea finally did test the Musudan in 2016, the first four tests failed.

There is further evidence that North Korea was sensitive to the international costs. North Korea's tests of missiles in the 2000s correlated strongly with nuclear explosions. North Korea conducted missile tests on only two occasions between August 1998 and February 2014—July 2006 and July 2009. North Korea's first and second nuclear tests also occurred in those years. There is no technical reasons for these events to be correlated. North Korea tested missiles in periods when it was also prepared to pay a relatively high cost, in terms of political isolation, for testing a nuclear weapon. It was not willing to do so on the more frequent basis necessary to sustain a technically driven testing program.

At the same time, North Korea was not willing to forgo the development of new capabilities, including a missile-deliverable warhead and a new generation of an intermediate-range ballistic missile. With tests held back for purposes of political demonstration, North Korea operationalized an unreliable nuclear deterrent. At this stage, North Korea's concept of enough appears to emphasize the fact of certain capabilities but places relatively little weight on the reliability of those capabilities. This choice is curious from the

CHAPTER 5

perspective of deterrence literature. The problem of preventive war has long been a significant concern among scholars who believe that the spread of nuclear weapons will be destabilizing. As a state approaches the nuclear threshold, calls for preventive war should increase, particularly among military leaders. There is ample evidence, for example, that some military leaders in the United States pushed for preventive action against the Soviet Union in the early 1950s and, later, against China.

A state that tests a nuclear weapon that fails should face the most severe threat of preventive war, having made an unambiguous declaration of its intent to acquire a balance-altering nuclear capability as well as an admission that the capability is just out of reach. North Korea's test of a Scud-based long-range missile capable of reaching parts of the United States, the Taepodong-2, failed in 2006. And its subsequent test of a nuclear weapon also failed. North Korea would seem to have been in a tough spot, given the relative power of the United States and South Korea. Yet no invasion occurred. The Bush administration in 2006 was mired in unpopular wars in Iraq and Afghanistan, while also managing a nuclear crisis with Iran. And South Korea, a necessary partner in any invasion, was led by Roh Moo-hyun, who had a strong political preference for diplomacy. There was little appetite for disarming North Korea.

There is another aspect, however: the effect of North Korea's latent deterrent. There does not seem to be much indication that Bush administration officials seriously discussed a preventive war in 2006. But this may be because the Bush administration had already "baked in" the assumption that North Korea's latent deterrent was, in important ways, a real one. And that may explain the decision to allow North Korea's capabilities to grow. This is evident in how individuals within the Bush administration framed the decision to withdraw from the Agreed Framework, even as they were invading Iraq for attempting to acquire precisely the same capability. When asked directly about North Korea's effort to recover the plutonium from the spent fuel, the then-secretary of state Colin Powell argued that North Korea was already a nuclear power. "What are they going to do with another two or three nuclear weapons?" Powell asked rhetorically on *Meet the Press*, "We now believe they have a couple of nuclear weapons and have had them for years."[86] More hawkish members of the Bush administration made a similar argument, though in favor of a different policy approach. John Bolton recalls arguing that "Since we judged the North had already reprocessed enough plutonium to make several weapons even before all this news, I didn't see that even the 'worst case reaction' as [Assistant Secretary of State James] Kelly called it, would make the slightest difference."[87] An implicit

---

86. Colin L. Powell, interview on NBC's *Meet the Press* with Tim Russert, December 29, 2002.
87. John Bolton, *Surrender Is Not an Option: Defending America at the United Nations and Abroad* (New York: Simon & Schuster, 2007), 115. Bolton misstates the intelligence assess-

notion of what it means to have nuclear weapons is doing an enormous amount of lifting in both of these dismissals. This implicit notion is also at odds with the specific technical understanding of the requirements for possessing a reliable operational force.

The result was that this period, like the previous, ended with diplomacy. After the missile launch and nuclear explosion in 2006, North Korea participated in a new diplomatic forum, the Six Party Talks, and agreed to a much weaker set of limitations that required the temporary disablement of its declared facilities for producing plutonium. That agreement was envisioned as a step toward a more ambitious resolution; however, it ultimately foundered over concerns relating to verification and collapsed in 2009 as North Korea greeted the incoming Obama administration with a second nuclear test and another space launch.

The second phase of North Korea's nuclear program dragged on for several more years during the Obama administration, which largely replicated the approach of the Bush administration, with similar results. After a long period of refusal to engage with North Korea—a period described as "strategic patience"—the United States and North Korea reached something called the Leap Day Deal in 2012.[88] This largely replicated the pattern of previous agreements, offering another freeze in North Korean nuclear capabilities in exchange for an easing of sanctions. Rather than an agreement in a formal sense, the deal was codified in a pair of unilateral statements. The differences between the two statements were immediately obvious, as the North Korean statement reserved the right to conduct space launches—something North Korea did a few weeks later. With the Leap Day Deal dead, North Korea conducted another nuclear explosion in 2013.

THE PATH TO MINIMUM DETERRENCE AND THE 2018 SINGAPORE SUMMIT

North Korea moved into the next phase of its nuclear development before the existing diplomatic process had completely ended. North Korea's ambitions were growing. As early as 2010, there were suggestions in North Korean statements that the country ultimately sought a thermonuclear weapon, and the ability to deliver it against the United States. In 2012 North Korea displayed the first of two mockups of a road-mobile ICBM that used a clustered pair of engines from the then-untested Musudan missile. By 2013, the chances of a diplomatic agreement were dead. Obama administration officials had abandoned diplomacy, arguing that striking a deal with Iran should

---

ments at the time, which were that "the North has one or possibly two weapons using plutonium it produced prior to 1992."

88. "Insight: Obama's North Korean Leap of Faith Falls Short," Reuters, March 30, 2012, https://www.reuters.com/article/us-korea-north-usa-leap-idUSBRE82T06T20120330.

CHAPTER 5

take priority, believing a deal with Tehran would be the best way to restart negotiations with North Korea, while Kim Jong Un made a series of visits and announcements that highlighted the role of North Korea's strategic rocket force. Most notably, Kim announced that he had approved a plan to target locations in the United States. The announcement came with an image that showed a map of the United States, revealing four targets: Pearl Harbor, San Diego, Washington, DC, and Barksdale Air Force Base.

The target map is interesting because it represents a concept of deterrence that is strikingly consistent with one presented by two North Korean defectors in the late 1990s. Washington is an obvious target. Barksdale was where President Bush went on September 11, 2001. Although that was a spur of the moment decision, North Korea may have concluded that this was a fallback location for the US president in a conflict. These targets represent the idea that deterrence against an effort to remove Kim Jong Un would imperil the president of the United States. The other two targets—Pearl Harbor and San Diego—are where the US Pacific fleet is based. These targets represent an extension of the targeting strategy that one of the defectors outlined. "Those missiles," Choi explained, describing missiles to target South Korea and Japan, "will be used to prevent the U.S. supplies reaching the Korean Peninsula and, therefore, ensuring the complete victory for North Korea." The inclusion of Pearl Harbor and San Diego demonstrates continuity between the impression held by defectors in 1997 and the current regime.

Similarly, Kim Jong Un has also posed with maps showing targets in South Korea, Japan, and Guam. In these instances, North Korean state media has conveyed that the use of nuclear weapons against US forces in South Korea and Japan is intended to interdict invading forces and their logistics. North Korea has taken pains to go beyond possessing capabilities to presenting these capabilities as an operational force that is capable of carrying out a specific task related to a theory of victory. The notion of enough has, in one important way, changed. Yet, in another important way, the notion of enough remains similar. In 2017, North Korea developed yet another series of missiles based on a different Soviet-era engine—the RD-250. This engine, like the Scud and Musudan before it, has been imported, reverse engineered, and then used in multiple missiles—the Hwasong-12 IRBM, the Hwasong-14 ICBM, and a clustered pair in the Hwasong-15 ICBM. Yet North Korea has flight tested these missiles only a handful of times—nine times across three missiles. The Hwasong-15, with its cluster of engines, has been flight tested once. A larger version with multiple warheads, the Hwasong-17, has not been tested at all as of February 2022.

In 2017, North Korea also successfully tested a thermonuclear weapon with a yield of around 200 kilotons. Kim Jong Un posed with a mockup of the weapon to demonstrate that it was small enough to arm a ballistic missile. North Korean state media also showed a short clip of the device being placed in a test tunnel. This device was also tested once. These are extremely limited test pedigrees for a nuclear weapons capability. The United States and other nuclear powers have successfully tested nuclear weapons and ballistic missiles, only to find problems in subsequent tests. And yet Kim Jong Un declared the completion of his nuclear force, apparently closed the nuclear test site at Punggye-ri, and engaged in three summits with Donald Trump. During this time, Kim dismantled the engine test stand at Sohae and offered to close the nuclear facility at Yongbyon. But like previous diplomatic engagements, this effort, too, has collapsed.

The parties left Hanoi empty-handed, North Korea has reassembled the test stand at Sohae and resumed engine testing, and statements since by North Korean officials indicate that new capabilities will be tested in the future. In the wake of the collapse, North Korean officials have given us the clearest hint yet as to how they think about this question of enough. Repeatedly, North Korean officials described the country's offers—to refrain from nuclear and missile testing, to close certain facilities, and so on—as political gifts to President Trump. In doing so, they have come far closer to asserting that they were seeking the tacit agreement outlined by Rabinowitz: that Washington would turn a blind eye to North Korea's nuclear capabilities provided that Pyongyang did not test or otherwise brandish these capabilities.

Conclusions

The late Tom Schelling was fond of complaining that nuclear explosions were described incorrectly as "tests." In his view, they were more correctly viewed as demonstrations, conducted for political more than technical reasons. Evidence from India, Pakistan, and North Korea underscores this observation and helps fill it out. New states self-determine enoughness based primarily on political ends more than technical benchmarks. Even before operationalizing minimally credible deterrents, these states have seen latent nuclear capabilities and rudimentary deterrence as enough for the time being. The balancing act being performed is not political interests against technical ones, but rather among political interests—almost exclusively, with technical issues treated as a detail to be dealt with otherwise.

These states, as a result, often settle on what Schelling called uncertain retaliation.[89] They appear to eschew numerical metrics in favor of political judgments. In some instances, this may reflect an international political and legal environment that imposes a political cost on overt displays of capability, but in others it reflects a view that nuclear explosions, missile flight tests, and unit exercises can be used for political gain. Decision makers in these states value these political benefits and costs more than they value increased

89. Schelling, *The Strategy of Conflict*.

reliability. After all, increased reliability must itself be understood as something that contributes to fundamentally political ends.

Even before North Korea had demonstrated a minimally credible intercontinental ballistic missile capability in 2017, it viewed nuclear testing as a useful means of establishing resolve and buttressing its pursuit of political objectives vis-à-vis the United States and other states in the region. Though India and Pakistan navigated periods of uncertainty about each other's nuclear capability—especially in the 1980s, as their nuclear deterrents coalesced into their weaponized forms—perceptual gaps between actual and imagined capabilities did not alter their political objectives. In the years immediately preceding their 1998 breakouts, both India and Pakistan had calculated that their recessed nuclear weapons capabilities provided enough deterrent effects given their political objectives. Across all three countries, there is evidence that even capabilities with limited demonstration and testing were perceived by their possessors as creating significant political effects.

New nuclear states appear to have internalized the dramatic effects of nuclear weapons early on in their pursuit to develop and deploy them. They have been satisfied with even low levels of credibility, believing significant deterrent effects have begun to manifest and observing adversaries undertaking investments in their own conventional and nuclear capabilities to respond. It is in this earliest period of nuclear possession—and development—that a state's conception of what is enough is most flexible. But over time, new nuclear states acclimate themselves to the ardors of nuclear possession and face familiar struggles. India and Pakistan, for instance, now find themselves in the throes of a spiraling security dilemma, where much like the United States and the Soviet Union in the first half of the Cold War, both states continue to invest in nuclear and nonnuclear capabilities to attain advantage and assure survivability.

North Korea continues to increase the size of its nuclear arsenal while also seeking newer and better delivery systems, including tactical nuclear weapons. These contemporary dynamics suggest that as new nuclear states mature, their conception of sufficiency may shift. Although the initial satisfaction that new nuclear states may have with an uncertain retaliatory capability may seem encouraging in terms of stability, the subsequent twenty-plus-year history of nuclear possession by India, Pakistan, and North Korea suggests that, over time, new nuclear states gradually become more like the old ones. This may reflect any number of factors from the bureaucratic influence of military-industrial interests, to the falling political costs as other states adjust to the reality of a state's nuclear status, to the propensity to arms race—something evident in both the relatively symmetric India-Pakistan relationship and the considerably asymmetric US-North Korea relationship.

There are differences among new nuclear states, especially in the earliest periods of nuclear possession. These differences may not reflect a state's self-conception of nuclear enoughness so much as how their adversaries make sense of the new nuclear state's capabilities. Where examples across our three cases diverge considerably, it is likely because the adversaries are so different. In the early 2000s, voices within the Bush administration treated North Korea as having something akin to a minimum deterrent long before North Korea itself saw its capabilities in this regard. But it was precisely this perception that may have allowed Pyongyang to deploy certain capabilities with low/no testing. In crises with Pakistan in the late-1980s, India appeared to have, by contrast, underrated what later became known: that Pakistan's nuclear weaponization efforts have proceeded apace and that Islamabad likely had a fully weaponized nuclear capability by the height of the Brasstacks Crisis, when its fears of an Indian preemptive strike were heightened. This dynamic repeated itself in May 1998, when the top leadership of the Bharatiya Janata Party spoke of India's nuclear capability as if New Delhi was expecting an apparent nuclear monopoly. Those illusions were shattered later that same month when Pakistan conducted its first tests. New Delhi's apparent complacency contrasts with Pakistan's reaction to the 1974 Indian PNE, which Islamabad interpreted as highly threatening despite Indian attempts to publicly present the event as nonthreatening. It is a puzzle that decision makers in the United States, where there is a high emphasis on testing for reliability, should regard North Korea's capabilities as politically significant, while Indian decision makers did not judge Pakistan's capabilities in the same way.

These examples underscore the point that measures of arsenal size must be understood through the perception of the states themselves. And that a new nuclear state's self-perception of enoughness may have little to do with how its adversaries reason about their capabilities. This tendency is complicated by the fact that the tendency to view tests and exercises as demonstrations increases the uncertainty experienced by adversaries. New nuclear states overwhelmingly prefer opacity about their capabilities to the benefits from demonstration. This tendency persists well into their possession of a rudimentary deterrent and after. Where some clarity emerges, it tends to be in the form of doctrinal statements on nuclear weapons and other forms of overt signaling.

This situation stands in contrast to much of the academic writing about nuclear deterrence and signaling as well as how these issues are described in policy circles. Western opinions have largely reflected Wohlstetter's sense that the balance of terror is fragile and highly sensitive to changes in the technical balance of power and capabilities. The experience of new nuclear states suggests a markedly different approach, one that finds the balance of terror in the political calculations of leaders rather than in the calculations made by analysts.

CHAPTER 6

Survivability in the New Era of Counterforce

Christopher Clary

This chapter examines whether the ability of nuclear forces to survive first strikes has eroded in politically meaningful ways in the new era of counterforce. Do advances in the accuracy of nuclear and non-nuclear delivery systems combine with new capabilities in remote sensing to make "the task of securing nuclear arsenals against attack much more challenging," as Keir Lieber and Daryl Press allege?[1] Or do these changes fail to erode the foundation of nuclear deterrence, just as past technological advances failed to do?

I argue that there is a continued material basis for the nuclear revolution. The new era of counterforce, like past eras, is likely to generate sufficient hope and hype to spur significant investments and even doctrinal evolution in an attempt by conventionally superior powers to escape the nuclear revolution's strictures; nevertheless, it remains unlikely that leaders in a crisis would ever be assured of counterforce success and therefore would be unlikely to attempt a counterforce strike. The action portion of the action-reaction cycle is likely to be significant for conventionally superior powers interested in disarming strikes, whereas the reaction portion is likely to be comparatively modest because the costs of technologies and systems necessary for first strike success still remain greater at the margin than the associated costs of technologies and systems necessary for survivability. As with the advent of thermonuclear weapons, spy satellites, ballistic missiles, and multiple independently maneuverable reentry vehicles (MIRVs), the con-

---

1. Keir Lieber and Daryl Press, "The New Era of Counterforce: Technological Change and the Future of Nuclear Deterrence," *International Security* 41, no. 4 (Spring 2017): 9–49; a revised version of which appears in Lieber and Press, *The Myth of the Nuclear Revolution* (Ithaca: Cornell University Press, 2020), chap. 3.

sequence of this new technological era is likely to be arms jogging and occasional arms racing that fails to erode the foundations of nuclear deterrence, even in asymmetric nuclear relationships. The greatest danger that these new technologies might unleash nuclear cataclysm is not that they cause a first strike but rather that reactionary steps, such as increasing the size and readiness of nuclear arsenals, modestly increase the danger of nuclear accidents and terrorism.

As in other areas of nuclear competition, these effects all occur in the shadow of continued US efforts to maintain nuclear primacy.[2] US counterforce capabilities stimulate concerns in Russia, China, North Korea, and (to a considerably lesser extent) Pakistan. Their responses, in turn, have implications for India, France, and the United Kingdom. Thus, while the analysis that follows will take the nuclear dyad as the primary unit for assessment, especially the US-China dyad, each dyad is merely part of a larger cascade that starts with US moves and the countermeasures those moves engender, with effects that percolate through the entire nuclear system.[3]

This chapter proceeds in four parts. First, it briefly reviews recent scholarship questioning the ease of constructing and maintaining a survivable second-strike nuclear force. Second, it assesses survivability during the old era of counterforce to show that states often accepted prolonged periods without reliable second-strike forces that were concealed or hardened against adversary first strike. Third, it examines each of the major technologies associated with the new era of counterforce before turning to countermeasures available to targeted nuclear states. Fourth, it examines why arms racing might be rational even if deterrence is not fundamentally jeopardized by new technologies.

New Worries about Nuclear Survivability

Since at least the 1950s, there has been debate about how difficult it is for two nuclear weapons powers to deter each other. One principal line of argumentation in that debate, arguably the most important one, involved whether a nuclear weapons state could ever engage in a first strike that would eliminate the retaliatory second-strike forces of its adversary under any plausible scenario. This element contained within it a subsidiary debate about how much destruction would have to be visited on the adversary—and hence

---

2. Keir Lieber and Daryl Press, "The Rise of U.S. Nuclear Primacy," *Foreign Affairs* 85, no. 2 (2006): 42–54.
3. Michael Krepon, "Missile Defense and the Asian Cascade," in *The Impact of Missile Defenses in Southern Asia*, ed. Michael Krepon and Chris Gagné, 61–95 (Washington, DC: Henry L. Stimson Center, 2002).

how many deliverable nuclear weapons would have to survive—to deter any political impulse to strike first.[4]

In the early years after Hiroshima and Nagasaki, the predominant Western thinking on nuclear deterrence concluded that its requirements were easily obtained. Though this school of thought has been most prominently associated with Bernard Brodie or P. M. S. Blackett, the breadth of this thinking was fairly wide, encompassing dozens of prominent intellectuals. The counterview is closely associated with one individual, Albert Wohlstetter, though his views would eventually come to dominate thinking on deterrence, especially within the US government.[5] Brodie, Blackett, and others were largely unconcerned with survivability and, as a consequence, nuclear asymmetry, but Wohlstetter argued that deterrence was "precarious" and the result of a "delicate balance of terror."[6] This was a radical shift from more relaxed thinking about the requirements of deterrence. Perhaps the apotheosis of that earlier, pre-Wohlstetter view is captured in journalist Richard Rovere's argument that "If the Russians had ten thousand warheads and a missile for each, and we had ten hydrogen bombs and ten obsolete bombers . . . aggression would still be a folly that would appeal only to an insane adventurer."[7] (Rovere could not know at the time that Chinese nuclear strategy would eventually come quite close to testing his proposition.) Wohlstetter, by contrast, argued that deterrence was "neither inevitable nor impossible but the product of sustained intelligent effort, attainable only by continuing hard choice." It would require costly and complex systems that could survive a nuclear first strike or be able to launch while under attack.

This had implications for thinking about nuclear proliferation, Wohlstetter was quick to point out. "Though a wider distribution in the ownership of nuclear weapons may be inevitable, or at any rate likely, it is by no means inevitable or even very likely that the power to deter an all-out thermonuclear attack by Russia will be widespread. This is true even though a minor power would not need to guarantee as large a retaliation as we in order to deter attack on itself. Unfortunately, the minor powers have smaller re-

---

4. Secretary of Defense McNamara, for instance, favored a requirement to maintain a capacity "to destroy, after a well-planned and executed Soviet surprise attack on our Strategic Nuclear Forces, the Soviet Government and military controls, plus a large percentage of their population and economy (e.g. 30% of their population, 50% of their industrial capacity, and 150 of their cities." Quoted in Lawrence S. Kaplan et al., *History of the Office of the Secretary of Defense*, vol. 5, *The McNamara Ascendency, 1961–1965* (Washington, DC: Department of Defense, 2006), 319.

5. For an informed introduction to the debate, see Rajesh Basrur, "Nuclear Deterrence: The Wohlstetter-Blackett Debate Re-Visited," RSIS Working Paper no. 271 (April 15, 2014), https://www.rsis.edu.sg/wp-content/uploads/rsis-pubs/WP271.pdf.

6. Albert Wohlstetter, "The Delicate Balance of Terror," *Foreign Affairs* 37 (January 1959): 211–234.

7. Rovere quoted in Wohlstetter, "The Delicate Balance of Terror," 213–214.

sources as well as poorer strategic locations." As a consequence, Wohlstetter posited, "Mere membership in the nuclear club might carry with it prestige, as the applicants and nominees expect, but it will be rather expensive, and in time it will be clear that it does not necessarily confer any of the expected privileges enjoyed by the two charter members."[8] For a variety of reasons, contemporary advocates of Wohlstetter-like arguments regarding the necessity of a fairly large and diverse US nuclear arsenal also tend to be much more concerned about nuclear proliferation than Wohlstetter was.[9]

The question of whether a damage-limiting disarming strike was possible did not fully go away, but the emphasis of the debate did shift in the public discourse in the late 1970s and 1980s. One way that a first strike might limit damage was not merely through the targeting of adversary forces, but also by targeting adversary command and control networks. The resulting retaliation would be disjointed, and each successful hit on a command and control node had, at least the potential, of having multiplicative effects far greater than successfully destroying a missile silo or a bomber base. Some argued this generated dangerous first strike incentives for adversaries, though they were countered by others who argued damage-limitation strikes worked best if the partially disarmed side could negotiate de-escalation to preserve what was left of their country. Targeting command and control networks had the principal downside of killing the counterparts necessary for intra-war negotiations.[10]

More recently, revisionist scholars have called into question whether assured destruction was firmly accepted by US nuclear planners and, importantly, if US counterforce developments led to meaningful doubts within Soviet planners about the survivability of their nuclear forces. In an argument most closely associated with Brendan Rittenhouse Green and Austin Long, these revisionists argue that there was a second Cold War arms race that followed the earlier race of the 1950s and 1960s. While the first race had been a scramble to acquire assured destruction capabilities, provoked in part by Wohlstetter's intervention, this second race included investments in precise counterforce capabilities, missile defenses, and sophisticated command and control systems for nuclear warfighting.[11] They suggest that the

---

8. Wohlstetter, "The Delicate Balance of Terror," 228–229.
9. Compare Matthew Kroenig, *The Logic of American Nuclear Superiority: Why Strategic Superiority Matters* (New York: Oxford University Press, 2018) and Kroenig, *A Time to Attack: The Looming Iranian Nuclear Threat* (New York: St. Martin's Press, 2014).
10. Bradley Thayer, "The Risk of Nuclear Inadvertence: A Review Essay," *Security Studies* 3, no. 3 (1994): 428–493.
11. Brendan Rittenhouse Green, *The Revolution That Failed: Nuclear Competition, Arms Control, and the Cold War* (Cambridge: Cambridge University Press, 2020); Green and Austin Long, "The Geopolitical Origins of U.S. Hard-Target—Kill Counterforce Capabilities and MIRVs," in *The Lure and Pitfalls of MIRVs: From the First to the Second Nuclear Age*, ed. Michael Krepon, Travis Wheeler, and Shane Mason (Washington, DC: Stimson Center, May 2016),

Soviet Union rationally feared these developments and responded accordingly.[12] Others disagree and suggest the Soviet Union only minimally reacted to late Cold War developments.[13]

Green and Long's arguments are distinct from, but related closely to, a series of arguments by Keir Lieber and Daryl Press that the United States stands—or at least stood—on the verge of "attaining nuclear primacy vis-à-vis its plausible great power adversaries" and more recently that there was a broader shift toward a "new era of counterforce." Green and Long were primarily interested in late Cold War developments, whereas Lieber and Press suggest post–Cold War developments may have generated even more profound shifts. Lieber and Press identify several reasons for US primacy against other great powers, principally improving US missile defenses, increasingly accurate ballistic missile delivery systems, and in later work improvement in sensors to locate stationary and mobile nuclear forces.[14]

If this new era of counterforce endangers survivability, how different is it from earlier eras? Has survivability largely been intact, only to be eroded by new technological developments? Or might this new era echo earlier periods where second-strike nuclear forces were perhaps less secure and hence less assured than conventional wisdom might suggest?

The Historically Slow Road to Survivability

One way to consider the implications of a new era with questionable survivability is to examine what happened during earlier periods when survivability was in doubt. What if we take Lieber and Press's twin requirements of concealment or hardening as the metric to measure when states achieved survivability? How quickly did nuclear weapons powers acquire forces that could retaliate even after a first strike? Since stationary forces, however well-concealed through camouflage and operational security precautions, are likely to be exposed over time through lapses and intelligence breakthroughs, I use mobility—either via land—or sea-based systems—as a proxy for concealment. By hardening, I use vertical underground silos as the standard, though many countries experimented with horizontal "coffin" silos, or roll-

---

19–54; Long and Green, "Stalking the Secure Second Strike: Intelligence, Counterforce, and Nuclear Strategy," *Journal of Strategic Studies* 38, nos. 1–2 (2015): 38–73.

12. Green and Long, "The MAD Who Wasn't There: Soviet Reactions to the Late Cold War Nuclear Balance," *Security Studies* 26, no. 4 (2017): 606–641.

13. Pavel Podvig, "Did Star Wars Help End the Cold War? Soviet Response to the SDI Program," *Science and Global Security* 25, no. 1 (2017): 3–27.

14. Lieber and Press, "The New Era of Counterforce"; and Keir A. Lieber and Daryl G. Press, "The End of MAD? The Nuclear Dimension of U.S. Primacy," *International Security* 30, no. 4 (Spring 2006): 7–44.

out-to-launch, or elevate-to-launch silos before most transitioned to either mobile systems or launches from within underground, vertical silos. Table 6.1 lays out those milestones for all nine nuclear powers.

The superpowers initially relied on some combination of secrecy, inaccuracy, and eventually large numbers to protect their nuclear forces in the first nuclear decade. Neither the United States nor the Soviet Union shifted to serious hardening, in the form of silo-based ballistic missiles, until the early 1960s, in part because the intellectual antecedents of why they might need to do so had not been formulated. Before then both states relied either entirely on bombers or bombers supplemented with a limited number of missiles arrayed at soft, fixed, above-ground sites (readily identifiable from air or space and initially requiring cumbersome fueling procedures). Missiles at sea, difficult to detect and mobile, were deployed on a similar timetable for the superpowers, though the United States had a limited carrier-based bomber capability within a few years of having an operational nuclear device. The distances involved in the superpower competition—Moscow is 7,000 kilometers from Anchorage and 8,000 kilometers from Washington, DC—meant that the technical advances necessary for a superpower to threaten the other from homeland to homeland were daunting. Although the United States could and did forward-base nuclear assets in Europe and the Soviet Union attempted to do so in the Caribbean in 1962, such forward assets were more vulnerable to attack. They were practically easier for the other superpower to reach, they might be rendered inaccessible through political changes in the host nation, and their destruction by the adversary might "limit" a nuclear war to the soil of allies rather than the superpowers themselves.[15] Thus there was a ten- to fifteen-year window between when superpowers had operational nuclear explosive devices and when they could reliably deliver them in a second strike from their territorial homeland. In fact, concerns about the survivability of the bomber leg led the United States to maintain airborne nuclear alerts from 1958 until 1968, when a string of accidents finally convinced US policymakers that the dangers of such an alert outweighed the survivability benefits.

The next two nuclear powers—the United Kingdom and France—similarly experienced a lag in fielding survivable forces, even though they started their journeys later, meaning more intellectual and technological elements associated with building such forces were in place. Neither US ally could reliably threaten their principal Soviet adversary with nuclear weapons in the immediate aftermath of nuclear weapons acquisition. For Britain, its geographic proximity to the Soviet Union (London is approximately 2,500 kilometers from Moscow) combined with its political-military relationship

---

15. See Wohlstetter's long discussion on problems associated with forward basing in "Delicate Balance of Terror."

Table 6.1 Time to Survivable Delivery Systems

Operational milestones (vs. primary adversary's homeland)	United States (vs. USSR)	USSR/Russia (vs. United States)	United Kingdom (vs. USSR)	France (vs. USSR)	China (vs. USSR pre-1989/US post-1989)	Israel (vs. Egypt, Jordan, and Syria)	India (vs. Pakistan)	Pakistan (vs. India)	North Korea (vs. United States)
First nuclear explosive device	1945	1949	1952	1960	1964	1966	1974	1984[1]	2006
Nuclear-capable bomber	1945 (B-29)	1949 (Tu-4)	1955 (Valiant)	1964 (Mirage IV[2])	—[3]	1968 (A-4[4])	1981 (Jaguar[5])	1984[6]	—
Soft-based missile	1959 (Atlas D)	1960 (R-7A)	—	—	1975 (DF-4[7])	—	—	—	—
Silo-based missile	1963 (Titan II)	1963 (R-16U)	—	1971 (SSBS S2)	1981 (DF-5)	1972 (Jericho-I[8])	—	—	—
Land-mobile missile	—	1985 (RT-2PM)	—	—	2007 (DF-31)	1972 (Jericho-I)	1995 (Prithvi-I)	2003 (Ghauri)	2017 (Hwasong-14[9])
Sea-launched ballistic missile	1961 (Polaris)	1963 (R-21[10])	1968 (Polaris)	1971 (M1 MSBS)	2016 (JL-2[11])	1999 (Unknown Cruise Missile)	2013 (Dhanush)	—	—
Time until operational delivery system	0 years	0 years	3 years	4 years	11 years	2 years	7 years	0 years	11 years
Time until survivable-delivery system	16 years	14 years	16 years	11 years	17 years	6 years	21 years	19 years	11 years

Notes:

Nuclear capable bomber refers to both (1) a bomber able to take at least a one-way trip to principal adversary's capital or significant portion of the population and (2) a bomber-deliverable device.

Soft-based missile includes launch pads, lift-to-launch silos with liquid fueling, or rollout-to-launch with liquid fueling.

Sea-launched ballistic missile year includes both operational missile and operational submarine (i.e., first deterrent patrol).

Survivable system timeline refers to the earliest operational system that is silo-launched, land-mobile, or sea-launched, even in cases (such as SSBS S2) where the small number of silos led to serious survivability concerns or where submarines were loud and might be vulnerable (as with Soviet subs).

[1] Pakistan did not conduct overt nuclear tests until 1998 but conducted its first successful series of cold tests in 1984. Feroz Hassan Khan, *Eating Grass: The Making of the Pakistani Bomb* (Stanford: Stanford University Press, 2012), 189.

[2] With aerial refueling.

[3] China could only reach targets in the Soviet/Russian Far East with its Tu-16/H-6 bombers. It had perhaps 2 Tu-16s in 1964 and began domestic production of the H-6 in 1968.

[4] Israel agreed "not to use any aircraft supplied by the U.S. as a nuclear weapons carrier" in 1968, though many observers do not view that promise as credible in crisis. See Hans Kristensen and Robert S. Norris, "Israeli Nuclear Weapons, 2014," *Bulletin of the Atomic Scientists* 70, no. 6 (2014): 105.

[5] Kampani argues that integration with the Jaguar and Mirage-2000 took much longer than typically understood, and that India did not have a reliable air delivery capability until 1996. Narang, by contrast, argues that India could have used transport aircraft *in extremis* even earlier than the Jaguar acquisition. See Gaurav Kampani, "New Delhi's Long Nuclear Journey: How Secrecy and Institutional Roadblocks Delayed India's Weaponization," *International Security* 38, no. 4 (2014): 79–114 and Vipin Narang, *Nuclear Strategy in the Modern Era: Regional Powers and International Conflict* (Princeton: Princeton University Press, 2014), chap. 4.

[6] The initial bomb was large and could only be delivered, with questionable accuracy, by transport aircraft until Pakistan completed design and testing of a smaller weapon in 1995. Khan, *Eating Grass*, 186, 189.

[7] Some sources refer to the DF-4 as silo-based, but a late 1980s DIA document identifies the DF-4/CSS-3 silos as either "elevate to launch" or "rollout to launch." DIA, "Chinese Strategic Forces," n.d. [late 1980s?], https://www.dia.mil/FOIA/FOIA-Electronic-Reading-Room/FOIA-Reading-Room-China/FileId/39740/.

[8] There are reports of Israel silo-basing a portion of the force, though early CIA documents also discuss a "missile under mountain" concept that appears similar to some reports of Chinese basing concepts with the DF-4 and DF-5. See CIA, *Free World Sounding Rockets, Ballistic Missiles, and Satellite Launch Vehicles*, FMSAC-STIR/69-1, February 1969, https://www.cia.gov/library/readingroom/docs/DOC_0001028023.pdf.

[9] Neither the Hwasong-14 nor any other North Korean system capable of reaching most of the United States, is likely operational in the traditional sense. The US government uses the term "initial threat availability" to describe missile systems that have had a successful flight test, and hence might be available for adversary use even if they are not deployed. See Ankit Panda, *Kim Jong Un and the Bomb: Survival and Deterrence in North Korea* (New York: Oxford University Press, 2020), 207–208.

[10] The R-11FM, a modified Scud, was first operational in 1959 but had a short range (170 kilometers) with a nuclear payload. I also exclude the 600-kilometer-range R-13, which entered into service in 1961. The R-21, with a range 1,300 kilometers, was arguably not usable under most scenarios involving the US homeland. It was not until 1974, with the entry into service of the R-29, that the Soviet Navy possessed an ICBM-class SLBM.

[11] The JL-1 carrying Xia-class submarine never undertook a deterrent patrol, and the comparatively short-range Xia could not reach US targets from Chinese coastal waters. The JL-2, while longer range, also would require deep patrols by Jin-class submarines to reach US shores. A patrol appears to have taken place in 2015, though US sources are ambiguous as to whether the Jin-class submarine carried nuclear weapons. Hans Kristensen and Matt Korda, "Chinese Nuclear Forces, 2019," *Bulletin of the Atomic Scientists* 75, no. 4 (2019): 175.

CHAPTER 6

with the United States offered it a distinct path to a survivable force compared to the two superpowers. Britain tested a nuclear explosive device by 1952; however, it could not reliably deliver a nuclear weapon to the Soviet Union until it acquired a bomber with sufficient range in 1955. Britain pursued the US-origin Skybolt air-launched ballistic missile to increase the reliability of its bomber-oriented deterrent but had to shift to the US-origin Polaris submarine-launched ballistic missile (SLBM) following the Skybolt's cancellation by the Kennedy administration. Britain did not field an operational submarine with associated SLBM until 1968, or sixteen years after its first successful nuclear explosive test.

France tested its first nuclear explosive in 1960 but did not have a bomber-deliverable device until 1963 or 1964. Like the superpowers, France pursued both silo-based land missiles and submarine-launched ballistic missiles for greater survivability, with both systems operational by 1971, eleven years after France's first nuclear test. Although France's silo-based missiles were nominally "survivable," in a sense they were hardened against anything but proximate, large nuclear blasts, the realities of the Soviet arsenal meant they were in practice "very vulnerable to a first strike."[16] French planners contented with the argument that their destruction would require a sufficiently large nuclear attack to justify any retaliatory attack from remaining French nuclear forces.[17] In other words, any Soviet attack would have to be sufficiently large that it would kill large numbers of French civilians, thus eliminating any moral concerns some future French leader might have about using the residual French nuclear arsenal in a way that killed large numbers of Soviet civilians.

China conducted its first nuclear test in 1964 but faced considerably larger distances than either the United Kingdom or France to reach the territorial core of its principal adversaries, initially the United States (more than 8,000 kilometers from eastern China to the US West Coast) and subsequently the Soviet Union (approximately 3,500 kilometers from western China to Moscow). Unlike the first four nuclear powers, China did not first acquire a bomber capable of reaching the territorial heartland of its principal adversary before fielding missile systems capable of doing so. Its Soviet-origin Tu-16 and indigenous equivalent H-6 had an approximately 2,600-kilometer range, and thus could only reach Soviet cities in Siberia (such as Novosibirsk) or the Soviet Far East (Vladivostok) or the cities of US allies in Asia (such as Japan). While subsequent H-6 variants had more efficient engines and could be aerially refueled, bringing Moscow into theoretical range, China acquired longer-range, liquid-fueled missiles before it had a bomber delivery capa-

---

16. David Miller, *The Cold War: A Military History* (New York: St. Martin's Press, 1998), 143.
17. Robbin F. Laird, *France, the Soviet Union, and the Nuclear Weapons Issue* (Boulder, CO: Westview Press, 1985), 48.

bility. Even then, when the DF-4 (CSS-3) was deployed in 1975, it was acquired initially in exceptionally small numbers, and its roll-out-to-launch or elevate-to-launch basing modes combined with its liquid-fueling likely made it vulnerable to the much larger Soviet and US nuclear forces. The follow-on, longer-range DF-5 faced similar vulnerability because of its liquid fuel and exceptionally small numbers, even if it was silo-based.[18] It was not until the fielding of the mobile, solid-fuel DF-31 in the late 2000s—more than four decades after China's first nuclear test—that China arguably had a truly survivable weapon, though even then it was fielded in such small numbers that even a tiny failure of concealment might have endangered the force.

Israel, primarily concerned with nearby adversaries, was able to acquire delivery systems, especially survivable mobile missile forces, on a faster timeline than the five prior nuclear weapons states, as a consequence of both its status as a later nuclear acquirer (benefiting from two decades of post–World War II developments in missile and rocket technology) and the less daunting ranges that it needed to traverse in order to deliver weapons onto its neighboring adversaries. Shorter-range missiles are easier to design with sufficient compactness to make them mobile, and Israel fielded the Jericho-I system as early as 1972, though many sources suggest its guidance system was unreliable for some period after its nominal operational status.

India tested its initial nuclear explosive device in 1974. That device may have fizzled, was unworkably large for a weapon, and would have been of uncertain reliability irrespective of the delivery vector. Though India may have been able to deliver that device against its primary adversary, Pakistan, using transport aircraft on what would have essentially been a suicide mission for the crew, it did not acquire a fighter-bomber capable of undertaking the mission until it acquired the Jaguar in 1981 and Mirage-2000 in 1985. Gaurav Kampani argues even this timeline understates how long it took India to develop a delivery capability and argues that India did not have a proven bomb design integrated onto an air platform until 1996, though his sources seem to suggest that some sort of device might have been deliverable by a skilled pilot earlier.[19] Around that time, India's liquid-fueled short-range ballistic missile, the Prithvi-I, was operational, giving it a mobile platform for

---

18. See Director of Central Intelligence (DCI), "Communist China's Weapons Program for Strategic Attack," NIE 13-7-71, October 28, 1971, https://www.cia.gov/library/readingroom/docs/DOC_0001098170.pdf; DCI, "PRC Defense Policy and Armed Forces," National Intelligence Estimate, NIE 13-76, November 11, 1976, https://www.cia.gov/library/readingroom/docs/DOC_0001097855.pdf; Defense Intelligence Agency, "Chinese Strategic Forces," n.d. [late 1980s?], https://www.dia.mil/FOIA/FOIA-Electronic-Reading-Room/FOIA-Reading-Room-China/FileId/39740/; see also M. Taylor Fravel and Evan S. Medeiros, "China's Search for Assured Retaliation: The Evolution of Chinese Nuclear Strategy and Force Structure," *International Security* 35, no. 2 (2010): 48–67.

19. Gaurav Kampani, "New Delhi's Long Nuclear Journey: How Secrecy and Institutional Roadblocks Delayed India's Weaponization," *International Security* 38, no. 4 (2014): 79–114.

use against Pakistan, though one where the problems associated with liquid fuel would have made the system vulnerable in practice. Even this timeline, of roughly two decades between the first nuclear weapons test and survivable delivery mode, is generous in assessing Indian capabilities against Pakistan. India may not even today have a reliable, survivable delivery means to reach China's eastern cities.[20]

Unlike China and India, which had to contend with nuclear or nuclear-aspiring competitors in opposite directions, Islamabad only focused on deterring one adversary: India. Although Pakistan did not conduct overt nuclear weapons tests until May 1998, it had conducted successful "cold" tests by 1984, and by that same year could, in theory, deliver a nuclear payload to India via transport aircraft (C-130s) or fighter aircraft (Mirage-IIIs and—Vs and F-16s) already in its inventory.[21] It did not have the capability to reach New Delhi with a missile with any reliability until at least January 2003, when it formally inducted the mobile, liquid-fueled Ghauri, a derivative of the North Korean Nodong missile. Though the Ghauri had been tested in April 1998, even before Pakistan's overt nuclear tests, there are some indications those initial flight tests failed.[22] Despite its formal induction in 2003, the Ghauri's four additional flight tests between 2004 and 2006 suggest it may not have been even fully operational at that point.[23] Thus it may not have been until March 2003, with the induction of the Shaheen solid-fuel missile (itself reportedly a Chinese M-9 derivative) that Pakistan obtained a reliable missile delivery system.

South Africa's small nuclear arsenal was quite distinct from all of the others discussed above since it consisted of only six assembled weapons and seventh planned but shelved. South Africa feared proxy dangers in its neighborhood (specifically Angola) rather than direct threats from the Soviet Union and its Cuban ally, since South Africa's arsenal was apparently designed to provide a catalytic option to its leaders to encourage US intervention rather than to directly deter the Soviet Union or Cuba, and since South Africa represents arguably the only true case of nuclear reversal. South Africa had assembled weapons in 1979, though Vipin Narang observes they did not have a "truly aircraft-deliverable nuclear weapon" until 1982. South Africa's Buccaneer bombers could reach most of southern Africa, including all of Angola, but South Africa had no way to directly threaten—even on a suicide mission—Cuba or the Soviet Union. South Africa dismantled its pro-

---

20. Christopher Clary and Vipin Narang, "India's Counterforce Temptations: Strategic Dilemmas, Doctrine, and Capabilities," *International Security* 43, no. 3 (Winter 2018–2019): 7–52.

21. Feroz Hassan Khan, *Eating Grass: The Making of the Pakistani Bomb* (Stanford: Stanford University Press, 2012), 189; International Institute for Strategic Studies, *Military Balance* (London: IISS, 1984), 107.

22. "North's Missiles Tied to Musharraf Blunder," *Japan Times*, January 28, 2013.

23. Khan, *Eating Grass*, 245.

gram beginning in 1990 until that task was completed by September 1991, before it ever had an operational delivery system capable of reaching its principal adversaries. South Africa neither pursued nor developed a survivable system that could reasonably be expected to survive a surprise first strike.[24]

Although all other nine nuclear powers developed aircraft-deliverable systems—though some, such as China, may never have had the ability to reach adversary capitals with them or others, such as Israel, may have built an air-deliverable option without relying on it—all available information suggests North Korea leaped directly and solely to missiles.[25] In theory, North Korea could use some of its approximately eighty Hong-5 (Il-28) light bombers for a nuclear delivery mission, but those aircraft could at best reach US bases in South Korea and Japan—and even that is doubtful since the US Central Intelligence Agency assessed nearly five decades ago that the bombers' "relatively slow speed makes them highly vulnerable to interceptors and ground-based air defenses."[26] Though there was speculation that North Korea's first announced nuclear weapons test in 2006 fizzled with substantially less than its designed yield, North Korea's subsequent five tests beginning in 2009 appear to have succeeded. Even so, North Korea likely did not have the ability to deliver such a weapon reliably to the US homeland until 2017. By late July of that year, North Korea had tested a missile that could reach major population centers in the western United States and, by November, it had tested a missile that could reach all of the United States.[27] Whether any of these longer-range systems are truly operational remains unclear as of 2021, with re-entry vehicle technology in particular identified by US intelligence officials and outside experts as an area where North Korea may have sufficient expertise but has not yet demonstrated it.[28] North Korea has conducted launches from submarines and submerged barges in its developmental sea-launched ballistic missile program. At best, North Korea has demonstrated a 1,900-kilometer range SLBM capability, making this a questionable survivable deterrent against the US homeland given the capabilities of the Korean People's Navy.[29]

---

24. Vipin Narang, *Nuclear Strategy in the Modern Era: Regional Powers and International Conflict* (Princeton: Princeton University Press, 2014), 210; Philipp C. Bleek, *When Did (and Didn't) States Proliferate: Chronicling the Spread of Nuclear Weapons* (Cambridge, MA: Project on Managing the Atom, 2017), 14–15.

25. Hans M. Kristensen and Robert S. Norris, "North Korean Nuclear Capabilities, 2018," *Bulletin of the Atomic Scientists* 74, no. 1 (2018): 44.

26. Central Intelligence Agency, *Warsaw Pact Air Power: Forces for Use in Central Europe*, SR IR 73-22, December 1973, 15, https://www.cia.gov/library/readingroom/docs/1973-12-01b.pdf.

27. David Wright, "North Korea's Longest Missile Test Yet," November 28, 2017, https://allthingsnuclear.org/dwright/nk-longest-missile-test-yet.

28. See Kristensen and Norris, "North Korean Nuclear Capabilities, 2018."

29. Ankit Panda, "North Korea Finally Unveils the Pukguksong-3 SLBM: First Takeaways," *Diplomat*, October 3, 2019.

CHAPTER 6

To summarize, and as table 6.1 shows, the median nuclear weapons-possessing state took three years before it could field an operational delivery system (and associated deliverable weapon) following the acquisition of a functional nuclear explosive device, while the median nuclear weapons power took much longer, sixteen years, before it had a system that met the standards of hardening or mobility that we typically associate with survivability. Yet humanity survived this earlier era of questionable survivability. This may be because, as Jeffrey Lewis and Ankit Panda observe in their chapter in this volume, leaders of nuclear states often hold some view of sufficiency that only requires a nonzero chance of nuclear retaliation—far less than the 100 percent probability of retaliation under all scenarios that militaries seem to prefer.

How to think about this period and its dangers? This era does appear to be associated with some of the better known preventive war crises and nuclear threats—the Soviet Union's threat against the United Kingdom and France during the 1956 Suez Crisis, the Soviet attempt to base missiles in Cuba in 1962 (before its first silo-based missile is operational), the Soviet Union's counterproliferation musings over China in 1969 coincident with their serious border clash, and India's apparent contemplation of preventive action in 1986–1987 against Pakistan.

The 1969 Sino-Soviet crisis involved perhaps the most serious consideration of one nuclear state of a counterproliferation strike on another confirmed nuclear state. Those states had a strong, growing ideological disagreement and jockeyed for global status. They had a preexisting territorial dispute, which had resulted in a deadly clash—albeit over territory of at most modest strategic value. The Soviet Union may have feared that the Cultural Revolution presaged a period of Chinese recklessness that might include unpredictable use of its small nuclear arsenal. The stakes were incredibly high. At the same time, the nuclear asymmetry was as stark as it could be with the Soviet Union having perhaps 200 warheads for every one Chinese warhead. Moreover, China had an incredibly limited—perhaps functionally nonexistent—way to deliver those warheads, since it possessed range-restricted, slow, vulnerable bombers, and even these could only reach targets in the Soviet east rather than core cities of Moscow or Leningrad. Although the United States expressed concern about Soviet feelers of nuclear escalation against China, decision makers in Moscow might have bet that no US leader would want to invite nuclear cataclysm by protecting China from Soviet aggression. The Soviet Union's close alliance with China only a decade earlier meant that its intelligence had a unique knowledge of the location and disposition of Chinese nuclear and conventional military forces. Yet despite all this, nuclear deterrence appears to have held. Perhaps it was Soviet unwillingness to have to deal with a post-attack China, a still daunting problem given China's size and population.

Perhaps it was fear of US interference. Even fifty years later, the record is muddled.[30]

Many of these same dilemmas would exist—some much more pronouncedly—if the United States contemplated counterproliferation strikes against North Korea, the current most asymmetric dyad in the system. Already North Korea likely has a greater capacity to destroy major American cities than China did in 1969. And the stakes of any US-North Korean confrontation are almost certainly less than those that motivated the Sino-Soviet crisis. If the 1969 crisis did not go nuclear, and if that stark nuclear asymmetry did not stop the Chinese ambush that began the whole crisis, is a future crisis likely to have more dangerous dynamics?

Having successfully exited this much more transparent window of vulnerability without cataclysm, it seems perhaps improbable that comparatively less vulnerability would generate greater risk taking in the future. However, to assess that claim requires a more careful examination of what distinguishes the new era of counterforce from the nuclear past.

What Is New about the New Era of Counterforce?

If prior periods of questionable survivability did not ultimately generate dangerous crisis instability, might this new period be different? Are the underlying technological changes sufficiently different to generate a different result? This section examines those changes before concluding that while hardening's significant survivability advantages have substantially eroded, mobility still retains them, largely invalidating the political implications of the new era of counterforce.

THE DANGER TO HARDENED TARGETS

Lieber and Press argue, "Of the two key strategies that countries have employed since the start of the nuclear age to keep their arsenals safe, hardening has been negated, and concealment is under great duress."[31] They are partially correct. Hardening appears to offer less meaningful enhancements to survivability, especially against the United States. In particular, decades of US efforts at missile accuracy were recently amplified by the US rollout of compensating fuzes, first for its SLBMs and perhaps for its ground-based missiles. These compensating fuzes have "vastly increase[d] the chances that

---

30. See Lyle Goldstein, "Do Nascent WMD Arsenals Deter? The Sino-Soviet Crisis of 1969," *Political Science Quarterly* 118, no. 1 (2003): 53–80.
31. Lieber and Press, *Myth of the Nuclear Revolution*, 92.

the target will be destroyed, even though the arriving warheads have essentially the same ballistic accuracy."[32] Taking these and other developments into account even counterforce skeptics, such as Charles Glaser and Steve Fetter, conclude in their examination of the US-China nuclear competition, "Although there may be some residual uncertainty, reasonable Chinese planners would have to assume that all operational silos have been or will be identified by the United States, and that its silo-based ICBMs are vulnerable to preemptive attacks."[33]

The political effects of this technological shift are likely to be muted, however, because only three nuclear states today rely on hardening, in the form of silos, to protect even a portion of their nuclear force in peacetime, crisis, and war—the United States, Russia, and China. Among those, China was quite skeptical historically of the utility of silos given its relatively small force, and there are reports that at least some Chinese weaponeers had referred to silos as "missile tombs" as early as the 1970s.[34] The fact that China appears to be significantly expanding its silo construction suggests two possibilities.[35] First, they may seek to harden a portion of the force to serve as a secure, second strike against less capable adversaries, such as Russia or India. Second, they may seek for the silos to serve a modest tripwire or so-called sponge role.[36] Silos are and will remain difficult to destroy with purely conventional means for even the United States and may not be destroyable through conventional means by less advanced militaries. By forcing an adversary to target silos with nuclear warheads, China is able to force a counterforce aspirant to cross the nuclear threshold, making it more rational for China to respond similarly. Even for a state like the United States that may be able to target silos conventionally, doing so would require a small subset of munitions, making conventional counterforce challenging against silos if not impossible.[37] Given the difficulties of conventional counterforce, new silos—even those without nuclear-armed missiles in them—would require diverting US nuclear weapons toward their destruction and

32. Hans M. Kristensen, Matthew McKinzie, and Theodore Postol, "How US Nuclear Force Modernization Is Undermining Strategic Stability: The Burst-Height Compensating Super-Fuze," *Bulletin of the Atomic Scientists*, March 1, 2017.
33. Charles L. Glaser and Steve Fetter, "Should the United States Reject MAD? Damage Limitation and U.S. Nuclear Strategy toward China," *International Security* 41, no. 1 (2016): 63.
34. Lewis and Hua, "China's Ballistic Missile Program," 24–25.
35. Joby Warrick, "China Is Building More Than 100 New Missile Silos in Its Western Desert, Analysts Say," *Washington Post*, June 30, 2021; William Broad and David Sanger, "A 2nd New Nuclear Missile Base for China, and Many Questions about Strategy," *New York Times*, July 26, 2021.
36. David Wright et al., *Rethinking Land-Based Nuclear Missiles: Sensible Risk-Reduction Practices for US ICBMs* (Washington, DC: Union of Concerns Scientists, 2020), 17.
37. James M. Acton, "Conventional Prompt Global Strike and Russia's Nuclear Forces," *Independent Military Review*, October 4, 2013, https://carnegieendowment.org/2013/10/04/conventional-prompt-global-strike-and-russia-s-nuclear-forces-pub-53213.

away from use against potential mobile counterforce targets, on the margin increasing the survival odds for those mobile platforms.

Even so, the slow negation of hardening might endanger not just silos but also bunkers, caves, or underground storage sites where mobile launchers or warheads are stored. Here mobility and uncertainty provided the majority of the protection to such mobile systems in any event, something discussed in the next section.

THE CONTINUING DIFFICULTY OF MOBILE TARGETS

The primary strategy for concealment, the second path to survivability, is mobility. If most nuclear states rely primarily on mobility—be it in the form of submarines, ground-based mobile missiles, or dispersible aircraft—rather than hardening for survivability, the question, then, is whether that strategy is truly under "great duress." There is a tradeoff between hardening and mobility since mobile targets are difficult to harden. As a consequence, "If mobile forces are discovered, they tend to be easy to destroy."[38]

Unlike with hardening, where Lieber and Press identify a true technological shift, concealment as a survival strategy is not under great duress but rather modest strain. While finders are growing cleverer and more capable, hiders have a wide variety of tricks still available to confound them. This section offers two primary arguments in favor of concealment's continued ability to assure survivable forces. First, even if systems are "discovered," it is often necessary to have exquisite detail about their location in order for successful targeting. Knowing that a system might be in a small area may often be insufficient to find and destroy that system. Second, any process that might discover hiding mobile systems is also likely to generate so many false positives that successful targeting of true positives becomes impossible. Scholars have examined the problem of false positives in early warning systems, but they have not focused as much attention on the problem of false positives in counterforce targeting.[39] In both domains—early warning and targets—the possibility of false positives should encourage substantial caution in leaders.

The Rocky Road from Discovery to Destruction. If signals or human intelligence offers a counterforce aspirant fairly precise information about the location of a mobile system, how easy is it to go from that discovery to the actual

---

38. Lieber and Press, *Myth of the Nuclear Revolution*, 69.
39. Lora Saalman, "Fear of False Negatives: AI and China's Nuclear Posture," *Bulletin of the Atomic Scientists*, April 24, 2018, https://thebulletin.org/2018/04/fear-of-false-negatives-ai-and-chinas-nuclear-posture/; Michael C. Horowitz, Paul Scharre, and Alexander Velez-Green, "A Stable Nuclear Future? The Impact of Autonomous Systems and Artificial Intelligence," working paper, December 2019, https://arxiv.org/pdf/1912.05291.pdf.

CHAPTER 6

destruction of the mobile system? It is more difficult than it might first appear. As an analogy to explicate that difficulty, we might examine past US success against mobile targets whose location was established within a very small area. In the aftermath of the 1991 Gulf War, the Defense Science Board estimated that locating a system within an area of two square kilometers would be sufficient to offer a veteran F-15E crew a "pretty good chance" of finding a mobile target.[40] Nevertheless, that estimate itself likely was overly optimistic, despite being ostensibly based on the 1991 experience. In fact, exercises prior to the 1991 Gulf War (Touted Gleem) demonstrated that US aircrews could not successfully target a mobile launcher even when they were given the precise coordinates of the target. Moreover, during the 1991 war US aircrews visually observed forty-two Scud launches, in only eight of them was any target attacked; and it is possible if not probable that none of those eight attacks was successful.[41] Discovery is harder than it first appears.

In 2001, the RAND Corporation considered the problem of countering mobile Chinese conventional ballistic missiles. Here the danger of repeated launches motivated their thought exercise, so an initial launch might serve as the intelligence input that then could prompt an aircraft to attempt to locate and destroy the launcher. This exact scenario is less salient in the case of a nuclear-tipped missile, though multiple nuclear-armed missiles per launcher are still at least a theoretical possibility. Instead, the 2001 RAND thought exercise—where the heat signature and plume associated with a missile launch is the intelligence input—offers a useful analogy to think about the problems associated with aircraft tasking following any reasonably precise and timely location information being available to a potential counterforce attacker.

Consistent with the RAND analysis, we might assume that under best case conditions, it would take one minute from locating the transporter erector launcher (TEL) precisely to transmit a potential launch location to forward-deployed aircraft. In the RAND analysis, this input comes from the missile launch itself, but we could also imagine satellites, ground sensors, spies, or drones providing the information, with varying lag times for each. We might further assume that a transporter-erector-launcher crew requires five minutes to tear down following launch and move out or hide. Here, too, the analogy is about the length of time the TEL is stationary, and less important the precise reasons that it is so. In the RAND analogy, the target was stationary for four minutes after the aircraft learned of its location. How much area can an attack aircraft cover in four minutes? At 0.8 Mach, an aircraft can go almost sixty kilometers in four minutes, meaning that each

40. Thomas A. Keaney and Eliot A. Cohen, *Gulf War Air Power Survey*, vol. 2, *Operations and Effects and Effectiveness* (Washington, DC: GPO, 1993), 336n159.
41. Keaney and Cohen, *Gulf War Air Power Survey*, 2:335–336.

aircraft can patrol a circular area of 11,000 square kilometers. Depending on transit times from bases to patrol areas, it might take four aircraft to maintain continuous air patrols by just one aircraft. Thus to patrol an area the size of North Korea to hunt TELs immediately post-launch (or some similar time-sensitive input), it might require eleven aircraft on patrol and thirty-three in transit or on the ground, certainly doable for something like a US-North Korea confrontation. For more challenging targets, such as US-China or India-Pakistan contingencies, the ratios quickly become unworkable. RAND's 2001 analysis calculated several hundred US aircraft would be required to search for ballistic and cruise missile launchers in China that could reach US bases calculated using the range of fielded systems at that time—the search area would be larger now since more longer-range Chinese systems are now online. Alternatively, given Pakistan's large size, it might require eighty aircraft to be on continuous patrol, with an additional 240 on the ground or in transit for a similar Indian mission, or nearly half of India's ground attack aircraft. In practice, given the long flight times to southwestern Pakistan, and India's small tanker fleet, such a mission would likely exceed Indian capabilities even if the opportunity cost for other missions were ignored. In addition, all of these analyses would require a permissive threat environment, something that would require the defeat of counterair aircraft and surface-to-air missile systems, something that would likely take weeks to achieve in US-China scenarios and many days in US-North Korea or India-Pakistan scenarios, during which TELs could operate in relative safety.[42] The point of this analysis is to show how difficult it is to actually destroy a mobile target if it remains mobile even if exquisitely detailed intelligence about its location is obtained.

Too Many False Positives. Given these difficulties, RAND proposed an alternative operational concept to discover and destroy mobile targets—one that would require a series of weapons still in development. Extending their analysis for this operational concept helps elucidate how daunting the problem of false positives is today and is likely to remain.

The first stage of RAND's operational concept was space- or UAV-based radars that could serve as ground moving target indicators (GMTI). Post-launch (or some similarly precise input) such sensors could then look for moving targets near the estimated launch coordinates. Both the GMTI and post-launch queuing rely on well-established technologies. But RAND further assumed that automatic target recognition (ATR) algorithms will work with a high rate of success at identifying TELs among all potential moving vehicles—they posit an 80 percent chance of correctly identifying a moving

---

42. Alan J. Vick et al., *Aerospace Operations Against Elusive Ground Targets* (Santa Monica, CA: RAND Corporation, 2001), 65–66.

CHAPTER 6

TEL (true positive), a 20 percent chance of incorrectly identifying a moving truck as a TEL (false positive), and a 5 percent chance of identifying a moving car as a TEL (false positive). It is difficult to know whether these ATR assumptions are plausible given contemporary imaging and processing capabilities, but they seem useful as a notional baseline.

These reasonably charitable assumptions yield an incredible number of false positives—with TELs vastly outnumbered by non-TELs. It is important to get a sense of the scale of false positives to understand why it is not possible to target "everything that moves" even if there is a substantial ATR screen to try to find TELs. Taking RAND's 2001 assumptions about China as a baseline, they offer 40 percent of trucks and 20 percent of cars operate in rural areas while 100 percent of TELs do. They further propose that 50 percent of the time trucks are moving in rural areas while 20 percent of the time cars are moving and only 10 percent of TELs do so. Assuming 100 TELs and plugging in 2018 data for Chinese vehicle registration data generates 1,113,600 cars falsely identified as TELs, 331,200 trucks or buses falsely identified as TELs, and 8 of 10 moving TELs (with another 90 TELs stationary in this example) correctly identified as TELs. In other words, there are approximately 180,000 non-TEL targets identified for every TEL. The scale of China's vehicle inventory means that better identification does not quickly resolve this problem of vastly more false positives. Even assuming trucks and cars are only falsely identified as TELs 1 time in 10,000 (0.01%) still generates something on the order of 100 false positives to every true positive. This process would be more tractable (though perhaps still impossibly difficult) against a country like North Korea with comparatively fewer vehicles, with countries like Pakistan in between on the feasibility spectrum. (Pakistan in 2015 had approximately 2.7 million cars on the road and 500,000 trucks or buses.)

To curtail the number of false positives RAND further conceptualized that each potential target is imaged by a robust constellation of synthetic aperture radar (SAR) and inverse synthetic aperture radar (ISAR) sensors. They assume imaging a single moving target on a smooth road takes about 0.33 seconds, but note that vehicles traveling on rough roads often creates difficulty for ISAR imaging, prolonging the time to collect the image and perhaps making it impossible. Even setting aside the issue of rough roads, though, imaging all potential targets assuming a persistent set of SAR-ISAR sensors could take many minutes. Using their 80/20/5 percent assumption, generates 1.5 million potential targets, which would take 135 hours to image. Again, the large number of false positives means this problem does not quickly become more tractable even if the time decreases that it takes to image any individual targets to something quite small, like 1/10th or 1/100thof a second. More sensors able to work in parallel rather than the series assumed in these calculations do not radically alter the basic problem.

Note that Lieber and Press essentially do not consider this problem. They note that space-based SAR "can produce high-resolution images of stationary TELs and enough resolution of moving vehicles to determine that a target is 'truck-sized," which they then argue might be "sufficient for a strike" especially given the stakes involved.[43] This seems to reduce the problem to one of rules of engagement or the laws of armed conflict. Although those ethical issues are substantial given the scope of false positives, even if one were entirely unconcerned with civilian truckers being killed in the thousands the challenge of false positives is so severe as to make the search and destruction of mobile targets infeasible.

Mobile TELs will likely be accompanied in close proximity by other vehicles, to provide security, supplies, fuel, and command and control. This constellation of vehicles may generate a more unique signature that yields fewer false positives. Awareness of this problem likely will yield pressures on the potential target state to attempt to reduce these signatures, though many of the easiest solutions to that problem might rely on additional communications between vehicles in a missile launch unit, potentially creating signal emissions that might ease targeting through other intelligence means. Even so, as anyone who has passed a truck carrying an oversized load on the highway can attest, multivehicle convoys surrounding a large vehicle are not so rare in daily life. In addition, the presumably large number of military units moving around the country during any real-life crisis or war may additionally generate false positives quite difficult for even a very capable searcher to disqualify. Any overreliance on convoys and vehicle constellations for targeting decisions in turn means that isolated vehicles have a greater chance of survival, perhaps incentivizing states toward a mixed deployment strategy.

Assuming some manageable number of targets is identified, RAND then posits that a hypersonic vehicle can be used to launch a number of Man-in-the-Loop, Variable-Autonomy, Anti-Armor Weapons (MILVAW) to attack those targets that persist past the screening process. Again, both the hypersonic vehicle and the MILVAW are hypothetical or at best early developmental systems.[44] Even this would require many sorties since most of the MILVAWs would be expended on false positives even in the very best-case scenarios.

Much of the above discussion focuses on false positives generated from moving targets, but the potential for false positives from static targets is also present, and something that adversaries may consciously exploit through the use of decoys. There is an extensive debate about the efficacy of Serbian decoys during Operation Allied Force in 1999; yet it is apparent that the

---

43. Lieber and Press, *Myth of the Nuclear Revolution*, 87, 155n72.
44. Steve Trimble, "U.S. Army Flickr Page Inadvertently Reveals Hypersonic Weapon Concept," *Aviation Week and Space Technology*, June 7, 2020, https://aviationweek.com/defense-space/sensors-electronic-warfare/us-army-flickr-page-inadvertently-reveals-new-hypersonic.

NATO initial battle damage assessment of having destroyed 150 Serbian tanks had to be revised down to 110 and eventually 93.[45] Credible NATO military sources say the true number may have been an order of magnitude lower still, with one former NATO staff officer assessing the true figure may have been as low as twelve tanks.[46] The difference between destroying 150 nuclear delivery vehicles and 110 delivery vehicles may be the difference between a splendid first strike and a decent damage-limiting one. The difference between destroying 150 delivery vehicles and only twelve would be cataclysmic for any counterforce aspirant.

An Unfair Race between Hiders and Finders. Lieber and Press argue that in this game of hiders and finders, the latter have one great advantage—namely, counterforce aspirants typically are the stronger and better resourced in a nuclear dyad, since weaker nuclear states typically expend effort on maintaining arsenal survivability rather than denying it to their foes.[47] This is true, though arguably the relative resource advantage was more pronounced for the combined forces of NATO against tiny Serbia in 1999 than it is for any current nuclear state with any of its nuclear rivals. Moreover, the concealment, camouflage, and decoy (CCD) technology necessary to defeat sensors is often much, much less expensive than the sensor technology needed to defeat CCD. Serbia used the insides of tetrapak milk cartons (reduce, reuse, recycle) to create radar signatures and sun-heated water receptacles to generate heat signatures for its decoys.[48] Advances in hyperspectral imaging may make it possible to defeat decoys, but this also produces strains on the overall network of sensors—perhaps requiring a SAR platform to then cue a hyperspectral imagery platform that can then report back to a munitions carrying platform, all amidst a very serious crisis or war.[49]

Moreover, CCD tactics do not begin or end with decoys. Even something as simple as building multiple covered shelters for a launch system would multiply the number of targets that would need to be destroyed in order to have confidence in attack success. The United States considered fairly elaborate "multiple protective shelter" schemes for the MX missile, including elaborate operational procedures to "preserve location uncertainty" of the true missile that involved missile decoys.[50] John Wilson Lewis and Hua Di

---

45. Benjamin Lambeth, *NATO's Air War for Kosovo: A Strategic and Operational Assessment* (Santa Monica, CA: RAND Corporation, 2001), 130–131.

46. MAJ Robert H. Gregory, "Turning Point: Operation Allied Force and the Allure of Air Power" (MA thesis, Command and General Staff College, 2014), 184.

47. Lieber and Press, *Myth of the Nuclear Revolution*, 90.

48. Lambeth, *NATO's Air War for Kosovo*, 130.

49. Steven M. Bergman, "The Utility of Hyperspectral Data to Detect and Discriminate Actual and Decoy Target Vehicles" (MA thesis, Naval Postgraduate School, 1996).

50. Office of Technology Assessment, *MX Missile Basing* (Washington, DC: GPO, 1981), chap. 2.

report that China in the 1980s, apparently after studying the US schemes, "decided to build a large number of bogus silos. All the fake silos were shallow holes disguised to look like the real thing."[51] North Korea has long been suspected of having built redundant bunkers and decoy shelters for its missiles, as well as a multidecade history of producing "numerous decoy vehicles and missiles."[52]

Hiders have other tricks to conceal ground-based mobile missiles, too. Sensors aboard unmanned aerial vehicles (UAV) and satellites may face restricted lines of sight if missile launchers are deployed in mountainous terrain. Such terrain consequently decreases the number of potential sensors that might identify a mobile missile, thus increasing the time lag between sensor revisit of a particular location. In addition, to the extent that space- or UAV-based GMTIs present a major survivability challenge, they could be mitigated by the application of a low-observable (stealth) covering affixed to the vehicle that decreases radar reflection.[53] Such a stealth launcher strategy might work in concert with the false positive problem since a TEL that appears even somewhat smaller on radar (through a reduced radar cross-section) might then require more actually smaller trucks and cars to be imaged to distinguish stealth TELs from actual cars. This is just one concrete manifestation of what is likely to be a sensitivity-specificity tradeoff facing counterforce aspirants. The more sensitive they make algorithms to ensure they do not miss a true launcher, the more nonlaunchers they will find. Anything hiders do to make launchers look more like nonlaunchers, be it stealth coatings or more quotidian steps such as superficial exteriors to make a TEL look like a mobile crane or a box truck, amplifies this challenge.

For either moving or static mobile ground-based targets, then, the problem of false positives is a large one—likely a prohibitive one—for the counterforce contemplator. This problem does not go away for aircraft-delivered weapons or submarine-launched ones. In many ways, aircraft-delivered weapons present similar challenges to mobile ground targets. Aircraft have a home base that may have nuclear weapons storage on site. The loading of nuclear warheads on aircraft will likely not be visible to adversary states. Weapons may be stored underground, and aircraft can be loaded in hangars out of sight of pesky satellites.[54] In peacetime, aircraft are vulnerable at their home bases,

---

51. Lewis and Hua, "China's Ballistic Missile Programs: Technologies, Strategies, Goals," *International Security* 17, no. 2 (1992): 25.

52. International Institute for Strategic Studies, *The Conventional Military Balance on the Korean Peninsula* (London: IISS, 2018), 24; Joseph S. Bermudez Jr., "A History of Ballistic Missile Development in the DPRK," *Occasional Paper* no. 2 (Monterey, CA: Center for Nonproliferation Studies, 1999), 28.

53. Li Bin, "Tracking Chinese Strategic Mobile Missiles," *Science and Global Security* 15 (2007): 20–24.

54. There are reports that at least some of India's air-delivered nuclear bombs are stored underground at select airbases. Narang, *Nuclear Strategy in the Modern Era*, 104.

but it would take an especially ruthless and unpredictable adversary to be able to exploit that vulnerability. In crisis and war, those aircraft can disperse to other airfields, including civilian ones, and in theory they can disperse to highways with some practice and effort.[55] The US and other air forces have explored inflatable decoys, which might complicate the identification of real versus fake satellite airfields.[56] Aircraft can maintain airborne alert, though many counterforce target states do not have the requisite number of aircraft with sufficient range (or with sufficient airborne refueling) to make airborne alert attractive as a survivability tool compared to dispersal. Large airbases with widespread hangar complexes present a similar shell game as decoy silos or shelters, with the notable difference that the runways present a shared vulnerability for all of the hangars. Even if an aircraft remains flyable after a strike, it cannot takeoff without a functional runway. Though here, too, deception options are imaginable. In World War II, for instance, the British Royal Air Force deployed fake craters on runways to confound German battle damage assessment, something that may be harder with modern sensors.[57]

Ballistic missile submarines were identified as the almost idealized survivable basing mode in the Cold War. While that image of ultimate survivability may have been true—and may continue to be true—for US nuclear missile submarines, it is less certain if the image was valid for the Soviet submarine fleet. Since all nine nuclear weapons states field operational nuclear weapons-carrying submarines or are developing such capabilities the survivability of sea-based weapons may vary quite considerably from dyad to dyad. However, only in dyads involving the United States (US-Russia, US-China, and US-North Korea being the most salient) or perhaps the India-Pakistan dyad does it seem conceivable that a counterforce aspirant might obtain reasonable confidence in its ability to find and track all or most nuclear missile submarines, and hence destroy them if necessary as part of a broader counterforce effort.[58] The United States has a variety of advantages with passive sensors that are likely to encourage adversary states to pursue

---

55. See Pakistani examples in Clary and Narang, "India's Counterforce Temptations," 44–45.
56. Alan J. Vick, *Air Base Attacks and Defensive Counters: Historical Lessons and Future Challenges* (Santa Monica, CA: RAND Corporation, 2015), 42–43.
57. Vick, *Air Base Attacks and Defensive Counters*, 40–41.
58. Cote argues even India is unlikely to be able to find Pakistani submarines, and concludes, "SSBNs deployed by states not in the cross hairs of the United States are likely to be quite survivable." Owen R. Cote Jr., "Invisible Nuclear-Armed Submarines, or Transparent Oceans? Are Ballistic Missile Submarines still the Best Deterrent for the United States?," *Bulletin of the Atomic Scientists* 75, no. 1 (2019): 35. On the India-Pakistan dyad, see Diana Wueger, "India's Nuclear-Armed Submarines: Deterrence or Danger?" *The Washington Quarterly* 39, no. 3 (2016): 77–90; and Christopher Clary and Ankit Panda, "Safer at Sea? Pakistan's Sea-Based Deterrent and Nuclear Weapons Security," *Washington Quarterly* 40, no. 3 (2017): 149–168.

bastion models for their nuclear submarines. This, in turn, necessitates long ranges for all potential nuclear competitors; ranges that two of the three most likely nuclear competitors of the United States (China and North Korea) have not fielded in operational sea-launched ballistic missiles. Even if China or North Korea do field sufficiently long-range missiles at some future date, there are other challenges associated with implementing a bastion strategy. Russia (and formerly the Soviet Union) could implement a bastion model in the Barents Sea or the Sea of Okhotsk, where they controlled all surrounding landmasses. China's comparable bodies of water—the South China Sea, East China Sea, or Yellow Sea—abut a chain of US allies and partners in Vietnam, the Philippines, Taiwan, Japan, and South Korea.[59] North Korea's situation is not more favorable.

During the Cold War, the US Navy with roughly 100 nuclear attack submarines felt reasonably confident that it could track the majority, if not all, of the 10 to 20 percent of the roughly sixty-five Soviet ballistic missile submarines at sail during peacetime. The ability of the US Navy to maintain that capability in crisis and war was less certain, as the Soviet Union flushed a much larger number of ballistic missile submarines out of port and presumably engaged in much more aggressive anti-submarine warfare tactics against US attack submarines.[60] The ratio of attack submarines to ballistic missile-carrying targets has only improved in a more favorable direction for the United States, depending on how much risk the United States is willing to take with other competitors as it prepares for crisis with any one nuclear foe. Russia with ten nuclear-powered missile submarines, China with four, and North Korea with one developmental diesel-electric missile submarine would compete against a US Navy operating nearly seventy nuclear-powered attack submarines. Despite these advantages, would any US leader be confident that all adversary ballistic missile submarines could be destroyed before they could launch their missiles? Each Chinese Type-094 submarine is outfitted with twelve JL-2 missiles—each capable of destroying a large city. Each Russian submarine can carry up to sixteen missiles, each of which can carry multiple warheads. The stakes are enormous. Could a submarine slip out of port in the context of concerted efforts by other elements of that state's navy to draw away hunter-killer submarines? Certainly. In the process of targeting a missile submarine could the attacker find itself targeted and destroyed? Also, yes. Thus even underwater naval superiority—even underwater naval dominance—may not yield certainty.

---

59. ChinaPower, Center for Strategic and International Studies, "Michael McDevitt: Does China have an effective sea-based nuclear deterrent?," April 19, 2016, https://www.youtube.com/watch?v=ihC3pcr5jns.

60. See discussion in Owen Cote Jr., "The Third Battle: Innovation in the U.S. Navy's Silent Cold War Struggle with Soviet Submarines," *Newport Papers* 16 (2003): 73–76.

CHAPTER 6

RESPONSES TO THE NEW ERA OF COUNTERFORCE

If hiders have considerable low-cost advantages over finders, then what are the political implications of this new era of counterforce? Do the hiders' advantages nullify the effects of the technological shifts ably demonstrated by Lieber and Press? No, because there are very likely greater dangers to the nuclear forces of weaker foes in peacetime and early crisis. There are six likely responses to that greater danger.

The first and second responses involve the number of nuclear eggs and the number of baskets, respectively, that weaker nuclear states view as sufficient for survivability. At the margin, counterforce pressures encourage states to have modestly more warheads (more eggs) and considerably more baskets (peacetime storage locations). This complicates the targeting problem for counterforce aspirants by increasing the number of peacetime targets. It may make sense to have more baskets than eggs. Although the marginal cost of producing a nuclear warhead is often relatively small, maintaining all of the associated personnel and equipment to support a delivery vehicle for that warhead can be quite expensive. Building covered storage sheds all around the country, and associated security arrangements, may be a comparatively modest expense. The more places that nuclear warheads may be dispersed to in peacetime and crisis, the more locations that are vulnerable to insider or outsider threats. A few highly secure centralized locations generate more signatures for finders to find, and hence more numerous, less secure, dispersed locations may prove beneficial, with unclear net results for nuclear safety and security.

The economies of scale achieved by storing several nuclear eggs in the same basket are nontrivial and likely to be attractive for all nuclear states in peacetime. The third step counterforce targets may take is to maintain higher readiness in peacetime so that such forces can be dispersed more quickly if a sudden crisis emerges. This, too, has implications for dangers associated with the warhead. Many nuclear states started with nuclear weapons disassembled and de-mated during peacetime, but subsequently many of those states concluded the benefits of enhanced readiness outweighed the safety and control advantages of those earlier more recessed postures. The new era of counterforce reinforces that tendency.

The fourth step counterforce targets are likely to take—and largely already have taken—is to rely more heavily on concealment rather than hardening for survivability. Thus mobility—already the preferred survivability mode for the majority of nuclear powers—will only become more attractive as silos are increasingly easy to find and destroy.

The fifth step follows naturally from those that precede it: rapid dispersal. A more ready force is in part useful because it can be dispersed more rapidly in a crisis, both to multiple bases not typically used in peacetime but also off the beaten path to locations where mobility and secrecy make it hard for anyone to predict where a mobile unit is heading. More rapid dispersal in wartime, though, generates dangers. Nuclear-armed missiles will be on the road, nuclear-armed missiles will be underway at sea, nuclear-armed planes will take off and land from unfamiliar airfields, increasing the dangers of accidents all along the way. The signatures associated with dispersal will be worrying for observers, and preparations for dispersal may generate counterforce temptations while delivery systems remain in better understood peacetime bases.

The sixth possible step may not be possible for all nuclear dyads and, if implemented, would be among the most dangerous possible countermeasures: launch-on-warning (LOW) or launch-under-attack postures.[61] The US Defense Department has considered China's interest in more silos as a sign of its interest in LOW.[62] For dyads such as India and Pakistan, the traditional early warning indicators of radar signatures or missile launch plumes may not permit decision making or the initiation of retaliatory launches given the incredibly short missile flight times. For all nuclear adversaries confronting the United States, LOW is at least conceivable, if perhaps unwise, given the vulnerability of the early warning systems themselves to attack and the seemingly high rate of false alarms based on the limited accounts we have of the US and Soviet/Russian systems. LOW postures if adopted or even feigned would add to the potential risk and operational complexity confronting any counterforce contemplating state.

Yield Not to Temptation

The temptations of counterforce for damage limitation are real and may motivate expensive arms procurement, especially by more powerful states, in peacetime. Would a leader actually authorize a shot in crisis, though? Here the enormous uncertainty generated by the hiders' advantage appears to yield caution in deep crisis. Even if a nuclear state has exquisite intelligence about the nuclear operations of its adversary, it is difficult to have sufficient certainty in the accuracy of that intelligence to bet national survival on it. As Robert Jervis notes, "Deception is fairly easy and the knowledge that it is possible degrades the value of accurate information."[63] Soviet leader Josef Stalin, after all, discounted information about the US nuclear weapons

---

61. For discussion of what these terms mean in practice, see Steven Starr et al., "New Terminology to Help Prevent Accidental Nuclear War," *Bulletin of the Atomic Scientists*, September 29, 2015.

62. Office of the Secretary of Defense, *Military and Security Developments involving the People's Republic of China* (Washington, DC: Department of Defense, 2020), 88–89.

63. Robert Jervis, *Why Intelligence Fails: Lessons from the Iranian Revolution and the Iraq War* (Ithaca: Cornell University Press, 2010), 2.

development effort in part because he did not believe the United States would so easily permit the penetration of its program.

How could any leader know that his or her nation's forces were targeting all of the adversary's? How could they be confident that misinformation had not been slipped into the system or that the intelligence was out of date? Setting aside whether each target could be located and destroyed in sufficient time, the completeness of the target set itself is difficult to know without inside information from within the nuclear stewards of an enemy power.

Although much is made of the failure of the Scud hunt, less is made of the fact that in the 1991 Gulf War targeting against fixed nuclear weapons-related infrastructure was substantially incomplete. Of twenty-one facilities identified by UN inspectors in the month immediately after the war, only eight (38 percent) had been identified by US targeters by the termination of hostilities on February 28, 1991, with an additional eight (for a combined 76 percent) being identified shortly after. Nuclear weapons states have likely been under focused surveillance by their principal adversaries for some time; Iraq in 1991 had been under intense surveillance since at least Operation Desert Shield in October 1990; nevertheless, those months of preparation were insufficient to identify, let alone destroy, a majority of Iraqi nuclear-related sites by the end of February 1991.[64]

This uncertainty of knowing with assuredness the size and scope of the adversary's arsenal, along with other aspects associated with the fog and friction of war, means that the political implications of this new era will be muted—though not altogether absent. P. M. S. Blackett was correct in his skepticism of operations research style analyses because, he stressed, "however ingenious a theoretical model might be, it could seldom resemble a real operation enough to give any confidence in any deductions from it."[65]

To say that arms racing will be muted is not to say that compensatory moves and countermeasures will be absent, nor is it to imply other sources of vertical proliferation do not exist. This chapter has focused on survivability, but survivability is only one driver of arms procurement. States that seek to use nuclear weapons to deter limited conventional attacks or that attempt to extend deterrence guarantees to their overseas allies have tougher tasks than merely retaining survivable second-strike weapons.[66] Their arsenals will reflect those more challenging aspirations.

Even muted competition entails some reaction in the face of counterforce aspirations by an opponent. States concerned with survivability will work to improve readiness and dispersal and delivery systems that permit greater

---

64. Keaney and Cohen, *Operations and Effects and Effectiveness*, 328.
65. Blackett, 1961 unpublished manuscript, quoted in Basrur 2014, https://www.rsis.edu.sg/wp-content/uploads/rsis-pubs/WP271.pdf, 3.
66. See Lieber and Press, *Myth of the Nuclear Revolution*, 5; Green, *The Revolution That Failed*, 51.

mobility. They may, on the margin, increase warhead and delivery system numbers. They may invest in modestly expensive technologies to ensure residual forces that survive a first-strike attempt can defeat missile defenses. But all of these efforts by the counterforce target involve comparatively modest expenditures. Even if the counterforce aspirant is running, the counterforce target likely will merely have to jog to stay competitive. This fundamental asymmetry of effort to maintain survivability generates considerable stability even in a world where the United States strives for primacy amidst a new technological era of counterforce.

CHAPTER 7

The Fulcrum of Fragility

Command and Control in Regional Nuclear Powers

Giles David Arceneaux and Peter D. Feaver

Command and control systems are the operational means by which a state conducts the management, deployment, and potential release of nuclear weapons.[1] These operational features of a state's nuclear arsenal directly impact important dimensions of nuclear strategy and strategic stability, such as a state's ability to survive an initial attack and retaliate with nuclear force. Command and control systems that are robust enough to accomplish this demanding mission reinforce nuclear deterrence. Command and control vulnerabilities, however, can present leaders with a "use them or lose them" dilemma that could escalate a crisis into conflict.[2] Command and control systems also constitute the primary defense against the accidental or unauthorized use of nuclear weapons. The structure of a state's command and control arrangements underpin core concepts of nuclear strategy such as strategic stability and arsenal safety and security.

Despite the importance of command and control systems for maintaining nuclear safety and stability, the causes and consequences of command and control in regional nuclear powers remain poorly understood. Whereas scholars have made significant progress in explaining other aspects of nuclear strategy and proliferation, operational level outcomes such as nuclear

---

1. Vipin Narang, *Nuclear Strategy in the Modern Era: Regional Powers and International Conflict* (Princeton: Princeton University Press, 2014), 4.

2. Bruce G. Blair, *Strategic Command and Control: Redefining the Nuclear Threat* (Washington, DC: Brookings Institution Press, 1985); John D. Steinbruner, "National Security and the Concept of Strategic Stability," *Journal of Conflict Resolution* 22, no. 3 (September 1978): 411–428.

command and control systems have received far less attention in academic debates.[3] As a result, our understanding of nuclear command and control has made comparatively little progress since the immediate aftermath of the Cold War, during which time the subject was a matter for lively debate.[4]

This chapter evaluates the operational challenges facing regional nuclear powers and how states develop their command and control systems to address these challenges. First, we present a conceptual framework for classifying command and control systems in regional nuclear powers. Second, we discuss how the domestic and international constraints on command and control in regional nuclear powers compare to the experience of the Cold War superpowers. Third, we empirically evaluate command and control systems in each of the regional nuclear powers. Finally, we conclude with practical assessments of the challenges that command and control systems pose for crisis stability in current and future proliferators. Ultimately, we find that although regional nuclear powers develop command and control systems in response to a different set of pressures than the Cold War superpowers, command and control remains the "fulcrum of fragility"—a critical variable in determining the instability of the nuclear world, especially in crises.

Nuclear Command and Control: Old Problems and New Challenges

When developing command and control systems, all nuclear states face a fundamental problem known as the always/never dilemma: nuclear weapons should always launch when ordered, but never without proper authorization.[5] On the one hand, nuclear weapons should be reliable. Nuclear forces should be resilient to preemption or decapitation efforts by an adversary and capable of responding under any circumstances.[6] On the other

---

3. Erik Gartzke and Matthew Kroenig, "Nukes with Numbers: Empirical Research on the Consequences of Nuclear Weapons for International Conflict," *Annual Review of Political Science* 19 (May 2016): 408.
4. For key works, see Peter D. Feaver, "Command and Control in Emerging Nuclear Nations," *International Security* 17, no. 3 (Winter 1992/93): 160–187; Peter D. Feaver, "Neooptimists and the Enduring Problem of Nuclear Proliferation," *Security Studies* 6, no. 4 (Summer 1997): 93–125; Peter D. Feaver, "Proliferation Optimism and Theories of Nuclear Operations," *Security Studies* 2, nos. 3–4 (Spring/Summer 1993): 159–191; David J. Karl, "Proliferation Pessimism and Emerging Nuclear Powers," *International Security* 21, no. 3 (Winter 1996/97): 87–119; Scott D. Sagan, "The Perils of Proliferation: Organization Theory, Deterrence Theory, and the Spread of Nuclear Weapons," *International Security* 18, no. 4 (Spring 1994): 66–107; Scott D. Sagan and Kenneth N. Waltz, *The Spread of Nuclear Weapons: An Enduring Debate*, 3rd ed. (New York: W.W. Norton, 2013); Jordan Seng, "Less Is More: Command and Control Advantages of Minor Nuclear States," *Security Studies* 6, no. 4 (Summer 1997): 50–92.
5. Peter D. Feaver, *Guarding the Guardians: Civilian Control of Nuclear Weapons in the United States* (Ithaca: Cornell University Press, 1992), 3–28.
6. John D. Steinbruner, "Nuclear Decapitation," *Foreign Policy*, no. 45 (Winter 1981/82): 16–28.

hand, the nuclear arsenal should be safe and secure. Nuclear weapons should not detonate accidentally due to errors in management or design, nor should they be used without proper political authorization.[7]

The always/never dilemma suggests that efforts to ensure the reliability of a nuclear arsenal can challenge the safety and security of a nuclear arsenal, whereas attempts to increase arsenal safety and security very likely reduce arsenal reliability. For instance, political leaders can improve arsenal reliability by predelegating the ability to use nuclear weapons to lower-level military commanders to reduce the time required to respond to an attack, but this arrangement requires fewer layers of authorization to use nuclear weapons and increases the likelihood of unwanted nuclear use. Alternatively, leaders can implement robust administrative oversight over the mobilization and employment of nuclear forces to protect against unwanted nuclear use, but these measures increase the time required to respond to an attack and the arsenal becomes more vulnerable to preemption and decapitation. Leaders can adopt a mixture of such measures, but the always/never dilemma ultimately forces tradeoffs between arsenal reliability, safety, and security in all nuclear states.

Command and control systems represent the primary institutional means for addressing the always/never dilemma.[8] Studies built on the US experience during the Cold War identify two ideal types of command and control: assertive and delegative. Assertive control refers to systems where political leaders exercise centralized administrative control over nuclear use decisions and physical control of nuclear assets.[9] Assertive control favors the never side of the always/never dilemma by increasing safeguards against accidental and unauthorized use; however, these measures produce slower mobilization and response times that make nuclear forces less reliable. In contrast, delegative control grants decision making autonomy and physical control of nuclear assets to lower-level commanders.[10] Delegative control favors the always side of the always/never dilemma by enabling peripheral commanders to increase arsenal readiness. These measures improve arsenal reliability but increase the likelihood of accidental or unauthorized use by reducing the barriers to nuclear use.

RECONCEPTUALIZING NUCLEAR COMMAND AND CONTROL

The traditional assertive/delegative framework portrays command and control systems as temporally static, suggesting that states either assert po-

---

7. For a full discussion of accidental and unauthorized use, see Feaver, *Guarding the Guardians*, 13–15.
8. Feaver, *Guarding the Guardians*, 29–66.
9. Feaver, *Guarding the Guardians*, 9–11.
10. Feaver, *Guarding the Guardians*, 7–9.

litical control over nuclear forces or delegate nuclear use capability to peripheral commanders. In practice, however, lower-level military operators are ultimately required to deliver nuclear weapons, and all states must eventually delegate control to conduct a nuclear strike. The appropriate question for classifying command and control systems is not whether states delegate nuclear use capability to lower levels of command but rather when such delegation occurs.[11]

The timing of delegation is most significant with respect to the onset of a crisis. States possess three options for when to delegate the ability to use nuclear weapons: during peacetime, before a crisis emerges; early in a crisis, when political tensions become severe and military forces mobilize; or late in a crisis, after significant conventional or even nuclear warfighting. Classifying command and control systems according to the timing of delegation expands the traditional assertive/delegative framework to include three analytically distinct arrangements: delegative, conditional, and assertive control.

The first type, delegative control, refers to the peacetime delegation of nuclear use capability. At all times, lower-level military operators possess physical control of the nuclear warheads and delivery platforms required to conduct a nuclear strike. These platforms are typically unconstrained by use-control technologies such as permissive action links (PALs).[12] Administratively, the military custodians of nuclear assets possess the ability to use nuclear weapons at any time, even if not the authority. Delegative control increases arsenal reliability by enabling lower-level military operators to launch a nuclear strike under any conditions. These systems face persistent threats of unwanted nuclear use, as these states almost exclusively rely on military professionalism to avoid accidental and unauthorized use.

The second type, conditional control systems, delegates the ability to use nuclear weapons early in a crisis. During peacetime, leaders centralize administrative authority, physically disperse nuclear components, and often implement at least modest technical controls. Early in a crisis—as tensions begin to mount, conventional force mobilizations begin, or some other escalatory measures ensue—these states rapidly assemble deliverable nuclear weapons and delegate nuclear use ability to lower-level military commanders and the custodians of nuclear weapons. Conditional control systems face three challenges that are distinct from other command and control arrangements. First, the process of increasing arsenal readiness early in a crisis may signal malign intent to an adversary and increase the likelihood of

---

11. Giles David Arceneaux, "Beyond the Rubicon: Command and Control in Regional Nuclear Powers" (PhD diss., Syracuse University, 2019).
12. On PALs, see Peter Stein and Peter Feaver, "Assuring Control of Nuclear Weapons: The Evolution of Permissive Action Links," CSIA Occasional Paper no. 2, CSIA Publications, Cambridge, MA, 1987.

crisis escalation.[13] Second, the rapid inclusion of military influence in nuclear decision making weakens political oversight of nuclear operations and creates opportunities for national policy and military operations to diverge as a crisis begins, which makes crisis de-escalation more difficult.[14] Third, the transition from centralized to decentralized control occurs as actors begin to face pervasive uncertainty, thereby increasing the likelihood of misperception. Combined, these challenges for conditional control create distinct pathways that increase the likelihood of conflict escalation.[15]

The final type, assertive control systems, delegates nuclear use capability late in a crisis. These states promote highly centralized administrative control over nuclear operations and often physically de-mate and disperse nuclear weapons to guarantee political control over nuclear decisions throughout the crisis. Assertive control systems often include technical controls such as PALs to separate the administrative control of nuclear forces from the physical possession of nuclear weapons, thereby allowing leaders to maintain centralized control deeper into a crisis.[16] These measures make assertive command and control systems highly resilient against accidental and unauthorized nuclear use but also make a nuclear arsenal vulnerable to decapitation.

Explanations for Nuclear Command and Control

The United States built its command and control systems from the outset of its nuclear program, but it was not until late in the Cold War that scholars developed the foundations of the public research program on nuclear command and control.[17] After the Cold War ended, analysts extended lessons from the superpower experiences—especially those of the United States—to conceptualize and explain command and control systems in regional nu-

---

13. Bruce G. Blair, "Alerting in Crisis and Conventional War," in *Managing Nuclear Operations*, ed. Ashton B. Carter, John D. Steinbruner, and Charles A. Zraket (Washington, DC: Brookings Institution Press, 1987), 75–78.

14. Blair, "Alerting in Crisis," 113–119.

15. On contemporary challenges for crisis escalation, see the relevant chapters in this volume: Vipin Narang and Heather Williams, "Thermonuclear Twitter?"; Christopher Clary, "Survivability in the New Era of Counterforce"; Mark S. Bell and Nicholas L. Miller, "The Limits of Learning in the New Nuclear Age."

16. Donald R. Cotter, "Peacetime Operations: Safety and Security," in Carter, Steinbruner, and Zraket, eds., *Managing Nuclear Operations*, 46.

17. Cold War-era studies include Blair, *Strategic Command and Control*; Paul Bracken, *The Command and Control of Nuclear Forces* (New Haven: Yale University Press, 1983); Carter, Steinbruner, and Zraket, eds., *Managing Nuclear Operations*; Feaver, *Guarding the Guardians*; Scott D. Sagan, *The Limits of Safety: Organizations, Accidents, and Nuclear Weapons* (Princeton: Princeton University Press, 1993).

clear powers.[18] At that time, the literature largely broke down into two camps: optimists, who argued that the new nuclear powers would find ways of managing their nuclear arsenals at least as well as the superpowers did, versus pessimists, who argued that the superpower record was hardly reassuring and that new nuclear powers faced constraints that would render their arsenals even more dangerous. Research on nuclear strategy and operations goes further, arguing that simple extrapolation from the US or Soviet experience and binaries such as optimism versus pessimism can obscure interesting variation in the behaviors of regional nuclear powers.[19]

The early theories of command and control in regional nuclear powers predicted that their systems would vary because the new nuclear powers would develop different strategies based on the geostrategic context, would face different resource and other domestic political constraints, and could learn from the US and Soviet experience.[20] We now know that is true. During the Cold War, the United States and the Soviet Union adopted a range of postures close to the maximalist end of the escalation spectrum—such as massive retaliation, flexible response, and damage limitation—that relied on massive arsenals and first-use capabilities to deter conventional and nuclear conflict.[21] By contrast, regional nuclear powers have adopted alternative nuclear postures that allow for significantly smaller arsenals and experience a wider range of strategic pressures on command and control systems.[22] Likewise, whereas the United States and Soviet Union developed their command and control infrastructures with "virtually unlimited resources," regional nuclear powers experience financial constraints that can force tradeoffs between support for nuclear weapons capabilities and robust arsenal safety and security processes.[23] Finally, whereas the superpowers

---

18. Feaver, "Command and Control in Emerging Nuclear Nations"; Scott D. Sagan, "The Origins of Military Doctrine and Command and Control Systems," in *Planning the Unthinkable: How New Powers Will Use Nuclear, Biological, and Chemical Weapons*, ed. Peter R. Lavoy, Scott D. Sagan, and James J. Wirtz (Ithaca: Cornell University Press, 2000), 16–46; Seng, "Less Is More."

19. Paul Bracken, *The Second Nuclear Age: Strategy, Danger, and the New Power Politics* (New York: Times Books, 2012); Toshi Yoshihara and James R. Holmes, eds., *Strategy in the Second Nuclear Age: Power, Ambition, and the Ultimate Weapon* (Washington, DC: Georgetown University Press, 2012).

20. Feaver, "Command and Control in Emerging Nuclear Nations."

21. Notable overviews include Lawrence Freedman, *The Evolution of Nuclear Strategy*, 3rd ed. (New York: Palgrave Macmillan, 2003); Charles L. Glaser, *Analyzing Strategic Nuclear Policy* (Princeton: Princeton University Press, 1990); and Scott D. Sagan, *Moving Targets: Nuclear Strategy and National Security* (Princeton: Princeton University Press, 1989).

22. On nuclear strategy in regional nuclear powers, see Narang, *Nuclear Strategy in the Modern Era*.

23. Feaver, "Command and Control in Emerging Nuclear Nations," 186; Lewis Dunn, "Containing Nuclear Proliferation," Adelphi Paper no. 263, International Institute for Strategic Studies, London, 1991, 20.

CHAPTER 7

Table 7.1 Competing Explanations for Nuclear Command and Control

Explanation	Measurement	Predicted Outcome
External threat environment	Nuclear threats	Arsenal and command vulnerabilities to nuclear attacks produce more delegative control
	Conventional threats	Presence of a proximate and conventionally superior adversary produces more delegative control
Strategic rationale	Nuclear use doctrine	First-use nuclear doctrines require more delegative control
Domestic politics	Civil-military relations	Greater military organizational autonomy and political influence produces more delegative control
	Domestic instability	Greater domestic instability produces more assertive control

indigenously developed the administrative, physical, and technical means of nuclear command and control, regional nuclear powers can potentially study these Cold War models to identify and evaluate arsenal management practices.[24]

This chapter evaluates the explanations of command and control in regional nuclear powers that were presented only in skeletal form three decades ago in light of what is now known about command and control outside of the United States and the Soviet Union. We focus on three categories of factors that may influence command and control decisions in regional nuclear powers: (1) the state's external threat environment, (2) the strategic rationale of the arsenal, and (3) the domestic political environment. Table 7.1 summarizes these alternative explanations.

EXTERNAL THREAT ENVIRONMENT: ARSENAL VULNERABILITY AND CONVENTIONAL THREATS

A state's external threat environment might shape command and control systems in two ways. First, an influential security-based argument emphasizes the effects of arsenal vulnerability on command and control decisions.[25] From this perspective, states with nuclear arsenals that are vulnerable to preemption or decapitation face challenges to the survivability and responsiveness of their nuclear forces. States with greater arsenal vulnerability experience

---

24. Peter Feaver refers to this as the "vicarious learning" model. Feaver, "Command and Control in Emerging Nuclear Nations," 172–174.
25. Feaver, "Proliferation Optimism and Theories of Nuclear Operations," 165–167; Sagan, "The Origins of Military Doctrine and Command and Control Systems," 39–42.

increased time-urgency, referring to the degree to which a state believes its arsenal must be ready for rapid use.[26] Time-urgency is particularly pronounced in states with small arsenals, limited geographic depth, and nuclear-armed adversaries, as these conditions generate "use them or lose them" pressures on states to safeguard against an adversary's preemptive strike.[27] The arsenal vulnerability factor suggests that states with more vulnerable nuclear arsenals will adopt more delegative command and control frameworks that bolster arsenal reliability, while more secure nuclear arsenals permit more assertive control measures that emphasize arsenal safety and security.

Second, severe conventional threats may shape nuclear command and control systems in regional nuclear powers.[28] Whereas the US and Soviet homelands were largely safe from conventional incursion during the Cold War, conventional military invasions have posed threats to the survival of states such as Pakistan and Cold War-era France. Furthermore, fears of foreign-imposed regime change through conventional means are believed to powerfully influence North Korea's nuclear policy, suggesting that conventional threats to state security and regime survival are both likely to factor into nuclear command and control decision making.[29] A conventionally superior adversary can quickly seize territory, destroy forces, sever lines of communication, and threaten regime change in regional nuclear powers. States facing such threats experience incentives to lower the nuclear threshold to deter conventional attacks. By lowering the threshold to nuclear use, regional nuclear powers can more clearly signal to adversaries that no room exists underneath the nuclear umbrella for conventional conflict, as even limited conventional disputes will risk escalation to the nuclear level. As a result, severe conventional threats encourage more delegative patterns of command and control that allow states to lower the nuclear threshold.

STRATEGIC RATIONALE: NUCLEAR POSTURE

Based on this threat environment and based on other aspects of the state's grand strategy—for instance, whether the state is a status quo or revisionist power—the state develops a strategic rationale for its nuclear arsenal, and this directly affects the shape of the command and control system. Regional nuclear powers have historically employed one of three strategic nuclear postures: (1) catalytic postures that seek to mobilize third-party intervention

---

26. Feaver, "Command and Control in Emerging Nuclear Nations," 178.
27. Feaver, "Command and Control in Emerging Nuclear Nations," 178; Sagan, "The Origins of Military Doctrine and Command and Control Systems," 39–40.
28. On the effects of conventional military threats on nuclear command and control systems, Arceneaux, "Beyond the Rubicon."
29. For example, see Megan Specia and David E. Sanger, "How the 'Libya Model' Became a Sticking Point in North Korea Nuclear Talks," *New York Times*, May 16, 2018.

on a state's behalf during a crisis, (2) assured retaliation postures that aim to guarantee secure second-strike capabilities after an adversary's nuclear attack, and (3) asymmetric escalation postures that envision the first use of nuclear weapons in a conflict.[30]

For purposes of explaining command and control systems, the key difference between these nuclear postures is whether they rely on first-use or second-use nuclear strategies. First-use strategies anticipate using nuclear weapons first in a conflict, most likely in response to conventional attacks. Late-use strategies, in contrast, plan to withhold nuclear weapons until an adversary has conducted a nuclear strike or appears imminently likely to do so. States with nuclear postures that envision early-use capabilities require the delegation of authority to peripheral commanders, whereas late-use doctrines permit assertive political control over the arsenal.[31]

DOMESTIC POLITICS: CIVIL-MILITARY RELATIONS AND DOMESTIC INSTABILITY

Domestic politics constitutes the final basket of factors shaping command and control and here two dimensions are of greatest importance. First, the patterns of civil-military relations within a state can exert strong pressures on command and control decisions. This is especially true in states where military organizations have influence over nuclear decision making and can promote policies that serve the military's interests. In such cases, the bureaucratic politics of military organizational interests and biases can have profound effects on nuclear doctrine. Military organizations possess three core interests that may be pursued through political channels: (1) access to material resources, (2) autonomy over the management of internal military affairs, and (3) command of operational and tactical decisions regarding the use of force.[32] Military organizations also possess procedural biases that shape doctrinal preferences, including reliance on organizational routines designed to address specific tasks and issues and an emphasis on operational-level military issues.[33] These interests and biases lead military organizations to systematically prefer offensive military doctrines that increase the military's access to resources, enhance military autonomy, and facilitate operational coordination

---

30. On these regional power nuclear postures, see Narang, *Nuclear Strategy in the Modern Era*, 27–46.

31. Narang treats command and control systems as a descriptive component of nuclear posture in his theory. Narang, *Nuclear Strategy in the Modern Era*, 22.

32. Richard K. Betts, *Soldiers, Statesmen, and Cold War Crises* (New York: Columbia University Press, 1991), 71–75; Barry R. Posen, *The Sources of Military Doctrine: France, Britain, and Germany Between the World Wars* (Ithaca: Cornell University Press, 1984), 41–59; Sagan, "The Perils of Proliferation," 75–76.

33. Posen, *The Sources of Military Doctrine*, 44–48.

within the military.[34] In nuclear states, offensive doctrines correspond to more delegative patterns of command and control that provide the military with physical control over nuclear assets and administrative autonomy over nuclear use decisions.[35] The civil-military relations hypothesis argues that higher levels of military influence in nuclear decision making will produce more delegative command and control systems.

A second domestic explanation for command and control in regional nuclear powers emphasizes the importance of domestic political instability. Several regional nuclear powers have experienced significant periods of domestic instability while possessing nuclear forces, including China, Pakistan, and apartheid-era South Africa.[36] Domestic sources of instability such as military coups, armed rebellion, and mass protests can pose significant threats to the survival of political regimes and directly threaten the safety and security of nuclear forces.[37] As a result, political leaders facing severe domestic instability possess incentives to centralize control over nuclear weapons. Centralized control allows leaders to institutionally exclude and withhold resources from potential domestic rivals, exploit the domestic political value of nuclear weapons for regime support, and strengthen the physical safety and security of nuclear forces.[38] Thus, higher levels of domestic instability should lead to more assertive patterns of command and control in regional nuclear powers.

Command and Control in Regional Nuclear Powers

In this section, we describe the command and control arrangements of each regional nuclear power, including the United Kingdom, France, China, Israel, apartheid-era South Africa, India, Pakistan, and North Korea, presented in the order in which they acquired nuclear weapons. We draw on the best publicly available sources, but much remains unknown or uncertain, even

---

34. Sagan, "The Origins of Military Doctrine and Command and Control Systems," 18–23.
35. Arceneaux, "Beyond the Rubicon," 42–46.
36. Henry D. Sokolski and Bruno Tertrais, eds., *Nuclear Weapons Security Crises: What Does History Teach?* (Carlisle, PA: Strategic Studies Institute and U.S. Army War College Press, 2013).
37. On the dual imperatives of internal and external threats to a regime's rule, see Sheena Chestnut Greitens, *Dictators and Their Secret Police: Coercive Institutions and State Violence* (Cambridge: Cambridge University Press, 2016), 3–71.
38. Cameron S. Brown, Christopher J. Fariss, and R. Blake McMahon, "Recouping after Coup-Proofing: Compromised Military Effectiveness and Strategic Substitution," *International Interactions* 42, no. 1 (January 2016): 1–30. Peter D. Feaver, "Nuclear Command and Control in Crisis: Old Lessons from New History," in Sokolski and Tertrais, eds., *Nuclear Weapons Security Crises*, 221; Christopher Clary, *Thinking about Pakistan's Nuclear Security in Peacetime, Crisis and War* (New Delhi: Institute for Defense Studies and Analyses, 2010), 3–4.

CHAPTER 7

in arsenals that are many decades old. For each case, we also identify the presence of key explanatory factors identified in the previous section. This section concludes by briefly evaluating the probative value of the competing explanations.

UNITED KINGDOM

The United Kingdom has employed delegative command and control systems throughout its nuclear history.[39] The UK relied on air-delivery systems from 1956 through 1969 for strategic deterrence after forming its V-bomber squadrons capable of targeting the Soviet Union.[40] From 1969 on, the UK has deployed nuclear-powered ballistic missile submarines (SSBNs) as the core of its nuclear arsenal, with Trident II submarine-launched ballistic missiles (SLBMs) currently serving as the only operational delivery platform in the UK's nuclear arsenal.[41]

The UK's command and control practices over its nuclear bombers demonstrated a reliance on delegative control. Administratively, the Royal Air Force (RAF) possessed the means to prepare for nuclear use without civilian direction.[42] In practice, the chief of air staff could mobilize the RAF's nuclear bomber force to conduct a nuclear strike or proceed to a holding area and await further instructions from Bomber Command.[43] Physically, the RAF received its first operational nuclear weapons in 1953 and maintained custody of the fissile cores and weapons casings required to assemble a nuclear bomb.[44] Technically, the RAF's nuclear weapons were free from any electronic controls.[45]

Delegative control procedures have remained in place since the UK transitioned to sea-based strategic deterrence in 1969. Administratively, each prime minister writes a "letter of last resort" upon assuming office that is held in a safe aboard each SSBN and provides directions to SSBN commanders in case communications with political leadership are severed.[46] These

---

39. Our analysis focuses exclusively on the UK's national command and control arrangements. On the role of British nuclear weapons in NATO missions, see Shaun R. Gregory, *Nuclear Command and Control in NATO: Nuclear Weapons Operations and the Strategy of Flexible Response* (New York: St. Martin's Press, 1996), 103–129.

40. Lawrence Freedman, "British Nuclear Targeting," *Defense Analysis* 1, no. 2 (June 1985): 85.

41. Robert S. Norris and Hans M. Kristensen, "The British Nuclear Stockpile, 1953–2013," *Bulletin of the Atomic Scientists* 69, no. 4 (July/August 2013): 70–72.

42. Stephen Twigge and Len Scott, "Learning to Love the Bomb: The Command and Control of British Nuclear Forces, 1953–1964," *Journal of Strategic Studies* 22, no. 1 (March 1999): 31–35.

43. Twigge and Scott, "Learning to Love the Bomb," 36, 39.

44. Twigge and Scott, "Learning to Love the Bomb," 33–35.

45. Twigge and Scott, "Learning to Love the Bomb," 45.

46. Niklas Granholm and John Rydqvist, "Nuclear Weapons in Europe: British and French Deterrence Forces," FOI-R-4587-SE (April 2018), 26.

letters provide SSBN crews with the administrative capability to conduct a nuclear strike.[47] Physically, the Royal Navy possesses complete control over its SLBMs while on deterrent patrols. Technically, the UK's SLBMs remain unconstrained by technical controls.[48] Combined, these delegative command and control systems reflect the UK's belief that the peacetime delegation of nuclear use capability bolsters the credibility of its strategic nuclear deterrent.[49]

External threats fail to explain the UK's continued reliance on delegative control over time. Although the collapse of the Soviet Union dramatically reduced external threats to UK security, delegative control measures remained in place. Similarly, the strategic rationale perspective also fails to explain it. Although the UK currently de-targets its SLBMs during peacetime to promote a late-use posture that could potentially require days to launch, the SSBN crew still possesses the necessary targeting information during peacetime.[50] Domestic political considerations provide the most consistent explanation of delegative control over time in the UK. Specifically, the longstanding involvement of British military organizations in nuclear decision making aligns with the UK's delegative control systems. For example, the military-led Herod Committee devised arrangements that would place all nuclear weapons components under RAF custody before Britain possessed nuclear weapons.[51] Over time, Britain's military forces successfully resisted the implementation of technical controls such as PALs and guaranteed that the military custodians of nuclear forces possess unimpeded control over nuclear weapons, suggesting that bureaucratic inertia may also contribute to the persistence of long-established patterns of delegative control.[52]

FRANCE

France tested its first nuclear weapon on February 13, 1960, and subsequently developed a complete nuclear triad before eventually eliminating land-based missiles after the end of the Cold War.[53] Unlike the United States and the United Kingdom—similarly advanced Western democracies and formal

---

47. For a description of the process required to launch SLBMs, see Gregory, *Nuclear Command and Control in NATO*, 118.
48. UK Ministry of Defense, "Nuclear Weapons Security—MoD Statement," November 17, 2007.
49. Gregory, *Nuclear Command and Control in NATO*, 117.
50. John Gower, "United Kingdom: Nuclear Weapon Command, Control, and Communications," NAPSNet Special Reports, September 12, 2019, 5.
51. Twigge and Scott, "Learning to Love the Bomb," 32.
52. Meirion Jones, "British Nukes Were Protected by Bike Locks," *Newsnight*, November 15, 2007.
53. Narang, *Nuclear Strategy in the Modern Era*, 169.

military allies of France—details regarding French nuclear command and control practices remain extremely limited, especially with respect to post–Cold War practices.[54]

France seemed to exercise delegative control over its nuclear forces during the Cold War. Administratively, French presidents have historically proclaimed their authority over nuclear use decisions, while some analysts argue that presidents can devolve administrative authority to other senior political leaders.[55] Physically, France's tactical nuclear weapons were under military control during peacetime and military operators possessed full operational custody of nuclear weapons.[56] The First Army controlled France's land-based Pluton missiles, while the Tactical Air Force (Force Aérienne Tactique) controlled France's air-launched tactical weapons.[57] Technically, it is unclear whether tactical nuclear weapons entailed use-control technological constraints during the Cold War.[58] The French president possessed an enabling code that would authenticate the origins of the order to use nuclear weapons, but it appears that military operators could launch nuclear weapons without awaiting this authentication code.[59]

France's command and control arrangements are more difficult to discern in the post–Cold War environment. In 1996, France reclassified all nuclear weapons as strategic and deemphasized the role of tactical or prestrategic weapons.[60] The key point of disagreement between analysts relates to command and control procedures for France's SSBNs: some scholars suggest that SSBN crews possess full operational control of nuclear weapons, while others argue that SSBN crews cannot launch missiles without enabling codes from political leaders.[61] Similarly, scholars disagree on whether the French president can unilaterally authorize nuclear use or must consult senior military officials to order a nuclear strike.[62]

Because of the paucity of data, any assessments about the causal weight of different constraints are necessarily provisional. That said, external threats—especially the conventional threat posed by the Soviet Union dur-

---

54. Benoît Pelopidas, "France: Nuclear Command, Control, and Communications," NAPSNet Special Reports, June 10, 2019.
55. Gregory, *Nuclear Command and Control in NATO*, 130–133.
56. Gregory, *Nuclear Command and Control in NATO*, 137.
57. Robbin F. Laird, "French Nuclear Forces in the 1980s and 1990s," Professional Paper 400 (Alexandria, VA: Center for Naval Analyses, August 1983), 22–23.
58. Narang, *Nuclear Strategy in the Modern Era*, 160.
59. Gregory, *Nuclear Command and Control in NATO*, 131; Narang, *Nuclear Strategy in the Modern Era*, 160.
60. Bruno Tertrais, "France," in *Governing the Bomb: Civilian Control and Democratic Accountability of Nuclear Weapons*, ed. Hans Born, Bates Gill, and Heiner Hänggi (New York: Oxford University Press, 2010), 112.
61. Shaun Gregory, "French Nuclear Command and Control," *Defense Analysis* 6, no. 1 (March 1990): 59; Narang, *Nuclear Strategy in the Modern Era*, 159; Tertrais, "France," 113.
62. Tertrais, "France," 112; Pelopidas, "France."

ing the Cold War—and a strategic rationale that envisioned early use both pushed France towards delegative control.[63] Similar to the United Kingdom, the likely persistence of delegative control after the collapse of the Soviet Union suggests that while external threats likely contributed to the initial development of delegative control measures, those threats cannot explain the endurance of delegative control. Furthermore, although France experienced a coup attempt that directly impinged on the nuclear arsenal, such domestic constraints do not appear to have produced a corresponding level of assertive control.[64]

CHINA

China tested its first nuclear weapon on October 16, 1964, becoming the final legally recognized nuclear weapons state under the Treaty on the Non-Proliferation of Nuclear Weapons.[65] Land-based ballistic missiles constitute the main operational leg of China's nuclear arsenal.[66] Although recent modernization efforts have introduced uncertainty in the nature of Chinese command and control procedures—especially with regards to China's emerging submarine-based nuclear capabilities—analysts generally accept that China has historically exercised highly assertive control over its nuclear forces.[67]

Administratively, nuclear operations occur under the authority of the chairman of the Central Military Commission (CMC).[68] China's political leaders have historically prioritized political control over nuclear forces. John Lewis and Xue Litai note this emphasis on centralized administrative control: "A launch will automatically be aborted if any step violates the verification requirements."[69] Furthermore, unlike other services in the People's Liberation Army (PLA), the CMC directly commands the PLA Rocket Force to guarantee political oversight of nuclear operations.[70] Physically, nuclear warheads are de-mated from delivery platforms and geographically dispersed to guarantee that lower-level military actors cannot use nuclear

---

63. Narang, *Nuclear Strategy in the Modern Era*, 154–169.
64. Feaver, "Nuclear Command and Control in Crisis," 212–214.
65. Fiona S. Cunningham and M. Taylor Fravel, "Assuring Assured Retaliation: China's Nuclear Posture and U.S.-China Strategic Stability," *International Security* 40, no. 2 (Fall 2015), 12.
66. Hans M. Kristensen and Matt Korda, "Chinese Nuclear Forces, 2019," *Bulletin of the Atomic Scientists* 75, no. 4 (July 2019): 172.
67. Fiona Cunningham, "Nuclear Command, Control, and Communications Systems of the People's Republic of China," NAPSNet Special Reports, July 18, 2019.
68. Bates Gill and Evan S. Medeiros, "China," in Born, Gill, and Hänggi, eds., *Governing the Bomb*, 137.
69. John Wilson Lewis and Xue Litai, *Imagined Enemies: China Prepares for Uncertain War* (Stanford, CA: Stanford University Press, 2008), 198–199.
70. Cunningham, "Nuclear Command, Control, and Communications Systems of the People's Republic of China."

weapons without political approval.[71] A political commissar oversees nuclear warheads at China's nuclear storage facilities and only releases these warheads to the PLA's missile units upon the direction of CMC and Politburo leaders.[72] Technical use-control devices likely exist on China's current nuclear weapons and are either indigenously developed or the product of Russian assistance.[73]

China has faced extensive periods of external threats to its nuclear arsenal and command and control systems, ranging from its 1969 border conflict with the Soviet Union to more recent vulnerabilities to US nuclear forces.[74] China has employed assertive control throughout its nuclear history, thereby opposing the predictions of the external threats explanation. The strategic rationale argument, however, correctly anticipates that China's reliance on a late-use doctrine of assured retaliation should produce assertive control. Domestic politics also correspond to China's assertive control measures, with the domestic instability produced by the Cultural Revolution leading to more assertive control early in China's nuclear program and the exclusion of military organizations from nuclear decision making remaining central to assertive control.[75]

ISRAEL

As a matter of policy, neither Israel nor the United States has formally declared Israel as a nuclear weapons state. In practice, however, Israeli leaders have cultivated the widespread belief that Israel likely possesses nuclear weapons. We adopt the now-standard convention among academic specialists by writing as though Israel has a nuclear arsenal.

Due to Israel's nuclear opacity, Avner Cohen—a leading scholar on Israel's nuclear program—notes that "Virtually nothing is publicly known about Israel's nuclear command and control structure."[76] To the extent that data

---

71. Mark A. Stokes, *China's Nuclear Warhead Storage and Handling System*, Project 2049 Institute Monograph, March 12, 2010, https://project2049.net/wp-content/uploads/2018/05/chinas_nuclear_warhead_storage_and_handling_system.pdf.

72. Stokes, *China's Nuclear Warhead*, 5.

73. Cunningham, "Nuclear Command, Control, and Communications Systems of the People's Republic of China."

74. On the 1969 Sino-Soviet border dispute, see M. Taylor Fravel, *Strong Borders, Secure Nation: Cooperation and Conflict in China's Territorial Disputes* (Princeton: Princeton University Press, 2008), 201–209. On China's acceptance of nuclear vulnerabilities, see Wu Riqiang, "Living with Uncertainty: Modeling China's Nuclear Survivability," *International Security* 44, no. 4 (Spring 2020): 84–118.

75. Mark A. Stokes, "Securing Nuclear Arsenals: A Chinese Case Study," in Sokolski and Tertrais, eds., *Nuclear Weapons Security Crises*, 65–85.

76. Avner Cohen, "Israel," in Born, Gill, and Hänggi, eds., *Governing the Bomb*, 157–158.

on Israeli nuclear operations are available, however, command and control systems appear to be assertive in nature.[77] Administratively, civilian elites retain exclusive nuclear use authority. In 1962, Prime Minister David Ben-Gurion chaired a meeting that resulted in an explicit decision to strictly separate conventional military operations from nuclear planning, thereby allowing for strict political control over nuclear use decisions.[78] Exclusive civilian control remains a pillar of Israel's command and control procedures and appears to apply during peacetime and late into conventional crises.[79] Physically, Israel maintained its nuclear weapons in a disassembled state during the early years of its nuclear program, with the civilian-led Israel Atomic Energy Commission controlling the nuclear cores and the Israel Defense Forces operating the delivery platforms.[80] The physical separation of nuclear warheads from land and air-based delivery platforms likely remain in effect, but it is unclear whether Israel employs any such controls over its submarine-based nuclear capabilities.[81] Technically, Israel likely developed a PAL equivalent in the 1980s.[82]

Paradoxically, despite its history of wars and vulnerability to terrorism, Israel's external threat environment today is sufficiently benign to permit more assertive command and control practices. The absence of a conventionally superior or nuclear-armed adversary reduces time-urgency pressures and facilitates assertive control. Israel's assured retaliation posture also enables assertive control measures and offers support for the strategic rationale argument.[83] Domestic politics, in contrast, offers a poor explanation for assertive control in Israel. Specifically, despite traditionally high levels of military autonomy and influence in national security policymaking that should predict more delegative patterns of command and control, the Israel Defense Forces have been unable to shape nuclear doctrine since the inception of Israel's nuclear weapons program.[84] This judgment is caveated by the high degree of uncertainty and opacity surrounding the Israeli program.

---

77. Cohen, "Israel," 152–170.
78. Avner Cohen, *Israel and the Bomb* (New York: Columbia University Press, 1998), 148–151; Avner Cohen, *The Worst-Kept Secret: Israel's Bargain with the Bomb* (New York: Columbia University Press, 2010), 62–67.
79. Avner Cohen, "Israel's NC3 Profile: Opaque Nuclear Governance," NAPSNet Special Reports, October 11, 2019.
80. Seymour M. Hersh, *The Samson Option: Israel's Nuclear Arsenal and American Foreign Policy* (New York: Random House, 1991), 84.
81. Hans M. Kristensen and Robert S. Norris, "Israeli Nuclear Weapons, 2014," *Bulletin of the Atomic Scientists* 70, no. 6 (November 2014): 101. Cohen, "Israel's NC3 Profile."
82. Cohen, "Israel," 158.
83. Narang, *Nuclear Strategy in the Modern Era*, 199–201.
84. Cohen, "Israel," 154–156.

CHAPTER 7

SOUTH AFRICA

South Africa is the only state to indigenously develop and subsequently dismantle its nuclear arsenal. South Africa developed its first nuclear device in 1979 and ultimately assembled six air-deliverable nuclear bombs in the 1980s.[85] South Africa began dismantling its nuclear weapons in 1989 and fully decommissioned all nuclear weapons by 1991.[86]

South Africa managed its nuclear arsenal through highly assertive measures. Administrative control procedures emphasized centralized political control over South Africa's nuclear weapons.[87] To access, assemble, and deploy nuclear weapons, the president would issue simultaneous orders to the minister of defense and the minister of energy affairs, who would then relay authentication codes along a parallel chain of command that included representatives from the South African Defense Force, the Atomic Energy Corporation, and the Armaments Corporation of South Africa. This division of administrative oversight guaranteed that nuclear weapons remained centrally controlled. Physically, South Africa split its nuclear weapons into two components: one half containing the nuclear warhead and a second half containing the gun assembly and uranium missile to initiate the detonation process. Both halves were stored in separate vaults and separate from delivery platforms.[88] Technically, each nuclear weapon contained a mechanical lock that served as a safe-ing mechanism that blocked the uranium missile from initiating a nuclear reaction unless the lock was removed.[89]

South Africa did not face major external threats while in possession of nuclear weapons.[90] The employment of assertive control aligns with the predictions of the external threats explanation, which predicts that a benign security environment facilitates assertive control. South Africa's late-use doctrine also correlates with assertive control, as predicted by the strategic rationale explanation.[91] Furthermore, high levels of domestic instability—especially in the twilight of the apartheid regime—also appear to explain the regime's intense centralization of political control over nuclear decision making.[92]

---

85. Nic von Wielligh and Lydia von Wielligh-Steyn, *The Bomb: South Africa's Nuclear Program* (Pretoria: Litera, 2015), 171.
86. David Albright, "South Africa and the Affordable Bomb," *Bulletin of the Atomic Scientists* 50, no. 4 (July 1994): 46.
87. Von Wielligh and von Wielligh-Steyn, *The Bomb*, 504–505.
88. Von Wielligh and von Wielligh-Steyn, *The Bomb*, 172.
89. Hannes Steyn, Richardt Van Der Walt, and Jan Van Loggerenberg, *Armament and Disarmament: South Africa's Nuclear Experience*, 2nd ed. (New York: iUniverse, 2005), 89.
90. James Barber and John Barratt, *South Africa's Foreign Policy: The Search for Status and Security, 1945–1988* (New York: Cambridge University Press, 1990), 247–346.
91. Peter Liberman, "The Rise and Fall of the South African Bomb," *International Security* 26, no. 2 (Fall 2001), 54–58.
92. For an elaboration on this argument, see Arceneaux, "Beyond the Rubicon," 136–165.

INDIA

India tested a nuclear device in 1974 but did not acquire the operational means to air-deliver a nuclear weapon until approximately 1988.[93] India has since diversified its arsenal to include land-based ballistic missiles and submarine-launched ballistic missiles.[94] Throughout its nuclear weapons program, India has managed its nuclear arsenal through highly assertive command and control measures that only delegate nuclear use capability to lower levels late in a crisis.[95]

India's administrative controls strongly emphasize centralized political control. The 1999 draft nuclear doctrine grants the prime minister strict control over nuclear use decisions.[96] India also strictly separates its chains of command for nuclear and conventional operations to facilitate civilian oversight of nuclear operations.[97] Physically, India has historically disassembled and de-mated its nuclear weapons from delivery platforms.[98] At least through the mid-2000s, the Department of Atomic Energy maintained custody of the fissile pits, and the Defense Research and Development Organization managed non-fissile components, such as nuclear triggers and detonators.[99] Since then, India has increased its reliance on canisterized systems that pre-mate warheads to delivery platforms, suggesting that physical control may be a weakening pillar of assertive control.[100] Technically, nuclear forces are likely protected by an indigenously developed PAL equivalent that requires a code at the final stages of deployment to arm and prepare the nuclear weapon for release across all platforms.[101] These codes are centrally managed to prevent lower-level commanders from bypassing the designated chain of command and to guarantee political oversight.

External threats do not appear to have significantly shaped India's command and control systems. Despite persistent border disputes with China and Pakistan—two nuclear-armed adversaries—India has maintained

---

93. George Perkovich, *India's Nuclear Bomb: The Impact on Global Proliferation* (Berkeley: University of California Press, 1999), 293; Dong-Joon Jo and Erik Gartzke, "Determinants of Nuclear Weapons Proliferation," *Journal of Conflict Resolution* 51, no. 1 (February 2007): 167–194.

94. Hans M. Kristensen and Matt Korda, "Indian Nuclear Forces, 2018," *Bulletin of the Atomic Scientists* 74, no. 6 (November 2018): 361–366.

95. For a detailed discussion of assertive control in India, see Arceneaux, "Beyond the Rubicon," 61–97.

96. Government of India, "Draft Report of National Security Advisory Board on Indian Nuclear Doctrine," August 17, 1999.

97. Narang, *Nuclear Strategy in the Modern Era*, 107.

98. Ashley J. Tellis, *India's Emerging Nuclear Posture: Between Recessed Deterrent and Ready Arsenal* (Santa Monica, CA: RAND Corporation, 2001), 401–428.

99. Narang, *Nuclear Strategy in the Modern Era*, 101.

100. Christopher Clary and Vipin Narang, "India's Counterforce Temptations: Strategic Dilemmas, Doctrine, and Capabilities," *International Security* 43, no. 3 (Winter 2018/19): 7–52.

101. Narang, *Nuclear Strategy in the Modern Era*, 106–107.

assertive control over its nuclear forces.[102] The strategic rationale argument, in contrast, correctly anticipates that India's late-use nuclear doctrine should produce assertive control.[103] Domestic politics also appear to play a significant role in India's employment of assertive control measures, as the purposeful and systematic exclusion of military influence in nuclear decision making has allowed political leaders to centralize control over India's nuclear forces.[104]

PAKISTAN

Pakistan employs conditional command and control arrangements over its nuclear arsenal. Conditional control allows Pakistan to centralize oversight of nuclear use decisions during peacetime, while also enabling the rapid delegation of nuclear use authority during crises to deter conventional aggression and bolster arsenal reliability.

Administrative control in Pakistan is centralized during peacetime. The prime minister officially chairs Pakistan's National Command Authority, which is responsible for policy formulation and the oversight of nuclear forces.[105] Although civilian leadership possesses de jure authority over nuclear operations, the military-led Strategic Plans Division ultimately exercises de facto authority over nuclear use.[106] Early in crises, Pakistan's command and control systems allow for the rapid devolution of nuclear use capability to lower-level commanders and enable field commanders to authorize nuclear use.[107] Physically, Pakistan's warheads are partially disassembled during peacetime, with the fissile cores and detonators separated from one another and dispersed across an unknown distance.[108] At a minimum, warheads are de-mated from delivery platforms to provide physical control during peacetime.[109] As crises escalate, Pakistan is likely to begin assembling weapons and mating those weapons to delivery platforms to increase the readiness of its nuclear forces, and Pakistan's military can quickly prepare nuclear weapons

---

102. On why external threats have not caused India to adopt more delegative control, see Arceneaux, "Beyond the Rubicon," 82–88.
103. Narang, *Nuclear Strategy in the Modern Era*, 94–120.
104. Arceneaux, "Beyond the Rubicon," 88–94.
105. "Pakistan Announcement of Nuclear-Weapons Command-and-Control Mechanism," Associated Press of Pakistan, February 3, 2000, http://www.acronym.org.uk/old/archive/spmech.htm.
106. Narang, *Nuclear Strategy in the Modern Era*, 84.
107. Mahmud Ali Durrani, "Pakistan's Strategic Thinking and the Role of Nuclear Weapons," Cooperative Monitoring Center Occasional Paper, no. 37, Sandia National Laboratories, Albuquerque, NM, 2004, 33.
108. Christopher Clary and Ankit Panda, "Safer at Sea? Pakistan's Sea-Based Deterrent and Nuclear Weapons Security," *Washington Quarterly* 40, no. 3 (Fall 2017): 153.
109. Naeem Salik, *Learning to Live with the Bomb: Pakistan: 1998–2016* (Karachi: Oxford University Press, 2017), 189.

for deployment in the event of a crisis. Pakistan's primary technical control over nuclear forces is a PAL-like device that aims to prevent unauthorized use.[110] These Pak-PALs are likely simple code-lock devices that lock subcomponents of the weapon or block the fusing space to prevent a nuclear detonation.[111] Pak-PALs can be bypassed to allow for nuclear use in the absence of authorization codes from political authorities.[112] The military custodians of nuclear forces likely include technical teams on base with the capacity to bypass these locks and enable nuclear use as crises escalate.[113]

External threats appear to play a significant role in explaining Pakistan's conditional control arrangements. Specifically, Pakistan's significant conventional inferiority with respect to India encourages the early delegation of nuclear use ability.[114] The strategic rationale argument also correctly predicts that Pakistan's first-use nuclear posture would enable nuclear delegation early in a crisis.[115] Domestic politics appear to play a significant role in Pakistan's nuclear decision making as well, but with different factors creating opposing pressures. The Pakistan Army's outsized political influence enables the military to adopt more delegative control, whereas longstanding fears of domestic instability and threats to arsenal safety and security promote more assertive control procedures.[116] Pakistan's employment of conditional control appears to be an attempt to balance the competing pressures that encourage the peacetime centralization of control over nuclear forces and incentives for delegation early in a crisis to guarantee arsenal reliability.[117]

NORTH KOREA

North Korea became the most recent state to acquire deliverable nuclear capabilities after testing its first nuclear device in 2006.[118] Although developments in North Korea's delivery platforms are observable to outside analysts, little information is available on the country's nuclear command and control capabilities.

---

110. Narang, *Nuclear Strategy in the Modern Era*, 88.
111. For descriptions of Pak-PALs, see: Clary, *Thinking about Pakistan's Nuclear Security in Peacetime, Crisis and War*, 15; Durrani, "Pakistan's Strategic Thinking and the Role of Nuclear Weapons," 33.
112. David O. Smith, "The Management of Pakistan's Nuclear Arsenal," *Nonproliferation Review* 21, nos. 3–4 (October 2014): 283.
113. Narang, *Nuclear Strategy in the Modern Era*, 89.
114. Arceneaux, "Beyond the Rubicon," 122–127.
115. Narang, "Posturing for Peace?"
116. Christopher Clary, "The Safety and Security of the Pakistani Nuclear Arsenal," in *Pakistan's Enduring Challenges*, ed. C. Christine Fair and Sarah J. Watson (Philadelphia: University of Pennsylvania Press, 2015), 98–127.
117. Arceneaux, "Beyond the Rubicon," 98–135.
118. Hans M. Kristensen and Robert S. Norris, "North Korean Nuclear Capabilities, 2018," *Bulletin of the Atomic Scientists* 74, no. 1 (January 2018): 41–51.

The available evidence suggests that North Korea employs conditional command and control systems. Administratively, the chairman of the Workers' Party exercises the final authority over nuclear use decisions. As North Korea's state-run Korean Central News Agency (KCNA) reported, "nuclear weapons can be used only by a final order of the Supreme Commander of the Korean People's Army (KPA)."[119] North Korea institutionalized centralized peacetime control in 2012 by creating the Strategic Rocket Forces Command, a military body with equal status to the other KPA services that reports directly to the supreme leader.[120] At the same time, the KCNA emphasizes that nuclear weapons must remain "on standby so as to be fired any moment."[121] Given North Korea's doctrinal emphasis on preemptive strikes, it appears likely that Kim Jong Un would rapidly decentralize control early in a crisis and delegate nuclear use capability to lower-level commanders.[122] Physically, the Central Military Committee (CMC) of the Workers' Party of Korea manages nuclear warheads during peacetime. Once the supreme leader authorizes the release of nuclear weapons, military operators can obtain warheads from the CMC and mount the warheads to their delivery platforms.[123] Technically, no evidence exists to suggest that North Korea employs technical constraints on its nuclear weapons.[124]

External threats provide strong incentives for North Korea to adopt more delegative command and control systems. North Korea's conventional and nuclear vulnerabilities to the United States generate pressures on state security and regime survival and correctly anticipate that North Korea should adopt more delegative control. The strategic rationale argument also appears to receive some support from the North Korea case, as indications of a first-use nuclear posture would also expect more delegative control.[125] Neither external threats nor strategic rationale can explain the peacetime centralization of political control that is inherent to North Korea's conditional control arrangements. Domestic politics appear to explain such peacetime central-

---

119. "Law on Consolidating Position of Nuclear Weapons State Adopted," Korean Central News Agency, April 1, 2013, https://kcnawatch.org/newstream/1451896124-739013370/law-on-consolidating-position-of-nuclear-weapons-state-adopted/.

120. Andrew O'Neil, "North Korea's Dangerously Rudimentary Nuclear Command-and-Control Systems," *Interpreter*, August 14, 2017.

121. "Kim Jong Un Guides Test-Fire of New Multiple Launch Rocket System," Korean Central News Agency, March 4, 2016, https://kcnawatch.org/newstream/252244/kim-jong-un-guides-test-fire-of-new-multiple-launch-rocket-system/.

122. Léonie Allard, Mathieu Duchâtel, and François Godement, "Pre-Empting Defeat: In Search of North Korea's Nuclear Doctrine," Policy Brief, European Council on Foreign Relations, 2017, 7; Nathan Beauchamp-Mustafaga, "North Korea's Weak Nuclear C2 Challenges Korean Crisis Stability," Pacific Forum Brief no. 22, March 14, 2017.

123. Myeongguk Cheon, "DPRK's NC3 System," NAPSNet Special Reports, June 6, 2019.

124. Beauchamp-Mustafaga, "North Korea's Weak Nuclear C2 Challenges Korean Crisis Stability."

125. Allard, Duchâtel, and Godement, "Pre-Empting Defeat."

ization of nuclear use ability, as the Kim dynasty's enduring fears of domestic threats to the regime's continued political rule encourage greater political oversight.[126] Like Pakistan, North Korea provides an example of how states use conditional control arrangements to simultaneously address competing pressures for early—and late-crisis delegation.

EVALUATING THE EXPLANATIONS

The evidence presented in this section demonstrates that regional nuclear powers have adopted a wide range of command and control systems, with multiple states adopting assertive, conditional, and delegative control systems. Furthermore, the evidence supports the chapter's argument that regional nuclear powers require direct analysis to explain command and control decisions, rather than relying on deductive extensions of Cold War frameworks. Table 7.2 summarizes how the alternative explanations empirically perform in each regional nuclear power.

The empirical analysis reveals two findings regarding the effects of external threats on command and control arrangements. First, nuclear threats provide at best a weak explanation for variation in regional nuclear power command and control systems. For example, despite potential arsenal and command vulnerabilities that should produce more delegative control, states such as China and India employ strictly assertive control measures that undermine the nuclear threats hypothesis. Second, conventional threats to state security and regime survival are more pronounced and influential in regional nuclear powers. All regional nuclear powers that have faced severe conventional threats—including France during the Cold War, Pakistan, and North Korea—have adopted conditional or delegative control systems that increase arsenal readiness. Whereas nuclear threats powerfully shaped command and control decisions in the Cold War superpowers, conventional threats serve as the more prevalent external threat to regional nuclear powers and appear to powerfully shape command and control decisions.

The strategic rationale hypothesis obtains mixed results after empirical analysis. On the one hand, late-use doctrines in India, China, and apartheid-era South Africa clearly align with highly assertive command and control systems. On the other hand, several cases deviate from the expectations of the strategic rationale hypothesis. For example, although the United Kingdom employs a late-use doctrine that should enable assertive control, British policymakers delegate nuclear use ability to military custodians of nuclear weapons during peacetime. Furthermore, although Pakistan and

---

126. Daniel Byman and Jennifer Lind, "Pyongyang's Survival Strategy: Tools of Authoritarian Control in North Korea," *International Security* 35, no. 1 (Summer 2010): 44–74; Scott Snyder, "North Korea's Challenge of Regime Survival: Internal Problems and Implications for the Future," *Pacific Affairs* 73, no. 4 (Winter 2000/2001): 517–533.

CHAPTER 7

Table 7.2 Empirically Evaluating Explanations for Nuclear Command and Control

Explanation	Measurement	Summary of Case Outcomes
External threat environment	Nuclear threats	Aligns with outcomes in some cases (Israel, South Africa, Pakistan) but fails to explain assertive control in cases where states face nuclear threats (China, India) and the persistence of delegative control after nuclear threats weaken (United Kingdom, France).
	Conventional threats	Clearly influential in explaining early delegation in some cases (France during the Cold War, Pakistan) and assertive control in others (e.g., China, South Africa, India). Fails to explain persistence of delegative control after conventional threats dissipate (United Kingdom, France).
Strategic rationale	Nuclear use doctrine	Aligns with outcomes in many cases (e.g., China, France, South Africa, India). Cannot explain why Pakistan's first-use doctrine does not provide predelegation or the persistence of delegative control in Britain, despite a late-use doctrine.
Domestic politics	Civil-military relations	Influential and important in several cases (e.g., United Kingdom, China, India), but fails to predict assertive control in cases with influential militaries (Israel, South Africa).
	Domestic instability	Correctly predicts assertive control in countries facing domestic challenges (China during the Cultural Revolution, apartheid-era South Africa) but cannot explain the range of variation in domestically stable states (i.e., delegative control in the United Kingdom and assertive control in India).

North Korea both appear to possess nuclear doctrines that envision first-use, both countries stop short of fully delegative control measures and employ conditional control systems that maintain centralized control during peacetime. The strategic rationale hypothesis offers some leverage for explaining command and control in regional nuclear powers, but an initial investigation of the data suggests that the strategic rationale explanation is at best incomplete.

The evidence presented here also shows that domestic politics affect command and control outcomes in a wide range of regional nuclear powers. Indeed, the nature of civil-military relations and levels of domestic instability vary more widely in regional nuclear powers than the Cold War superpowers, and both factors yield significant findings. First, the civil-military relations hypothesis correctly predicts that states in which the military enjoys greater organizational autonomy will adopt more delegative control systems, as observed in the United Kingdom and Pakistan. Conversely, states are more likely to adopt assertive control in countries where political leaders purposefully reduce the autonomy and influence of a military organization, such as India and China. The civil-military relations hypothesis, however, appears insufficient to explain command and control outcomes. For example, despite the Pakistan Army's complete control over nuclear decision making, Pakistan nevertheless employs conditional control arrangements that promote centralized control during peacetime. Despite the central political role of the South African Defense Force in apartheid-era South Africa, civilian leaders exercised highly assertive control that challenges the civil-military relations hypothesis.[127]

Domestic instability provides a second domestic-level explanation of command and control in regional nuclear powers. Domestic challenges to the apartheid regime in South Africa and China's Cultural Revolution provide clear examples of domestically unstable regimes adopting highly assertive control measures, as predicted by the domestic instability hypothesis.[128] Pakistan and North Korea provide examples of states facing severe domestic instability that have adopted conditional control arrangements. Although conditional control allows these states to assert control over nuclear forces during peacetime, the ability to rapidly delegate command early in a crisis shows that domestic instability alone cannot explain variation in regional nuclear power command and control systems.

The empirical analysis also reveals a third potential domestic-level explanation for the cases: the inertia of bureaucratic politics from a state's earliest design choices appear to persist even when the factors that drove initial command and control decisions no longer obtain. We see evidence of this kind of bureaucratic politics at work in all of the country cases, but perhaps especially Britain and France, the oldest of the regional nuclear powers. In these cases, delegative control arrangements remain in place despite a significantly more benign threat environment after the Cold War. The history of US nuclear command and control suggests that evolution is possible, but the general lack of variation in many explanatory variables and the presence of bureaucratic inertia suggest that changes in regional nuclear power command and control systems will be case-specific rather than general trends.

This evaluation of the alternative explanations for command and control in regional nuclear powers also highlights three broader takeaways. First, the wide range of observed variation in command and control frameworks

---

127. On the political influence of the South African military during this period, see Philip H. Frankel, *Pretoria's Praetorians: Civil-Military Relations in South Africa* (Cambridge: Cambridge University Press, 1984).

128. Mark A. Stokes, "Securing Nuclear Arsenals: A Chinese Case Study," in Sokolski and Tertrais, eds., *Nuclear Weapons Security Crises*, 65–85.

CHAPTER 7

demonstrates the utility of our conceptual framework. By emphasizing the timing of delegation with respect to crisis onset, we are able to more precisely differentiate between assertive, conditional, and delegative command and control systems in regional nuclear powers. Second, although several factors such as conventional threats, strategic rationale, civil-military relations, and domestic instability appear to influence command and control decisions in regional nuclear powers, further research is needed to identify the conditions under which these explanations shape command and control outcomes. Each variable appears to have a mixed record in predicting command and control outcomes, which suggests that further research on cases such as Pakistan and North Korea—both of which likely employ conditional control in response to severe external threats and domestic political instability—could help resolve the longstanding question of how regional nuclear powers will respond when facing opposing pressures on command and control systems.[129] Third, the analysis indicates the enduring challenges of empirically evaluating command and control systems in regional nuclear powers. Although more data are currently available than when regional nuclear powers began developing their arsenals, the secrecy surrounding nuclear command and control systems remains a barrier to empirical analysis and requires analysts to accept lower levels of confidence when developing theories of nuclear operations in regional nuclear powers.

Nuclear Command and Control in the Twenty-First Century

Rather than following the Cold War superpower script, regional nuclear powers have instead adopted a wide array of nuclear command and control arrangements. Regional nuclear powers face similar tradeoffs to those encountered by the Cold War superpowers and have drawn certain lessons from the US and Soviet experiences, but regional nuclear powers have modified these lessons to suit their own purposes. This chapter illustrates these points by providing a new conceptual framework for command and control systems and providing an initial empirical analysis to identify the factors that lead regional nuclear powers to adopt assertive, conditional, or delegative command and control arrangements.

Although data limitations continue to constrain the ability of outside analysts to evaluate nuclear command and control systems in regional nuclear powers—especially in inaccessible or secretive countries like North Korea and Israel—the practices of some recent proliferators such as India and Pakistan have emerged through official public statements and interviews by individual researchers with political and military elites in these countries. Information on

---

129. Feaver, "Command and Control in Emerging Nuclear Nations," 181.

nuclear command and control in the Cold War superpowers was limited for the first three decades of the nuclear age before scholars obtained extensive and reliable empirical evidence. Scholars can expect a similarly gradual increase in data availability in regional nuclear powers over time and should continue to revise theoretical and conceptual frameworks as these new data become available. Other potential sources of data include recent revelations about how states manage other weapons of mass destruction, such as chemical weapons, although further research will be necessary to determine the extent to which the command and control of different weapons types translate into the nuclear realm.[130]

The empirical record is mixed for the post-Cold War predictions of both proliferation optimists and pessimists. In contrast to the expectations of the proliferation optimism school, several regional nuclear powers have adopted command and control frameworks that are markedly delegative in nature, such as France and the United Kingdom. Other states such as Pakistan and likely North Korea envision first-use nuclear doctrines that delegate nuclear use capability to peripheral military commanders early in a crisis. These command and control arrangements enable lower-level commanders to use nuclear weapons without political approval and increase the likelihood of a conventional crisis escalating across the nuclear threshold. As pessimists feared, regional nuclear powers experience a variety of domestic and international pressures that encourage leaders to consider command and control systems that prioritize arsenal reliability over safety and security.

As optimists predicted and contrary to the worst fears of pessimists, however, regional nuclear powers have thus far managed their nuclear arsenals without experiencing the accidental or unauthorized use of nuclear weapons. Furthermore, political crises involving regional nuclear powers have not escalated out of control and across the nuclear threshold. Although the operational configuration of command and control systems in regional nuclear powers aligns with several expectations of the proliferation pessimism school, the absence of nuclear use offers support for the proliferation optimism school.

Although nuclear optimists have thus far correctly predicted the absence of purposeful or inadvertent nuclear use, empirical trends in recent proliferators provide cause for concern. Notably, conditional control arrangements in Pakistan and North Korea provide examples of new challenges to crisis stability, as these arrangements create avenues to unwanted escalation during crises. Furthermore, Pakistan and North Korea also face significant challenges

---

130. As an example, Saddam Hussein appears to have predelegated the ability to use chemical weapons in the event of a decapitation attack on his regime. Benjamin Buch and Scott D. Sagan, "Our Red Lines and Theirs," Foreign Policy, December 13, 2013, https://foreignpolicy.com/2013/12/13/our-red-lines-and-theirs/.

regarding long-term domestic political stability that could threaten to throw nuclear-armed countries into domestic political turmoil. In short, despite the good fortune that the world has received to avoid nuclear use, significant reasons for concern remain. To paraphrase Winston Churchill, perhaps both optimists and pessimists have something about which to be modest.

Improving our understanding of the causes of variation in regional nuclear power command and control systems also provides the foundations for anticipating the effects of command and control systems on important outcomes in international security. In particular, this chapter's theoretical and empirical discussion of conditional control arrangements reveals two emerging challenges for nuclear security. First, conditional control systems provide pathways to inadvertent nuclear escalation that are not captured by the traditional binary measurement of assertive and delegative control. For instance, the process of decentralizing the ability to use nuclear weapons early in a crisis may signal malign intent to an adversary.[131] An adversary would likely view actions such as mating warheads to delivery platforms and dispersing nuclear assets as offensive in nature and could choose to escalate an ongoing crisis to preempt a nuclear attack. Furthermore, the rapid delegation of nuclear use capability from centralized political authorities to military operators would weaken political oversight of nuclear decision making and increase the likelihood of divergence between political goals and military actions as political leaders attempt to reduce tensions while the military prepares for conducting nuclear operations.[132] Second, the empirical analysis in this chapter shows that conditional control arrangements are now a prominent form of command and control in regional nuclear powers. Pakistan and North Korea—the two most recent states to develop nuclear weapons—seemingly employ conditional control arrangements that have the potential to foster crisis escalation and have engaged in numerous crises with nuclear adversaries.[133] These cases show that the challenges presented by conditional command and control systems are likely to persist and deserve greater attention within the scholarly and policy communities to foster strategic stability in future crises.

---

131. Blair, "Alerting in Crisis and Conventional War," 75–78.
132. Blair, "Alerting in Crisis and Conventional War," 113–119.
133. For instance, Pakistan and India were mired in the Balakot crisis in 2019, and North Korea engaged in a series of escalating threats with the United States in 2017. Williams and Narang, "Thermonuclear Twitter?"

CHAPTER 8

The Limits of Nuclear Learning in the New Nuclear Age

Mark S. Bell and Nicholas L. Miller

The idea of nuclear learning offers a powerful reason for optimism about the future nuclear landscape. According to the nuclear learning argument, new nuclear-armed states learn over time that nuclear weapons are good for deterring invasion or nuclear attack but not much else. In Kenneth Waltz's words, "the slow spread of nuclear weapons gives states time to learn to live with them . . . and to understand the limits they place on behavior."[1] Others acknowledge that learning takes time and may even require states to learn from potentially dangerous crises, but still retain the optimistic view that states learn stabilizing (and normatively pleasing) lessons over time.[2] Indeed, nuclear learning is merely one application of a broader literature that suggests states can learn—a "descriptive term for identifying any new inference drawn by an individual based on observation, experience, or mentoring"—and craft smarter foreign policies as a result.[3]

---

1. Kenneth N. Waltz, "The Spread of Nuclear Weapons: More May Be Better," *Adelphi Papers* 21, no. 171 (1981): 26.
2. Joseph S. Nye Jr., "Nuclear Learning and U.S.-Soviet Security Regimes," *International Organization* 41, no. 3 (1987): 371–402; Michael C. Horowitz, "The Spread of Nuclear Weapons and International Conflict: Does Experience Matter?," *Journal of Conflict Resolution* 53, no. 2 (2009): 234–257; Michael D. Cohen, *When Proliferation Causes Peace: The Psychology of Nuclear Crises* (Washington, DC: Georgetown University Press, 2017).
3. We take this definition from Jeffrey W. Knopf, "The Concept of Nuclear Learning," *Nonproliferation Review* 19, no. 1 (2012): 85. For example, George W. Breslauer, "Ideology and Learning in Soviet Third World Policy," *World Politics* 39, no. 3 (1987): 429–448; Jack Levy, "Learning and Foreign Policy: Sweeping a Conceptual Minefield," *International Organization* 48, no. 2 (1994): 279–312; Janice Gross Stein, "Deterrence and Learning in an Enduring Rivalry: Egypt and Israel, 1948–73," *Security Studies* 6, no. 1 (1996): 104–152; Daniel Sobelman, "Learning to Deter: Deterrence Failure and Success in the Israel-Hezbollah Conflict, 2006–16," *International Security* 41, no. 3 (2016/2017): 151–196.

CHAPTER 8

The question of whether nuclear learning can allow states to settle into stable patterns of deterrence is theoretical but has important policy implications in the new nuclear era. For example, advocates of nuclear learning argue that the policy challenges associated with new nuclear-armed states such as North Korea are a short- or medium-term problem rather than a long-term one. If the international community can get through an initial period of instability, stable patterns of deterrence will then emerge as both sides learn. Michael Cohen's argument is representative: "Leaders in Pyongyang and Tehran may develop nuclear weapons and authorize assertive foreign policies in the short term, [but] this behavior is unlikely to continue over the long run," with leaders subsequently "authoriz[ing] restrained foreign policies."[4] Similarly, Michael Horowitz argues that "new nuclear states appear the most 'risky.'"[5] Experienced nuclear states, and future relations among established nuclear-armed states, by contrast, should not be objects of substantial concern.

Despite the prominence of the nuclear learning argument and its importance to policy debates, it has rarely been subjected to direct critique.[6] In this chapter, we argue that the nuclear learning argument is built on weak theoretical and empirical foundations. Moreover, in the new nuclear era, nuclear learning is even less likely than in the past. We show that there are theoretical reasons to believe nuclear learning should occur rarely, if at all, and is particularly unlikely in the new nuclear era. We also show that the nuclear learning argument fails to make sense of the historical record by briefly examining the US-Soviet case as well as the more recent cases of India and Pakistan. The evidence suggests that while these states may sometimes have learned lessons about nuclear weapons, they were not generally the stabilizing ones anticipated by nuclear learning advocates.

---

4. Cohen, *When Proliferation Causes Peace*, 24.
5. Horowitz, "The Spread of Nuclear Weapons and International Conflict," 250.
6. For examples of partial or implicit critiques of nuclear learning, see Scott D. Sagan, *The Limits of Safety: Organizations, Accidents, and Nuclear Weapons* (Princeton: Princeton University Press, 1993), chap. 5, which finds limited learning with respect to preventing nuclear accidents; and Peter D. Feaver, "Command and Control in Emerging Nuclear Nations," *International Security* 17, no. 3 (1992/1993): 160–187, which argues that learning does not appear to explain the evolution of states' nuclear command and control arrangements. For more direct critiques of nuclear learning that focus on the specific cases of India and the Cuban Missile Crisis, respectively, see Frank O'Donnell, "India's Nuclear Counter-Revolution: Nuclear Learning and the Future of Deterrence," *Nonproliferation Review* 26, no. 5–6 (2019): 407–426 and Benoît Pelopidas, "The Unbearable Lightness of Luck: Three Sources of Overconfidence in the Manageability of Nuclear Crises," *European Journal of International Security* 2, no. 2 (2017): 240–262. Even some advocates of nuclear learning identify areas where learning was limited. For example, Nye finds little learning between the United States and the Soviet Union when it comes to achieving arms race stability or converging on stabilizing nuclear force structures.

The Nuclear Learning Argument

Scholars offer different interpretations of the nuclear learning argument, but several core features are common across the various arguments. First, the behavior of nuclear-armed states changes; as Horowitz argues, "the length of time countries have nuclear weapons may influence both the way they think about how to use their nuclear arsenal and the way they are perceived by adversaries."[7] Second, those changes are in the direction of stability; the behavior of nuclear-armed states moderates over time, allowing stable patterns of interstate relations to emerge. More specifically, nuclear learning advocates suggest that states learn that nuclear weapons are primarily useful for deterrence, take steps to reduce the risk of accidents and miscalculation, adopt nuclear postures emphasizing retaliation, and accept mutual vulnerability instead of pursuing costly arms races. In short, nuclear learning has a progressive character to it, which suggests that the arc of state policy bends toward wise, careful, and restrained policies. In contrast to the value-neutral definition of learning offered above, the nuclear learning literature (implicitly or explicitly) adopts a more normative view of learning, anticipating (and, indeed, requiring) that particular lessons be learned.[8] Third, those changes in behavior are attributable to learning; it is the development of "new beliefs, skills, or procedures" occurring due to "observation and interpretation of experience" that drive changes rather than other factors.[9] The nuclear learning argument is consistent with broader understandings of nuclear weapons that emphasize the transformative political effects that follow from the technological properties of nuclear weapons.[10] Such arguments rely on assumptions that nuclear learning occurs because they require leaders to realize the merits of—and pursue—the particular policies and postures that nuclear weapons demand.

Beyond these core features, important differences exist between different accounts of nuclear learning. For example, different scholars identify different mechanisms driving the process of learning: Cohen identifies leaders' psychological reactions to nuclear crises, Nye emphasizes individuals at all levels of government collectively coming to understand the appropriate policies to pursue in the nuclear realm, while Horowitz's account emphasizes

---

7. Horowitz, "The Spread of Nuclear Weapons and International Conflict," 235.
8. On the distinction between normative and value-neutral views of learning, see Knopf, "The Concept of Nuclear Learning."
9. This definition of learning is from Levy, "Learning and Foreign Policy," 283.
10. See, for example, Bernard Brodie, ed., *The Absolute Weapon: Atomic Power and World Order* (New York: Harcourt Brace, 1946); Robert Jervis, *The Meaning of the Nuclear Revolution: Statecraft and the Prospects of Armageddon* (Ithaca: Cornell University Press, 1989).

rational states learning the uses and limits of nuclear weapons through trial and error.[11] Similarly, scholars disagree about whether states can learn vicariously from the experiences of others or whether they can only learn from their own experiences.[12]

The Rarity of Nuclear Learning

Despite the prominence of the nuclear learning argument, there are strong theoretical reasons to expect nuclear learning to occur only rarely. First, states are generally poor at learning lessons, and we should expect learning lessons about nuclear weapons to be particularly difficult. Second, there are many lessons that states might learn from nuclear weapons and little reason to expect states to learn the particular lessons that lead to stability. Third, as long as some states deviate from learning stabilizing lessons, other states face weaker incentives to do so. Further, all of these arguments are particularly applicable in the new nuclear era.

OBSTACLES TO NUCLEAR LEARNING

Large government bureaucracies are not humans and, as Jack Snyder argues, "do not literally learn in the same sense that individuals do."[13] Although this is widely understood in the literature on organizational learning, it poses particular challenges for states and for learning in the nuclear realm. States may well face incentives to learn. As Waltz argued, states should be socialized to the behaviors demanded by an international system in which they must provide for their own security.[14] However, whether nuclear-armed states feel these incentives is more questionable. Nuclear-armed great powers face the weakest incentives for learning; their power allows them to make mistakes and still survive.[15] Advocates of nuclear learning argue that nuclear weapons have the very effects—deterring major attacks and securing a state's core interests—that should most weaken the pressures to socialize and learn.

---

11. Cohen, *When Proliferation Causes* Peace; Nye, "Nuclear Learning"; Horowitz, "The Spread of Nuclear Weapons and International Conflict."

12. On the possibility of vicarious learning, see Feaver, "Command and Control in Emerging Nuclear Nations."

13. Jack Levy, "Learning and Foreign Policy," *International Organization* 48, no. 2 (1994): 287.

14. Kenneth N. Waltz, *Theory of International Politics* (Long Grove, IL: Waveland Press, 1979), 74–77.

15. Jonathan Kirshner, "The Economic Sins of Modern IR Theory and the Classical Realist Alternative," *World Politics* 67, no. 1 (2015): 160; Randall L. Schweller, "Entropy and the Trajectory of World Politics: Why Polarity has become Less Meaningful," *Cambridge Review of International Affairs* 23, no. 1 (2010): 146–147.

More broadly, since 1945, the threat of state death—the most powerful force incentivizing socialization—has largely disappeared.[16]

Even if pressures to learn remain, states possess a number of features that make them poor learners.[17] And we should expect states would be particularly poor learners in the nuclear realm.[18] First, although all government bureaucracies exhibit tendencies that inhibit learning, the military and technical bureaucracies that often control nuclear weapons are particularly susceptible to biases, groupthink, and resisting the evaluation needed to promote learning.[19] More substantively, the particular biases that militaries typically exhibit—notably, toward favoring offensively oriented strategies—will generally push in the opposite direction to what advocates of nuclear learning would recommend. In theory, robust civilian control of nuclear weapons could ameliorate these tendencies, but nuclear-armed states often grant—or feel strategic pressures to grant—their militaries substantial autonomy with respect to nuclear weapons.[20]

Second, nuclear strategy, procurement, and, in some cases, the very existence of nuclear weapons is subject to high levels of secrecy. Secrecy does not preclude learning, but it makes it harder; learning is inhibited when much relevant information is highly classified. Further, many of those who do possess the clearances and access to relevant information will be from the military and thus subject to the biases identified above that push against learning of the sort that the nuclear learning argument demands. The secrecy associated with nuclear weapons thus interacts with the biases of the military to make nuclear learning unlikely.[21]

Third, nuclear weapons operate in the background of international politics. They are rarely brandished explicitly and even more rarely used directly. As a

---

16. Tanisha M. Fazal, *State Death: The Politics and Geography of Conquest, Occupation, and Annexation* (Princeton: Princeton University Press, 2007).

17. On the dynamics inhibiting learning within organizations, and an application to states, see, respectively, Aaron Wildavsky, "The Self-Evaluating Organization," *Public Administration Review* 32, no. 5 (1972): 509–520; Stephen Van Evera, "Why States Believe Foolish Ideas: Non-Self-Evaluation by States and Societies," in *Perspectives on Structural Realism*, ed. Andrew K. Hanami (Palgrave Macmillan, 2003).

18. These mechanisms are discussed in more detail in Mark S. Bell, "Explaining the Stability of U.S. Nuclear Thinking: Grand Strategy, Nuclear Weapons, and Policy Change," paper presented at the Nuclear Studies Research Initiative conference, Hamburg, Germany, December 2019.

19. For example, Barry R. Posen, *The Sources of Military Doctrine: France, Britain, and Germany between the World Wars* (Ithaca: Cornell University Press, 1984); Jack Snyder, "Civil-Military Relations and the Cult of the Offensive, 1914 and 1984," *International Security* 9, no. 1 (1984): 108–146.

20. Feaver, "Command and Control in Emerging Nuclear Nations;" Vipin Narang, *Nuclear Strategy in the Modern Era: Regional Powers and International Conflict* (Princeton: Princeton University Press, 2014).

21. On the influence of secrecy on learning, see Sagan, *Limits of Safety*, 209–210.

result, their role in particular events is often highly ambiguous. Consider, for example, the continued debate about whether nuclear weapons caused Japanese surrender at the end of World War II, the only occasion on which nuclear weapons have been directly used against an adversary.[22] This ambiguity makes nuclear weapons an unusually tricky subject for learning, especially since nuclear learning does not simply require "factual learning" about technological or physical features of nuclear weapons or their effects.[23] The nuclear learning argument requires states to make much more challenging judgments about the utility of nuclear weapons in different crises, the political effects of different nuclear postures, the circumstances in which it is appropriate to threaten or use nuclear weapons, and so on—what Levy describes as "causal learning."[24] Horowitz, for example, argues that states learn from "nuclearized interactions that helps leaders effectively identify the situations in which their nuclear arsenals are likely to make a difference."[25] To expect leaders to come to reasonable conclusions about such matters seems optimistic given the ambiguity of the historical record, especially given well-established tendencies for individuals both to filter information to fit their pre-existing beliefs and to avoid acknowledging the limits of their ability to control dangerous events.[26]

LEARNING THE WRONG LESSONS

Second, even if states face incentives to learn, will they learn the particular lessons that lead to stability? The nuclear learning argument implicitly adopts a normative rather than value-neutral view of learning and thus argues that nuclear learning is a stabilizing process. However, there is no a priori reason that learning necessarily results in normatively attractive lessons being learned, especially in contested domestic and geopolitical environments in which hardliners may advocate for policies at odds with those the nuclear learning argument requires. As Joseph Nye acknowledges, "negative, as well as positive, learning can occur."[27] Similarly, lessons learned can be subsequently unlearned or revised by political entrepreneurs or new leaders.

---

22. For example, Ward Wilson, "The Winning Weapon? Rethinking Nuclear Weapons in Light of Hiroshima," *International Security* 31, no. 4 (2007): 162–179.
23. The term "factual learning" comes from Knopf, "The Concept of Nuclear Learning," 81.
24. Levy, "Learning and Foreign Policy," 285.
25. Horowitz, "The Spread of Nuclear Weapons and International Conflict," 239.
26. See, e.g., Pelopidas, "The Unbearable Lightness of Luck." See also the discussion of the evolution of Robert McNamara's thinking about the Cuban Missile Crisis in Richard Ned Lebow and Benoît Pelopidas, "Facing Nuclear War: Luck, Learning and the Cuban Missile Crisis," in *The Oxford Handbook of History and International Relations*, ed. Mlada Bukovansky, Edward Keene, Maja Spanu, and Christian Reus-Smit (Oxford: Oxford University Press, forthcoming).
27. Nye, "Nuclear Learning and U.S.-Soviet Security Regimes," 379–380.

With respect to nuclear weapons, there is "a vast range of things that one might learn," not all of which would lead to more stable relations among nuclear-armed powers.[28] North Korea might reasonably have learned that in addition to deterring attack, nuclear weapons have coerced the United States into diplomatic concessions and weakened the US-South Korea alliance.[29] The United States might reasonably have learned from the Cold War that intense nuclear competition, arms racing, and an aggressive nuclear posture help it prevail over geopolitical rivals.[30] And Pakistan appears to have learned that nuclear weapons limit the risk of retaliation and thus facilitate revisionist aggression against an adversary.

By arguing that states should learn the stabilizing lessons of nuclear weapons over the destabilizing ones, the nuclear learning argument assumes that states are inherently inclined toward pursuing policies that promote stability and thus will learn particular lessons over others. Although some nuclear-armed states may prize stability in their relationships, it is not clear that all (or even most) do, or that they are willing to prioritize stability at any cost. Powerful states such as the United States prize their freedom of action, and the stability that nuclear learning theorists expect to emerge may often be directly inimical to US interests.[31] More broadly, states use nuclear weapons to facilitate a wide range of foreign policies, many of which seek to revise aspects of the status quo.[32] The intensity of geopolitical competition between nuclear powers could play a key role, too; periods of détente could facilitate learning positive, stabilizing lessons, while periods of heightened hostility could incentivize states to overturn the status quo using aggressive nuclear policies. If so, states (or, at least, segments of political actors within states) may actively resist learning stabilizing lessons and learn other lessons instead or actively seek to unlearn. Thus, even if we accept the possibility of nuclear learning, we should not expect such learning to necessarily lead to more stable relations among nuclear-armed states.

THE DIFFICULTY OF CROSS-NATIONAL LEARNING

Third, even if individual states have the capacity to learn important lessons about nuclear weapons, and they correctly learn the stabilizing lessons

---

28. Jeffrey Knopf, "The Concept of Nuclear Learning," 81.
29. See, e.g., Mark S. Bell, "North Korea Benefits from Nuclear Weapons. Get Used to It," *War on the Rocks*, October 2, 2017, https://warontherocks.com/2017/10/north-korea-benefits-from-nuclear-weapons-get-used-to-it/.
30. Brendan Rittenhouse Green, *The Revolution that Failed: Nuclear Competition, Arms Control, and the Cold War* (Cambridge: Cambridge University Press, 2020).
31. Matthew Kroenig, *Exporting the Bomb: Technology Transfer and the Spread of Nuclear Weapons* (Ithaca: Cornell University Press, 2011).
32. Mark S. Bell, *Nuclear Reactions: How Nuclear-Armed States Behave* (Ithaca: Cornell University Press, 2021).

that the nuclear learning argument requires, it does not follow that nuclear learning will be a reliable feature of an international system in which nuclear-armed states interact strategically.[33] First, if powerful states seek to teach other states the lessons that the nuclear learning argument requires, they may trigger resistance from states skeptical of their intentions. For example, the United States might seek to teach North Korea or Pakistan about the benefits of rigorous safety and command and control systems, but both countries might reasonably view such lessons as a thinly veiled effort to render their arsenals less easily deployed in a crisis and more vulnerable to preemption. In addition, powerful states may not wish to provide any sort of help for fear of legitimizing new nuclear states and undermining broader nonproliferation efforts.[34] This is reinforced by Article I of the Nuclear Non-Proliferation Treaty (NPT), which bars nuclear weapon states from assisting others in acquiring or producing nuclear weapons—a clause the United States interpreted as preventing them from helping countries such as Pakistan learn about security features like permissive actions links (PALs).[35] Second, and more broadly, nuclear learning is not necessarily self-reinforcing across states. When one state learns the lessons advocated by the nuclear learning argument, other states do not necessarily face incentives to themselves learn the same lessons. In fact, the opposite may be true: adversaries may have incentives to exploit states who restrain their behavior in the way that nuclear learning advocates suggest. The policies of India and Pakistan offer an example of these dynamics. India initially adopted policies close to those anticipated by the nuclear learning argument. Pakistan has used nuclear weapons differently: to facilitate aggression. This asymmetric learning, in turn, places India under pressure to unlearn the lessons that previously moderated its nuclear posture. We discuss this case further below.

THE PARTICULAR CHALLENGES OF LEARNING
IN THE NEW NUCLEAR ERA

The above arguments are particularly applicable in the new nuclear era in comparison to the Cold War. First, the bilateral relationship between the

---

33. For an additional argument emphasizing the importance of "international learning," see Jeffrey W. Knopf, "The Importance of International Learning," *Review of International Studies* 29, no 2 (2003): 185–207.
34. Feaver, "Command and Control in Emerging Nuclear Nations," 184; Peter Feaver and Emerson Niou, "Managing Nuclear Proliferation: Condemn, Strike, or Assist?," *International Studies Quarterly* 40, no. 2 (1996), 209–233; and Nicholas L. Miller, "North Korea and the Problem of Managing Emerging Nuclear Powers," *Lawfare*, March 25, 2018, https://www.lawfareblog.com/north-korea-and-problem-managing-emerging-nuclear-powers.
35. See, for example, David Sanger and William Broad, "U.S. Secretly Aids Pakistan in Guarding Nuclear Arms," *New York Times*, November 18, 2007, https://www.nytimes.com/2007/11/18/washington/18nuke.html.

United States and the Soviet Union offered a certain simplicity that should have facilitated nuclear learning. For example, the geographic distance between the two countries; the relative domestic political stability in each country; and the extensive avenues for communication between the two countries, should all have been conducive both to nuclear learning and to the stabilizing policies that the nuclear learning argument recommends. By contrast, the current nuclear era is characterized a greater number of nuclear powers, many of which interact with multiple other nuclear-armed adversaries in close geographic proximity, have weak domestic institutions, and contentious civil-military relations. The complexity of the new nuclear era should be expected to make nuclear learning particularly challenging. Second, technological change may increasingly facilitate aggressive, counterforce-oriented nuclear postures.[36] In such a world, states with smaller arsenals may be particularly vulnerable to states which reject the lessons that nuclear learning advocates propose. An equilibrium in which nuclear-armed states learn to exist in stable relationships may be less plausible than one in which states actively seek to undermine the lessons that nuclear learning advocates hope that states will learn. Third, the greater disparities in the nuclear arsenals of plausible adversaries in the new nuclear era (such as between the United States and North Korea, or the United States and China) increase incentives for first nuclear use and for the aggressive nuclear policies that make first use credible.[37] This further reduces the likelihood of states learning the merits of purely retaliatory forces. Fourth, new nuclear powers are by definition illegitimate under the NPT, which makes them more likely to embrace secrecy in their nuclear arsenal and strategy.[38]

Nuclear Learning in Practice

The sections above demonstrate the theoretical obstacles that stand in the way of nuclear learning. It is possible, of course, that states have nonetheless overcome these obstacles. We use the US-Soviet and India-Pakistan cases to evaluate this possibility. These cases involve hostile relationships in which we might expect learning to be difficult, but these are also cases that scholars have pointed to as being ones in which learning has occurred, and in which it is most important that nuclear learning occur if it is to offer

---

36. Keir A. Lieber and Daryl G. Press, "The New Era of Counterforce: Technological Change and the Future of Deterrence," *International Security* 41, no. 4 (2017): 9–49.
37. Mark S. Bell and Julia Macdonald, "How to Think about Nuclear Crises," *Texas National Security Review* 2, no. 2 (2019): 40–65.
38. See Avner Cohen and Benjamin Frankel, "Opaque Nuclear Proliferation," *Journal of Strategic Studies* 13, no. 3 (1990): 14–44.

a reliable pathway to the reduction of nuclear risks.[39] We focus on whether these states learned that nuclear weapons are only useful for deterrence, that steps should be taken to reduce the risk of accidents and miscalculation, and that mutual vulnerability should be accepted in lieu of costly arms racing.[40] We show that they mostly did not. In the case of India-Pakistan, the trends have pointed in the opposite direction, with both countries adopting increasingly aggressive and risky nuclear policies over time. Many of the theoretical mechanisms outlined above have played a role in this process. For example, secrecy inhibited Pakistan's learning process; Pakistan learning the wrong lessons put pressure on India to adopt more aggressive policies; and crises between the two countries have led them to double down on aggressive nuclear policies rather than converge on more stabilizing policies.

THE US-SOVIET CASE

Did the United States and the Soviet Union learn the lessons that the nuclear learning argument expects?

First, if the nuclear learning argument were correct, the United States and the Soviet Union should have learned that nuclear weapons are only useful for deterrence and should not be used or brandished except in the most extreme circumstances. For example, Nye points to US and Soviet leaders becoming less inclined to use nuclear weapons for political or coercive effect over time, a claim consistent with some datasets and analyses that suggest the limited effectiveness of nuclear threats.[41] However, a reduction in the frequency of nuclear crises is not necessarily evidence of learning and can be just as easily explained by the resolution of core political disputes that drove US-Soviet tensions in the 1950s and early 1960s.[42] Once that political agreement began to fragment, US-Soviet tensions rose again in the "second Cold War" of the 1980s. More broadly, high-level consideration of the use of nuclear weapons and coercive nuclear signaling and risk taking has occurred regularly since the 1960s. President Richard Nixon considered using nuclear weapons in Vietnam on multiple occasions and alerted US nuclear forces to send coercive signals in October 1969 and during the 1973 Arab-

---

39. Nye, "Nuclear Learning," and Cohen, *When Proliferation Causes Peace*.

40. These correspond to the areas discussed by Nye and also encompass the arguments made by Cohen and Horowitz. Nye also examines learning in the area of nonproliferation policy, which we exclude since assessing the proliferation intentions and capabilities of others is conceptually distinct from managing one's own nuclear arsenal and learning how to use it and, indeed, is more amenable to successful learning. See Nicholas L. Miller, "Learning to Predict Proliferation," *International Organization*, 72, no. 2 (2022): 487–507.

41. Nye, "Nuclear Learning," 386; Todd S. Sechser and Matthew Fuhrmann, *Nuclear Weapons and Coercive Diplomacy* (New York: Cambridge University Press, 2017).

42. Marc Trachtenberg, *A Constructed Peace: The Making of the European Settlement, 1945–1963* (Princeton: Princeton University Press, 1999).

Israeli War.⁴³ The Carter administration reportedly mulled using tactical nuclear weapons in the event of a Soviet invasion of Iran, and after the Cold War, the United States issued threats of nuclear use to relatively weak non-nuclear adversaries, including Iraq and Iran.⁴⁴

Second, did the superpowers learn the importance of secure second-strike forces and accepting nuclear parity rather than pursuing primacy? In this area, it is clear that little learning occurred. Both the United States and the Soviet Union retained postures designed for first nuclear use throughout the Cold War. Indeed, to the extent there was a trend over the course of the Cold War, it was toward developing more limited—and more usable—options for first nuclear use.⁴⁵ Like the United States, the Soviet Union initially envisioned massive use of nuclear weapons and gradually shifted toward limited nuclear options as the Cold War progressed.⁴⁶ Further, neither the United States nor the Soviet Union fully abandoned the idea of achieving superiority.⁴⁷ The United States, especially, has never fully accepted mutual vulnerability and continually sought nuclear superiority through counterforce, missile defense, and damage limitation capabilities.⁴⁸

Third, did the superpowers learn about the potential for nuclear accidents and miscalculations and move to adopt stronger mechanisms of control over weapons and crisis management practices? There is some evidence of such learning: for example, the installation of PALs to reduce the risk of unauthorized use, establishing a hotline for high-level crisis communication, and

---

43. See Nina Tannenwald, "The Nuclear Taboo: The United States and the Normative Basis of Nuclear Non-Use," *International Organization* 53, no. 3 (1999): 455–458; Scott D. Sagan and Jeremi Suri, "The Madman Nuclear Alert: Secrecy, Signaling, and Safety in October 1969," *International Security* 27, no. 4 (2003): 150–183; Barry M. Blechman and Douglas M. Hart, "The Political Utility of Nuclear Weapons: The 1973 Middle East Crisis," *International Security* 7, no. 1 (1982): 132–156; Sagan, *Limits of Safety*, 221–222.

44. Daniel Ellsberg, *The Doomsday Machine: Confessions of a Nuclear War Planner* (New York: Bloomsbury, 2017), 321–330.

45. See, for example, Scott D. Sagan, *Moving Targets: Nuclear Strategy and National Security* (Princeton: Princeton University Press, 1989).

46. See, for example, John Battilega, "Soviet Views of Nuclear Warfare: The Post-Cold War Interviews," in *Getting MAD: Nuclear Mutual Assured Destruction, Its Origins and Practice*, ed. Henry Sokolski (Carlisle, PA: Strategic Studies Institute, 2004), 151–164.

47. Brendan R. Green and Austin Long, "The MAD Who Wasn't There: Soviet Reactions to the Late Cold War Nuclear Balance," *Security Studies* 26, no. 4 (2017): 606–641; Battilega, "Soviet Views of Nuclear Warfare," 163.

48. Austin Long and Brendan Rittenhouse Green, "Stalking the Secure Second Strike: Intelligence, Counterforce, and Nuclear Strategy," *Journal of Strategic Studies* 38, no. 1–2 (2015): 38–73; Long and Green, "The MAD Who Wasn't There"; Keir A. Lieber and Daryl G. Press, "The End of MAD? The Nuclear Dimension of U.S. Primacy," *International Security* 30, no. 4 (2006): 7–4; Niccolo Petrelli and Giordana Pulcini, "Nuclear Superiority in the Age of Parity: US Planning, Intelligence Analysis, Weapons Innovation and the Search for a Qualitative Edge 1969–1976," *International History Review* 40, no. 5 (2018): 1191–1209; Francis J. Gavin, "Rethinking the Bomb: Nuclear Weapons and American Grand Strategy," *Texas National Security Review* 2, no. 1 (2018): 74–100.

CHAPTER 8

agreements intended to reduce the dangers of accidental nuclear war and incidents at sea.[49] At least on the US side, there appears to have been a reduced rate of accidents involving nuclear weapons, from nineteen in the 1950s to twelve in the 1960s, and only one between 1970 and 1980.[50] There is less evidence on Soviet accidents with nuclear weapons, but it appears that they continued to experience problems until the end of the Cold War. For instance, there were three separate cases of Soviet submarines exploding or catching fire in the 1980s alone, at least two of which were nuclear-armed at the time.[51] Beyond accidents, dangerous miscalculations and near-misses occurred regularly in the second half of the Cold War. In 1979, the accidental insertion of a training tape into a computer led the North American Aerospace Defense Command to conclude a large-scale Soviet nuclear attack was incoming, with national security adviser Zbigniew Brzezinski only a few minutes from waking President Jimmy Carter to discuss launching a nuclear response when the mistake was discovered.[52] The following year, a series of computer chip malfunctions again led to false alarms of a nuclear attack.[53] Scott Sagan concludes from these events that although some learning took place, "the learning process was *severely* constrained," while Benoît Pelopidas concludes that even the most dangerous event of the Cold War—the Cuban Missile Crisis—did not lead to meaningful learning about the limits of controllability in nuclear crises.[54] On the Soviet side, the 1980s saw multiple dangerous false alarms. In 1983, Soviet satellites detected what appeared to be incoming US nuclear missiles, and the officer receiving this information elected to ignore standard operating procedures rather than alert Soviet decision makers.[55] A few months later, the Able Archer NATO military exercise led Soviet officials to seriously consider whether the United States was preparing to launch a nuclear first strike.[56] In the aftermath of the Cold War, the United States and Russia cooperated extensively on nu-

49. Nye, "Nuclear Learning," 390–391.
50. "U.S. Nuclear Weapons Accidents: Danger in our Midst," *Defense Monitor* 10, no. 5 (1981): 1–12.
51. "Broken Arrows: Nuclear Weapons Accidents," Atomic Archive, http://www.atomicarchive.com/Almanac/Brokenarrows_static.shtml.
52. See Sagan, *The Limits of Safety*, 229–231; and Eric Schlosser, "World War Three, By Mistake," *New Yorker*, December 23, 2016, https://www.newyorker.com/news/news-desk/world-war-three-by-mistake.
53. Sagan, *The Limits of Safety*, 231–233.
54. Sagan, *The Limits of Safety*, 246; Pelopidas, "The Unbearable Lightness of Luck."
55. See Carl Lundgren, "What Are the Odds?," *Nonproliferation Review* 20, no. 2 (2013): 365–366.
56. See, e.g., Dmitry Adamsky, "The 1983 Nuclear Crisis—Lessons for Deterrence Theory and Practice," *Journal of Strategic Studies* 36, no. 1 (2013): 4–41; Nate Jones, ed., *Able Archer 83: The Secret History of the NATO Exercise that Almost Triggered Nuclear War* (New York: New Press, 2016).

clear security; however, this cooperation broke down as geopolitical tensions resurged following Russia's annexation of Crimea.[57]

The US-Soviet relationship was not characterized by unstinting hostility or by consistently escalatory policies. For example, US-Soviet cooperation on preventing proliferation, the Reagan-Gorbachev statement that "a nuclear war cannot be won and must never be fought," and the periodic pursuit of arms control all tempered the trends we identify above. Nonetheless, overall, the US-Soviet case offers only limited support for the nuclear learning argument.

INDIA

After testing a crude nuclear device in 1974 and assembling nuclear weapons for the first time in the late 1980s, India initially adopted nuclear policies that conformed to the expectations of nuclear learning advocates. India maintained a small arsenal and adopted a posture optimized for retaliation rather than first use, storing its nuclear weapons in separate components at different locations and under centralized civilian control, thus reducing the odds of unauthorized use.[58] After India tested a series of nuclear devices in May 1998, leading Pakistan to respond in kind, the BJP government led by Prime Minister Atal Vajpayee appears to have concluded that overt nuclearization would stabilize its relationship with Pakistan and prevent major conflict, exactly the sort of lesson advocates of nuclear learning arguments expect. As Vajpayee put it in 1999, "Now both India and Pakistan are in possession of nuclear weapons. There is no alternative to but to live in mutual harmony. The nuclear weapon is not an offensive weapon. It is a weapon of self-defense. It is the kind of weapon that helps in preserving the peace."[59] Consistent with this perspective, in February 1999 India and Pakistan agreed to the Lahore Declaration, which called for a series of confidence building measures and other steps to reduce the risk of conflict. The declaration noted that "the nuclear dimension of the security environment of the two countries adds to their responsibility for avoidance of conflict" and committed Indian and Pakistani leaders to dialogue on nuclear doctrine, a moratorium on nuclear tests, and measures to reduce the risk of nuclear accidents and miscalculation.[60]

---

57. See Mariana Budjeryn, Simon Saradzhyan, and William Tobey, "25 Years of Nuclear Security Cooperation by the US, Russia, and Other Newly Independent States," *Russia Matters*, June 16, 2017, https://www.russiamatters.org/analysis/25-years-nuclear-security-cooperation-us-russia-and-other-newly-independent-states.

58. Narang, *Nuclear Strategy in the Modern Era*, 94–103.

59. Quoted in Timothy Hoyt, "Kargil: The Nuclear Dimension," in *Asymmetric Warfare in South Asia: The Causes and Consequences of the Kargil Conflict*, ed. Peter Lavoy (New York: Cambridge University Press, 2009), 150.

60. Hoyt, "Kargil: The Nuclear Dimension," 154–155.

CHAPTER 8

The Kargil conflict, which broke out a few months later, began the process of changing Indian views on its nuclear weapons.[61] Shortly after the war concluded, India released a draft nuclear doctrine that formalized its no-first-use policy and declared, "the fundamental purpose of Indian nuclear weapons is to deter the use and threat of use of nuclear weapons."[62] However, this obscured the rethinking about the utility of nuclear weapons that was occurring within the Indian government. Indian leaders concluded from the Kargil conflict that Pakistan was using its nuclear arsenal for aggressive purposes, using it as a shield to provide cover for conventional and sub-conventional operations while limiting India's ability to retaliate.[63] The conflict demonstrated that limited war was possible under the nuclear shadow, that India could prevail in such a conflict, and pushed Indian officials to develop a doctrine of limited war and conclude that its nuclear weapons might be useful for compellence in addition to deterrence. After a terrorist attack on the Indian parliament in December 2001, India launched a massive military mobilization, demanded Pakistan take steps to crack down on terrorists on its territory, tested nuclear-capable ballistic missiles, and made threats to destroy Pakistan if it used nuclear weapons.[64] Pakistan's concessions were mostly cosmetic, reinforcing India's belief that it needed to increase its capability to escalate and coerce Pakistan under the nuclear shadow.[65]

Shortly thereafter, in early 2003, India updated its nuclear doctrine, promising "massive" as opposed to "punitive" retaliation, permitting first use of nuclear weapons in response to biological or chemical attacks, and clarifying that it would use nuclear weapons in response to a nuclear attack on Indian forces even if they were operating outside Indian territory.[66] This latter change, as Sagan observes, implies that India's nuclear weapons could support an offensive operation inside Pakistani territory, convincing Pakistan that if it resorted to nuclear use—even on its own territory—it would face a devastating response.[67] These doctrinal changes were driven not just by Pakistan's aggressive behavior, but also the models provided by more established nuclear powers like the United States, which also reserved the option of using nuclear weapons in a wide variety of circumstances, includ-

61. O'Donnell, "India's Nuclear Counter-Revolution," 422.
62. O'Donnell, "India's Nuclear Counter-Revolution," 417.
63. Rajesh Basrur, "The Lessons of Kargil as Learned by India," in *Asymmetric Warfare in South Asia*, ed. Peter Lavoy (New York: Cambridge University Press, 2009), 322.
64. Hoyt, "Kargil: The Nuclear Dimension," 162–164; and Basrur, "The Lessons of Kargil as Learned by India," 325–328.
65. Hoyt, "Kargil: The Nuclear Dimension," 165; and O'Donnell, "India's Nuclear Counter-Revolution," 422–423.
66. O'Donnell, "India's Nuclear Counter-Revolution," 415.
67. Scott Sagan, "The Evolution of Pakistani and Indian Nuclear Doctrine," in *Inside Nuclear South Asia*, ed. Scott Sagan (Stanford, CA: Stanford University Press, 2009), 250.

ing in response to a chemical or biological attack.[68] This change was followed by the adoption of a more aggressive conventional doctrine, which was designed to allow India to swiftly retaliate against Pakistani provocations.[69] Collectively, these policy shifts demonstrate the fragility of nuclear learning when one state in a dyad learns the wrong lessons; Pakistan's use of nuclear weapons to facilitate conventional aggression created incentives for India to adjust its own policies in a more aggressive direction.

These trends have continued since the mid-2000s. After the Pakistani-backed 2008 terrorist attack in Mumbai, India considered retaliatory responses but ultimately was deterred by the possibility of Pakistani nuclear use. As Clary and Narang document, this experience, coupled with previous Pakistani-backed attacks, has led Indian officials to increasingly flirt with a counterforce nuclear strategy and possible first use against Pakistan's long-range nuclear assets. As they put it, "If India could convince Pakistan that its ability to launch a disarming strike were credible, this might nullify Pakistani nuclear threats, permitting punitive conventional attacks that could restore Indian deterrence of Pakistani sub-conventional attacks." This has involved a range of changes to India's nuclear force structure, including storing a portion of its arsenal fully assembled and at a higher state of readiness, increasing the accuracy of its missiles, enhancing its surveillance capacity, working on multiple independently targetable reentry vehicles, and investing in missile defense systems to protect against Pakistani nuclear attack. Though intended to create a more effective deterrent against Pakistan, this evolving nuclear posture entails serious risks, including giving Pakistan stronger incentives to strike first in a crisis and increasing pressures for arms racing.[70]

As of 2016, India has deployed a nuclear-armed submarine, *Arihant*. In theory this could help stabilize the nuclear balance by offering a secure second strike. However, it could also increase the risk of accidents, erode civilian control over India's nuclear arsenal, and create incentives for pre-delegation.[71] India's arsenal has also grown substantially in numbers over the last few decades, from between 25 and 40 in 2000 to about 150 today.[72] Although India initially prided itself on avoiding the arms racing, aggressive nuclear doctrines, and hair-trigger alert levels adopted by the superpowers during the Cold War, it has increasingly moved in that direction—driven by Pakistan's resistance to learning the lessons expected by nuclear learning theorists.

---

68. Scott Sagan, "The Case for No First Use," *Survival* 51, no. 3 (2009): 175–176.
69. Walter Ladwig III, "A Cold Start for Hot Wars? The Indian Army's New Limited War Doctrine," *International Security* 32, no. 3 (2007/2008): 158–190.
70. Clary and Narang, "India's Counterforce Temptations," 14–15.
71. Diana Wueger, "India's Nuclear-Armed Submarines: Deterrence or Danger?" *Washington Quarterly* 39, no. 3 (2016): 77–90.
72. SIPRI Yearbook 2000 and SIPRI Yearbook 2020, https://www.sipri.org/yearbook/archive.

CHAPTER 8

Meanwhile, in the conventional realm, India has shown more willingness to take risks, backed by nuclear threats to deter Pakistani escalation. In 2016, in retaliation for an insurgent attack on Indian troops in Kashmir, the Indian military crossed the Line of Control and conducted a so-called surgical strike against Pakistani forces and militants near the border—a line they notably had not crossed during the Kargil War.[73] Even more dramatically, in the Balakot crisis of 2019, India launched air strikes against a militant camp in Pakistan in response to a suicide attack against Indian police officers in Pulwalma, Kashmir. During the crisis India alerted its nuclear forces, began to track Pakistani naval assets, and considered launching missiles against Pakistani targets.[74] A few months later, Indian prime minister Narendra Modi bragged about his actions, arguing that "Pakistan and its supporters have been threatening us for long with its nuclear capability but the IAF [Indian Air Force] called its bluff with its strikes. Those days are gone when India would give in to threats."[75] To the extent that India appears to be learning from these crises, it is that it can—and, indeed, that it should—take the initiative in crises, that escalation even at high levels can be controlled, and that risk-taking can help it to achieve its political goals despite the associated risks of nuclear use.

PAKISTAN

Like India, Pakistan's view on the political utility of nuclear weapons has changed over time—but not in the direction expected by nuclear learning arguments. When it initially acquired a small, covert arsenal in the late 1980s, Pakistan adopted a strategy aimed at drawing in US intervention to defuse crises with India. According to Narang, "this nuclear posture calls for the use of nuclear weapons—first-use if necessary—only as a last resort in the event of a mortal conventional or nuclear threat to the state's existence," the narrow set of circumstances that nuclear learning arguments suggest nuclear-armed states should eventually converge on.[76] Like India, Pakistan stored its nuclear weapons disassembled in separate components (though under military custody), reducing the risk of unauthorized or hasty use.[77]

---

73. Ankit Panda, "Lessons from India's 'Surgical Strikes,' One Year Later," *The Diplomat*, September 29, 2017, https://thediplomat.com/2017/09/lessons-from-indias-surgical-strikes-one-year-later/.
74. O'Donnell, "India's Nuclear Counter-Revolution," 408–409.
75. Yusuf Unjawhala, "Modi's Nuclear Threat Is Not the End of No First Use, It's from Obama and Theresa May Playbook," *The Print*, April 25, 2019, https://theprint.in/opinion/modis-nuclear-threat-isnt-end-of-indias-no-first-use-its-from-obama-theresa-mays-playbook/226789/.
76. Narang, *Nuclear Strategy in the Modern Era*, 61.
77. Feroz Hassan Khan, *Eating Grass: The Making of the Pakistani Bomb* (Stanford: Stanford University Press, 2012), 332; Narang, "Posturing for Peace," 65.

After losing US patronage following the Soviet withdrawal from Afghanistan in 1989, Pakistan concluded it could no longer rely on third parties to protect it from Indian conventional superiority, shifting toward a more aggressive nuclear posture, which sought to deter Indian attack by threatening the first use of nuclear weapons. This shift was cemented by India's nuclear tests in May 1998, which gave Pakistani leaders the political cover to conduct tests and demonstrate the country's nuclear capabilities.[78] In order to make this posture credible, Pakistan has developed a diverse array of missile systems for delivering tactical warheads.[79] It has also moved toward a delegative approach to controlling its arsenal, seeking to ensure that nuclear weapons can be readied, transported, and used quickly in a crisis, potentially without an order from political authorities. This increases the risk of accidents, unauthorized use, and the theft of nuclear weapons.[80]

If Pakistan utilized this posture simply to deter large-scale Indian aggression, it would be partly consistent with the nuclear learning argument—that states should learn to only threaten to use nuclear weapons under the most extreme circumstances. Instead, Pakistan has concluded that its nuclear arsenal provides it with a shield that enables aggressive operations against India—both directly and indirectly through proxies. It has also repeatedly demonstrated a willingness to threaten nuclear use before conflicts reach high levels of escalation. Shortly after shifting its nuclear posture in 1998, Pakistan initiated the Kargil conflict, briefly discussed above. Islamabad had already been supporting an insurgency in Kashmir, in part based on the notion that its nuclear arsenal could limit the Indian response, but the Kargil operation represented the most aggressive operation against India since 1965.[81] Scholars have concluded that Pakistan's nuclear weapons were at least one factor convincing Pakistani leaders to go forward with the operation. According to Timothy Hoyt, Pakistani leaders "most likely calculated that India would be slower to respond, in part, because of its perception of the effects of nuclear weapons on the military rivalry."[82] Russell Leng concurs, arguing that Pakistan believed India "would be restrained by fear of triggering a full-scale conventional war, which, in turn, could escalate to nuclear war."[83] S. Paul Kapur reaches a similar conclusion, based

---

78. Narang, *Nuclear Strategy in the Modern Era*, 76–77.
79. See Mansoor Ahmed, "Pakistan's Tactical Nuclear Weapons and Their Impact on Stability," *Carnegie Endowment for International Peace*, June 30, 2016, https://carnegieendowment.org/2016/06/30/pakistan-s-tactical-nuclear-weapons-and-their-impact-on-stability-pub-63911.
80. Narang, "Posturing for Peace," 65–70.
81. S. Paul Kapur, "Ten Years of Instability in a Nuclear South Asia," *International Security* 33, no. 2 (2008): 75.
82. Hoyt, "Kargil: The Nuclear Dimension," 153.
83. Russell Leng, "Realpolitik and Learning," in *The India-Pakistan Conflict: An Enduring Rivalry*, ed. T. V. Paul (New York: Cambridge University Press, 2005), 116.

on the statements of Pakistani officials and analysts.[84] In the course of the conflict, Pakistani leaders made veiled nuclear threats, for example, that Pakistan would "not hesitate to use any weapon in [its] arsenal to defend [its] territorial integrity."[85] Despite the fact that it lost the conflict and was forced to withdraw from the positions it had seized in Kargil, Pakistan did not conclude that using its nuclear arsenal as a shield for aggression was ineffective, as nuclear learning arguments would expect. Instead, "Pakistan publicized its new command and control arrangements, ensuring that nuclear weapons would be closely controlled and readily available to military commanders in a crisis . . . Pakistan sought to negate India's efforts at escalation dominance by lowering the nuclear threshold and increasing nuclear risks."[86]

Learning from the Kargil conflict may have been inhibited in Pakistan by the government-enforced secrecy surrounding the conflict, in particular the desire to maintain the fiction that it was insurgents rather than Pakistani forces that had started the conflict. As Hasan-Askari Rizvi notes, the civilian government led by Nawaz Sharif "did not institute any official or semiofficial inquiry of the Kargil operation largely because it feared opposition from the military."[87] More broadly, secrecy hampered the development of Pakistani nuclear doctrine. As Naeem Salik puts it, the desire to keep Pakistan's nuclear program covert meant that "issues related to prospective nuclear doctrine and strategy, command and control, and safety and security could not be discussed in public. This emphasis on secrecy even discouraged in-house deliberations on these issues in the military as well as civilian institutions."[88] "Indeed, though Pakistan had the advantage of hindsight and a whole body of literature available especially on the development of US and NATO nuclear doctrines its doctrinal development lagged far behind its weapons development."[89]

Two years later, Pakistan-backed terrorists attacked the Indian parliament, and Pakistani leaders explicitly threatened nuclear use if India responded by entering Pakistani territory.[90] Pakistan carried out three tests of nuclear-

84. Kapur, "Ten Years of Instability in a Nuclear South Asia," 74–77.
85. Quoted in Vipin Narang, "Posturing for Peace? Pakistan's Nuclear Postures and South Asian Stability," *International Security* 34, no. 3 (2009–2010): 61.
86. Hoyt, "Kargil: The Nuclear Dimension," 163.
87. Hasan-Askari Rizvi, "The Lessons of Kargil as Learned by Pakistan," in *Asymmetric Warfare in South Asia*, ed. Peter Lavoy (New York: Cambridge University Press, 2009), 333.
88. Naeem Salik, "The Concept of Nuclear Learning: Pakistan's Learning Experience," in *Nuclear Learning in South Asia: The Next Decade*, ed. Feroz Hassan Khan, Ryan Jacobs, and Emily Burke (Monterey, CA: Naval Postgraduate School, 2014), 42–43.
89. Naeem Salik, "The Evolution of Pakistan's Nuclear Doctrine," in *Nuclear Learning in South Asia: The Next Decade*, ed. Feroz Hassan Khan, Ryan Jacobs, and Emily Burke, 73.
90. Narang, "Posturing for Peace," 62.

capable missiles, and at the height of the crisis, Pakistani president Pervez Musharraf reportedly believed an Indian attack was imminent.[91] While the two nations stood on the brink of war, Lt. General Khalid Kidwai, the head of Pakistan's Strategic Plans Division that oversees the country's nuclear arsenal, outlined a broad set of scenarios under which Pakistan would use nuclear weapons, including if (1) India took significant portions of Pakistani territory, (2) destroyed major portions of the Pakistani military, (3) undertook "economic strangulation" of Pakistan, or (4) caused major internal unrest in Pakistan.[92] Contrary to the expectations of nuclear learning arguments, Pakistan relied on nuclear weapons not only to provide a cover for aggressive operations but also to deter Indian actions far short of major invasion.

Pakistan has continued to provide backing for insurgent and terrorist attacks against Indian targets, including the 2008 Mumbai attack that killed more than 150 people. After the 2019 Pulwama attack, as a crisis simmered with India, Pakistani prime minister Imran Khan issued a veiled nuclear threat, warning, "with the weapons you have and the weapons we have, can we afford miscalculation? Shouldn't we think that if this escalates, what will it lead to?"[93] After the Indian government revoked the autonomy of the portion of Kashmir under its control in late 2019 and began a repressive crackdown, Khan again raised the specter of nuclear war, publishing an op-ed in the *New York Times* calling for international opposition to India's move and cautioning of the "consequences for the whole world as two nuclear-armed states get ever closer to a direct military confrontation . . . World War II happened because of appeasement at Munich. A similar threat looms over the world again, but this time under the nuclear shadow."[94]

Meanwhile, the Pakistani arsenal has grown substantially. By 2011, it boasted "the world's fastest growing nuclear stockpile."[95] The Pakistani arsenal increased from between 15 and 20 warheads in 2000 to around 160 in 2020.[96] Qualitatively, Pakistan has continued to advance its delivery capabilities, including developing a nuclear-armed submarine force, which could

91. Khan, *Eating Grass*, 350.
92. Khan, *Eating Grass*, 351–352.
93. Annie Waqar, "Nuclear War Between India and Pakistan? An Expert Assesses the Risk," *The Conversation*, March 6, 2019, https://theconversation.com/nuclear-war-between-india-and-pakistan-an-expert-assesses-the-risk-112892.
94. Imran Khan, "The World Can't Ignore Kashmir. We Are All in Danger," *New York Times*, August 30, 2019, https://www.nytimes.com/2019/08/30/opinion/imran-khan-kashmir-pakistan.html.
95. Hans Kristensen and Robert Norris, "Pakistan's Nuclear Forces, 2011," *Bulletin of the Atomic Scientists* 67, no. 4 (2011), 91.
96. SIPRI Yearbook 2000 and SIPRI Yearbook 2020, https://www.sipri.org/yearbook/archive.

increase the risk of unauthorized use and inadvertent escalation were India to attack a submarine it wrongly believed was conventionally armed.[97]

Like India, Pakistan's nuclear policies have tended in the opposite direction to that predicted by nuclear learning arguments. Pakistan may have learned lessons about the impact of nuclear weapons, but they are not the stabilizing ones expected by advocates of nuclear learning. This, in turn, has caused India to follow suit and adopt more aggressive and risk-acceptant policies. As a 2020 Stimson Center report on South Asia crisis dynamics put it, learning in the region over the past twenty years has been "inconsistent," "highly uneven in scope and quality," and has "sometimes incentivized belligerence over restraint."[98]

Conclusion

The nuclear learning argument appears overly optimistic. The theoretical barriers to nuclear learning are substantial, and those barriers appear particularly relevant in the new nuclear era. Empirically, the nuclear learning argument also appears weak. The progressive lessons expected by nuclear learning arguments were not generally learned in the US-Soviet case. And in the case of India and Pakistan, trends have moved in the opposite direction to that expected by theorists of nuclear learning. To the extent that the four countries seem to have learned common lessons, it is that policies that increase nuclear risks can be useful for deterrence and compellence, and that competitive arms racing is central to effective geopolitical competition.

Looking ahead, there is little reason for optimism about the future of nuclear learning. If the public statements of North Korean officials are to be believed, they learned from witnessing the fate of Saddam Hussein and Muammar Qaddafi that nuclear weapons would protect them while disarmament could spell their doom.[99] This is consistent with the expectation of nuclear learning arguments, which hold that nuclear weapons are effective at deterring invasion. Beyond this lesson, though, North Korea has strong strategic reasons to adopt a nuclear posture that looks quite different from what nuclear learning theorists expect. Because of the disparity in

---

97. Christopher Clary and Ankit Panda, "Safer at Sea? Pakistan's Sea-Based Deterrent and Nuclear Weapons Security," *Washington Quarterly* 40, no. 3 (2017): 149–168.

98. Sameer Lalwani, Elizabeth Threlkeld, Sunaina Danziger, Grace Easterly, Zeba Fazli, Gillian Gayner, Tyler Sagerstrom, Brigitta Schuchert, Chloe Stein, and Akriti Vasudeva, "From Kargil to Balakot: Southern Asian Crisis Dynamics and Future Trajectories," *Stimson Center*, February 2020, https://www.stimson.org/2020/from-kargil-to-balakot-southern-asian-crisis-dynamics-and-future-trajectories/.

99. See, e.g., Mark McDonald, "North Korea Suggests Libya Should Have Kept Nuclear Program," *New York Times*, March 24, 2011, https://www.nytimes.com/2011/03/25/world/asia/25korea.html.

arsenal size with the United States, conventional force imbalances, and past US talk about a preventive war, North Korea is likely to optimize its nuclear forces for first use rather than retaliation, which would involve delegating authority under certain conditions, thereby increasing the risks of accident, theft, miscalculation, or unauthorized use.[100] Beyond North Korea, the United States has withdrawn from or undermined a range of arms control treaties that have played a role in restraining the arms races that nuclear learning advocates counsel against. Finally, under the pressure of potent US counterforce capabilities, China—a country that has historically pursued a nuclear posture close to that which nuclear advocates recommend—appears to be investing in substantial additional nuclear forces and investing in more accurate, shorter-range, and nuclear warfighting-oriented capabilities such as the DF-26 missile.[101]

Our argument does not rule out the possibility that nuclear-armed states can exist in relationships characterized by stable deterrence. However, nuclear learning should not be viewed as an automatic (or even particularly likely) route to such relationships. The inherent optimism of the nuclear learning argument offers a false promise to those hoping that the new nuclear era will be characterized by greater stability and fewer dangers than the Cold War.

---

100. Vipin Narang, "Why Kim Jong Un Wouldn't be Irrational to use a Nuclear Weapon First," *Washington Post*, September 8, 2017.

101. On China's historic nuclear posture, see M. Taylor Fravel and Evan S. Medeiros, "China's Search for Assured Retaliation: The Evolution of Chinese Nuclear Strategy and Force Structure," *International Security* 35, no. 2 (2010): 48–87. On more recent developments, see, for example, Joby Warrick, "China Is Building More Than 100 New Missile Silos in Its Western Desert, Analysts Say," *Washington Post*, June 30, 2021; Austin Long, "Myths or Moving Targets? Continuity and Change in China's Nuclear Forces," *War on the Rocks*, December 4, 2020, https://warontherocks.com/2020/12/myths-or-moving-targets-continuity-and-change-in-chinas-nuclear-forces/.

Conclusion

The Dangerous Nuclear Future

Vipin Narang and Scott D. Sagan

It is often said that every child is born into a different family. Similarly, every nuclear weapons state is born into a different nuclear world. Each new nuclear state adds to the complexity of nuclear balances, the range of real and potential rivalries, the risks of normal accidents, and the pressures for existing nuclear states to act against emerging threats. Since the end of the Cold War, the nuclear weapons club has grown by "only" three members: India, Pakistan, and North Korea. However, this obscures that other states—Iraq, Libya, Syria, and Iran—tried to acquire nuclear weapons, and efforts to thwart their nuclear programs created significant turbulence, and a generation-defining war, in the international system. And new nuclear aspirants remain on the horizon as the risk of nuclear contagion grows, increasing the likelihood of the spread of nuclear weapons. Iran's nuclear journey seems far from over, and its mere retention of a potential nuclear weapons program appears to be incentivizing neighbors such as Saudi Arabia and Turkey to at least contemplate acquiring their own nuclear weapons options. Meanwhile, concerns over the reliability of the US' extended deterrence commitments, after the Trump administration's testy relations with alliance partners, may generate motivations for independent nuclear weapons programs among US allies such as Japan, South Korea, or even Germany. Russia's invasion of Ukraine in February 2022 and the subsequent war further increased the risk of nuclear proliferation, both among NATO states threatened by Russia and among potential proliferators elsewhere, who have witnessed three states give up nuclear weapons programs or weapons—Iraq, Libya, and at least nominally Ukraine—only to later suffer a devastating attack.

What are the risks in this emerging nuclear era? Some are novel risks as the system structure, information environment, leadership characteristics, and technologies change; some are enduring risks—such as nuclear accidents and preemptive war incentives—intensified by the growing number of nuclear states, ongoing military conflicts with rivals, and asymmetries between them. Put together, these challenges significantly reduce confidence that deterrence and luck will continue to spare the world its first deliberate or accidental use of nuclear weapons since August 1945. This volume has assembled a distinguished set of scholars to analyze the dynamics of this emerging nuclear era. The conclusions are worrying.

Declining Confidence in Deterrence

The arguments and evidence presented by different authors in this volume, especially when assessed together, substantially erode our confidence that classical deterrence theory—premised on rational actors behaving on the basis of cost-benefit calculations—will apply and lead to stability in the emerging nuclear era. Consider the following factors: the growing prevalence of personalist dictatorships driven by pathology and incomplete or incorrect information; many states facing multiple nuclear adversaries and operating in a novel information environment where misinformation can be maliciously planted or otherwise spread rampantly; and each state possessing small nuclear arsenals which they fear may not be reliable or survivable or over which they may not retain firm command and control. Each of these factors alone, and especially in combination, generate risks that our standard strategies of nuclear deterrence are simply unequipped to manage or address.

NEW DETERRENCE CHALLENGES IN THE NEW NUCLEAR ERA

Some of the chapters have highlighted novel challenges as a growing number of nuclear states, particularly smaller powers sometimes with volatile domestic politics and often with intense local rivalries, appear on the nuclear landscape. Talmadge highlighted the difficulty of navigating multipolar nuclear interactions, both as the structure of the system trends to multipolarity at the great power level with arms competition between the United States, Russia, and China, but also as new nuclear states emerge in regional subsystems, often driven to nuclear weapons due to the presence of an intense regional rivalry. Although the presence of nuclear weapons may reduce the risk that state leaders will plan to initiate a major war with a nuclear rival, the growing number of nuclear powers increases the risk that they may stumble into a war.

The case of the 2019 Balakot crisis between India and Pakistan highlights this risk. The crisis illustrates that new nuclear states may increasingly attempt to push the line with how far they can go against their nuclear adversaries. This crisis was the first use of Indian military airpower against mainland Pakistan in almost half a century and the first time a nuclear weapons state has bombed the undisputed territory of another nuclear weapons state. Although both nations believe that they were able to carefully control escalation, if any one of a number of incidents had gone slightly awry—if the captured Indian Air Force pilot had been killed, if the Pakistan Air Force had accidentally hit a civilian target in its retaliation, if India had fired surface-to-surface missiles, if India's ballistic nuclear submarine on patrol had had an accident—there could have been a sharp increase in the risk of escalation and potentially advertent or inadvertent nuclear weapons use. Then in 2020, India was locked in an intense standoff with China, another nuclear power, on the Line of Actual Control, and over twenty Indian soldiers were killed by the People's Liberation Army for the first time in almost half a century. Intense conflict between three nuclear powers simultaneously is no longer a remote possibility.

The fragility of deterrence in the new nuclear era is also illustrated by one unfortunately realistic scenario. In January 2018, the Hawaii emergency management system issued an incoming missile warning alert adding, "this is not a drill." US political and military leaders did not react precipitously because redundant warning systems did not confirm the missile attack, professional operators in Hawaii promptly acknowledged the mistake, and no one in Washington expected a North Korean missile attack on Hawaii. But imagine that this incident occurred in North Korea rather than the United States. None of the three mitigating factors would apply. North Korea relies on an unreliable radar system for warnings of attack, with no redundant satellite-based missile warning system. North Korean officials would be less likely to acknowledge operational failures because you can get killed, not just fired, for making mistakes in the DPRK. And finally, the North Koreans did fear a possible US first strike in 2017 and 2018, in part because President Trump was threatening "fire and fury" if North Korean nuclear and missile tests continued.

Moreover, any conflict on the Korean Peninsula would now bring three nuclear powers into close contact—the United States, China, and North Korea. Would China stand idly by as its only formal ally, North Korea, was potentially facing—or in the midst of—being disarmed of its nuclear weapons by the United States in a counterforce strike? Our theories and expectations of risk from the Cold War are ill-equipped for this new nuclear era, where the hypothesized stabilizing effect of survivable nuclear forces may be offset by more vulnerable forces and a growing risk of an advertent or inadvertent nuclear use. Just at the structural level alone, we should expect higher frequency, complexity, and intensity of interactions between nuclear states.

Then, on top of the sheer increase in frequency and intensity of interaction between multiple nuclear states in multipolar environments, a number of new nuclear powers and nuclear aspirants—from Kim Jong Un's North Korea to Saddam's Iraq, to Assad's Syria to Qaddafi's Libya—are, or were, led by personalist dictators whose risk profile, as McDermott shows us, is fundamentally different from the picture of the "rational actor model" assumed to be present in both superpowers in the Cold War. Other personalist leaders—Turkey's Erdogan and Saudi Arabia's Mohammed Bin Salman—are suspected of seeking nuclear weapons or at least a nuclear option.[1] These types of leaders often suffer from pathologies such as megalomania, narcissism, and paranoia that may make their behavior unpredictable in a crisis. Not only are such leaders more likely to misperceive innocuous information as personal challenges or threats to them, but they may be more likely to escalate a crisis if they believe they have been challenged or humiliated. Vladimir Putin is such a personalist authoritarian, and his living in a bubble of deception and delusion, surrounded by "yes men," may have been a major factor leading to his disastrous decision to invade Ukraine in February 2022.[2]

These risks are unfortunately not limited to personalist dictatorships, as a growing trend of what could be called "aspiring personalist strongmen" in major power nuclear states—including Trump's United States to Modi's India—suggests that leaders in even mature nuclear states can make decisions on a whim and engage in risky nuclear behavior. These types of leaders fundamentally challenge notions of rational deterrence. Traditional cost-benefit calculations may not drive behavior when emotion, revenge, and narcissism dominate leadership calculations. These were concerns during the Cold War, but even Mao and Stalin had large party and military bureaucracies under them that somewhat tempered their tendencies to make rash decisions.

President Trump's alarmingly rash and vengeful decision-making tendencies highlighted that there are dangers in a policy of sole authority for the use of nuclear weapons, even in the United States. In the days before the January 6, 2021, insurrection on Capitol Hill, concerns about Trump's potential use of military force, including nuclear weapons, grew so large that General Mark Milley, the chairman of the Joint Chiefs of Staff, summoned senior officers to review the procedures for launching nuclear weapons. Milley reportedly acknowledged that the president had the legal authority to order the use of nuclear weapons but insisted that commanders contact him before following any such orders.[3] It is not clear what Milley intended to do if Trump ordered a nuclear strike—encourage officers to disobey orders,

---

1. David E. Sanger and William J. Broad, "Erdogan's Ambitions Go Beyond Syria. He Says He Wants Nuclear Weapons," *New York Times*, October 20, 2019, https://www.nytimes.com/2019/10/20/world/middleeast/erdogan-turkey-nuclear-weapons-trump.html; Mark Mazzetti, David Sanger and William J. Broad, "U.S. Examines Whether Saudi Nuclear Program Could Lead to Bomb," *New York Times*, August 2, 2020, https://www.nytimes.com/2020/08/05/us/politics/us-examines-saudi-nuclear-program.html.

2. Scott D. Sagan, "The Most Dangerous Man in the World," *Foreign Affairs*, March 8, 2022, https://www.foreignaffairs.com/guest-pass/redeem/-8OnSjLcQTw.

3. Isaac Stanley-Becker, "Top General Was so Fearful Trump Might Spark War That He Made Secret Call to His Chinese Counterpart, New Book Says," *Washington Post*,

seek to reverse a presidential decision, or call for initiation of the Twenty-Fifth Amendment—but his concern about a potentially unhinged president is clear.

The future may bring more nuclear states being led by personalist (overwhelmingly male) leaders and more states operating in a novel information environment, which can both spark crises and act as a catalyst in one. Narang and Williams unpack the new social media and media environment in which misinformation and disinformation, and hysteria, can spread virally and put pressure on leaders and governments to escalate. Social media is not a monolithic phenomenon, but a variety of open and closed platforms that spread information and misinformation—which can be maliciously manipulated and which then cross-pollinate more mainstream media outlets—are novel phenomena with which governments must now contend in crises. Some closed social media platforms, like chat tools, make it easy for governments to propagate face-saving lies easier, while more open platforms such as Twitter make it more difficult to sustain those lies. And all of this is flying around every second, all day, during and after crises and can spin up virulent nationalism that may make it difficult for governments to easily de-escalate crises or provide justifications for personalist dictators to escalate if they want to. In addition, social media is increasingly being used by leaders to communicate with the public or signal to each other. A July 2020 Twitter breach in which hackers had the ability to take over and tweet from almost any account was a terrifying reminder of the power of these tools. Luckily, the hackers just wanted cryptocurrency. But what if they wanted to start a war? They could have taken over President Trump's infamous Twitter account and tweeted, "It's over for Kim Jong Un." With few alternative avenues for intelligence and information and fearing a surprise US attack that could threaten his regime and nuclear forces, it is reasonable to fear that Kim Jong Un might launch a thermonuclear-armed intercontinental ballistic missile (ICBM), thinking it was his last act of revenge against the United States.[4]

How good has the United States, in particular, been in predicting which new states will populate the current and emerging nuclear landscape? Zegart points out that the rise of open-source intelligence (OSINT) outside of traditional government channels complicates traditional proliferation prediction and intelligence and produces both advantages and disadvantages over past government monopolies of intelligence. On the one hand, the rise of OSINT sleuths has increased the chance that a "hider" might be discov-

---

September 14, 2021. https://www.washingtonpost.com/politics/2021/09/14/peril-woodward-costa-trump-milley-china/.

4. For a fictional but realistic account of such a conflict, see Jeffrey Lewis, *The 2020 Commission Report on the North Korean Nuclear Attacks on the United States: A Speculative Novel* (New York: Houghton Mifflin, 2018).

ered, adding to the collection capabilities of national intelligence agencies.[5] The more eyes there are on a state and a program, the less likely it will be able to hide any potential proliferation activities, especially as the red lights start flashing brighter as the nuclear weapons program makes progress. This has been successful in the cases of North Korea and even Iran. The 2021 public disclosure and discovery of China's massive potential silo expansion was also accelerated by OSINT researchers, bringing into the public domain what government officials had only been able to previously hint at cryptically.[6]

On the other hand, OSINT tools are imperfect as well, and may even backfire, producing more, not fewer, proliferation intelligence failures and dangerous crises. First, hiders may still be able to hide. In 2007 Syria was able to hide the construction of a nuclear reactor—a replica of North Korea's Yongbyon reactor built with North Korean assistance—from private sources and US intelligence agencies alike. Syria made the cube look like an old Crusader's fort, not defending it or even placing a security perimeter around it—nothing to tip satellites off that there was anything worth defending there. It took a fortuitous Mossad operation in Vienna, breaking into the head of the Syrian Atomic Energy Agency's laptop where they discovered selfies with North Korean scientists—what were North Koreans doing in northern Syria?—and pictures of the reactor hall and core.

Second, while OSINT tools may increase the chance that such hiders will be caught, hiders learn as well, and it will be a constant cat and mouse game. Zegart provides worrisome examples of proliferating states becoming better at hiding their activities after private proliferation watchers revealed their intelligence. Some emerging nuclear states may therefore benefit from the OSINT revolution by learning how to adapt and improve their clandestine activities.

Third, the growth in OSINT transparency has a further downside. It may make it difficult for governments to sustain convenient fictions that enable de-escalation, as OSINT sleuths expose facts that undermine claims, embarrass governments, or otherwise undermine victory narratives. For example, in the 2019 Balakot crisis, foreign imagery analysts cast significant doubts on India's claim that it killed hundreds of terrorists at Balakot—it appears that India's missiles may have entirely missed the structure—and on India's claim that it shot down a Pakistan Air Force F-16, both of which India's government

---

5. See Vipin Narang, "Strategies of Nuclear Proliferation: How States Pursue the Bomb," *International Security* 41, no. 3 (Winter 2016/2017): 110–150.

6. See Joby Warrick, "China Is Building More Than 100 New Silos in Its Western Desert, Analysts Say," *Washington Post*, June 30, 2021, https://www.washingtonpost.com/national-security/china-nuclear-missile-silos/2021/06/30/0fa8debc-d9c2-11eb-bb9e-70fda8c37057_story.html; David E. Sanger and William J. Broad, "A 2nd New Nuclear Missile Base for China, and Many Questions about Strategy," *New York Times*, July 26, 2021, https://www.nytimes.com/2021/07/26/us/politics/china-nuclear-weapons.html.

sold as substantial retaliation for the Pulwama terrorist attack. OSINT analysts have consistently found evidence that North Korea's nuclear and missile program is progressing, contrary to the claims of President Trump, who tweeted, "There is no longer a nuclear threat from North Korea," after the 2017 Singapore summit. In some cases, convenient fictions sustain diplomacy and de-escalation, and OSINT tools have the potential to undermine this. Imagine if there had been OSINT analysts and tools during the Cuban Missile Crisis—would exposing the extent of the Soviet deployment have raised pressure for US preventive action, or would evidence that the United States removed Jupiter missiles from Turkey as a quid pro quo have undermined the perception of Kennedy's handling of the crisis?

All of these novel features, in isolation, would pose a challenge to our classical notions of deterrence: two rational players, with full information, who keenly observe and calculate the cost-benefit of every action for their nation and act accordingly. But what happens when there are more than two players—some of whom we may be able to identify, but some not—who are not rational in the traditional sense because the ends they seek are driven by personal psychology and emotion and not national interest, and where information is manipulated or incorrect? This is the nuclear era we are entering.

ENDURING DETERRENCE CHALLENGES WITH NEW TWISTS

In addition to the novel features of the emerging nuclear era, the volume has highlighted some enduring features which will continue to complicate and challenge the notion of stable deterrence among nuclear weapons powers with new twists. Some are technological, and some are structural.

For any nuclear state, but particularly for new nuclear states, the immediate technological question is "how much is enough" to achieve a nuclear weapons capability that can achieve a state's deterrent goals? Lewis and Panda show that what one government thinks is enough may differ from what its adversary thinks is enough, and when and where there are discrepancies, crisis dynamics can be very complicated. Contrary to what is widely assumed in the literature, deterrence stability does not require both rivals to *have* secure second-strike capabilities. Instead, it requires both rivals to *believe*, with high confidence, that both they and their rivals have such capabilities. And those beliefs must be widespread within the governments, otherwise some senior decision-makers may advocate for preventive war and others for caution.

Lewis and Panda examine the empirical record of Indian and Pakistani nuclearization, and North Korea's nuclear weapons development, and show that periods where there was a gap in perceptions of enoughness can lead to dangerous crisis dynamics. After 1974, Pakistan had to account for the possibility that India was effectively a nuclear weapons capable state, but

Indian leaders knew that it was not. India was, therefore, potentially able to reap some deterrent benefits against Pakistan well before it actually had a deliverable nuclear weapon. At the same time, and more dangerously, India did not believe Pakistan had enough nuclear weapons capability to deter in the late 1980s. This may have led India to be much more aggressive toward Pakistan during the Brasstacks Crisis, when some Indian officials may have contemplated baiting Pakistan into a conflict in order to preventively strike the Kahuta enrichment facility, mistakenly believing that Pakistan was not yet a nuclear weapons capable state, even though it was.[7]

A similar dynamic may exist with the North Korean leadership, which claims it has completed its deterrent but about which some in the United States harbor doubts, especially on the reliability of the weapons, reentry vehicle technology, and ICBM. The question of enoughness is not new, but the current incarnation is: because of norms and regimes that largely proscribe nuclear and missile testing, new and emerging nuclear weapons powers have to demonstrate enoughness with fewer—or maybe zero—tests. Long gone are the days when China and France could announce a new capability to the world by detonating a weapon above ground at Lop Nur or on a Pacific island. The challenge of proving to themselves and others that new and emerging nuclear states have enough to deter is sharper in the new nuclear era, with the attendant deterrence challenges when there are perceptual discrepancies between nuclear states and their adversaries on this question.

The dynamics analyzed by Lewis and Panda also raise important concerns about nuclear weapons operational safety and reliability. If new nuclear states feel compelled to deploy military capabilities, before they have been fully tested or incorporated into safe organizational procedures for the sake of deterrence, they are sacrificing a degree of protection against nuclear accidents. This problem existed during the Cold War—for example, when the United States rushed ICBMs into operational readiness during the Cuban Missile Crisis—but it appears to be a more common risk accepted by new nuclear states who lack the resources and time to make their arsenals have higher margins of safety.[8]

Once a state has developed its initial nuclear forces, the next challenge, as Clary illuminates, is how to develop survivable nuclear forces in the so-called new era of counterforce as intelligence platforms and precision strike capabilities—conventional, cyber, and nuclear—have put pressure on the

---

7. See Scott D. Sagan, "The Perils of Proliferation in South Asia," *Asian Survey* 41, no. 6 (November/December 2001): 1068–1071.

8. Scott D. Sagan, *The Limits of Safety: Organizations, Accidents, and Nuclear Weapons* (Princeton: Princeton University Press, 1993), 81–91.

survivability of new and emerging nuclear states' forces. These forces are often initially small and may lack diverse and survivable basing modes. Clary casts significant doubt on the ability of the new era of counterforce technologies to fully deliver on their promise because, as proponents of the theory of the nuclear revolution argued decades ago, survivability may still be easier and cheaper to obtain and maintain than it is to threaten. However, that does not mean that the pursuit of counterforce and damage limitation strategies—perhaps not through standard hard kill targeting but also through conventional or cyber capabilities that may seek to render an arsenal impotent—is not real, and the siren song of counterforce may be diffusing beyond the United States to smaller nuclear powers such as India.

What does this mean? In peacetime, it will put pressure on the smaller nuclear powers—including those that may have underlying domestic volatility, such as Pakistan and North Korea—to build up and diversify their nuclear forces and quickly close their windows of vulnerability. It may force them to undertake riskier deployment patterns that involve moving nuclear weapons around during peacetime, so they cannot be targeted or force them to go to sea quicker than they are ready to seek more survivable platforms than on land, with significant risks of accidents or unauthorized use. More nuclear weapons on more varied platforms in countries that may face domestic political uncertainty or terrorism can be incredibly worrisome, putting pressure on these states to securely manage their nuclear growth in the search for survivability. In crises, states worried about survivability can have itchy trigger fingers. Even if they may objectively be able to survive a first strike—though with North Korea that may be an open question—the uncertainty alone may lead them to much riskier crisis behavior and use them or lose them fears. And this particular risk may be amplified with the types of leaders McDermott identifies. In the new nuclear era, survivability is less automatic than it may have been in the past, and this can lead to concerning peacetime and crisis behaviors.

This leads directly to the Arceneaux and Feaver chapter on command and control, or how new nuclear states think about managing and controlling their nuclear forces. Particularly for states with small forces and rudimentary command and control architectures, worried about survivability, what are the kinds of arrangements and procedures that they may erect? The key insight of this chapter is that the classic assertive/delegative dichotomy is too static. All states ultimately delegate the ability to use nuclear forces at some point in a conflict; the question is when. States worried about internal threats, such as perhaps Pakistan and North Korea, may adopt highly assertive command and control structures during what they perceive to be peacetime. But because they may worry about the survivability of both their command and control structures—which might be the first things blinded in a war—and nuclear forces, they may flex out their nuclear force quickly and delegate early in a crisis to end-users and thereafter lose negative control.

It is this transformation of the command and control and the nuclear force in a crisis, particularly in states that are not accustomed to it, that might run exceptional risks. First, there may no longer be one threshold for use but twenty, as any commander in control of a nuclear weapon can use it if he fears the end is coming. Second, these transformations are exceedingly rare and would occur under precisely the scenario under which you would not want to be practicing for the very first time: under the psychological stress of a potential war. The concerns about survivability highlighted in Clary's chapter increase the likelihood that new nuclear states will adopt risky command and control procedures in crises to ensure the force does not fail impotent. This is one more reason to worry that new and emerging nuclear weapons states will present significant risks of inadvertent nuclear use.

But surely new and emerging nuclear states will be socialized into the tenets of the theory of the nuclear revolution and learn to manage these risks and behave like stereotypically rational states over time, right? Bell and Miller pour cold water on that hope and show that states rarely learn the right lessons from crises or previous experiences. In an important chapter, they show that nuclear states are just as immune to learning the right lessons—how to reduce risk and avoid escalation risks—as any other type of states. India and Pakistan have had a series of significant crises but seem to draw conclusions that suit their narratives—often that escalation is possible and good—rather than internalizing accurate assessments of the risks that they have just run. Although history may not repeat itself between nuclear weapons powers and rivals, it tends to rhyme.

The biggest concern highlighted by Bell and Miller is that new nuclear states may not seek to avoid crises but to win them. This suggests that there is no reason to expect the frequency or intensity of crises to fall over time in many nuclear rivalries. And, over time, that frequency may one day lead to a catastrophic outcome. If one reruns the Balakot crisis ten times, for example, a majority of the time one might expect a bloodier outcome. But states tend to believe that they walk away from crises only slightly bruised due to skill, not luck. One day, however, that luck may run out given the likely increase in the frequency and intensity of crises in the new nuclear era.

In the Cold War, Thomas Schelling famously identified a solution to the problem of how to make nuclear threats credible given the danger of escalation, calling for "the threat that leaves something to chance."[9] The problem, of course, is that the threat that leaves something to chance leaves something to chance. Do we want to face a future with such risks hanging over us? Do we have a choice?

---

9. Thomas C. Schelling, "The Threat That Leaves Something to Chance," in *The Strategy of Conflict* (Cambridge, MA: Harvard University Press, 1960): 187–204.

CONCLUSION

Mitigating Risks in the New Nuclear Age

We have no choice but to recognize these emerging nuclear risks and do what we can to reduce them when possible and manage them when necessary. Fortunately, mitigation measures exist that may help reduce the growing risk of deliberate and accidental or advertent nuclear use in this more complicated, more dangerous nuclear age. Some, such as crisis management efforts and arms control, are aimed at reducing the risk that existing nuclear powers intentionally escalate or inadvertently stumble into nuclear use. Others are aimed at slowing the expansion of the nuclear weapons club: redoubling efforts on nonproliferation and, where necessary, leaving open the option of targeted counterproliferation, which serves as a potential deterrent to proliferators as well as retains limited force options to delay or terminate their programs. Finally, if the nuclear states renew their commitment, under Article VI of the Nonproliferation Treaty (NPT), to work in "good faith" toward the goal of nuclear disarmament, more non-nuclear states could be encouraged to cooperate in nonproliferation policies.

CRISIS MANAGEMENT AND OPERATIONAL ARMS CONTROL

The frequency, intensity, and unpredictability of nuclear crises are likely to increase in the new nuclear age. The growing number of nuclear actors with ongoing hostile rivalries, the propensity for personalist leaders to be more risk-acceptant or volatile than previous nuclear leaders, information asymmetries, uncertainty and deliberate misinformation in the new media environment, and the fear that small arsenals may be threatened in a conflict may lead some nuclear states to have itchier trigger fingers than in the past where nuclear weapons may have induced caution. Obviously, crisis prevention is ideal. But there will inevitably be crises between nuclear powers, where the risk of advertent or inadvertent nuclear use may lurk—perhaps early—in the course of the crisis. What are some steps to help manage nuclear crises when they inevitably break out?

First, one important lesson from the 1960s has been forgotten and needs to be highlighted. After the Cuban Missile Crisis, the United States submitted an important working paper to the Eighteen Nation Disarmament Committee on December 12, 1962 outlining a series of crisis management recommendations, which are worth revisiting today for all existing and new nuclear powers.[10] The introduction to the report remains highly relevant today: "The

---

10. "Reduction of the Risk of War through Accident, Miscalculation, or Failure of Communication," United States Working Paper Submitted to the Eighteen Nation Disarmament Committee, December 12, 1962, in United States Arms Control and Disarmament Agency,

technology and techniques of modern warfare are such that much reliance is inevitably placed on the ability to respond rapidly and effectively to hostile military action. Events which may occur in connexion [sic] with the efforts of one state to maintain its readiness to respond to such action may, in varying degrees and with varying consequences, be misconstrued by another. The initiating state may have underestimated the ambiguity of such events and may have miscalculated the response they would call forth. The observing state may misinterpret them and feel compelled to act."[11] The report recommended advance notification of military movements with verification protocols, the establishment of working hotlines between adversaries so that information and signals can be conveyed directly in real-time rather than through telegram (in the 1960s) or Twitter (today). These remain important tools, and emphasis should particularly be placed on reliable and authenticated modes of communication between potential nuclear adversaries to reduce the risks of misperception or miscalculation, which might force states to assume the worst at the worst possible moment in a crisis.

This is more difficult than it sounds. For example, despite the existence of a hotline between India and Pakistan, at the height of the 2008 attack on Mumbai, someone spoofed a call from Indian foreign minister Pranab Mukherjee to Pakistani president Asif Zardari threatening a major Indian attack, sending Zardari into a panic and nearly spinning the crisis to war.[12] US secretary of state Condoleezza Rice called Mukherjee and berated him. Except, it turns out, Mukherjee had not made the call. Similarly, there is no evidence that the United States has the ability to communicate with North Korea's Kim Jong Un in real time, in extremis, other than perhaps Twitter, which is a risky platform on which to rest the future of the world. If Washington was conducting a routine exercise but detected nuclear movements in North Korea, which it feared could be due to misperception, would there be a way to reassure Kim of benign US intentions before it was too late? Advance notification and verification protocols and ensuring reliable and authentic modes of communication to enable potential nuclear adversaries to manage crises in real-time and avoid misperceptions and miscalculations will become increasingly important in the coming decades. This may mean considering more careful and considered use of Twitter in crises, due both to its vulnerability to direct hacking and to malicious actors using it to spread misinformation that may risk escalation.

Documents on Disarmament 1962 (Washington, DC: United States Printing Office, 1963), 1214–1225, http://unoda-web.s3-accelerate.amazonaws.com/wp-content/uploads/assets/publications/documents_on_disarmament/1962_V_II/DoD_1962%20VOL_II.pdf.
 11. "Reduction of the Risk of War," 1214.
 12. See Saeed Shah, "Mysterious Phone Call Brought Nuclear Rivals to the Brink in Mumbai," *Guardian*, December 7, 2008, https://www.theguardian.com/world/2008/dec/08/india-pakistan-mystery-telephone-call.

CONCLUSION

Second, the United States could reengage in military-to-military talks, negotiated agreements, and even joint exercises, when feasible, to reduce the risk that dangerous military interactions could lead to unintended escalation with adversaries in crises. During the Cold War, for example, the United States and the Soviet Union negotiated the 1972 Agreement on the Prevention of Incidents on and over the High Seas and the 1987 Agreement on the Prevention of Dangerous Military Activities.[13] Not only should the United States seek to establish "rules of the road" for exercises, surveillance at sea, and procedures to follow if accidental overflights over with North Korea, but it should also encourage other states (such as South Korea and North Korea and India and Pakistan) to engage in such "operational arms control" measures.[14]

Third, as a critical third party in many potential nuclear crises, the United States, in particular, should take care not to green light escalation. In the Balakot crisis between India and Pakistan, prior to India's historic strike on Pakistan's mainland territory at Balakot, President Trump stated almost approvingly that "India is looking at something very strong," and National Security Adviser John Bolton reportedly told his counterpart, Ajit Doval, that he supported India's right to self-defense, which Indian officials interpreted as a green light for retaliation.[15] This was a departure from previous administrations, which universally cautioned Indian restraint after a perceived Pakistan-backed provocation and would send high level officials to the region as a deterrent to escalation by putting skin in the game. Had the Trump administration urged Indian restraint, it is still likely that India may have retaliated. But it is possible that the target would have been confined to the disputed territory of Pakistan-held Kashmir, generating less pressure for escalation. The United States is the world's most important crisis broker, and as the new nuclear age unfolds, it will have to be much more careful and calibrated in how its extension of support to states may be interpreted as a green light for escalation, which can increasingly run risks of nuclear mobilization or use.

---

13. See Sean M. Lynn-Jones, "A Quiet Success for Arms Control: Preventing Incidents at Sea," *International Security* 9, no. 4 (Spring 1985): 154–184; and Kurt M. Campbell, "The U.S.-Soviet Agreement on the Prevention of Dangerous Military Activities," *Security Studies* 1, no. 1 (1991): 109–131.

14. See P. R. Chari, "CBMS in Post-Cold War South Asia," Regional Center for Strategic Studies, Colombo, Sri Lanka, reprinted for Stimson Center, June 14, 2012, https://www.stimson.org/2012/cbms-in-post-cold-war-south-asia/.

15. See Joshua T. White, "The Other Nuclear Threat: America Can't Escape Its Role in the Conflict between India and Pakistan," *Atlantic*, March 5, 2019, https://www.theatlantic.com/ideas/archive/2019/03/americas-role-india-pakistan-nuclear-flashpoint/584113/.

NUCLEAR ARMS CONTROL, DOCTRINE, AND DISARMAMENT STEPS

In addition to reducing the risk that nuclear weapons are accidentally or intentionally used in a crisis, another mitigation strategy is to reduce the number and types of nuclear platforms that existing nuclear weapons powers possess. This has two benefits. First, it reduces the chance of accidents and inadvertent use by reducing the number of nuclear weapons in a state's inventory. Second, and relatedly, minimal survivable forces are easier to securely manage from a command and control perspective. With leaner, but nevertheless effective, nuclear force structures, there is a lower chance of accidents and for loss of negative control in a crisis—that is, ensuring that a nuclear weapon is not employed when the appointed authority does not intend it to be.

With new nuclear states, such as North Korea, Washington is often reluctant to discuss arms control for fear of being accused of de facto accepting its status as a nuclear weapons state. Nevertheless, there are nontrivial peacetime and crisis benefits to shifting the discussion from the elimination of the North Korean arsenal to arms control. As with India and Pakistan after their 1998 nuclear tests, the United States continues to insist on a cap, rollback, and eliminate approach with North Korea. Given the continued growth and improvement of North Korea's nuclear and missile arsenal and concerns over the disposition of that arsenal in a crisis or if Kim were to ever lose power, it is even more reasonable to start with the goal of slowing the growth of the arsenal before seeking caps and reductions.[16]

One enduring but growing problem for existing and new nuclear states is the extensive reliance on dual-use delivery capabilities, which have both conventional and nuclear roles. On the one hand, using the same attack aircraft or missile for conventional and nuclear missions is cost effective, especially for resource-strapped regional states. And some states have convinced themselves that ambiguity about platforms, when moved, can enhance crisis deterrence by suggesting a threat that leaves something to chance. But the price of that ambiguity is potentially unintentional escalation as the adversary has no choice but to assume that nuclear assets may be being moved, and be forced to reciprocate, generating additional risk. In the new nuclear era, the perceived deterrence benefits of ambiguity will likely be swamped by the additional risks of this so-called discrimination problem—the adversary may not be able to discriminate whether the dual-use missile is tipped with a conventional or a nuclear warhead, but it cannot afford to guess wrong and

---

16. See John K. Warden and Ankit Panda, "Goals for Any Arms Control Proposal with North Korea," *Bulletin of Atomic Scientists*, February 13, 2019, https://thebulletin.org/2019/02/goals-for-any-arms-control-proposal-with-north-korea/.

may therefore have no choice but to assume the latter. One confidence-building measure is for nuclear powers to clearly and solely assign nuclear delivery systems for nuclear missions and to convey those assignments to adversaries to avoid misperceptions.

At the major power level, a renewed commitment to great power arms control, such as a further extended or successor to the New START treaty with Russia and perhaps some trilateral arms control arrangement including China, would both help limit and verify great power nuclear deployments as well as establish a model for smaller nuclear states. In addition, it is important for the major nuclear powers to adhere to a nuclear testing moratorium, even in the absence of a Comprehensive Test Ban Treaty in force. Periodic discussions in US administrations about a resumption of yield-producing nuclear tests are concerning, as tests are both technically unnecessary and would be counterproductive, opening the floodgates for other nations to test and disproportionately advance their nuclear programs.[17] North Korea remains the only state to conduct detectable-yield nuclear tests in the twenty-first century. Maintaining the major power testing moratorium norm is an important mitigation strategy to slow the progress of nuclear aspirants, but also to slow the pace of nuclear modernization in existing nuclear weapons powers, particularly more compact warhead designs for MIRVed missiles.

Furthermore, the existing nuclear powers could usefully commit to reduce the role of nuclear weapons in their military doctrines and to follow the laws of armed conflict in nuclear targeting plans.[18] In an important, but not well-remembered speech, the then vice president Joseph Biden announced in January 2017 that "it's hard to imagine a plausible scenario in which the first use of nuclear weapons by the United States would be necessary—or make sense. President Obama and I are confident we can deter—and defend ourselves, and our Allies, against—non-nuclear threats through other means."[19] This was as close to a no-first-use commitment as any US administration has ever given, though it still fell short of one.

The Trump administration's 2018 Nuclear Posture Review (NPR), by contrast, expanded the kinds of scenarios in which nuclear weapons might be used, including hints of nuclear responses to large-scale non-nuclear strategic attacks, including cyber-attacks, that killed large numbers of US or allied

---

17. See John Hudson and Paul Sonne, "Trump Administration Discussed Conducting First U.S. Nuclear Test in Decades," *Washington Post*, May 22, 2020, https://www.washingtonpost.com/national-security/trump-administration-discussed-conducting-first-us-nuclear-test-in-decades/2020/05/22/a805c904-9c5b-11ea-b60c-3be060a4f8e1_story.html.

18. Jeffrey G. Lewis and Scott D. Sagan, "The Nuclear Necessity Principle: Making US Targeting Policy Conform with Ethics & the Laws of War," *Daedalus* 145, no. 4 (2016): 62–74.

19. Biden speech, Carnegie Endowment for International Peace, January 11, 2017, as quoted in Fred Kaplan, *The Bomb: Presidents, Generals, and the Secret History of Nuclear War* (New York: Simon and Schuster, 2020), 258–259.

civilians.[20] Although the Trump NPR did recommit the United States, as first announced by the Obama administration in 2013, to follow the laws of armed conflict in all nuclear targeting and employment plans, the legality of using nuclear weapons to retaliate against civilian populations in belligerent reprisal has been disputed.[21] Other nuclear weapons states, such as Russia and China, who ratified the 1977 Additional Protocol of the Geneva Conventions without reservations, could usefully be challenged to address the legality of their nuclear doctrine in future NPT Review Conferences or other international forums.

Finally, when they ratified the NPT, the United States (along with the UK, Russia, France, and China) states committed to "pursue negotiations in good faith on effective measures relating to cessation of the nuclear arms race at an early date and to nuclear disarmament."[22] During the Obama administration, many non-nuclear weapons states grew impatient with the slow pace of disarmament and became increasingly alarmed by calls for new nuclear weapons systems after Trump's election in 2016. These concerns accelerated the negotiation of the Treaty on the Prohibition of Nuclear Weapons, making possession and use of nuclear weapons illegal by signatories, which was approved by 122 states in the UN General Assembly in 2017.[23]

None of the nuclear weapons states nor any allies covered by nuclear security guarantees have signed this nuclear ban treaty. Nor do they intend to do so in the future. The new danger is that with a nuclear ban treaty in place, the non-nuclear weapons states may feel less incentive to bargain with the nuclear weapons states in future NPT review conferences, that is, accepting improved inspections on nonproliferation steps for additional steps in the direction of nuclear disarmament. This is exactly what happened during the 2010 NPT Review Conference.[24] The United States could reduce this risk by recommitting to a step-by-step approach to nuclear disarmament and

---

20. See U.S. Department of Defense, *Report on Nuclear Employment Strategy of the United States Specified in Section 491 of 10 U.S.C.*, Washington, DC, June 12, 2013, 4–5 and U.S. Department of Defense, *Nuclear Posture Review*, Washington, DC, February 2018, 23, https://media.defense.gov/2018/Feb/02/2001872886/-1/-1/1/2018-NUCLEAR-POSTURE-REVIEW-FINAL-REPORT.PDF.

21. See Scott D. Sagan and Allen S. Weiner, "The Rule of Law and the Role of Strategy in U.S. Nuclear Doctrine," *International Security* 45, No. 4 (Spring 2021): 126–166, doi.org/10.1162/isec_a_00407; and Christopher A. Ford, John R. Harvey, Franklin C. Miller, Keith A. Payne, Bradley R. Roberts, Scott D. Sagan, and Allen S. Weiner, "Are Belligerent Reprisals against Civilians Legal?," *International Security* 46, No. 2 (Fall 2021), 166–172, https://doi.org/10.1162/ise.

22. "Treaty on the Non-Proliferation of Nuclear Weapons (NPT)," https://www.un.org/disarmament/wmd/nuclear/npt/text.

23. "Treaty on the Prohibition of Nuclear Weapons," https://www.un.org/disarmament/wmd/nuclear/tpnw/.

24. See Scott D. Sagan and Jane Vaynman, eds., "Arms, Disarmament and Influence: the International Impact of the 2010 U.S. Nuclear Posture Review," *Nonproliferation Review*, Special Issue (March 2011).

CONCLUSION

working with other nuclear states to negotiate multilateral approaches toward that long-term goal. Commitments by the non-NPT member nuclear states to negotiations toward step-by-step nuclear disarmament—including North Korea—could also help dispel the criticism that the United States is rewarding Pyongyang by accepting its current status as a nuclear state for its past failure to comply with NPT commitments.

NONPROLIFERATION

In addition to managing the arsenals of and crises between existing nuclear powers, preventing new entrants into the nuclear club—both US adversaries as well as its allies—remains a critical mitigation strategy to reducing the systemic risk of nuclear use in the new nuclear age. Traditional diplomatic vehicles such as the Nuclear Nonproliferation Treaty (NPT) and the International Atomic Energy Agency's (IAEA) additional protocol mechanisms, which commit a state to stringent monitoring and verification, are crucial to disincentivizing states from pursuing nuclear weapons in contravention of their international legal obligations. However, after North Korea cheated and withdrew from the NPT before acquiring nuclear weapons, it is unclear whether the NPT can survive any more future cheaters and withdrawers who successfully acquire nuclear weapons—and, by definition, any state that acquires nuclear weapons in the future will have been a member of the NPT who either cheated or withdrew or both. Any future nuclear weapons states will therefore pose a challenge to the very regime that is designed to prevent additional members of the club.

As such, other diplomatic initiatives such as the 2015 Joint Comprehensive Plan of Action (JCPOA) with Iran may become more valuable in the emerging nuclear era, bringing a cheater back off the path to nuclear weapons with a bespoke agreement that incentivizes a state to suspend, and rollback, its pursuit of nuclear weapons despite its past activities.[25] All of these diplomatic initiatives are backed by an important and increasingly sophisticated enforcement tool: unilateral and multilateral sanctions.[26] The coercive threat of sanctions may deter many states from attempting to pursue nuclear weapons in the first place, but the remaining states, which nevertheless persist, have likely priced in the cost of sanctions, making them the toughest cases. Maintaining an effective sanctions regime over time and space without facing defection from other actors—often Russia and China—is difficult. This enhances the value of initiatives such as the JCPOA, which

25. Iran, United States, Russia, China, United Kingdom, France, Germany, "Joint Comprehensive Plan of Action," July 14, 2015, https://2009-2017.state.gov/documents/organization/245317.pdf.
26. See Nicholas L. Miller, *Stopping the Bomb: The Sources and Effectiveness of US Nonproliferation Policy* (Ithaca: Cornell University Press, 2018).

can verifiably push back a state's nuclear program—extending the so-called breakout time or time required to acquire enough fissile material for a nuclear weapon—in exchange for sanctions relief. In the future, the combination of intelligence to detect potential proliferators, as Zegart's chapter shows, plus the threat of sanctions and subsequent diplomatic and economic inducements may be the most viable nonmilitary template to keep adversaries from acquiring the bomb.

Another crucial but often underappreciated US nonproliferation tool to keep its allies non-nuclear is credible extended deterrence guarantees. This has so far been an important constraint on German, South Korean, and potentially Japanese nuclear weapons pursuit. Although allied appetite for reassurance is often infinite, the Trump administration's insistence on greater burden sharing and its threats to remove US troops from Germany and the Korean Peninsula in 2020 raised questions about the sustained credibility of US extended deterrence commitments. Although Japan and Germany would face significant domestic political hurdles on a path to an independent nuclear weapons capability, a majority of the South Korean public, for example, has supported, and continues to support, an independent nuclear deterrent.[27] Despite some US advocates of, for example, an independent South Korean nuclear capability, maintaining credible commitments to its formal allies is an important nonproliferation tool for the United States, and one that will need reinforcing and repairing after the Trump administration.[28] Keeping adversaries and allies alike disincentivized to try to pursue nuclear weapons should remain a high foreign policy priority for the United States. Each additional nuclear state in the system—even if it is an ally—adds complexity to an already risky and complex dynamic.

COUNTERPROLIFERATION

In cases where nonproliferation efforts fail to prevent a state from pursuing nuclear weapons, the United States and its partners will have to consider counterproliferation efforts to delay or terminate a state's nuclear weapons program. These can range from sabotage efforts to slow or delay a program, as with the Stuxnet cyberattack on Iran, to limited military strikes that destroy a state's nuclear infrastructure, such as the Israeli surgical strike on the al-Kibar reactor in September 2007 perhaps just weeks before it may have become operational, to more comprehensive strikes against multiple nuclear

---

27. Lauren Sukin, "Credible Nuclear Security Commitments Can Backfire: Explaining Domestic Support for Nuclear Weapons Acquisition in South Korea," *Journal of Conflict Resolution* 20, no. 2, (2019): 1–32.

28. Jennifer Lind and Daryl G. Press, "Should South Korea Build Its Own Nuclear Bomb?," *Washington Post*, October 7, 2021, https://www.washingtonpost.com/outlook/should-south-korea-go-nuclear/2021/10/07/a40bb400-2628-11ec-8d53-67cfb452aa60_story.html.

CONCLUSION

facilities.²⁹ A case like Libya, where Qaddafi's scientists could not find the keys to an off-the-shelf turnkey centrifuge program and thus surrendered its capabilities before its centrifuges could even be unpacked, is exceptionally rare and unlikely to recur.³⁰ Future cases where military action may need to be considered may look more like the cases of Syria and Iran.

In Syria, the United States and Israel had noted a building in Syria's northeastern hinterland near the Euphrates in early 2007 but were not overly concerned—it seemed like any one of a number of neglected buildings, with no signatures or indicators that there was anything worth defending there. In March 2007, Israel was stunned to discover in a Mossad operation that this nondescript cube was a superstructure that was concealing an aboveground nuclear reactor in plain sight, a replica of North Korea's Yongbyon reactor being constructed with North Korean assistance. With no obvious connection to the Syrian electrical grid, both the United States and Israeli intelligence concluded that the reactor had only one purpose: to produce plutonium for a nuclear weapons program.³¹ But now that they knew what Syria was doing, what could the United States and Israel do about it?

Wary from the Iraq war, President Bush had little interest in a military operation that might risk a war with Syria. But he did not stop Israeli prime minister Ehud Olmert, who decided to take no chances. On September 6, four Israeli F-15s and four F-16s screamed low over the Syrian desert and leveled the building, which the IAEA later concluded was a graphite-moderated nuclear reactor that Syria was concealing. Israel risked major escalation with Syria—which, caught red-handed, simply remained quiet after the Israeli strike—but successfully destroyed the reactor, likely weeks before fuel was to be added, after which a military strike could have caused tremendous environmental damage. Had Israel not struck the al-Kibar reactor, it is likely the world would have had to contend with a potential Syrian nuclear weapons program for years. The tragedy of the Syrian civil war would be heightened by the possible use of nuclear weapons against the rebels, ISIS forces, or civilian populations.

Although the operation against al-Kibar was successful, few future proliferators may be as brazen and daring as Assad, who tried to conceal a single above-ground nuclear reactor—and nearly got away with it. Instead, the blueprint for a determined nuclear proliferator may be Iran, which dispersed, buried, and hardened uranium enrichment facilities and had an active nuclear weapons program until 2003, under the AMAD Plan.³² Against

29. Harel and Benn, "No Longer a Secret."
30. See Malfrid Braut-Hegghammer, *Unclear Physics: Why Iraq and Libya Failed to Build Nuclear Weapons* (Ithaca: Cornell University Press, 2016).
31. George W. Bush, *Decision Points* (New York: Crown Books, 2010), 421.
32. See Board of Governors, International Atomic Energy Agency, "Implementation of the NPT Safeguards Agreement and Relevant Provisions of Security Council Resolutions

such a state, a single surgical strike as was conducted against Syria may be infeasible. But many options have been pursued to slow and delay the Iranian program, including cyber capabilities under the Olympic Games program authorized under President Bush and accelerated by President Obama, as well as an alleged Israeli effort to assassinate Iranian nuclear scientists.[33] These did not eliminate Iran's capability, but it may have helped buy time. Indeed, Stuxnet may have slowed Iran's enrichment capability enough to allow moderates led by Rouhani to replace the hardline President Ahmadinejad and set the stage for the JCPOA. As the JCPOA risks crumbling with the Trump administration's withdrawal and with Iran nibbling away at its restrictions, there may come a day when the United States and its partners may have to consider military options to set back Iran's nuclear program and perhaps others like it.

Although prevention and counterproliferation became dirty words after the 2003 Iraq war—and without relitigating its causes or being apologists for it—it is possible to consider narrow counterproliferation military objectives that stop well short of wholesale regime change. In extremis, military options that restrict themselves to solely attacking nuclear infrastructure to set back a nuclear program, even if it cannot permanently destroy it, may be necessary to put on the table or execute. The North Korean case illustrates that such options become nearly impossible if they are not executed prior to acquisition. If all else fails, a variety of counterproliferation tools, from sabotage to limited military strikes, could continue to be developed and considered not only as a deterrent to pursuit but also to slow down a nuclear aspirant if necessary. These are not without risks of blowback or backfiring; they can harden a proliferator's resolve and drive a program further underground or accelerate it. But the growing dangers of the new nuclear age illustrate the need to redouble efforts to prevent new proliferators from reaching the finish line.

Conclusion

Our previous understanding of nuclear deterrence and nuclear risks is largely derived from a Cold War experience where two superpowers dominated the nuclear landscape. Though not without their own pathologies, the

---

in the Islamic Republic of Iran," GOV/2011/65, November 8, 2011, Annex: Possible Military Dimensions to Iran's Nuclear Programme.

33. David E. Sanger, "Obama Order Sped Up Wave of Cyberattacks on Iran," *New York Times*, June 1, 2012, https://www.nytimes.com/2012/06/01/world/middleeast/obama-ordered-wave-of-cyberattacks-against-iran.html; see also Ronen Bergman and Farnaz Fassihi, "The Scientist and the A.I.-assisted, Remote Control Killing Machine," *New York Times*, September 18, 2021, https://www.nytimes.com/2021/09/18/world/middleeast/iran-nuclear-fakhrizadeh-assassination-israel.html.

United States and the Soviet Union shared interest in avoiding nuclear war and managed—though barely at times—to succeed in doing so. But the contemporary and emerging nuclear era bears little resemblance to the Cold War. There are more nuclear powers, some with domestic political instability or led by pathological personalist dictators unconstrained by the checks and balances the United States and the Soviet Union possessed, with smaller and less sophisticated arsenals, but with more—and more intense—rivalries operating in a high-velocity internet-age where misinformation can be rampant.

We have been slow to appreciate the new risks posed by the new nuclear age, and how these different risks cumulate to generate a characteristically different and more dangerous nuclear age. This volume has outlined these new challenges and why the coming nuclear age will be different than the ones that preceded it. It has offered some potential mitigation strategies, but the challenges we face and that await us in this less stable, more volatile nuclear age are daunting. We are entering a new nuclear era of the extreme risk and must be even more cautious and smart in managing these risks than we were during the Cold War.

Acknowledgments

This book would not have been possible without the assistance of many individuals and organizations interested in making our collective nuclear future a little more secure. The book has its origins in the "Meeting the Challenges of the New Nuclear Age" project of the American Academy of Arts and Sciences, and we thank David Oxtoby, Francesca Giovannini, Kathryn Moffat, Poul Erik Christiansen, and Islam Qasem for their strong support. We thank Louise Henry Bryson and John E. Bryson, John F. Cogan, Jr., Lester Crown, Alan M. Dachs, Bob and Kristine Higgins, Richard Rosenberg, and Kenneth L. and Susan S. Wallach for their generous support of the project, which made this volume possible. We are also grateful to the American Academy of Arts and Sciences' Committee on International Security Studies for their feedback on the initial proposal for this volume.

Our first conference was held at Stanford University in the fall of 2019, and we thank Zachary Davis, Lynn Eden, Thomas Fingar, Peter Hayes, Sig Hecker, Herb Lin, Steve Miller, Reid Pauly, William Perry, Barry Posen, Brad Roberts, Allen Weiner, and Rodney Wilson for their participation and critiques of our first rough drafts. We also thank Lauren Sukin and Katie McKinney for serving as rapporteurs. Because of the Covid-19 pandemic, our second authors' conference was held virtually, and we benefited greatly from a group of expert discussants of each chapter. We thank Steve Fetter, Charles Glaser, Sir Lawrence Freedman, Brendan Green, Jill Hruby, Jeffrey Knopf, Austin Long, Steve Miller, Joshua Rovner, Paul Slovic, and Harold Trinkunas for supplying detailed commentary that improved each chapter.

At Cornell University Press, we thank Rodger Haydon, Michael McGandy, Robert Art, and an anonymous outside reviewer. We thank Katie McKinney for her excellent research assistance.

Finally, and most important, we thank each of the book's authors for researching, writing, revising, and then revising again, their chapters. The book was a team effort, and this group of scholars rose to the occasion in the midst of a global pandemic, and both challenged and supported each other to produce the best work possible.

Contributors

Giles David Arceneaux is an assistant professor of political science at the University of Colorado, Colorado Springs. He completed his doctorate in political science from Syracuse University, focusing on nuclear command and control.

Mark S. Bell is an associate professor of political science at the University of Minnesota, focusing on nuclear proliferation and strategy. He is the author of *Nuclear Reactions: How Nuclear-Armed States Behave*.

Christopher Clary is an assistant professor of political science at the University at Albany, State University of New York, and a nonresident fellow in the South Asia program of the Stimson Center in Washington, DC. He is the author of *The Difficult Politics of Peace: Rivalry in Modern South Asia*.

Peter D. Feaver is professor of political science and public policy at Duke University, where he directs the Program in American Grand Strategy. He has written extensively on civil-military relations, grand strategy, and nuclear command and control.

Jeffrey Lewis is director of the East Asia Nonproliferation Project (EANP) at the Middlebury Institute of International Studies at Monterey. He is the author of a novel about a nuclear war with North Korea, *The 2020 Commission Report on the North Korean Nuclear Attacks Against the United States*.

Rose McDermott is the David and Mariana Fisher University Professor of International Relations at Brown University, focusing primarily on political psychology. She is the author of five books and coeditor of two volumes. She is also the author of over 200 academic articles across a wide variety of disciplines encompassing topics such as gender, experimentation, national security intelligence, social identity, cybersecurity, emotion and decision-making, and the biological and genetic bases of political behavior.

Nicholas L. Miller is an associate professor in the Department of Government at Dartmouth College. He is the author of *Stopping the Bomb: The Sources and Effectiveness of US Nonproliferation Policy*.

Vipin Narang is the Frank Stanton Professor of Nuclear Security and Political Science at the Massachusetts Institute of Technology. He is author of *Nuclear Strategy in the Modern Era* and *Seeking the Bomb: Strategies of Nuclear Proliferation*.

Ankit Panda is the Stanton senior fellow in the Nuclear Policy Program at the Carnegie Endowment for International Peace in Washington, DC. He is the author of *Kim Jong Un and the Bomb: Survival and Deterrence in North Korea*.

Scott D. Sagan is the Caroline S.G. Munro Professor of Political Science and Senior Fellow at the Center for International Security and Cooperation at Stanford University. He is the author of, among other works, *Moving Targets: Nuclear Strategy and National Security*; *The Limits of Safety: Organizations, Accidents, and Nuclear Weapons*; and (with Kenneth N. Waltz) *The Spread of Nuclear Weapons: An Enduring Debate*.

Caitlin Talmadge is associate professor of security studies at Georgetown University, where she focuses on nuclear deterrence, civil-military relations, and military operations and strategy. She is the author of *The Dictator's Army*.

Heather Williams is a senior lecturer and associate professor in defence studies at King's College London. Along with work on social media and crisis escalation, her research focuses on arms control, emerging technologies, and deterrence and assurance.

Amy Zegart is the Morris Arnold and Nona Jean Cox Senior Fellow at the Hoover Institution and professor of political science (by courtesy) at Stanford University. She specializes in US intelligence, emerging technologies, and national security, grand strategy, and global political risk management. She is the author of *Spies, Lies, and Algorithms: The History and Future of American Intelligence*.

Index

Figures, notes, tables are indicated by f, n, and t following the page number.

Additional Protocol of Geneva Conventions (1977), 245
Advani, L. K., 138–139
Agreed Framework (1994), 140–141, 142–145
Agreement on the Prevention of Dangerous Military Activities (1987), 242
Agreement on the Prevention of Incidents on and over the High Seas (1972), 242
Ahmadinejad, Mahmoud, 249
Albright, David, 108, 110
Allcott, Hunt, 71–72, 71n31
alliances: counterforce and, 166; multipolar deterrence and, 18, 29–30, 38; nuclear contagion and, 230; nuclear learning and, 215
Antony, A. K., 136n49
Arab-Israeli War (1973), 218–219
Arceneaux, Giles David, 9, 182, 238
Argentina, US intelligence on nuclear weapons program in, 96–97
Armaments Corporation of South Africa, 198
arms control: crisis management and, 240–242; multipolar deterrence and, 26–31; nuclear arms control doctrine and disarmament, 243–246. *See also specific agreements and treaties*
al-Assad, Bashar, 7–8
assertive command and control: in China, 196, 203, 205; defined, 184–185, 186; in India, 199–200, 203, 205; in Israel, 197; in South Africa, 198, 203, 205
asymmetric nuclear balances, 4

Atomic Energy Corporation (South Africa), 198
ATR (automatic target recognition) algorithms, 171–172
autocracies, 7–8, 42. *See also specific countries*

Balakot crisis. *See* Pulwama/Balakot crisis
Basur, Rajesh, 136n49
Beg, Mirza Aslam, 135, 135n43
Beirut ammonium nitrate explosion (2020), 72
Bell, Mark S., 5–6, 9, 80, 209, 239
Ben-Gurion, David, 197
Berkowitz, Bruce, 116
Bhabha Atomic Research Center (India), 130, 137
Bhutto, Zulfikar Ali, 132–133
Biden, Joe, 88, 244
biological anthropology, 51
biological weapons, 46
Blackett, P. M. S., 156, 180
BlackSky (satellite firm), 101
Bolton, John, 148, 148–149n87, 242
Brasstacks Crisis (1986–1987), 134, 153, 237
Braut-Hegghammer, Malfrid, 39–40, 41
Britain. *See* United Kingdom
Brodie, Bernard, 127, 156
Brooks, Linton, 30
Brzezinski, Zbigniew, 220
Buch, Benjamin, 46
Burr, William, 35
Bush, George W., 16, 95, 141, 146, 248

255

INDEX

Cal Tech, 103
Carl Vinson (ship), 86
Carter, Jimmy, 219
catalytic nuclear war problem, 24
causal learning, 214
CCD (concealment, camouflage, and decoy) technologies, 174
cell phones, 102
CEM (Civil Emergency Message), 82
Center for International Security and Cooperation, 108
Center for Nonproliferation Studies, 103, 108, 117
Center for Strategic and International Studies, 111, 116
Central Intelligence Agency (CIA), 93–94, 165
Central Military Commission (China), 195
Central Military Committee (North Korea), 202
Chakma, Bhumitra, 133
chemical weapons, 46
China: Additional Protocol of Geneva Conventions and, 245; arms races and, 27, 28, 30; command and control systems in, 191, 195–196; concealment of nuclear forces in, 174–175; crisis and wartime behavior, 32, 33, 35–36; deterrence challenges and, 232; disinformation campaigns by, 114; domestic politics in, 191, 196; eroding foundations of nuclear stability and, 4, 7; hardened targets and, 168; India's nuclear weapons program and, 130; mobile nuclear forces in, 170, 171, 172; multipolar deterrence and, 14, 17, 18–19, 24–25, 37, 231; nuclear arms control and, 244; nuclear learning and, 229; nuclear modernization program, 1, 28; Nuclear Non-Proliferation Treaty and, 245; nuclear weapons program, 33; personalistic leadership in, 60; regime type and state structure in, 42; Sino-Soviet Crisis (1969), 166; social media and, 88; submarine forces in, 177; survivability issues and, 176; survivability of nuclear forces in, 160t, 162–163, 165; US counterforce capabilities and, 155; US intelligence on nuclear weapons program in, 96–97
Choi Juhwal, 144–145, 150
Churchill, Winston, 208
CIA (Central Intelligence Agency), 93–94, 165
Civil Emergency Message (CEM), 82
civil-military relations, 190–191, 197, 200–201, 204–205
Clary, Christopher, 9, 154, 223, 237–238
Clinton, Bill, 16, 140
CNN effect, 70

Coats, Daniel, 100
Cohen, Avner, 196
Cohen, Michael, 58, 210, 211, 218n40
Cold War. *See* Soviet Union
command and control, 9, 182–208; always/never dilemma and, 183–184; challenges of, 183–186; in China, 195–196; civil-military relations and, 190–191; deterrence challenges and, 238–239; domestic politics and, 188t, 190–191, 203–206, 204t; explanations for, 186–191, 188t, 203–206, 204t; external threat environment and, 188–189, 188t, 203–206, 204t; in France, 193–195; as "fulcrum of fragility," 183; future of, 206–208; in India, 199–200; in Israel, 196–197; in North Korea, 201–203; nuclear learning and, 210n6; in Pakistan, 200–201; reconceptualizing, 184–186; in regional nuclear powers, 191–203; in South Africa, 198; strategic rationale and, 188t, 189–190, 203–206, 204t; survivability of, 157–158; in United Kingdom, 192–193
compact fission device, 130, 130n20
compensating fuzes, 167–168
Comprehensive Test Ban Treaty, 244
computer modeling for nuclear intelligence, 102–103
concealment, camouflage, and decoy (CCD) technologies, 174
conditional control systems, 185–186; in North Korea, 202–204, 207; in Pakistan, 200–201, 203–204, 207
CORONA satellite program, 98–99
corruption, 40
Cote, Owen R., Jr., 176n58
Côte d'Ivoire political crisis (2010–2011), 72
counterforce, 9, 154–181; deterrence challenges and, 237–238; early warning indicators and, 178–179; hardened targets and, 167–169; mobile targets and, 169–177; multipolar deterrence and, 30; responses to, 178–179; survivability concerns and, 155–167, 160t; time constraints on, 158–167, 160t
counterproliferation, 9, 247–249
credibility of threats, 127–129, 128t
crisis management: ambiguous messaging and, 68; command and control systems and, 185–186, 239; deterrence and, 9; risk mitigation and, 240–242; social media and, 63–64, 88
crowdsourcing, 102, 103
Cuban Missile Crisis, 5, 25, 69, 93, 94, 95–96, 220

damage limitation approach, 26, 29–30, 238. *See also* survivability
Dar, Adil Ahmad, 75

INDEX

deepfakes, 74, 114–115. *See also* misinformation/disinformation
de-escalation: command and control systems and, 186; crisis behavior and, 32–33; open-source intelligence and, 9, 236; Pulwama/Balakot crisis (2019), 80–81; social media and, 65, 87
Defense Research & Development Organization (India), 134, 136, 199
Defense Science Board (US), 170
delegative command and control, 184–185; in France, 194–195, 207; in North Korea, 202; in Pakistan, 205; in United Kingdom, 192–193, 203, 205, 207
democratization of intelligence, 98–103; automated analytics and, 102–103; internet connectivity and, 102; satellites and, 98–102, 101*f*
Department of Atomic Energy (India), 199
Department of Defense (US), 79, 84–85, 113, 179
deterrence regime: challenges in new nuclear era, 231–239; counterproliferation and, 247–249; crisis management and, 240–249; declining confidence in, 231–239; enoughness and, 124–127; new nuclear states learning, 9, 209–229; nonproliferation and, 246–247; nuclear arms control doctrine and disarmament, 243–246; recessed deterrents, 133–135, 152; resource constraints and, 125; restraining effects of, 2; risk mitigation and, 240–249; survivability and, 155–156
Di, Hua, 174–175
Digital Globe, 110
Dill, Janina, 6
disarmament: Eighteen Nation Disarmament Committee, 240–241; nuclear arms control doctrine and, 243–246; social status and, 57
disinformation. *See* misinformation/disinformation
Dobrynin, Anatoly, 34–35
domestic politics: command and control and, 188*t*, 190–191, 203–206, 204*t*; nuclear learning and, 217
Doval, Ajit, 242

echo chambers, 71
Edmondson, Amy, 59
Egypt, arms sales to North Korea, 143
Eighteen Nation Disarmament Committee, 240–241
Eisenhower, Dwight, 50n24, 97
electro-optical imagery, 100, 100n40
Ellsberg, Daniel, 55
enoughness, 123–153; credibility of threats and, 127–129, 128*t*; deterrence and, 124–127, 236–237; India-Pakistan conflict and, 129–140; North Korea and, 140–151
Erdogan, Recep Tayyip, 56, 233
escalation: command and control systems and, 187, 190, 208; nuclear intelligence on risks of, 93; social media and, 66–71
Euroconsult, 100
evolutionary psychology, 51, 54
external threat environment, 188–189, 188*t*, 203–206, 204*t*

Facebook: as closed platform, 64; escalation risks and, 66, 67; Hawaii missile alert (2018) and, 68; Korean Peninsula fake evacuation order (2017) and, 84, 85, 86; misinformation/disinformation on, 71–72, 71n31; political communication via, 63
factual learning, 214, 214n23
Feaver, Peter D., 9, 182, 238
Federal Emergency Management Agency (FEMA), 82, 82n60
Federation of American Scientists, 114
Fetter, Steve, 168
fog of war, 64
Force Aérienne Tactique (France), 194
France: command and control systems in, 193–195; counterforce capabilities in, 155; domestic politics in, 195; eroding foundations of nuclear stability and, 7; multipolar deterrence and, 17, 20–21; mutually assured destruction doctrine and, 23; Nuclear Non-Proliferation Treaty and, 245; nuclear taboo and, 6; as regional nuclear power, 20–21; survivability of nuclear forces in, 159, 160*t*, 162, 166; US intelligence on nuclear weapons program in, 96–97
Freedman, Lawrence, 69

Gabbard, Tulsi, 82, 83
Gandhi, Indira, 130, 132–133
Gandhi, Rahul, 75
Gandhi, Rajiv, 134, 139
Gentzkow, Matthew, 71–72, 71n31
Geo4Nonpro, 103
George, Alexander and Juliette, 50n24
Germany: deterrence regimes and, 247; nuclear contagion and, 7, 230; US intelligence on nuclear weapons program in, 96–97
Ghafoor, Asif, 77
Glaser, Charles, 168
GMTIs (ground moving target indicators), 171–172, 175
Goetz, Jennifer, 54n32

257

INDEX

Goodman, Allan, 116
Google Earth, 101–102, 117
Google Sketchup, 111
Gorbachev, Mikhail, 221
Great Britain. *See* United Kingdom
Green, Brendan Rittenhouse, 157–158
Greens, Stefan, 109
ground moving target indicators (GMTIs), 171–172, 175
groupthink, 59, 213
guilt vs. shame, 49

Hanham, Melissa, 103
Harvard University, 113
Hawaii Emergency Management Agency, 81–82
Hawaii missile alert (2018), 64–65, 74, 81–84, 88, 232
Hecker, Siegfried, 108, 110–111
Hibbs, Mark, 134n37
Hinderstein, Corey, 110
Hitler, Adolf, 47, 61
Hooper, Mira-Rapp, 30
horizontal proliferation, 92–93
Horowitz, Michael, 210, 211–212, 214, 218n40
Hoyt, Timothy, 225
Hussein, Saddam, 39, 45, 46, 59, 90–91, 93, 228
Hymans, Jacques, 39–40

IAEA (International Atomic Energy Agency), 91, 246
IAF. *See* Indian Air Force
IDF (Israel Defense Forces), 197
India: arms races and, 28–29; Brasstacks Crisis (1986–1987), 134, 153, 237; command and control systems in, 199–200; concealment of nuclear forces in, 175n54; counterforce capabilities in, 155; credibility of nuclear threat, 127–129, 128*t*, 137–138, 235–236; crisis and wartime behavior, 32, 241; deterrence regimes and, 129–140, 152–153, 231–232; domestic politics in, 200; eroding foundations of nuclear stability and, 4, 5, 7; Kargil war (1999), 64–65, 139, 222, 225–226; Kashmir insurgency (1988–1990), 134, 135; Lahore Declaration (1999), 221; mobile nuclear forces in, 171; multipolar deterrence and, 20; Mumbai terrorist attack (2008), 64–65, 139, 223, 227, 241; nuclear learning and, 210, 221–224, 239; nuclear taboo and, 6; nuclear weapons program, 1–2, 13, 93, 243; Operation Meghdoot (1984), 134; Pulwama/Balakot crisis (2019), 64, 74, 75–81, 224, 227, 231–232, 235–236, 242; as regional nuclear power, 20; shame and social sanction in, 51; survivability of nuclear forces in, 160*t*, 163–164, 236–237; US intelligence on nuclear weapons program in, 96–97
Indian Air Force (IAF), 77, 78–79, 132, 224
Indian Atomic Energy Commission, 134
Indo-Pacific Command (US), 82
information hoarding, 59
information threat theory of shame, 51
Instagram, 66
Institute for Science and International Security, 108, 110
intelligence. *See* open-source intelligence; satellite intelligence collection
International Atomic Energy Agency (IAEA), 91, 246
international relations theory, 15
inverse synthetic aperture radar (ISAR), 172
Iran: counterproliferation and, 247–248; crisis and wartime behavior, 32; disinformation campaigns by, 114; Joint Comprehensive Plan of Action and, 246–247; multipolar deterrence and, 20; Natanz nuclear site, 110, 112; nuclear contagion and, 7; nuclear weapons program, 2, 95, 109–110, 230; social media and, 63, 88; US intelligence on nuclear weapons program in, 96–97
Iraq: mobile missile forces in, 170, 180; multipolar deterrence and, 232; nuclear weapons program, 2, 46, 90–91; personalistic leadership in, 46; US intelligence on nuclear weapons program in, 96–97
ISAR (inverse synthetic aperture radar), 172
Israel: command and control systems in, 196–197; counterproliferation and, 247–248; crisis and wartime behavior, 32; domestic politics, 197; eroding foundations of nuclear stability and, 7; intelligence agency effectiveness in, 97; multipolar deterrence and, 17; nuclear taboo and, 6; shame and social sanction in, 51; survivability of nuclear forces in, 160*t*, 163, 165; US intelligence on nuclear weapons program in, 96–97
Israel Defense Forces (IDF), 197
Italy, nuclear reactors in, 143
Iyengar, P. K., 137

Jaish-e-Mohammed (JeM), 75, 76–77
Japan: arms races and, 30; deterrence regimes and, 247; North Korea's nuclear weapons program and, 150; nuclear contagion and, 7, 230; nuclear learning and, 214; nuclear reactors in, 143; US security commitments to, 38
Jasani, Bhupendra, 90–91
JeM (Jaish-e-Mohammed), 75, 76–77

INDEX

Jervis, Robert, 22, 179
Joint Comprehensive Plan of Action (JCPOA), 246–247
Joshi, Harsh, 131

Kahn, Herman, 129
Kampani, Gaurav, 163
Kanwal, Gurmeet, 131
Kapur, S. Paul, 225–226
Karber, Phillip, 113–114, 115
Kargil war (1999), 64–65, 139, 222, 225–226
Kashmir insurgency (1988–1990), 134, 135
KCNA (Korean Central News Agency), 202
Kelly, James, 148
Keltner, Dacher, 54n32
Kennedy, John F., 50n24, 69, 94, 116
Kent, Sherman, 93
Khan, A. Q., 94, 132
Khan, Feroz, 133–134, 135, 135n43
Khan, Imran, 227
Khrushchev, Nikita, 56, 69, 93, 116
Kidwai, Khalid, 227
Kimball, Jeffrey, 35
Kim Il Do, 144n78
Kim Il Sung, 142–143
Kim Jong Il, 145, 146
Kim Jong Un: command and control systems and, 202; minimum deterrence and, 150–151; as personalistic leader, 5, 39, 45, 48, 61; social media and, 74, 81, 83, 85; Trump and, 123, 151
Kim Yong-ham, 144n80
Kissinger, Henry, 34–35
Korea. *See* North Korea; South Korea
Korean Central News Agency (KCNA), 202
Korean People's Army (KPA), 202
Kristensen, Hans M., 114

Lahore Declaration (1999), 221
Laird, Melvin, 35
Lanoszka, Alexander, 67
Lashkar-e-Taiba (LeT), 139
launch-on-warning (LOW) systems, 179
Lawrence Livermore National Laboratory, 134n37, 138
Leap Day Deal (2012), 141, 149
Leng, Russell, 225
Levy, Jack, 214
Lewis, Jeffrey, 9, 108, 114, 123, 166, 236
Lewis, John Wilson, 174–175, 195
Libya: civil war in, 94; counterproliferation and, 248; multipolar deterrence and, 232; nuclear weapons program, 2, 93–94; US intelligence on nuclear weapons program in, 96–97
Lieber, Keir, 19n20, 154, 158, 167, 169, 174, 178
"limits of safety," 30–31

LinkedIn, 109
Litai, Xue, 195
Long, Austin, 157–158
Los Alamos National Laboratory, 134n37
LOW (launch-on-warning) systems, 179
LuoKogan, Aleksandr, 54n32

machine learning, 102–103
MAD (mutually assured destruction) doctrine, 4, 22–23
Managing the Atom Project, 113
Manhattan Project, 93
Man-in-the-Loop, Variable-Autonomy, Anti-Armor Weapons (MILVAWs), 173
Mao Zedong, 60, 61
Maritan (company), 109–110
Masashi, Okyuyama, 87n74
McDermott, Rose, 8, 39, 232–233, 238
McNamara, Robert, 156n4
Michishita, Narushige, 140, 147
Military Times on Korean Peninsula fake evacuation order (2017), 86
Miller, Nicholas L., 5–6, 9, 80, 209, 239
Milley, Mark, 233
MILVAWs (Man-in-the-Loop, Variable-Autonomy, Anti-Armor Weapons), 173
MIRVs (multiple independently maneuverable reentry vehicles), 154, 244
misinformation/disinformation: crowd-sourcing of intelligence and, 102; Korean Peninsula fake evacuation order (2017) and, 85; open-source intelligence and, 108–109; open vs. closed platforms and, 71–72; Pulwama/Balakot crisis (2019), 75–81; social media and, 8–9, 67–69, 70
Modi, Narendra, 75, 76, 77, 78, 79–80, 224
Montgomery, Alexander H., 96
Morell, Michael, 102
Mount, Adam, 96
Mubarakmand, Samar, 133–134, 135
Mukherjee, Pranab, 241
multiple independently maneuverable reentry vehicles (MIRVs), 154, 244
multipolar deterrence, 5, 8, 13–38; alliances and, 29, 38; arms races and, 26–31; counterforce and, 30; crisis and wartime behavior, 31–36; damage limitation approach and, 26, 29–30; emerging nuclear era, defined, 16–21; general deterrence, 22–26; "limits of safety" and, 30–31; peacetime behavior, 21–31; policy implications, 36–38; postwar predation problem and, 25, 26–27; regime type and, 43; state power vs. nuclear status, 16–17; tailored deterrence and, 16
Mumbai terrorist attack (2008), 64–65, 139, 223, 227, 241
Musharraf, Pervez, 227

259

INDEX

Mutual and Balanced Force Reductions talks, 38
mutually assured destruction (MAD) doctrine, 4, 22–23
mutual vulnerability, 5

Narang, Vipin, 1, 8–9, 63, 108, 126, 131, 164, 223–224, 230, 234
narcissism: in personalistic regime leaders, 40, 47, 48–49, 233; pride and, 54; shame and, 50
National Command Authority (Pakistan), 77–78, 80, 200
National Council for the Resistance of Iran (NCRI), 109, 110
National Geospatial Intelligence Agency, 103, 111
National Intelligence Estimate (2007), 95
National Technical Research Organization (NTRO), 78
NATO (North Atlantic Treaty Organization), 17, 38, 174, 220, 226
New START Treaty (2010), 37, 244
Nixon, Richard, 33–35, 50n24, 218
no first use doctrine, 19, 38
noncombatant evacuation operation order (NEO), 84–85
nongovernmental nuclear intelligence collection, 104–117; attributes of, 104–108, 105–107t; benefits of, 108–111; risks of, 112–117
nonproliferation, 9
nonstrategic nuclear weapons, 19
North American Aerospace Defense Command, 220
North Atlantic Treaty Organization. *See* NATO
North Korea: Agreed Framework (1994), 140–141, 142–145; arms races and, 30; command and control systems in, 201–203, 238; concealment of nuclear forces in, 174–175; counterproliferation and, 249; credibility of nuclear threat, 127–129, 128t; crisis and wartime behavior, 32; deterrence regimes and, 140–151, 152–153; domestic politics in, 202–203, 205, 207–208, 238; eroding foundations of nuclear stability and, 4, 6, 7; Hawaii missile alert (2018) and, 81, 83; ICBM test flight (2017), 123; Korean Peninsula fake evacuation order (2017) and, 74, 84–87; Leap Day Deal (2012) and, 141, 149; mobile nuclear forces in, 172; multipolar deterrence and, 20, 232; nuclear learning and, 210, 215, 216, 228–229; nuclear weapons program, 1–2, 103, 110–111, 110n69, 243; personalistic regime leader in, 7–8, 60; as regional nuclear power, 20; Singapore Summit (2018) and, 149–151, 236; Six Party Talks (2007) and, 141, 146–149; submarine forces in, 177; survivability of nuclear forces in, 160t, 165, 176; Syria's nuclear weapons program and, 235, 248; US counterforce capabilities and, 155; US intelligence on nuclear weapons program in, 96–97, 144, 144n78, 236
NPT. *See* Nuclear Non-Proliferation Treaty
NTRO (National Technical Research Organization), 78
nuclear contagion, 2, 7, 230
nuclear learning, 9, 209–229; cross-national learning difficulties, 215–216; defined, 209; deterrence challenges and, 239; learning the wrong lessons, 214–215; obstacles to, 212–214; in practice, 217–228; rarity of, 212–217; secrecy as barrier to, 213; theoretical analysis of, 211–212. *See also specific countries*
Nuclear Non-Proliferation Treaty (NPT), 7, 146, 195, 216, 245, 246–247
Nuclear Posture Review (US 2018), 244–245
nuclear taboo, 6
Nutt, Cullen, 97
Nye, Joseph S., Jr., 210n6, 211, 214, 218, 218n40

Obama, Barack, 16, 141, 149, 244–245
Olmert, Ehud, 248
open-source intelligence (OSINT), 9, 90–119; automated analytics and, 102–103; cell phones and, 102; computer modeling and, 102–103; crowdsourcing of, 102, 103; democratization of intelligence, 98–103, 101f; deterrence challenges and, 234–236; estimating nuclear threats, 92–97; internet connectivity and, 102; machine learning and, 102–103; nongovernmental nuclear intelligence collection, 104–117, 105–107t; policy implications, 118–119; satellites and, 98–102, 101f; surveillance cameras, 102
Open Street Map, 102
operational arms control, 9
Operation Allied Force (1999), 173–174
Operation Desert Shield (1990), 180
Operation Meghdoot (India 1984), 134
organizational learning, 57–60. *See also* nuclear learning
OSINT. *See* open-source intelligence
Oveis, Christopher, 54n32

Pabian, Frank, 91, 99, 110–111, 112
PAF (Pakistan Air Force), 78–79
Pakistan: arms races and, 28–29; Brasstacks Crisis (1986–1987), 134, 153, 237; command and control systems in, 191, 200–201, 238;

credibility of nuclear threat, 127–129, 128t, 138–139, 235–236; crisis and wartime behavior, 32, 241; deterrence regimes and, 129–140, 152–153, 231–232; domestic politics in, 5, 191, 201, 205, 207–208, 238; eroding foundations of nuclear stability and, 4, 5, 6, 7; Kargil war (1999), 64–65, 139, 222, 225–226; Kashmir insurgency (1988–1990), 134, 135; Lahore Declaration (1999), 221; mobile nuclear forces in, 171; multipolar deterrence and, 20; National Command Authority, 77–78, 80; North Korea's nuclear weapons program and, 145; nuclear learning and, 210, 215, 216, 224–228, 239; nuclear weapons program, 1–2, 13, 93, 243; personalistic leadership in, 60; Pulwama/Balakot crisis (2019), 64, 74, 75–81, 224, 227, 231–232, 235–236, 242; regime type and state structure in, 42; as regional nuclear power, 20; survivability of nuclear forces in, 160t, 163–164, 236–237; US counterforce capabilities and, 155
Pakistan Air Force (PAF), 78–79
PALs (permissive action links), 185, 216, 219
Panda, Ankit, 9, 123, 166, 236
Pant, Yogesh, 131
paranoia, 40, 47, 48–49, 233
Pelopidas, Benoît, 220
Pelosi, Nancy, 115
People's Liberation Army (China), 195–196, 232
Perkovich, George, 131–132
permissive action links (PALs), 185, 216, 219
personalistic regime leaders, 7–8, 39–62; deterrence challenges and, 232–233; impulsiveness, 39; loyalty privileged over competence by, 59; organizational constraints and, 40, 41–48; as poor learners, 40, 57–60; pride as psychological factor, 52–54; psychic numbing, 39; psychological mechanisms used by, 40, 48–57; regime type and state structure, 41–48, 58; security focus, 39; shame as psychological factor, 49–52; social status and, 54–57; vengefulness, 39, 49, 57
Planet (satellite firm), 100–101
postwar predation problem, 25, 26–27
Powell, Colin, 148
Press, Daryl, 19n20, 154, 158, 167, 169, 174, 178
pride: motivational role of, 53; as social pricing signal, 54
public opinion, social media and, 69–70, 73–74
Puccioni, Allison, 107

Pulwama/Balakot crisis (2019), 64, 74, 75–81, 224, 227, 231–232, 235–236, 242
Putin, Vladimir, 62, 72, 89, 233

al-Qaddafi, Muammar, 39, 45, 94, 228
QZone, 66n9

Rabinowitz, Or, 146, 151
RAF (Royal Air Force), 192, 193
RAND Corporation, 170–171, 172
Reagan, Ronald, 221
Reddit, 66n9
Rice, Condoleezza, 241
Richelson, Jeffrey, 96
Rizvi, Hasan-Askari, 226
Roberts, Gwynne, 90–92
Rodung Sinmun (North Korean news outlet), 83–84
Roh Moo-hyun, 148
Roosevelt, Franklin, 93
Rosen, Steven, 47
Rouhani, Hassan, 249
Rovere, Richard, 156
Rowen, Henry, 24
Royal Air Force (UK), 192, 193
Royal Navy (UK), 193
Russia: Additional Protocol of Geneva Conventions and, 245; arms races and, 27; credibility of nuclear threat, 127–129, 128t; crisis and wartime behavior, 32; disinformation campaigns by, 114; hardened targets and, 168; multipolar deterrence and, 14, 18–19, 24–25, 231; nuclear learning and, 220–221; nuclear modernization program, 1, 244; Nuclear Non-Proliferation Treaty and, 245; regime type and state structure in, 42; social media and, 88, 89; submarine forces in, 177; survivability issues and, 176; US counterforce capabilities and, 155. *See also* Soviet Union

Sagan, Scott D., 1, 6, 15, 30–31, 46, 80, 220, 222, 230
Salik, Naeem, 226
Salman, Mohammad bin, 39, 45, 233
SALT I and SALT II treaties, 38
sanctions, 246–247
Sandalow, David, 112–113
Santhanam, K., 137
SAR (Synthetic Aperture Radar), 100, 112, 172
satellite intelligence collection, 98–102, 101f; costs of, 101–102; electro-optical imagery, 100, 100n40; mobile missile force detection via, 175; resolution improvements, 99, 99n37, 108, 108n66; Synthetic Aperture Radar (SAR), 100, 112

INDEX

Saudi Arabia: crisis and wartime behavior, 32; multipolar deterrence and, 20; nuclear contagion and, 7, 230; as regional nuclear power, 20

Schelling, Thomas, 55, 68, 125, 129, 151, 239

Schmerler, Dave, 117

secure second-strike capability, 1

Serbia, mobile missile forces in, 173–174

shame: information threat theory of, 51; as social pricing signal, 54; social sanction and, 51–52

Sharif, Nawaz, 226

simple fission device, 130, 130n20

Singapore Summit (2018), 149–151, 236

Singh, Manmohan, 138

Single Integrated Operational Plan (SIOP), 24–25, 27

Sino-Soviet Crisis (1969), 166

Six Party Talks (2007), 141, 146–149

SLBMs (submarine-launched ballistic missiles), 162, 165, 167, 177, 192–193

social media, 8–9, 63–89; ambiguous messaging and, 68; analytical framework for, 71–74, 73t; cross-pollination with mainstream media, 70, 86–87; deterrence challenges and, 234; domestic vs. international audiences, 72–73; escalation risks, 66–71; open-source intelligence and, 92, 102; open vs. closed platforms, 64, 71–74, 73t; pride and, 53; short crisis vs. long crisis, 72, 73t

social status: failure and, 59; nuclear negotiations and, 61–62; nuclear weapons as signals of, 54–57

Soleimani, Qasem, 63, 63n1

South Africa: command and control systems in, 191, 198; credibility of nuclear threat, 127–129, 128t; eroding foundations of nuclear stability and, 7; survivability of nuclear forces in, 160t, 164–165; US intelligence on nuclear weapons program in, 96–97

South African Defense Force, 198, 205

South Korea: arms races and, 30; deterrence regimes and, 247; fake evacuation order (2017), 64, 74, 84–87; multipolar deterrence and, 20; North Korea's nuclear weapons program and, 148, 150; nuclear contagion and, 7, 230; nuclear learning and, 215; nuclear weapons program, 140, 142; US intelligence on nuclear weapons program in, 96–97; US security commitments to, 38

Soviet Union: arms races and, 26, 28; command and control systems in, 186–188; counterforce capabilities in, 157–158; credibility of nuclear threat, 127–129, 128t; crisis and wartime behavior, 33, 34–36, 242; Cuban Missile Crisis and, 94; eroding foundations of nuclear stability and, 3–4, 7; hardened targets in, 159, 160t; multipolar deterrence and, 17, 37; mutually assured destruction doctrine and, 23; North Korea's nuclear weapons program and, 142–143, 142–143n74, 145; nuclear learning and, 210n6, 217, 218–221; regime type and state structure in, 44; satellite intelligence programs, 98–99; Sino-Soviet Crisis (1969), 166; submarine forces in, 177; survivability of nuclear forces in, 159, 160t, 166; US intelligence on nuclear weapons program in, 96–97. *See also* Russia

stability-instability paradox, 5

Stalin, Josef, 44, 47, 61, 179–180

Stanford University, 108

Stanley Foundation, 119

Stars and Stripes on Korean Peninsula fake evacuation order (2017), 86–87

State Department (US), 16

Steinberg, Blema, 49–50

Steinbruner, John, 125

Stimson Center, 228

strategic rationale in command and control systems, 188t, 189–190, 203–206, 204t

Stuxnet, 247, 249

submarines, 176–177; command and control systems and, 192–193, 194; in India, 223; in Pakistan, 227; in Soviet Union, 220; submarine-launched ballistic missiles (SLBMs), 162, 165, 167, 177, 192–193

Subrahmanyam, K., 137

surveillance cameras, 102

survivability, 9, 154–181; of command and control systems, 157–158, 188–189; deterrence challenges and, 3–4, 237–238; early warning indicators and, 178–179; of hardened targets, 167–169; of mobile targets, 169–177; new worries about, 155–158; responses to new era of counterforce, 178–179; time constraints on, 158–167, 160t

Synthetic Aperture Radar (SAR), 100, 112, 172

Syria: counterproliferation and, 248–249; multipolar deterrence and, 232; nuclear weapons program, 2, 235; US intelligence on nuclear weapons program in, 97

Sznycer, Daniel, 51, 52

tailored deterrence, 16

Taiwan, US intelligence on nuclear weapons program in, 96–97

Talmadge, Caitlin, 5, 8, 13, 42, 231

Tannenwald, Nina, 6

TELs (transporter erector launchers), 170–173, 175

Tenet, George, 94
terrorist attacks: Mumbai attack (2008), 64–65, 139, 223, 227, 241; Pulwama/Balakot crisis (2019), 75–81; social media and, 72
TikTok, 66n9, 71
transporter erector launchers (TELs), 170–173, 175
Treaty on the Prohibition of Nuclear Weapons (2017), 245
Treverton, Greg, 95
Truman, Harry, 93
Trump, Donald: crisis management and, 242; Hawaii missile alert (2018) and, 81, 83–84; Korean Peninsula fake evacuation order (2017) and, 86; New START Treaty (2010) and, 37; North Korea and, 123, 151, 232; Nuclear Posture Review (2018), 16, 244–245; social media use by, 63, 63n1, 66, 72
Turkey: crisis and wartime behavior, 32; Erdogan's desire for nuclear weapons for status, 56; multipolar deterrence and, 20; nuclear contagion and, 7, 230; as regional nuclear power, 20
Twitter: escalation risks and, 66–67; hacking of accounts, 88, 234; Hawaii missile alert (2018) and, 81, 84; Korean Peninsula fake evacuation order (2017) and, 86; misinformation/disinformation on, 71–72, 71n31; as open platform, 63, 64, 71–72, 234; popularity of, 66n9; Pulwama/Balakot crisis (2019) and, 77, 78, 79, 80

UAVs (unmanned aerial vehicles), 175
Ukraine crisis (2014), 66–67, 221
Ukraine crisis (2022), 89, 230, 233
uncertain retaliation, 151
unipolarity, 13–14
United Kingdom: Calder Hall-type reactors exported by, 143; command and control systems in, 192–193; counterforce capabilities in, 155; eroding foundations of nuclear stability and, 7; multipolar deterrence and, 17, 20–21; mutually assured destruction doctrine and, 23; Nuclear Non-Proliferation Treaty and, 245; as regional nuclear power, 20–21; survivability of nuclear forces in, 159, 160t, 162, 166
United States: arms races and, 26–27, 28, 30; command and control systems in, 186–188; counterforce capabilities in, 155; credibility of nuclear threat, 127–129, 128t; crisis and wartime behavior, 32, 33–36, 242; eroding foundations of nuclear stability and, 3–4, 7; hardened targets and, 159, 160t, 167; India's nuclear weapons program and, 130; intelligence agency effectiveness in, 95–97; multipolar deterrence and, 14, 17, 18–19, 24–25, 37, 231; mutually assured destruction doctrine and, 23; nuclear learning and, 210n6, 215, 216, 217, 218–221, 229; nuclear modernization program, 1; Nuclear Non-Proliferation Treaty and, 245; nuclear taboo and, 6; satellite intelligence programs, 98–99; shame and social sanction in, 51; survivability issues and, 9; survivability of nuclear forces in, 159, 160t, 176; Vietnam War and, 33–36
University of California Santa Cruz, 103
University of Missouri, 103
unmanned aerial vehicles (UAVs), 175

Vajpayee, Atal, 221
Valentino, Benjamin, 6, 80
Van Der Löwe, Ilmo, 54n32
Van Kleef, Gerben, 54n32
Varthaman, Abhinandan, 78–79
vertical proliferation, 92
Vietnam War, 33–35, 49–50, 218
vulnerability of command and control systems, 188–189

Wallace, Terry, 91, 137
Wall Street Journal on deepfakes, 115
Waltz, Kenneth, 15, 23, 36, 209
Way, Christopher, 39–40, 44
Weeks, Jessica, 39–40, 42, 44
WhatsApp: as closed platform, 64; escalation risks and, 66; Korean Peninsula fake evacuation order (2017) and, 84; misinformation/disinformation and, 71, 72; political communication via, 63; Pulwama/Balakot crisis (2019) and, 75–76, 77, 78, 79, 80
Wheelon, Albert, 98
Williams, Heather, 8–9, 63, 234
Wilson, Woodrow, 50n24
WMDs (weapons of mass destruction), 90–91
Wohlstetter, Albert, 32n69, 125, 153, 156–157; "The Delicate Balance of Terror," 1
WorldView 3 satellite, 99

Yaqub-Khan, Sahabzada, 135
Young-Hwan Ko, 145
YouTube, 66, 67, 77
Yu, Chuan, 71–72, 71n31

Zardari, Asif, 241
Zegart, Amy, 9, 78, 90, 102, 234–235, 247
Zenit-2 satellite program, 98–99
Zhang, Hui, 113, 114
Zuckerberg, Mark, 115

www.ingramcontent.com/pod-product-compliance
Lightning Source LLC
Chambersburg PA
CBHW021853230426
43671CB00006B/369